DMU 0350410 01 X

AF750737

Labour Law and Industrial Relations i

Retaining 1992 ed. for Historical research. B. W. d Feb 08

Retain ?

Labour Law and Industrial Relations in Great Britain

by
Bob Hepple
Sandra Fredman

This book was originally published as a monograph in the International Encyclopaedia for Labour Law and Industrial Relations

Second Edition

1992

Kluwer Law and Taxation Publishers
Deventer · Boston

Kluwer Law and Taxation Publishers
P.O. Box 23, 7400 GA Deventer
The Netherlands
Tel.: +31 5700 47261
Fax: +31 5700 22244

Distribution in Canada and the USA
Kluwer Law and Taxation Publishers
6 Bigelow Street
Cambridge MA 02139
USA

Library of Congress Cataloging-in-Publication Data

Hepple, B.A.
Labour law and industrial relations in Great Britain / by Bob Hepple, Sandra Fredman.
– 2nd ed.
p. cm.
'Originally published as a monograph in the International encyclopaedia for labour law and industrial relations.'
Includes bibliographical references and index.
ISBN 90-6544-6419
1. Labor laws and legislation – Great Britain. I. Fredman, Sandra. II. Title.
KD3009.H47 1992
344.41'01 – dc20
[344.1041]

92-27370
CIP

Cover Design: Louis Rinck

ISBN 90 6544 6419

Table of Contents

List of Abbreviations 13

Acknowledgements 15

Preface 16

Introduction 17

I. General Features 17

§1. A Comparative Perspective 17
§2. Geography and Population 20
A. The countries 20
B. The people 21
§3. Political and Legal System 22
A. Constitution 22
B. Trade unions and the political system 23
C. Legal systems 24
D. European Community (EC) 24
§4. The Economy 28
A. General 28
B. The changing structure of the labour force 31

II. Definitions and Notions 33

§1. Industrial Relations 33
§2. Labour Law 33
§3. Social Law 35
§4. Collective Bargaining 35
§5. Negotiation and Consultation 36
§6. Procedural and Substantive Agreements 36
§7. Disputes of Rights and Disputes of Interest 37
§8. Voluntary and Compulsory Methods 38
§9. Conciliation, Arbitration, Mediation and Inquiry 39

III. THE HISTORICAL BACKGROUND 40

§1. The Traditional Voluntary System until the 1960s 40
A. The individualist tradition 40
B. Support for voluntary collective bargaining 42
C. The selective nature of regulatory legislation 44
§2. Things fall Apart: The 1960s and 1970s 46
§3. Legal Restriction and Market Individualism: the 1980s and early 1990s 50

IV. THE ROLE OF GOVERNMENTAL INSTITUTIONS IN THE SHAPING AND ADMINISTRATION OF LABOUR LAW AND INDUSTRIAL RELATIONS POLICY 53

§1. Advisory, Conciliation and Arbitration Service (ACAS) 53
§2. Central Arbitration Committee (CAC) 56
§3. Equal Opportunities Commission (EOC) and Commission for Racial Equality (CRE) 57
§4. Training and Enterprise Councils (TECs) 58
§5. Certification Officer (CO) 58
§6. Commissioner for the Rights of Trade Union Members (CROTUM) 59
§7. Department of Employment (DE) 59

V. INDUSTRIAL TRIBUNALS AND COURTS 61

§1. Jurisdiction of Tribunals 61
§2. Jurisdiction of Courts 62
§3. Composition of Tribunals 62
§4. Procedure 63
§5. Employment Appeal Tribunal (EAT) 64

VI. SOURCE OF LABOUR LAW 67

§1. Common Law 67
§2. Legislation 67
§3. Relation between Legislation and Common Law 68
§4. Codes of Practice 69
§5. Voluntary Sources 70

VII. PRIVATE INTERNATIONAL LABOUR LAW 71

§1. Scope and Sources 71
§2. Choice of Law Rules 72
§3. Application of Statutes 74
§4. Collective Labour Relations 75

Part I. The Individual Employment Relationship 77

CHAPTER I. FORMATION OF THE RELATIONSHIP 77

§1. Categories of Workers 77
A. Introduction 77
B. Contract of service or contract for services 78
C. Specific categories of worker 81
I. Employees 81
II. Workers 82
III. Public employees 82
IV. Office-holders 84
V. Manual workers 84
VI. Domestic servants 84
VII. Specific employments 85
VIII. Apprentices and trainees 85
IX. Casual or short-term workers 86
X. Temporary workers supplied by an intermediary 87
XI. Homeworkers 88
XII. Part-time workers 89
§2. Written Statement of Employment Terms 91
§3. Capacity to Contract and Restrictions on Employment 94
A. Children and young persons 94
B. Women 94
C. Foreign workers 95

CHAPTER II. THE SOURCES OF TERMS OF THE CONTRACT OF EMPLOYMENT 97

§1. Express and Implied Terms 97
§2. Terms Incorporated from Collective Agreements 98
§3. Terms Incorporated from Works Rules and Notices 101
§4. Terms Incorporated from Custom and Practice 102

CHAPTER III. THE DUTIES OF CO-OPERATION, FIDELITY AND CARE 103

§1. The Duty of Mutual Co-operation 103
A. The employee's duty to obey lawful and reasonable orders 103
B. The employer's duty to take steps to achieve the purposes of the employment relationship 104
C. The provision of work 105
§2. The Employee's Duty of Faithful Service 106
A. Misappropriation of property 106
B. Spare-time work 106
C. Trade secrets and confidential information 107

§3. The Duty of Reasonable Care 109
A. The employee's duty 109
I. The employer's claim for damages or an indemnity 109
II. The power of dismissal 110
B. The employer's duty 110

CHAPTER IV. WORKING TIME AND HOLIDAYS 112

§1. The Importance of Collective Agreements 112
§2. Statutory Restrictions on the Working Day 113
§3. Statutory Provisions Relating to Holidays 114
§4. Time Off Work 114
A. Union officials 114
B. Union members 115
C. Public duties 115
D. Redundant employees 115
E. Ante-natal care 115
F. Safety representatives 116
G. Claims for breach of rights 116
H. Excluded classes of employees 116

CHAPTER V. REMUNERATION AND BENEFITS 117

§1. Regulation of Remuneration 117
§2. Payment Systems 117
§3. Fringe Benefits 119
§4. Occupational Pensions 120
§5. Minimum Wage Legislation 122
§6. Payment and Calculation of Wages 125
A. A question of contract 125
B. The concept of a 'week's pay' 126
C. No agreement as to amount 126
D. Payment for incomplete periods 127
E. Manner of payment and deductions 127
F. Itemized pay statements 129
§7. Rights to Remuneration on Employer's Insolvency 130
§8. Remuneration during Lay-off and Short-time 130
A. Frustration of the contract 131
B. The employee is dismissed 131
C. The employee is dismissed but is re-engaged when work resumes 131
D. The employee is suspended from work 131
I. At common law 131
II. Guaranteed week collective agreements 132
III. Guarantee payments under the Employment Protection (Consolidation) Act 1978 133
IV. Social Security benefits 134
V. Redundancy payments 134

CHAPTER VI. INCAPACITY FOR WORK 135

§1. Statistics of Work Absence 135

§2. Income Maintenance during Absence from Work due to Sickness or Injury 135
A. Remuneration under the contract of employment 135
B. Social security benefits and statutory sick pay 137
C. Lump sum damages 139
§3. Maternity Pay 139
A. Under the contract of employment 139
B. Statutory Maternity Pay 140
§4. Suspension from Work on Medical Grounds 140
§5. Right to Return to Work 141
A. Sickness or injury 141
B. Pregnancy and confinement 142
§6. Protection of Seniority Rights 143

CHAPTER VII. JOB SECURITY 144

§1. Development of the Concept of Job Security 144
§2. Job Creation Measures 152
§3. Continuity of Employment 153
§4. Acquired Rights on Transfer of Undertakings 154
§5. Disciplinary Suspension from Work 158
§6. Methods of Termination of Employment 159
A. Frustration 159
B. By agreement 160
C. Dismissal by employer with notice 161
D. Dismissal by employer without notice 161
E. Variation of contract distinguished from dismissal 162
F. Termination by the employee 163
§7. Reasons for Dismissal and References 164
§8. Remedies for Wrongful Dismissal 165
§9. Unfair Dismissal 166
A. Reasons allowed for dismissal 167
B. Reasonableness 168
C. Remedies for unfair dismissal 171
D. Relationship with other claims 173
E. Exclusions from unfair dismissals legislation 174
§10. Redundancy 174
A. Meaning 174
B. Calculation of compensation and rebates 176
C. Exclusions 176
§11. Collective Redundancies 177

CHAPTER VIII. DISCRIMINATION 179

§1. The Development of the Legislation 179
§2. The Impact of the Legislation 181
§3. Grounds for Unlawful Discrimination 184
§4. The Concept of Discrimination 185
§5. Areas of Unlawful Discrimination 189
§6. Exceptions 189
§7. 'Reverse' Discrimination and Positive Action 191
§8. Enforcement 191
§9. Equal Pay 192
§10. Reform 198

CHAPTER IX. COMPETITION BY FORMER EMPLOYEES 200

CHAPTER X. INVENTIONS BY EMPLOYEES 202

Part II. Collective Labour Relations 205

CHAPTER I. TRADE UNION FREEDOM 205

§1. Government Policies 205
§2. The Right to Belong to and to Participate in the Activities of an Independent Trade Union 207
§3. The Right Not to Belong 209
§4. The Closed Shop 211
§5. Exclusion or Expulsion from the Union 215
§6. The TUC's Independent Review Committee 216
§7. Union-only Practices 216

CHAPTER II. TRADE UNIONS AND EMPLOYERS' ASSOCIATIONS 218

§1. Trade Union Membership 218
§2. Trade Union Structure 218
§3. Trades Union Congress 220
§4. Trade Union Amalgamations 221
§5. Definition and Objects of a Trade Union 222
§6. Expenditure on Political Objects 223
§7. Legal Classifications of Trade Unions 225
§8. Legal Status of Trade Unions 226
§9. Liability of Trade Unions in Tort 227
§10. Trade Union Rules 230
§11. Trade Union Elections 233
§12. Employers' Associations 235

CHAPTER III. WORKERS' PARTICIPATION IN THE ENTERPRISE 237

§1. The Concept of 'Workers' Participation' 237
§2. Industrial Democracy 239
§3. Safety Representatives and Safety Committees 242

CHAPTER IV. COLLECTIVE BARGAINING 244

§1. Levels and Extent of Bargaining 244
§2. The Role of Shop Stewards 248
§3. Legal Support for Collective Bargaining 250
§4. Collective Agreements 252

CHAPTER V. INDUSTRIAL ACTION 255

§1. Patterns of Industrial Action 255
§2. The Freedom to Strike 256
§3. Civil Liability 257
A. Contract and no-strike agreements 257
B. Loss of statutory rights 259
C. Tort 259
§4. The 'Trade Disputes' Immunity 263
§5. Restrictions on the Trade Disputes Immunity 266
A. Secondary action 266
B. Union-only practices 268
C. Ballots before industrial action 268
§6. Picketing 272
§7. Labour Injunctions 275
§8. Other State Intervention 276

Appendices 281

SELECTED BIBLIOGRAPHY 281

TABLE OF CASES 285

TABLE OF STATUTES 293

TABLE OF STATUTORY INSTRUMENTS AND ORDERS IN COUNCIL 295

Index 297

Table of Contents

List of Abbreviations

ACAS	Advisory, Conciliation and Arbitration Service
All ER	All England Law Reports
CA	Court of Appeal
CAC	Central Arbitration Committee
CBI	Confederation of British Industry
CIR	Commission on Industrial Relations
CO	Certification Officer
CRE	Commission for Racial Equality
DE	Department of Employment
EA 1980	Employment Act 1980
EA 1982	Employment Act 1982
EA 1989	Employment Act 1989
EA 1990	Employment Act 1990
ECJ	European Court of Justice
ECR	European Court Reports
EC	European Community
EOC	Equal Opportunities Commission
EPA 1975	Employment Protection Act 1975
EPCA 1978	Employment Protection (Consolidation) Act 1978
HL	House of Lords
ICR	Industrial Cases Reports (formerly Industrial Court Reports)
IRLR	Industrial Relations Law Reports
ITR	Industrial Tribunal Reports
JES	Job Evaluation Study
KIR	Knight's Industrial Reports
MLR	Modern Law Review
MSC	Manpower Services Commission
OJLS	Oxford Journal of Legal Studies

List of Abbreviations

QB	Queen's Bench Division of the High Court
RRA	Race Relations Act 1976
SDA	Sex Discrimination Act 1975
TLR	Times Law Reports
TUA 1984	Trade Union Act 1984
TUC	Trades Union Congress
TULRA 1974	Trade Union and Labour Relations Act 1974
TULRA 1976	Trade Union and Labour Relations (Amendment) Act 1976
TULRCA	Trade Union and Labour Relations (Consolidation) Act 1992

Acknowledgements

The authors of this monograph and the publishers gratefully acknowledge the permission of the Comptroller, Her Majesty's Stationery Officer to reproduce the Table in Part II, Chapter V from the *Employment Gazette*, and of Sweet & Maxwell Ltd. to draw on material in *Hepple and O'Higgins Employment Law* 4th ed. (1981). Some of the Introduction, Section III, originally appeared in Bob Hepple's contribution to *Industrial Relations in Britain* (ed. G. S. Bain), published by Basil Blackwell, 1983.

The authors wish to thank Andrew Glyn, Fellow and Tutor in Economics at Corpus Christi College, Oxford for contributing the section on the economy, and Philip Trott, solicitor, for his assistance with the section on foreign workers. We were extremely fortunate to have research assistance and help with indexing by Helen Gower. We would also like to thank Vivien Fairley and Sandra Cooper for secretarial assistance, and Joël Kendall and Keith Jones for help with proof-reading. Sandra Fredman has very special thanks for Alan Stein and Jeremy and Kim Fredman Stein.

Preface

Events move quickly in British labour law. With the election of a Conservative government for the fourth successive term in April 1992, new employment measures were immediately set in train. The Queen's Speech on 6 May 1992 outlined legislative proposals which will impose further restrictions on trade unions, both in respect of what remains of the freedom to take industrial action, and the relationship between unions and their members. These proposals largely reflect those in the preceding Green and White Papers and are to be enacted during 1992. Where relevant, such proposals are mentioned in the text as they appeared in the Green Paper *Industrial Relations in the 1990s* (Cm. 1692, July 1991). It should be noted, however, that not all the provisions will be enacted: the new Bill had not been published at the time of going to press.

At the same time, the patchwork of legislative provisions relating to collective labour law, found in the Trade Union Act 1913, the Trade Union and Labour Relations Act 1974, the Employment Protection Act 1975, the Employment Acts 1980–1990 and the Trade Union Act 1984, as well as parts of the Employment Protection Consolidation Act 1978 have usefully been consolidated in the Trade Union and Labour Relations (Consolidation) Act 1992. This is a pure consolidation measure and does not change the substantive law. At the time of going to press, it had been introduced in Parliament as the Trade Union and Labour Relations (Consolidation) Bill. Wherever possible, we have referred to it as TULRCA 1992 in the form of the Bill introduced on 19 May 1992.

Introduction

I. General Features

§1. A Comparative Perspective

1. A traveller making an organised tour of the world's systems of labour law and industrial relations is likely to begin the journey in Great Britain. This is the country in which industrial relations began, as the product of the first industrial revolution in history. It is here that labour law took shape. Great Britain was for a time not only the 'workshop' of the world, she was also an exporter of labour law. The 21 million British citizens who emigrated during the 19th and early 20th centuries to the United States, the British Colonies and overseas dominions, took with them not only the attitudes and behaviour they had learnt in the industries of the mother country. They also built on to the age-old English common law which, ideologically, epitomises the *laissez-faire* liberal capitalism which became ascendant in Great Britain between 1820 and 1850. So Great Britain is a natural starting point for any study of the labour laws and industrial relations of the United States and the Commonwealth countries, and also for a comparison of the common law with Roman-Germanic (civil law) systems.

2. Britain was the first country (1824) to legalise trade unions, and the liberal and utilitarian beliefs behind this era of toleration, in which collective bargaining could begin to develop, spread over the next 70 years to other parts of Europe. French and German workers, sponsored by their governments, came to Britain at the time of the Great Exhibition to study how the new reformist British trade unions worked. The 19th century British factories and workmen's compensation legislation served as a model in many parts of the world, as far apart as France and Japan. Stephan Bauer, first secretary of the International Association for Labour Legislation, described the adaptation of this model as being at least as important for humanity as the reception of the Roman law of property and obligations.[1] 'His claim was extravagant, not least because the British Acts cannot be compared with the Romanistic legal techniques which promoted national civil laws. But his analogy serves to emphasise the historical relationship between the labour laws of different countries.'[2] It was the pioneer of British socialism, Robert Owen, who can be regarded as the 'father' of international labour law because as early as 1818 he carried his campaign to end the exploitation of human resources into Europe and presented a petition to the Five Powers then meeting at Aix-la-Chapelle, appealing to them to regulate working hours throughout the Continent. His petition was dismissed, but when at the end of the century the movement was revived Britain played a leading role in the various conferences which culminated in the founding of the ILO in 1919. Successive British governments promoted international standards not infrequently based on British practice.

1. S. Bauer, 'Arbeiterschutzgesetzgebung', *Handwörterbuch der Staatswissenschaften* (ed. L. Elster, A. Weber, F. Wieser) 4th ed., vol. I, Jena 1924, p. 401.
2. B. Hepple in *The Making of Labour Law in Europe: a comparative study of 9 countries to 1945*, London 1986, p. 2.

3. When our traveller moves on to other parts of the capitalist world in which industrialization came later, under different social and political conditions, he or she will be quick to discover the many disadvantages of pioneering. By comparison with those countries British trade union organisation seems archaic, the structure of industrial relations appears to be chaotic, labour law is uncodified, the common law contract of service is still the cornerstone of legal thinking, and there is an absence of positive legal rights to organise, to bargain collectively and to strike. In 1954, Otto Kahn-Freund could write that 'there is, perhaps, no major country in the world in which the law has played a less significant role in the shaping of [labour-management] relations than in Great Britain, and in which today the legal professions have less to do with labour relations',[1] and in 1959 he again remarked on the British 'policy of abstention on the part of the law and the reluctance to apply legal sanctions'.[2] In some senses, this reference to 'abstention' of the law was misleading. For one thing, it was wrong to imply that the state was an essentially neutral party to industrial conflict. For another thing, there *was* a great deal of regulatory legislation on subjects such as health and safety in factories, mines and some other workplaces, minimum wages in 'sweated' trades, workmen's compensation for accidents, and the law of social insurance, the latter inspired by Bismarck's welfare system. However, as William Robson, a leading scholar, commented in 1935 'many foreign countries now lay down much higher legal standards in these and cognate matters than we do; and it is no longer possible to fall back on the complacent belief that whereas English law is enforced, the legislation of foreign countries is ignored in practice'.[3] Moreover, Kahn-Freund's *description* of British voluntarism could be regarded as an accurate one right up to the 1960s and, in some respects, even later. In the field of collective labour relations, British labour law unlike that in most comparable countries, conferred no positive rights to organise and to strike, despite the growing political power which the unions could have used, but did not, to secure these rights. Legal intervention was largely limited to a series of negative immunities from the judge-made common law, which was hostile to collective action, and to some relatively weak supports for collective bargaining.

1. O. Kahn-Freund, Chap. 11, 'The Legal Framework' in *The System of Industrial Relations in Great Britain* (eds. A. Flanders and H. A. Clegg), Oxford 1954, p. 44.
2. O. Kahn-Freund, 'Labour Law' in *Law and Opinion in England in the 20th Century* (ed. M. Ginsberg), London 1959, p. 238.
3. W. Robson, 'Industrial Law' *Law Quarterly Review* (1935) Vol. 51, p. 195 at p. 201.

4. Between 1963 and 1979 it seemed that Britain was feeling its way towards a more legally-regulated system of industrial relations. In 1963 Britain became the last country in Europe (apart from Ireland) to introduce statutory minimum periods of notice to terminate employment, and this was followed by a whole series of new rights, especially on unfair dismissal, for individual employees. The American model of anti-discrimination legislation was transplanted into the different social and legal climate of Britain, and membership of the EEC (from 1973) brought with it a new range of social legislation on matters such as collective redundancies, acquired rights on the transfer of undertakings and equal pay. For a time, between 1971–1974, it seemed that American Taft-Hartley style laws would serve as the main instrument for the restructuring of collective labour relations in Britain, but the Industrial Relations Act 1971 failed not least because it was based on the mistaken assumption that employers would use the law and that trade union leaders would co-operate with it. It was followed by a 'social contract' between the Labour Government (1974–1979) and the Trades Union Congress (reminiscent of such other famous accords as the Danish September 1899 agreement, the French Matignon Agreement (1936) and Grenelle *constat* (1968) and the German Margaretenhof agreement (1954)). This produced a great volume of new legislation and enhanced the role of the industrial tribunals (established in 1964) which like labour courts in other countries are composed of employer and worker members alongside a legally-qualified chairman.

5. This period was marked by a growing conflict between incomes policies, which interfered with collective bargaining, and reformist legislation, which aimed to support and encourage the development of collective bargaining. Since May 1979 Britain has had a right-wing Conservative Government which has abandoned both direct incomes policies and support for collectivism and has substituted a consistent strategy of legal restrictions on trade unions and the restoration of market regulation. It is the preoccupation of state policies since 1979 with the power of trade unions which distinguishes the response of Britain to the economic crisis from that of other Western European countries. In many countries the inflexibility of labour markets is seen as a major cause of the crisis, and measures have been adopted to reduce labour costs and to deregulate employment protection laws. The British government since 1979 has also resorted to measures of this kind, and this has, so far, involved the denunciation of no less than five ILO conventions (on public contracts, minimum wage-fixing machinery, the protection of wages, night work and underground work for women). In developments of this kind Britain has moved earlier and further than other Western European governments. The trend to deregulation is not unique, but in those other countries the systems of labour law have generally retained the values of democratic pluralism. Unions are still seen as the 'social partners' of the employers; collective bargaining remains at the centre of labour relations. In Britain, by contrast, the main thrust of the government's strategy has been built around attempts to weaken trade unions, through measures such as the privatisation of heavily-unionised public corporations, the devolution of industrial relations to the workplace where unions are relatively weak in a time of high unemployment, and legislation which severely restricts the freedom to organise, to bargain and to strike. These policies have been put dramatically to the test, notably in a series of conflicts between the unions and the law in the miners' strike (1984–1985) and in the disputes in the printing industry (1983–1986). In this new period the British government has shown a willingness to defy international standards, such as in its refusal to accept the findings of the ILO Committee on Freedom of Association in 1984 that the withdrawal of trade union rights for some civil servants constituted a violation of ILO conventions (*see* Part II, Chapter I, *below*). Britain has vigorously opposed attempts by the EC to extend its activities into the social sphere. Thus in December 1989, the UK government stood alone in refusing to support the Community's Charter of Fundamental Social Rights of Workers, and, since then has opposed several of the draft directives which have emerged under the Commission's Action Programme to implement the Charter. In December 1991, the UK objected to a new 'Social Chapter' in the Maastricht Treaty on European Union, leaving the other eleven Member States to reach their own Agreement on Social policy.

6. We must, however, start the exploration of modern British labour law at the beginning. This Introduction describes for those with no background knowledge the general features of the country, its political and legal systems and economy; some definitions of basic concepts; a brief historical sketch; a description of the main institutions, industrial tribunals and courts, and of the sources of labour law. There is also a short account of how British law deals with the problems which arise when more than one legal system may be relevant. Part I considers the law and practice of the individual employment relationship, and Part II collective labour relations and the law.

§2. Geography and Population

A. The Countries

7. The island of Great Britain comprises England (total area including inland water 130,367 square kilometers), Wales (20,763 square kilometers) and Scotland (including its many inhabited islands 78,773 square kilometers). Separated from Northwestern Europe by the natural 'moat' of the English Channel, the island has avoided foreign invasion since 1066. To the West, across the Irish Sea, lies Ireland which the British have colonised since early times.

8. England was united as a Kingdom 1,000 years ago and Wales became part of this Kingdom during the middle ages. The thrones of England and Scotland were dynastically united in 1603 and in 1707 a single Parliament was established for the whole of Great Britain. In 1800 the United Kingdom was completed by a union joining the Irish Parliament and that of Great Britain. In 1922 Southern Ireland (now the Republic of Ireland) became a self-governing country. The six counties of Northern Ireland had in 1920 been given their own subordinate Parliament and they have remained within the United Kingdom.

(This monograph is concerned only with Great Britain. Northern Ireland and the Republic of Ireland are the subject of separate monographs in this series.)

9. When studying British statistics it is important to note whether they refer to England alone, to England and Wales, to England, Wales and Scotland (i.e. Great Britain) or to the United Kingdom as a whole. United Kingdom statistics and other data sometimes include the Isle of Man (558 square kilometers) and the Channel Islands (194 square kilometers) which strictly are not part of the United Kingdom but are dependencies of the Crown.

B. The People[1]

10. In mid-1989, the estimated population of Great Britain was 55.6 million (with a further 1.6 million in Northern Ireland), compared with 54.7 million in mid–1973 (with 1.5 million in Northern Ireland). This can be contrasted with the figure of 38.2 million in the whole of the UK in 1906. The majority (about 47.7 million) live in England. The percentage of the population over retirement age has increased from 14.8 per cent in 1963 to 18.8 per cent in 1989, a figure of major importance in the allocation of resources.

1. These and other demographic statistics are derived from *Population Trends* (London, Central Office of Statistics, 1991).

11. The people of Great Britain were traditionally relatively homogeneous, with none of the linguistic, cultural or religious divisions which characterise either Northern Ireland or parts of Continental Europe. Living in a unitary state, whose boundaries have remained stable for centuries, most of the inhabitants share the English language (although in Wales there has been a revival in recent years of Welsh which now enjoys the status of an official language) and there is a fairly uniform system of free secular popular education up to the age of 16. The Anglican Church has been a state church since the sixteenth Century (as is the Presbyterian Church in Scotland) subordinate to the ruling political class; dissenting minorities secured rights to equal treatment during the 19th Century and non-conformism has had an important influence on sectors of the working-class, particularly in Wales. The British traditions of religious and cultural tolerance have meant that groups of political refugees, such as the Huguenots in the seventeenth Century, the East European Jews in the late nineteenth Century and the post-war Polish and Hungarian exiles, have been readily integrated. So Britain has escaped the phenomenon of religious, linguistic or racial divisions in the trade union and labour movements.

12. Race relations have, however, become an important factor in social and industrial life as a result of the influx, since the late 1950s, of economic migrants from the 'New Commonwealth' countries such as the West Indies, India and Pakistan. At the census held in 1981 4.5 per cent of the usually resident population were living in households whose head was born in the new Commonwealth or Pakistan, and in 1989, an estimated 2.57 million people described themselves as being of an ethnic origin other than white.[1] Most black

Britons are born or educated in Britain, and many are concentrated in the decaying 'inner cities' in poor housing and doing the worst jobs in a relatively small number of industries. Ethnic minorities are permanent residents in Britain and cannot be compared to migrant workers elsewhere in Europe. The period of immigration is over, largely due to the tightening of immigration controls, but Britain must now be characterised as ethnically heterogeneous. The pressure of these ethnic groups has sharpened awareness of the age-old problems of poor housing, low pay and law enforcement. Black workers are, however, playing an increasing part in the general trade union movement.

1. *Labour Force Survey* 1987–89.

§3. POLITICAL AND LEGAL SYSTEM

A. Constitution

13. The British Constitution is not to be found in a basic document or set of documents. It has evolved over the centuries and consists of Acts of Parliament and other legislation, judge-made common law and precepts and practices known as constitutional conventions. These conventions are political usages, not directly enforceable in courts of law. The most important feature of the constitution is parliamentary sovereignty. Parliament (which means effectively the democratically elected House of Commons because the largely hereditary House of Lords has only a delaying power) can enact any law on any subject; even the rules and conventions of constitutional law can be changed by ordinary legislation. This means that there are not the formal restraints against encroachment on individual liberties which exist in other liberal democracies – there is no entrenched bill of rights – and there are no constitutional 'rights' to strike or to associate in trade unions. Concern over issues such as the denial of the right to belong to trade unions at the Government Communications Headquarters by the Conservative Government in 1984, and earlier legislation by a Labour Government permitting compulsory trade union membership (the closed shop) has led in recent times to pressures for some limitation on executive and parliamentary power and for the formal entrenchment of certain individual rights. The United Kingdom Government is a party to the European Convention on Human Rights, but the terms of the Convention have not been enacted as part of domestic law.

14. Parliamentary government does not, however, mean government by Parliament. The public or civil service is non-partisan and serves the Government in office; its members enjoy security of employment irrespective of the political complexion of the party in power. The Government consists of members of both Houses of Parliament (mostly drawn from the Commons). The Cabinet is collectively responsible to the Commons; a Government that lost the support of a majority in the Commons would have to resign or call an election. The Government is not, however, the delegate of Parliament. Because of the way in which the two party system operates, the Government is generally able to command Parliamentary support for the implementation of its policies. Those who are baffled by the apparently sudden reversals of legislative policies – such as the repeal of the Industrial Relations Act in 1974 only three years after its enactment – should remember that apart from times of war or national emergency (as in 1931) there has not been a Coalition Government in Britain. Where major policy differences exist between the Conservative and Labour parties, it can be expected that the party with a parliamentary majority will be able to reverse the legislation initiated by its predecessor, as happened in the case of the Industrial Relations Act. At various times, however, the largest party in the Commons has had to rely on the parliamentary support of the small Liberal Party and the Scottish and Welsh Nationalists. For example, the minority Labour Government's labour relations legislation introduced in March 1974 could not be carried in full because of the absence of support from these smaller parties, and also because of the use of their delaying powers by the House of Lords in which there is a permanent majority of hereditary Conservative peers. The emergence in 1980 of a Social Democratic Party (SDP) in alliance with the Liberal Party briefly signalled the possibility that future governments might consist of a coalition of more than one political party. However, after the 1987 election, it became clear that the two main parties would continue to dominate the electoral scene. In fact, the years since 1979 have been characterised by the overwhelming predominance of the Conservative Party in Parliament, facilitated by the electoral system, which can produce far larger majorities in Parliament than the proportion of electoral support enjoyed by a particular party.

B. Trade Unions and the Political System

15. An understanding of the relationship between collective bargaining and legislation enacted by Parliament is impossible unless two vital facts are borne in mind. The first, which Professor Sir Otto Kahn-Freund has emphasised,[1] is that British trade unions won minimum labour standards, without the aid of legislation, before the franchise was extended to the town artisan in 1867 and to the country operative and miner in 1885. The suffrage never assumed the same importance in the formative period of the British unions as it did elsewhere in Europe; and the British unions came to rely on their industrial strength rather than the parliamentary struggle. The second fact is that the trade unions had given birth to their own leaders and their own pragmatic, reformist organizations, long before the Socialist movement assumed importance. The socialists who formed the Marxist Social Democratic Federation (SDF) in 1884 and the less orthodox Independent Labour Party (ILP) in 1893, faced an already established trade union leadership, predominantly Liberal in outlook. In 1900 a number of unions affiliated to the Trades Union Congress (TUC) combined with the SDF, ILP and Fabian Society to establish the Labour Representation Committee from which emerged the Labour Party. British trade unions are the products of the practical organization of wage earners and are not the creation of political parties nor are they the outcome of a socialist critique of society as in some other European countries.

1. O. Kahn-Freund, *Law and Opinion in the Twentieth Century* (ed. M. Ginsberg), London 1959; *Selected Writings*, London, 1978.

16. There is not an organizational link between the TUC and the Labour Party, although there is a regular liaison. Individual trade unions, representing about half the total affiliated membership of the TUC, are affiliated to the Labour Party. Trade union block votes exercise a decisive influence on Labour Party conferences and shifts in the political balance between right and left in unions can therefore be reflected in shifts in Labour Party policy. Although the number of unions affiliated to the Labour Party had dropped to 38 (representing 5.8 million votes) by 1988, the trade union share of the vote had increased to 90 per cent because of the decline in the number of members in constituency Labour parties. The Labour Party and its affiliated unions have been exploring various options in order to reduce the influence of the trade union block vote. Unions 'sponsor' (i.e. help with expenses) a considerable number of Labour MPs.

C. Legal Systems

17. England and Wales, on the one hand, and Scotland, on the other, have different systems of law, different legal professions and a different judiciary as well as different education systems and different local government organization. In order to extend this devolution of decision-making from London, there have been moves for the establishment of elected assemblies with limited law-making powers for Scotland and Wales. At present, Acts of Parliament do not extend to Scotland and Wales, unless they are expressly stated to do so. In practice nearly all labour legislation does expressly extend to the whole of Great Britain and it is only a few old Acts which are peculiar to a single law district. The English Common Law, by which is meant here all the law that is not the result of legislation, differs in some important respects from Scots law. One practical example is that in Scotland third parties may directly acquire rights under collective agreements, whereas the *jus quaesitum tertio* does not exist in English law. Scots law today is a hybrid system with roots in the Roman (civil) law as well as being under the living influence of the English Common Law. A brief description of the court system in each country, so far as relevant, will be found in para. 81. (*In this monograph only the rules of the English Common Law will be described and in general, not any special features of Scots law.*)

D. European Community (EC)

18. Britain has been a member of the EC since 1 January 1973. The effect on the British Constitution and the legal systems of England and Scotland is profound. Legislative power has been transferred from London to Brussels, in certain important matters, and the decisions of the European Court of Justice in Luxembourg on questions arising under the Treaty of Rome are binding on British courts. Above all, English lawyers are having to familiarise themselves with laws and practices expressed in the Continental legal idiom. Industrial relations are being affected not only by the generally higher social standards in other Member States, but also by regulations and directives made by the Community organs. The most important of these so far are the regulations made under Article 48 of the Treaty providing for the freedom of movement for workers within the Community, and under Article 51 relating to social security for migrant workers and a series of directives relating to equal pay and equal treatment for men and women (under Article 119), on harmonisation of the laws of Member States on collective redundancies, on safeguarding employees' rights in the event of transfers of undertakings, and on the protection of workers in the event of bankruptcy of the employer (under Articles 100 and 117). The Community Charter of Fundamental Social Rights of Workers (adopted by all the Member States except the UK) and the Commission's Action Programme (of 29 November 1989) is now spawning a number of initiatives and EC instruments which are likely to have a significant long-term effect on British labour law.[1] Although the UK opted out of the new 'Social Chapter' agreed at Maastricht in December 1991 by the other Member States, the existing EC Treaty (as slightly modified at Maastricht) will continue to be important, especially in the fields of health and safety and equal treatment. Important interpretative rulings by the European Court of Justice on subjects such as equal pay and equal treatment (*see* Part I, Chapter VII *below*) and the protection of the acquired rights of workers on the transfer of undertakings (*see* Part I, Chapter VIII *below*) have shifted the boundaries of British domestic law. The 'incoming tide' of EC law, as Lord Denning described it, is becoming an increasingly important source of regulation.

1. The texts will be found in *Social Europe* 3/90 (Brussels, EEC). The Charter and Action Programme have been widely commented upon in the UK: *see*, generally, Lord Wedderburn, *The Social Charter, European Company and Employment Rights: an outline agenda*, (London, Institute of Employment Rights, 1990), 'The Social Charter in Britain – Labour Law and Labour Courts?' (1991) 54 *Modern Law Review* 1, and 'European Community Law and Workers' Rights. Fact or Fake in 1992?' (1991) 13 *Dublin University Law Journal* 1; Bob Hepple, 'The Implementation of the Community Charter of Fundamental Social Rights,' (1990) 53 *Modern Law Review* 643, 'Social Rights in the European Economic Community: a British Perspective' (1990) 11 *Comparative Labour Law Journal* 425, and in (1989) 6 Recht der Arbeit 348; Erika Szyszczak, 'L'Espace Sociale Europeénne: Reality, Dreams, or Nightmares?' (1991) 33 *German Yearbook of International Law* 284.

19. The foundation of Community law is a set of treaties. It is a general principle of British law that a treaty entered into by the Government does not in itself affect British domestic law. Domestic law and international law are regarded as separate legal orders. In view of this the effect of Community law is specially defined in an Act of Parliament, the European Communities Act 1972. The Act provides three principal methods by which Community law may be given effect.

(1) Section 2(1) provides that directly effective or directly applicable Community law is binding in the UK. This includes secondary Community law and future Community law. The question whether a particular provision is 'directly effective' or 'directly applicable' is determined by Community law but it is for national courts to decide how to give effect to such rights. Articles 48,[1] 52,[2] 59[3] (freedom of movement) and 119[4] (equal pay) have been held to be directly effective, but articles 117 and 118 (harmonisation and co-ordination) are not.[5] Regulation 1612/68 on freedom of movement of workers is directly applicable,[6] as is Directive 63/221 on the same subject.[7] Directive 75/117 on equal pay has been held by the European Court of Justice to facilitate the

practical application of Article 119,[8] which is directly effective, but the Court has said that Directive 76/207 on equal treatment of men and women is not sufficiently precise to be relied upon in the absence of national implementing measures by an individual seeking a specific remedy for its infringement when such a remedy is not provided for under a national law.[9] A limitation on direct effectiveness of Directives is that they may be enforced only 'vertically' against 'organs of the state' and not 'horizontally' against private individuals.[10] In *Foster* v. *British Gas plc.*[11] the European Court of Justice held that an 'organ of the state' includes a body 'whatever its legal form, which has been made responsible pursuant to a measure adopted by the State, for providing a public service under the control of the State and has for that purpose special powers beyond those which result from the normal rules applicable in relations between individuals.' Following this guidance, the House of Lords held that the British Gas Corporation, prior to its privatisation, was an 'organ of the State', the fact that the Government did not possess executive or day-to-day control being irrelevant.[12] Even if a Directive is capable of having direct effects against an 'organ of the state', it will depend upon the wording of the particular Directive whether it applies to all kinds of public undertakings. For example, Council Directive 75/129 on collective redundancies does not apply to workers employed by public administrative bodies or establishments governed by 'public law', while Directive 77/187 on transfers of undertakings is silent on this point.

(2) Section 2(4) requires any court or tribunal to construe 'any enactment passed or to be passed' in the UK so as to be consistent with Community law. On two occasions the House of Lords has held that this method of giving effect to Community obligations does not apply to the construction of a UK statute (the Sex Discrimination Act 1975 and corresponding legislation in Northern Ireland) which was not passed in order to implement Community obligations.[13] To hold otherwise, Lord Bridge said, would mean 'effectively eliminating any distinction between Community law which is of direct effect between citizens of Member States and Community law which only affects citizens of Member States when it is implemented by national legislation.'[14] These decisions of the House of Lords now appear to have been overtaken by the case law of the ECJ. In the *Marleasing* case[15] (not concerned with employment law) the Court held that 'whether it is a question of provisions that predate the Directive or a later enactment, the national court called on to interpret national law is bound to do so retroactively to the greatest extent possible.' This clarifies the earlier ECJ ruling in the *van Colson* case[16] that national law must be interpreted in the light of the wording and purpose of the Directive. This 'purposive' interpretation was applied by the House of Lords in *Pickstone* v. *Freemans plc.*[17] to the Equal Pay Regulations 1983, which give effect to the Equal Pay Directive, notwithstanding doubts expressed by Lord Oliver as to whether Art. 119 EEC (which the Directive clarifies) is directly applicable in the context of an equal value claim. The distinction, in relation to 'purposive' construction, between Directives on the basis of their direct effects was ignored in *Litster* v. *Forth Dry Dock*

& Engineering Co. Ltd.[18] where the British Transfer of Undertakings (Protection of Employment) Regulations 1981 were purposively interpreted so as to give effect to the relevant EEC Directive in circumstances where the Directive could not have direct effects because enforcement was sought against a private sector employer. It is to be noted that the ECJ has also held that national courts are bound to take not only Directives but also Recommendations into consideration where they clarify the interpretation of national provisions adopted in order to implement them or where they were intended to supplement binding Community measures.[19]

(3) Section 2(2) enables the Government to implement Community obligations which are not directly effective by means of subordinate legislation made by Ministers of the Crown subject to parliamentary approval. This procedure was used to give effect to Directive 77/187 on safeguarding employees' rights in the event of transfers of undertakings;[20] and to remedy the infringement by the UK of Article 119[21] in respect of equal pay for work of equal value. The use of this procedure, rather than legislation by Parliament itself, has been severely criticised because it allows only for short debates and the ministerial order has to be accepted or rejected *in toto* without the possibility of amendment.

1. *Van Duyn* v. *Home Office*, Case 41/74 [1974] ECR 1337 (ECJ).
2. *Reynders* v. *Belgian State*, Case 2/74 [1974] ECR 631 (ECJ).
3. *Van Binsbergen*, Case 33/74 [1974] ECR 1299 (ECJ).
4. *Defrenne* v. *Sabena* (Defrenne II), Case 43/75 [1976] ECR 455 (ECJ).
5. *Defrenne* v. *Sabena* (Defrenne III), Case 159/77 [1978] ECR 1365 (ECJ).
6. *Van Duyn* v. *Home Office*, Case 41/74 [1974] ECR 1337 (ECJ).
7. *Ibid.*
8. *Jenkins* v. *Kingsgate Clothing*, Case 96/80 [1980] ECR 911 (ECJ); *Worringham* v. *Lloyds Bank Ltd*, Case 69/80 [1981] ICR 558 at 589 (ECJ).
9. *Van Colson and Kamann*, Case 14/83 [1984] ECR 1892; *Harz*, Case 79/83 [1984] ECR 1921 (EJC).
10. *Marshall* v. *Southampton and Southwest Hampshire AHA* [1986] IRLR 140, (ECJ).
11. [1990] IRLR 313, (ECJ)
12. *Foster* v. *British Gas plc*. [1991] IRLR 268, HL; but compare *Doughty* v. *Rolls-Royce plc*. [1992] IRLR 26, CA.
13. *Duke* v. *GEC Reliance Ltd* [1988] IRLR 118, HL and *Finnegan* v. *Clowney Youth Training Programme* [1990] IRLR 299, HL.
14. [1990] IRLR at 301.
15. ECJ, 13 November 1990.
16. *Van Colson* v. *Land Nordrhein-Westfalen*, Case 14/83, [1984] ECR 1891 at 1909.
17. [1988] IRLR 357, HL.
18. [1989] IRLR 161, HL.
19. *Grimaldi* v. *Fonds des Maladies Professionelles* [1990] IRLR 400, (ECJ).
20. Transfer of Undertakings (Protection of Employment) Regulations 1981 (SI 1981 No. 1794).
21. In *Commission of the European Communities* v. *United Kingdom*, Case 61/82 [1982] ICR 578, the ECJ held that the UK had failed to provide equal pay for work to which equal value is attributed as required by Art. 119. In a second infringement proceeding, *Commission of the European Communities* v. *United Kingdom*, Case 165/82 [1984] ICR 192, the ECJ held that the UK was not in compliance with Art. 4(b) of the Equal Treatment Directive 76/207. *See* para. 350, *below*.

19bis. After some controversy, it has been decided that the industrial tribunals have jurisdiction to deal with claims under directly applicable EEC law where this is related to their other statutory jurisdictions, for example in respect of equal treatment.[1] Where EC law is not clear then the court or tribunal may refer questions of law for preliminary ruling by the ECJ under Article 177 of the Treaty. Recent cases have emphasized the doctrine of supremacy of EC law: a national court or tribunal is required to set aside a rule of national law which is the sole obstacle to the effectiveness of rights under Community law.[2] Moreover, the Community principle of effectiveness means that national rules must not make it impossible in practice to exercise Community rights and the principle of non-discrimination means that the national rules governing actions for the enforcement of Community rights may not be less favourable than those governing the same cause of action on an internal matter.[3]

1. *Secretary of State for Scotland* v. *Greater Glasgow Health Board* [1991] IRLR 187, EAT; *McKechnie* v. *UBM Building Supplies (Southern) Ltd* [1991] IRLR 283, EAT.
2. *Factortame Ltd* v. *Secretary of State for Transport (No.2)*, Case 213/89, [1991] 1 All ER 70, (ECJ); *Thomas* v. *Adjudication Officer and Secretary of State for Social Security* [1990] IRLR 436, esp. at 445 per Sir Denys Buckley, and Slade LJ at 440–441. This new approach renders dubious the decision of a majority of the Court of Appeal in *Marshall* v. *Southampton and Southwest Hampshire AHA (No.2)* [1990] IRLR 481 (appeal to House of Lords pending) that reliance cannot be placed on the Equal Treatment Directive, Article 6, to override the limits on compensation in the British legislation.
3. A point re-emphasized in the *Dekker* case [1991] IRLR 27, (ECJ); *see* too, *Kowalska* v. *Freie und Hansestadt Hamburg*, [1990] IRLR 447, (ECJ) (declaration that collective agreement void not an adequate sanction).

§4. The Economy[1]

A. General

20. The outstanding feature of the British economy over the last hundred years has been its decline from the manufacturing workshop of the world to the status of a thoroughly second-rank economic power. Output per head is the most basic indicator of a country's productive power. A recent authoritative account of the pattern of productivity explains that 'the UK appears as the leader at the beginning of the period [1870], but is overtaken by the United States in the next decade, by Sweden between the wars, by France and Germany around 1960, by Italy around 1970 and Japan probably in the late 1970s'.[2]

1. Paras. 20–26 have been contributed by Andrew Glyn, Fellow and Tutor in Economics at Corpus Christi College, Oxford.
2. R. C. O. Matthews, C. H. Feinstein and J. C. Oddling-Smee, *British Economic Growth 1856–1973* (Oxford 1982), p. 33.

21. The UK's agricultural sector is small and highly productive, and some service sectors are relatively efficient. It is in manufacturing industry, crucial because of its importance in overseas trade, that the situation is particularly dire. In the mid–1980s, output per hour worked in UK manufacturing was about one half of the US level and two thirds that of Japan and Western Europe. This has been reflected in a disastrous decline in the UK's share of world manufacturing trade – from 25 per cent in 1950 to 8 per cent in the 1980s. Imports of manufactures now exceed exports.

22. Two factors have helped to mask this disastrous decline. First the great post-war boom of the 1950s and 1960s in the advanced capitalist countries dragged the UK along.[1] Between 1951 and 1973 UK production grew by 2.8 per cent per year, faster than in any previous peacetime period of comparable length. But behind this, UK manufacturing productivity grew at half the rate of the main European economies and one-third of the rate in Japan. Unlike its rivals the UK failed to catch up with the technical level achieved in the US. This has left the UK economy extremely exposed in the more difficult economic conditions faced by the advanced countries in the 1970s and 1980s. For a time the full impact of this weakened position was cushioned by the entirely fortuitous discovery of North Sea Oil. By 1985 the government was receiving nearly 7 per cent of its revenue from this source, some £10 billion, enough to pay the enormous social security costs of more than 3 million unemployed. In the context of the Conservative Government's deflationary policies, however, even North Sea Oil turned into a mixed blessing. For the impact on the balance of payments (£11 billion extra exports or reduced imports) was allowed to push the value of the pound up, making British manufacturing industry even less competitive.

1. *See* P. Armstrong, A. Glyn and J. Harrison, *Capitalism since 1945* (Oxford, 1991).

23. Looking for causes of the UK's economic failures has been a major preoccupation of UK economists. It would be generally agreed that the low level of UK investment has been of crucial importance. For it is investment in new machinery and factories which increases the productivity of labour by incorporating new technology. During the 1950s and 1960s the stock of capital in UK manufacturing grew at around 3.5 per cent per year, only two-thirds of the rate in Europe and one-third of that in Japan. But this immediately invites the question: why was UK investment so much lower? One answer might be low profits, and indeed by the early 1970s the profit rate in British manufacturing, around 10 per cent, was less than that in Europe and far below that of Japan. But this cannot be the fundamental explanation, for in the early 1950s the profit rate in Britain was around 20 per cent and the investment rate was even lower then. Indeed, the decline in profitability over the period has been attributed to low investment and the declining competitiveness which it brought.

24. The involvement of the City in overseas investment has often been blamed for starving British industry of finance. But there is little evidence that it has been shortage of finance which has constrained British firms. What does seem to be clear is that British industry, early in the post-war period, became locked into a low investment pattern from which it has been unable to break out. This is despite the greatly increased competition it has faced, both at home and from imports and in its export markets. Much energy has been dissipated on mergers, whose benefits in increased efficiency have been severely limited. The banks have never taken it upon themselves to develop and implement strategic plans for individual industrial sectors and governments' efforts have been limited to a few general investment incentives.

25. Not only has investment been low in total, but its effectiveness has not been up to international standards. The amount of output derived from each unit of investment has been as much as one-third below that of France and Germany. Studies of the motor industry in particular have suggested much lower productivity in British plants of identical design than those in Europe. Bad organization and management, poor training and bad industrial relations are favourite explanations. The latter finds some support in the fact that some large UK plants have been abnormally strike-prone by international standards. The fact that British unions entered the 1950s in an entrenched position (unlike those in most of Europe and Japan), but without a strong modernising ethos, may have reinforced the negative effects of sluggish and complacent management. However, surveys into the implementation of new technology have found workforce opposition to be a factor of negligible importance in comparison with factors such as low expected profitability, doubts as to whether the equipment would be fully used and lack of technical expertise. Most recently, attention has been focussed on the lack of training as a key factor in explaining manufacturing weakness in the UK.

26. The recent history of the British economy has to be viewed in this context. The Labour Government of 1974–1979 was elected on a policy of industrial interventionism. But these plans were abandoned in the teeth of hostile opposition from business (the Director-General of the CBI recently admitted that the employers' organisation had contemplated launching an 'investment strike'). In the context of deflationary policies and wage limitations the government supported firms in trouble and attempted to strengthen trade union rights in relation to employment preservation. The Conservative Government pursued the opposite policy of attempting to force rationalisation of industry by more deflation, high interest rates and a rise in the pound. Productivity grew rapidly in 1981–1982 as unemployment rose by about 2 million. There has been fierce rationalisation in the public sector, especially in steel and the coal industry where bitter strikes ended in defeat for the trade unions and sweeping job losses. In the 1980s, manufacturing industry achieved rapid productivity growth (more than 4 per cent per year). But this was achieved by closing plants and reducing manning levels rather than by sustained investment in new products and processes. The investment expansion which occurred at the end of the 1980s was concentrated in those areas of the service sector most closely tied to the consumption boom (retail trade and the financial sector. This consumer boom was based on cuts in tax for the better off and an explosion of consumer credit, sparked off by the deregulation of the financial sector). The mounting balance of payments deficit, which preceded the recession of 1990–1992, demonstrated how narrow this boom really was and that the 'Thatcher miracle' had utterly failed to revitalise manufacturing industry. Only an optimist would forecast that the 1990s will witness a lower average level of unemployment than the 2.4 million recorded in the 1980s.

B. The Changing Structure of the Labour Force

27. In 1990, there were approximately 25.6 million people in employment (including self-employed), about 46 per cent of the total population.[1] The most prominent characteristic of the early 1980s was the accelerated increase in unemployment figures, partly as a result of the strict monetary policies of the incumbent Conservative Government. Unemployment reached a peak of 3.41 million in January 1986 (12.3 per cent of the working population). It would have been higher still, at 3.78m., if calculated on the official basis used before November 1982, when certain persons previously classified as unemployed were excluded. In 1986, levels of unemployment began to fall; in April 1990, official unemployment stood at 1.51m (or 1.63m. on the earlier basis of calculation) amounting to 5.4 per cent the workforce. In particular, the number of long-term unemployed more than halved, to 178,000 in 1990. The unemployment figure is still higher than in previous decades. In the twenty years prior to 1967, the general unemployment level in Britain was among the lowest in the western world – usually between 1 and 2 per cent. Although unemployment has been growing since 1967, the peak figure in the 1970s was only 1.47m. (excluding students). One reason for the reduction from 1986 in the unemployment figure for under 18s is that figures do not include trainees on the virtually compulsory Youth Training Scheme programme. Since April 1990, the general unemployment figure has begun to rise again, and was 2.6 million or 9.4 per cent by March 1992.

1. All figures in this section are taken from statistics published in the *Employment Gazette* and in *Labour Research* (Labour Research Department, London).

28. For those in work there have been several significant changes in the structure of employment. Of particular importance has been the shift of the working population away from production industries to service industries. Employment in the manufacturing sector fell from 7.28 million in 1976 to 4.93 million in 1991. More than 70 per cent of total employment is now in the service sector, accounting for half of all working men and about 80 per cent of working women. These trends are reflected in the changing occupational structure of employment, which displays a marked shift away from manual towards non-manual occupations. By 1990, more than 65 per cent of the workforce were employed in non-manual occupations.

29. A second important change in the structure of the workforce has been the increase in the number of women workers. The female workforce has grown by more than 3 million since 1959, reaching 10.57 million in September 1990, and accounting for over 40 per cent of those in employment. The increase in working women has been parallelled by an increase in part-time work. There were just over 5.5 million part-time workers by 1990, as against about 3.2 million in 1971. This represents the highest proportion of part-time workers in the EC, apart from Denmark and the Netherlands. The part-time workforce is predominantly female with married women accounting for three-quarters of all part-time employees (as against one-quarter of full-timers) (*see further*, para. 127 *below*).

30. Another feature of the labour force is the relatively disadvantaged position of the ethnic minority population (*see* para. 337, *below*). About 80 per cent of the white male labour force are employees. The figure for Afro-Caribbean males is similar. About 74 per cent of other Black and Asian ethnic minorities are employees, but a relatively large proportion of the Asian male labour force are self-employed (23 per cent compared to 16 per cent for white males). Only just over half the Pakistani/Bangladeshi female labour force are in paid employment, but other ethnic minority females are represented in the labour force in roughly the same proportions as white females.[1] Unemployment rates for the ethnic minority groups tend to rise faster than those for whites at times when unemployment generally is rising (*see* para. 337 *below*).

1. The information in this paragraph is derived from the *Employment Gazette*, March 1991, p. 59–71.

31. Employment in the public sector which traditionally constituted an important portion of the workforce, has diminished significantly during the 1980s due to privatisation of nationalised industries and Government policy of 'slimming down' the public services. Between mid-1983 and mid-1989, the public sector share of the total workforce in employment fell from 29.4 per cent to 23.1 per cent.[1] In mid-1989, about 6.1 million people were employed in the public sector. The most dramatic decline has been in respect of public corporations, which employed 1.7m. in 1983, but only 0.8m. in 1989. This was largely due to an intensive programme of privatisation. The majority (nearly 60 per cent) of those employed in central government in mid-1989 were women, but women formed only 45 per cent of full-time employees. This reflects the large number of women working part-time in education and health. By contrast in public corporations women form less than one-sixth of the workforce; there are few part-time jobs in public corporations. In October 1989, 565,000 civil servants were employed in the civil service.

1. Central Statistical Office, *Economic Trends*, December 1989; *The Bulletin*, February 1990, p. 21.

32. Britain is sharply distinguished from other Western European and industrialised countries by the small proportion of the population engaged in agriculture. In 1990, 275,000 people were employed in agriculture, fishing and forestry, or 1 per cent of those in employment.[1]

1. *Monthly digest of statistics*, February 1991.

II. Definitions and Notions

§I. Industrial Relations

33. The reader who seeks any clear or explicit definition in Britain of basic notions, such as *industrial relations* and *labour law* will be disappointed. The subject of *industrial relations* has become an accepted area of academic study. But the scope of the subject has been determined empirically with attention being concentrated on the collective bargaining activities of trade unions.[1] Allan Flanders, elaborating Dunlop's analysis,[2] has defined industrial relations as a system of rules which appear 'in different guises in legislation and in statutory orders; in trade union regulations; in collective agreements and arbitration awards; in social conventions; in managerial decisions; and in "accepted custom and practice". In other words, the subject deals with certain regulated or institutionalised relationships in industry.'[3] Flanders' emphasis was on the *institutions of job regulation* excluding 'personal' and 'unstructured' relationships from the system of *industrial relations*. Since the 1960s, however, the prevailing conception of industrial relations has broadened to include the informal, largely unstructured relationships on the factory or shop floor which modify or even contradict the official institutions. The emphasis has increasingly been on the impact of informal work group relations, and unofficial 'custom and practice' as means of controlling jobs. An important landmark in this new approach was the Report of the Royal Commission on Trade Unions and Employers' Associations (1968)[4] which distinguished the formal system of industrial relations embodied in official institutions, from the informal system 'created by the actual behaviour of the trade unions and employers' associations, of managers, shop stewards and workers'.

1. Notably in H. A. Clegg, *The Changing System of Industrial Relations in Great Britain*, Oxford, 1979.
2. J. T. Dunlop, *Industrial Relations Systems*, New York, 1958.
3. A. Flanders, *Industrial Relations: What is wrong with the System?*, London, 1965.
4. Cmnd. 3623, 1968.

§2. Labour Law

34. This changing emphasis has also had an influence on the study of the law relating to industrial relations. Right down to 1939, legal studies were almost exclusively concerned with the common law of 'master and servant' (the earliest book on this subject by Matthew Dutton was published in Ireland in 1723),[1] and with legislation on safety and welfare and workmen's compensation for accidents. This *law of master and servant*, concerned exclusively with common law and, less often, legislation affecting the *individual employment relationship* has developed into what is today generally called '*employment law*'. This includes the rights and duties of individual employer and employee and is sometimes extended to such matters as the employer's vicarious responsibility to third parties for the torts (delicts) of his employees.

1. Matthew Dutton, *The Law of Masters and Servants in Ireland*, Dublin, 1723.

35. The legal aspects of relations between trade unions and employers and internal trade union matters were, however, little studied before 1939 and then only concerning specific legislation or case law. Books on *trade union law* usually focussed on the judicial interpretation of Acts of Parliament defining the legal status of trade unions and the protection of acts in so-called 'trade disputes'. There were also a few studies of the *practice of conciliation and arbitration*. This particularly narrow focus and the neglect of *collective labour law* can only be understood in the light of two factors. First, the pragmatic case by case orientation of English lawyers, who generally eschew the broader conceptual and doctrinal study of the subject; and secondly, the neglect of the sociology of law by English academic writers.

36. It was in this situation that Otto Kahn-Freund, a pupil of Hugo Sinzheimer, the great German exponent of industrial relations 'pluralism', arrived in England in 1933. He found in the London School of Economics the intellectual environment in which he was able to combine his experience as a judge of the Berlin labour court, his wide understanding of the sociology of Marx, Weber and others, with his study of English law and the British practice of collective bargaining. It is to him that the scientific study of *collective labour law* in Britain, a study filled with valuable comparative insights, owes its origin. Where English lawyers thought collective agreements not worth studying because they were never directly enforced in courts, Kahn-Freund found them a fascinating subject precisely because of the apparent 'abstention' by the law. He was able to generalise this into a theory of the absence of an intention to create legal relations (itself a Continental rather than English notion) in collective bargaining. In studying the legal support given to collective bargaining he expounded general principles such as that of 'voluntarism' – the aim of the law is to help the parties reach a settlement not to impose it – and that of the 'priority of autonomous institutions' – the law intervenes only if the parties' own machinery has failed to produce a result.[1]

1. A Bibliography of the writings of the late Professor Sir Otto Kahn-Freund (1900–1979) will be found in his *Selected Writings*, London, 1978. Many of his most important ideas are crystallised in his *Labour and the Law*, 2nd ed., London ,1977 (also available in German and Italian translations), and *Labour Relations: Heritage and Adjustment*, London, 1979. A 3rd ed. of *Labour and the Law*, ed. by P. L. Davies and M. Freedland, was published in 1983. Appraisals of his work will be found in F. Gamillscheg *et al.* (eds.), *In Memoriam Sir Otto Kahn-Freund*, Munich, 1980, and Lord Wedderburn, Roy Lewis and Jon Clark (eds.) *Labour Law and Industrial Relations: Building on Kahn-Freund*, Oxford, 1983. For his earlier period in Germany, *see* Roy Lewis and Jon Clark (eds. and Introduction), *Labour Law and Politics in the Weimar Republic. Selected German Writings of O. Kahn-Freund* (translated by J. Clark), Oxford, 1981.

37. The elaboration of general principles such as these, and the Continental and the United States influences, have resulted in a change of scope and emphasis of legally-based studies. The scope of what since the 1960s has tended to be called *labour law* (although the term *industrial law* is still not infrequently used to describe the same subject) is now defined in terms of the law which is used 'to regulate, to support and to restrain the power of management and the power of organised labour'.[1]

1. O. Kahn-Freund, *Labour and the Law*, 3rd ed., p. 15.

38. Labour law may now be understood in this way in academic studies, but legislation still uses a bewildering variety of descriptions of the same subject matter. For example, there was an Industrial Relations Act in 1971, but the repealing legislation dealing with some of the same topics is called the Trade Union and Labour Relations Acts 1974 and 1976. The Employment Protection Act 1975 covered not only a diverse range of individual employment rights (now consolidated in the Employment Protection (Consolidation) Act 1978), but also set up new institutions and gave legal support to trade unions and collective bargaining. The Employment Acts of 1980, 1982, 1988, 1989, 1990 and the Trade Union Act 1984 dealt with the rights of trade union members, picketing and industrial action as well as individual employment rights. The labour courts are known as 'industrial tribunals' and from them there is an appeal on questions of law to an Employment Appeal Tribunal.

§3. Social Law

39. This lack of uniformity is also reflected in the absence of any clear dividing line between labour law and *social law*. The latter concept is not even generally recognised in academic studies. In a wide sense it includes all studies of the operation of law in society; more narrowly it concerns the law affecting the working population as a whole, as distinct from those at work; more narrowly still it covers only *social security law*, that is the law relating to the administration of contributory and non-contributory state benefits for income maintenance. The term *welfare law* usually covers both social security and the law relating to personal welfare services. Legislation on contributory state benefits has, since 1946, been known as the National Insurance Acts, but in 1975 these were consolidated in the Social Security Act and amended in subsequent Social Security Acts.

§4. Collective Bargaining

40. The absence of agreed or statutory definition of the scope of study is matched by the lack of any precise definition of some of the main subjects of study. For example, the term 'collective bargaining' (which is said to have been invented by Mrs. Beatrice Webb in 1891)[1] was for many years regarded as the collective equivalent of industrial bargaining in the labour market:

> 'Instead of the employer making a series of separate contracts with isolated individuals he meets with a collective will, and settles, in a single agreement, the principles upon which, for the time being, all workmen of a particular group, or class, or grade, will be engaged.'[2]

1. In *The Co-operative Movement in Britain*, London, 1891, and subsequently developed by her and Sidney Webb, *Industrial Democracy*, London, 1898.
2. Sidney and Beatrice Webb, *Industrial Democracy*, p. 173.

41. This analysis was criticised by Allan Flanders[1] as being inadequate because it suggests that collective agreements commit someone to buy and sell labour, whereas in fact, collective agreements simply lay down the *terms* upon which individual workers sell their ability to work. This led Flanders to develop the alternative theory of collective bargaining as an 'institution for the joint regulation of labour management and labour markets'.[2] Against this view Alan Fox has argued that in collective bargaining there is:

> '(1) a bargaining process during which the parties deploy arguments, present evidence and issue threats; this may or may not end in
> (2) an agreement which adjusts the antithetical interests of buyer and seller. This may or may not be embodied in
> (3) a contract into which both parties decide to enter . . . In practice these elements often appear to be fixed in a single process . . . But it is important to distinguish them for analytic purposes.'[3]

Whatever the relative merits of these theories for understanding the phenomenon of collective bargaining, it has to be stressed that for certain legal purposes (such as trade union recognition) 'collective bargaining' has a much more limited definition excluding certain subjects such as bargaining about investment plans (*see below*, Part II, Chapter IV).

1. *British Journal of Industrial Relations*, 6 (1968), p. 1.
2. *British Journal of Industrial Relations*, 6 (1968), p. 1; for a defence of this definition against a Marxist criticism, *see* Clegg, *The Changing System of Industrial Relations in Great Britain*, Ch. 11.
3. *British Journal of Industrial Relations*, 13 (1975) p. 151.

§5. Negotiation and Consultation

42. A distinction has often been drawn in Britain between 'negotiation' and 'consultation'. The former refers to matters within the power of joint regulation by management and trade unions; the latter refers to subjects within the scope of managerial prerogative. The distinction is fluid and controversial. The scope of managerial prerogative has traditionally been wide in Britain, including matters such as health and safety and pensions. But these matters for 'consultation' have in several industries now become matters for 'negotiation'. In legal contexts, workers' participation in decision-making in Britain has generally been limited to 'consultation' (i.e. the right to be heard) before management decides (e.g. redundancy consultation, *see* Part I, Chapter VII) .

§6. Procedural and Substantive Agreements

43. The 'dynamic' structure of collective bargaining (*see below* para. 44) in Britain does not lend itself to any sharp distinction between *procedural* and *substantive* collective agreements. TULRCA 1992, s. 178(2)(g) lists as a possible subject of 'collective bargaining' (for certain legal reasons) 'machinery for negotiation and consultation, and other procedures, relating to any of the foregoing matters including the recognition by employers or employers' associations of the right of a trade union to represent workers in any such negotiation or consultation or in the carrying out of such procedures'. The world of industrial relations has borrowed this concept to describe *procedural* agreements. It covers both collective procedures and procedures to deal with individual grievances and individual discipline. *Substantive* agreements on the other hand relate to wages and other terms and conditions of employment.

§7. Disputes of Rights and Disputes of Interest

44. Britain is probably the only industrial country in which the distinction between disputes of rights and disputes of interest is not recognised. The reason for this is to be found in the dynamic method of collective bargaining, as distinguished from the contractual or static method, which is characteristic of British industrial relations. This typical British method, in Kahn-Freund's words:

> 'consists in the creation of a permanent bilateral body, known as a joint industrial council, a conciliation board, or a joint committee, on which both sides are represented by an equal number of members, sometimes (in a minority of cases) with an independent chairman presiding. To this body the parties give a constitution and a code of procedure, but they leave it to the body thus created by unanimous resolutions to settle the wages and the substantive conditions of the industry. . . .
>
> . . . Since the "dynamic" or "institutional" method consists in the passing of resolutions by a joint body which is always free to modify its own decisions, provided it does so unanimously, it encourages "open ended" agreements and discourages the fixing of time limits. More important, the body which lays down the conditions is often also the body which interprets its own resolutions. Over a large area of British industrial relations, the rule-making and the decision-making processes, the, as it were "legislative" and "judicial" functions are as indistinguishable as they were in the constitution of medieval England. Within these processes of institutional bargaining every dispute about existing "rights" can be turned into a dispute about "interests" by the simple device of solving it through a new and possibly retrospective resolution.'[1]

Although the ambiguity of procedures has tended to decrease since Kahn-Freund first described this 'common law' model of collective bargaining and the location of procedures has shifted from national to company or workplace level in the private sector, little else has changed in the practice of collective bargaining.[2]

1. *Labour and the Law*, 3rd ed., pp. 70–72.
2. K. Sisson and W. Brown in *Industrial Relations In Britain* (ed. G. Bain), Oxford, 1983, p. 150.

45. It is the absence of any clear distinction between these two types of dispute that goes a long way to explain why collective agreements in Britain are generally not regarded as contracts. Where English lawyers talk about 'disputes of right' in labour law they usually have in mind not disputes arising out of collective agreements, but the determination of rights arising from legislation.

§8. Voluntary and Compulsory Methods

46. The voluntary nature of much of the disputes settlement machinery in Great Britain is often cited as a distinctive feature of British industrial relations. The extent to which this reflects reality is discussed in the section on Historical Background (*below*, para. 49). At this point, it is necessary to analyse what 'voluntary' and 'compulsory' mean. At one end of a spectrum the word 'voluntary' suggests that disputes are resolved entirely by the parties themselves, using agreed procedures or industrial action without any third party intervention; at the other end of the 'voluntary' spectrum are negotiated settlements reached after third parties have assisted the employer and unions, with their consent, through means such as conciliation or mediation.

47. The anonym of 'voluntary' is 'compulsory' but as Kahn-Freund explained,[1] 'compulsory' is used in at least four different senses in Britain. (1) The parties must use a particular procedure prescribed by law, such as compulsory arbitration. In the twentieth century this has applied only in time of war. (2) One of the parties may invoke a particular procedure without the consent of the other side. The most prominent example is unilateral arbitration. From 1940 to 1980, in various forms, it was possible for representative trade unions or employers' organisations to invoke arbitration to oblige employers in otherwise well-organised industries to observe employment terms established by collective bargaining in that industry. The Employment Protection Act 1975 utilised unilateral arbitration of terms of employment as the final sanction against employers who failed to recognise independent trade unions or to disclose information to unions, once recognised, for purposes of collective bargaining. With the repeal of the extension and recognition provisions by the Employment Act 1980 (*see* Part II, Chapter IV) all that remains of unilateral arbitration is the almost unused provision relating to disclosure of information. (3) The results of a process (e.g. a collective agreement or arbitration award) are binding on one or both parties. As will be seen later, collective agreements are presumed not to be intended to be legally enforceable between the collective parties, but some of their provisions may take effect as binding obligations in individual contracts of employment (*see* Part I, Chapter II); only to this extent are they 'compulsory', and in this connection it should be remembered that it is possible (in theory, at least) for the individual employee and employer to opt out of the terms of the collective agreement. The awards of arbitrators are not legally enforceable, unless they take effect through individual contracts of employment (*see* Part I, Chapter II). This is expressly provided for in the case of unilateral arbitration, but may occur by implication in other cases. (4) No industrial sanctions may be used by either side during a defined period. This was the case under the Industrial Relations Act 1971 when a 'cooling-off' period could be imposed in certain emergency disputes but this was repealed in 1974. The Trade Union Act 1984 and later the Employment Act 1990 have achieved a similar objective by requiring pre-strike ballots in respect of virtually all strikes whether 'official' (i.e. union-backed) or unofficial (wildcat); the effect of this is a compulsory delay until a ballot has been held. In a wider sense, the removal of immunities from many traditional forms of industrial action by the Employment Acts 1980 to 1990 and the Trade Union Act 1984 (now found in TULRCA 1992) has removed the key element of freedom to impose social sanctions, which underpinned the so-called 'voluntary' system (*see* Part II, Chapter V).

1. Kahn-Freund, *Labour and the Law*, 3rd ed., p. 147.

§9. Conciliation, Arbitration, Mediation and Inquiry

48. Conciliation and arbitration are not defined by law in Britain, although machinery is provided by statute to implement these methods of dispute settlement (*see below*, paras. 460–463). However, these terms are a well-known part of industrial relations vocabulary.

Conciliation is a voluntary, informal process of dispute resolution, whereby an independent third party assists the parties to a dispute to clarify the points of disagreement and attempts to promote a settlement. No binding award is made and any agreement reached is the responsibility of the parties. *Arbitration* differs from conciliation in that reference is made to an independent third party to adjudicate on the dispute and come to a decision. In *voluntary arbitration*, the decision is not legally binding, but the parties have nevertheless embarked on the procedure on the understanding that they will abide by whatever decision is reached. In the case of *compulsory arbitration* (*see above*), the award is usually legally enforceable as an implied term in the contract of employment. *Mediation*, on the other hand, leads to a recommendation by the third party which the parties to the dispute are free to reject. In Britain, *arbitration* and *mediation* may involve the settlement of conflicts of interest and conflicts of right, a distinction which, as we have seen, is difficult to make in a British context. *Inquiry* or *investigation* of the facts of industrial relations matters by an individual or a committee (sometimes misleadingly called a 'court') and the making of recommendations for the settlement of a dispute is also known in Britain; this eventually leads to an agreement between the parties.

III. The Historical Background

§1. The Traditional Voluntary System until the 1960s

49. In order to understand modern labour law and industrial relations it is necessary to appreciate three features of the legal framework of industrial relations as it developed until the 1960s. The first is the tradition of individualism; the second is the tradition of support for voluntary collective bargaining and abstention of the law from industrial action; and the third is the selective nature of regulatory or 'protective' legislation.

A. The Individualist Tradition[1]

50. The notion of the individual contract of employment is central to the legal analysis of industrial relations. This fragmentation of industrial relations into millions of individual relationships, is not an accidental or modern phenomenon. It is deeply rooted in social and legal tradition. The conception of the reciprocal rights and duties of the parties flowing from their free exchange of promises arrived relatively late on the legal scene in Britain in comparison with the continental countries influenced by Roman law. The reason was the tradition of the Statute of Labourers passed by Edward III in 1351, following an Ordinance of 1349, later reinforced by the Elizabethan Statute of Artificers of 1563, and the tradition of the Poor Law Act 1601. Under these laws the 'servant's' status determined the obligation to work at wages arbitrarily fixed by justices of the peace, usually themselves masters. Servants were liable to punishment for not accepting the work, for not doing it according to directions, or for deserting the master. As late as 1850 Blackstone's definition of the master-servant relationship was still in vogue among lawyers and, according to that definition the relationship need not be based on contract: for example, a labourer could be compelled to serve by justices of the peace; a parish apprentice indentured under the Poor Law had to serve a master with whom he had no contract; and the mere condition of 'having no visible effects' could give rise to a direction to compulsory work.[1] The sanctions were criminal. When the Elizabethan statute fell into disuse, the legal basis for prosecutions against workers were the 19th-century Master and Servants Acts. It was the trade unions which were largely responsible for the modification and repeal of these penal laws by the Master and Servant Act 1867 and the Conspiracy and Protection of Property Act 1875 respectively. Trade union agitation arose primarily because of the effect of the laws on the freedom to strike: 'it was a recognised tactic of the employers, particularly in dealing with smaller strikes, to cause all the strikers to be arrested for breach of contract and then to confront them with the alternatives of returning to work on the employer's terms or suffering up to 3 months' imprisonment. Furthermore, as the law stood, a troublemaker might be silenced not just once but repeatedly'.[2] Between 1858 and 1875 an average of 10,000 prosecutions of workmen for breach of contract took place each year in England and Wales.[3]

1. This section draws extensively on B. Hepple, Ch. 16 in *Industrial Relations in Britain* (ed. G. S. Bain), Oxford 1983.
2. P. S. Bagwell, *Industrial Relations in 19th Century Britain*, Dublin 1974, p. 30.
3. D. Simon, 'Master and Servant' in *Democracy and the Labour Movement*, London 1954 p. 160.

51. The repeal of the Master and Servant Acts removed a major impediment to the development of the notion of freedom of contract between equal contracting parties by civil sanctions alone. However, the intellectual backwardness of the legal analysis of 'master and servant' relationships has had a lasting impact on the modern law. One consequence has been the patchy and inadequate coverage of labour law (*see* Part I, Chapter I, *below*). Another has been the inordinate complexity of labour law. The bulk of labour legislation in the l9th century developed outside the framework of the contract of employment. This 'atrophy' of the contract of employment, as Kahn-Freund called it,[1] is largely attributable to the absence of an explicit and flexible contract model in the formative period of labour law. The most important consequences of the heritage of ideas evolved over centuries under the influence of the Statute of Labourers, the Statute of Artificers, and the Poor Law is that the form of contract which emerged in the nineteenth century effectively guaranteed the rule-making powers of the employer. When the worker at the factory gate accepts an offer of employment, neither he nor the employer may be conscious that they have concluded a binding contract of service. In law they have done so although nothing was said about wages or hours of work, let alone such matters as holidays, sick pay, pensions or what is to happen if there is a stoppage of work due to a power failure. If there is no legislation in point, and no express agreement, it is left to the courts and tribunals to make sense of the contract by implying terms as to these matters. As indicated later (Part I, Chapter II), where there is collective bargaining the courts may be prepared to fill in the gaps by incorporating the relevant terms of the collective agreements as implied terms of the individual contract. The great success of collective bargaining in many industries has meant that the courts have rarely been called upon to imply terms. In reality, where there is no collective agreement or arbitration award or legislation, the superior economic power of employers enables them to dictate terms of the contract which the individual employees are in no position to contest through the courts, least of all when they are still working for the employer.The law of contract was developed by the courts, and the principal conceptual instrument they use to fill the gaps left by the parties is the implied intention of the parties. In a few extreme cases (such as contracts in restraint of trade) public policy is used to nullify a contract, but never to mould it. This means that the idea of positive legal regulation of the contract by imperative norms is alien to the common law approach: parties are even free to 'contract out' of protective legislation unless and until Parliament says they cannot do so. This is quite different from the continental legal systems which for two centuries have applied general imperative norms to all contracts and special norms to the contract of employment. Moreover, when British judges have sought to imply terms they have relied heavily on custom and practice. The task of discovering the custom is greatly simplified, as indicated later, when there is a collective agreement. Where none exists everyday obligations, such as the speed of work, the conditions of labour, and the subjection to discipline, are implied from what the parties do in practice, and that means in effect what the employer has laid down and applied in works rules, even informally. Some obligations, such as fidelity, the maintenance of mutual trust and confidence, and obedience to the employer's reasonable commands, are regarded as fundamental. They are implied as a matter of law from judicial precedents which have been influenced from the traditions of the law of 'master and servant'. The judicial perspective, even in recent times, has been unitary rather than pluralist, although under the impact of modern legislation there are some signs of change.

1. O. Kahn-Freund, 'Blackstone's neglected child: the contract of employment', *Law Quarterly Review* 93 (1977) 508 at p. 524.

B. Support for Voluntary Collective Bargaining

52. The traditional British system of industrial relations until the 1960s rested on a social consensus that the state's role should be minimal. Trade unions and strikes emerged from illegality at criminal law in a series of statutes from 1824 to 1875. However, the courts almost immediately began to develop a series of common law liabilities, with the effect that most industrial action, while not unlawful at criminal law, was likely to give rise to civil liability. Parliament responded, not by creating statutory rights to strike or organise, but by enacting immunities to specific common law torts if committed in the course of a trade dispute. Hence the law of industrial action until the 1970s consisted largely of legislative responses to judicial creativity. In Lord Wedderburn's words: 'This period saw the pendulum swing regularly back and forth between judge-made liabilities and cautious parliamentary protection.'[1] Thus, although the Conspiracy and Protection of Property Act 1875 stated that simple conspiracy was not a *crime* if done in the context of a trade dispute, the courts held that this did not prevent liability for the *civil tort* of conspiracy in taking industrial action.[2] In the same year, the *Taff Vale*[3] case made it possible to sue a trade union in respect of this tort. In addition, the tort of inducing breach of contract of employment made most organised action tortious.[4] The legislature responded with the Trade Disputes Act 1906, which gave immunity to any person acting in contemplation or furtherance of a trade dispute in respect of the torts of conspiracy, inducing breach of contract of employment or (for the avoidance of doubt) interfering with business. It also gave immunity for peaceful picketing if carried out in contemplation or furtherance of a trade dispute; and, significantly, a blanket immunity to trade unions from actions in tort. The limitations on political activities by unions established in the *Osborne*[5] case were countered by the Trade Union Act 1913. After the controversial case of *Rookes* v. *Barnard*[6] resuscitated the obsolete tort of intimidation, the Trade Disputes Act 1965 was passed to reverse its effect and to give immunity for intimidation in contemplation or furtherance of a trade dispute. This pattern led Kahn-Freund to describe the British system of labour law as 'abstentionist.' Similarly, the law gave support for voluntary collective bargaining without enacting specific legal rights.

The recognition of trade unions for collective bargaining was achieved without the aid of legislation or any significant demand for such legislation. Robson noted,[7] in 1935, that 'England is the home of trade unionism; it was on her soil that the practice of combined bargaining first arose; yet here alone is the collective contract still denied the elementary right of legal enforcement in the courts of law despite the fact that it is the recognised method of determining the conditions of employment of the vast majority of wage earners'. However, there was a certain amount of 'auxiliary' legislation designed to promote and support voluntary collective bargaining. This included the minimum wage-fixing machinery established in selected 'sweated' trades where collective bargaining was non-existent, originating with the Trade Boards Act 1909, the successive Fair Wages Resolutions of the House of Commons, from 1891, which imposed obligations on government contractors to pay 'fair' wages, of which collectively agreed terms were a primary guide, and the machinery established in 1896 and 1919 to encourage the use of voluntary conciliation and arbitration.

1. Lord Wedderburn *The Worker and The Law*, 3rd ed. Harmandsworth, 1986, p. 17.
2. *Quinn* v. *Leathrem* [1901] A.C. 495.
3. *Taff Vale Railway Company* v. *The Amalgamated Society of Railway Servants* [1901] A.C. 426.
4. *South Wales Miners' Federation* v. *Glamorgan Coal Company Ltd* [1905] A.C. 239.
5. [1910] A.C. 87.
6. [1964] A.C. 1129.
7. W. Robson, 'Industrial law' *Law Quarterly Review* 51(1935), p. 204.

53. It is a striking feature of Britain's war-time legislation, and of the policy of the first twenty years after the Second World War, that this served to consolidate the traditional voluntary system. The Conditions of Employment and National Arbitration Order No. 1305 severely restricted strikes and lock-outs and made it compulsory to submit disputes to arbitration. In practice, however, the peacetime system of voluntary collective bargaining remained intact. Moreover, the unions were more deeply involved in carrying out wartime measures such as the allocation of labour and paying out unemployment benefits for the Ministry of Labour. At plant level, joint production committees distributed work and administered discipline. Labour benefitted from this policy of 'tripartite corporatism'. Average earnings in real terms were 24 per cent higher in 1944 than in 1938 (due to extra overtime and bonuses) and membership in trade unions rose by about one-third during the War to bring it up to 8 million (45 per cent of the workforce). When a Labour government was elected with a massive majority in 1945, the unions did not seek any major changes in the traditional system. The only immediate measure was the repeal of the Trade Disputes and Trade Union Act 1927, which a Conservative government had imposed in the aftermath of the 1926 General Strike to outlaw 'political' sympathy strikes, to restrict financial support by union members for the Labour Party, and to forbid civil servant unions from affiliating to outside bodies such as the Trades Union Congress (TUC). The war-time Order 1305 remained in force, with union consent, until 1951 when it was repealed as the result of withdrawal of trade union support following the prosecution of some strikers. It was replaced by Order 1376 of 1951 which restored the freedom to strike and lock-out and allowed representative organisations to invoke unilateral arbitration in order to extend collective agreements; when the Order was replaced by permanent legislation in 1959 (under a Conservative administration) a modified form of such extension remained a feature of the law until 1980. Other legislative changes in the immediate post-war period also aimed to improve support for the traditional voluntary system. These included a new and amended Fair Wages Resolution of 1946, and a Wages Councils Act of 1945. The latter replaced the earlier trade boards legislation and enabled the renamed 'wages councils' to recommend that the Minister made a wages order not only where there was no collective bargaining machinery but also where such machinery was inadequate, as, for example, where it had collapsed leaving workers unprotected in times of depression. Trade union acquiescence in the consolidation of the voluntary system was closely linked to the implementation of Beveridge's proposals for a reformed comprehensive system of social security.

54. The welfare state, together with the voluntarist system of industrial relations, was part of the policy not only of the post-war Labour Government but also was accepted by the Conservative administrations from 1951–1964. In retrospect, it is possible to see that this 'rested upon a middle-class acquiescence in the current balance of industrial power'.[1] There was a stable economic basis for the social consensus. In the 1930s, despite high levels of unemployment, wage and salary earners in employment enjoyed relative prosperity, and Britain was cushioned from the economic crisis by its foreign assets. During the War Britain lost £7,000 million, a quarter of its national wealth, but the sporadic post-war economic crises were held in check by loans from the United States. Britain had not suffered military occupation or physical destruction as other European countries had, and there was no significant pressure for the renewal of industry and the 'modernization' of industrial relations. In that climate it is not surprising that there were no moves towards restructuring labour law, for example by introducing forms of co-determination of the kind which the British occupation forces, with British trade union advice, fostered in Germany. Even in the industries which the Labour Government nationalised (civil aviation, cable and wireless, coal, railways, long-distance road transport, electricity, gas, iron and steel and the Bank of England), the legislation went no further than to require the boards of the new public corporations to 'consult' with 'appropriate organisations' with a view to establishing and maintaining negotiation and arbitration procedures, provisions which have proved to be largely symbolic. Co-partnership or even more radical notions of workers' control formed no part of the traditional consensus.

1. K. W. Wedderburn, 'Labour Law and Labour Relations in Britain', *British Journal of Industrial Relations* 10 (1972) p. 270 at p. 275.

C. The Selective Nature of Regulatory Legislation

55. The primacy of voluntary collective bargaining meant that regulatory legislation, directly laying down rules of employment on matters such as wages, hours, health and safety, has tended to take second place. The policy of the law has been not to regulate by statute the terms of employment of those who are considered capable of protecting themselves. Legislation applied primarily to children and women and not to adult men. In the twentieth century, the principle has been to cover by direct regulation only those who are not protected by collective bargaining and to deal only with those subjects which do not appear to lend themselves to collective bargaining. Even where there is regulatory legislation, it has often been designed to allow for its replacement by approved collective agreements, which are at least as good in content as regulatory legislation. In any event, legislation can always be supplemented by collective bargaining on the same subject. The most important consequence of the approach has been the absence of the kind of comprehensive regulation that is to be found in other industrial countries of such matters as hours and holidays for all employees. Significantly, apart from the mining industry, the 8-hour day in Britain was achieved by collective bargaining rather than legislation. There was specific regulation of the hours of women and young persons in certain activities (see Part I, Chapter III) until 1986 and 1989 respectively, but with a few exceptions the hours of adult men have always been regulated by collective bargaining.

56. The reason for the selective use of the 'method of legal enactment' as a means of worker protection is to be found in the ebb and flow of struggle of unions and reform groups inside and outside Parliament, and the resistance by powerful groups of employers and intellectual supporters of *laissez-faire*. The earliest legislation, including the Regulation of Chimney Sweepers Act 1788 and the Health and Morals of Apprentices Act 1802, was concerned with child labour. The initial aim of the short-time committees from 1831 onwards was the 10-hour day for all employees, regardless of sex and age, but when the political reality of the time made this unattainable, the committees modified their aims to concentrate on the hours of work of women. The first major victory for the short-time committees was the Factories Act 1844 which equated women with young persons, restricted their hours, and required dangerous parts of machinery to be fenced, as well as strengthening the powers of the inspectorate which had been established by the Factories Act 1833. The opportunities for evasion were many and some loopholes were closed in 7 Acts passed between 1844 and 1856. Most important of all was the 'Ten Hours Act' of 1847 which conceded the main demand of the short-time committees. In the second half of the 19th century this legislation, which applied only to textile factories, was gradually extended to cover factories and workshops over a wide range of old and new manufacturing industries. At different times activities outside these industries were also regulated: mines from 1842 (but with effective inspection only from 1860), shops from 1886 (although the health and safety aspects of shop work were not covered until 1963), and standards comparable to factory legislation were not extended to agriculture until 1956. Surveying the scene in 1972, an official committee of inquiry, under the chairmanship of Lord Robens, found that there were 9 main groups of statutes supported by over 500 subordinate statutory instruments. These contained a mass of intricate and ill-assorted detail.

Some 5 million workers worked in premises not covered by any occupational health or safety legislation. A result of the recommendations of the committee was the comprehensive Health and Safety at Work etc. Act 1974. The existing legislation relating to health, safety and welfare is very slowly being replaced by this new comprehensive system, which is based on the philosophy of self-regulation. This does not, however, mean that there has been a significant shift to collective bargaining over these matters in place of statutory regulation. The legislation is based on the concept of 'consultation' with safety representatives and safety committees rather than bargaining (*see* Part II, Chapter III *below*).

§2. Things Fall Apart: The 1960s and 1970s

57. There were already signs in the late 1950s and early 1960s that the social consensus which had sustained the traditional voluntarist framework was under strain. The pressure of full employment had contributed to a shift of power to the workplace: employers anxious to retain and recruit labour did not need much prompting to accede to demands for pay increases made by shop stewards on behalf of workgroups. Shop stewards were increasingly identified by politicians and the media as the main cause of 'wages drift', increases in earnings not accounted for by central industry-wide negotiations, and so a serious impediment to the control of inflation which, together with the maintenance of full employment, was a major goal of successive governments from 1945. Trade unions were also blamed for their failure to control the relatively large number of unofficial ('wildcat') strikes in breach of agreed procedures, and for the inefficient use of manpower through the imposition of restrictive 'custom and practice' overmanning. The more deep-seated causes of Britain's post-war economic problems, such as the high levels of military spending and the insistence of the multinational enterprises on keeping Britain as an international financial centre and open economy with a high level of capital export and relatively little domestic investment, received much less attention in the public debate. Trade unions were unable to influence factors such as these, but they came to be seen as a major cause of Britain's relative economic failure. The preoccupation of successive governments was with the exchange rate and the balance of payments, and wage-induced inflation could be readily identified as a source of economic instability.

58. Two broad strategies were adopted to control this phenomenon. One was a succession of incomes policies, the other was the use of the law in order to influence the conduct of industrial relations. These strategies were not consistently applied, and, indeed, they were not infrequently discordant. The political parties, the trade unions and the employers were locked in ceaseless battle over these questions. In the period 1948 to 1979 there were no less than six different incomes policies: voluntary wage restraint under the Labour administration (1948–1950); a freeze on prices under the Conservatives (1956–1957); a 'pay pause' under the Conservatives (1961–1962); the Labour government's voluntary (1965) and later (1966–1967) compulsory incomes policy; the

Conservative's Counter-Inflation Acts (1972–1974); and Labour's 'social contract' with the TUC (1974–1976), followed by a unilateral policy (1977–1979) and a 'concordat' with the TUC (February-May 1979). Each of these policies had distinctive features and used different institutional devices. Some were voluntary and some of them had statutory support. All of them ended in failure. However, it is important to note that, while 'encroaching very directly upon the autonomy of collective bargaining',[1] these policies did not reshape labour law itself.[2] The Prices and Incomes Acts of 1966 and 1967 and the Counter-Inflation Acts of 1972 and 1973 nominally rested upon criminal sanctions, but these were never enforced; the traditional 'immunities' in respect of industrial action were not removed and, indeed, the Act of 1966 actually widened them. Moreover, the policies exempted either wholly or in part the machinery designed to help the low paid and to achieve equal pay for men and women. The negative restraints on the results of collective bargaining were accompanied by a series of positive measures to encourage or promote trade union growth and recognition: in the period from 1948 to 1979 union density among manual workers grew from 50.3 per cent to 63.0 per cent, and among white-collar workers from 33.0 per cent to 44.0 per cent.

1. P. Davies and M. Freedland, 'Editors' Introduction' to *Kahn-Freund's Labour and the Law*, 3rd ed., p. 7.
2. Lord Wedderburn, 'Labour Law Now – A Nudge and a Hold', *Industrial Law Journal* 13 (1984), p. 73.

59. Indirectly, however, incomes policies did have a major impact on the conceptual framework of labour law. Successive governments always tried to secure trade union consent to their incomes policies. This 'corporate bargaining' recognised the trade union interest in a wide range of policy issues outside the traditional 'economic' questions of terms and conditions of employment. In return for this political influence the unions were ready to accept periods of pay restraint and more state interference in 'free' collective bargaining. For example, during discussions with Prime Minister Heath in 1972 the unions demanded the repeal of the Industrial Relations Act (*below*) and some other legislation in return for agreement on pay restraint. Mr. Heath regarded this as too high a price, but the subsequent Labour government entered into a 'social contract' with the TUC. In return for a programme of social and legal reforms, the TUC agreed a policy of temporary pay restraint. The first stage of the reforms was the repeal of the Industrial Relations Act; the second was the enactment of a wide range of new legal rights for trade unions and workers in the Employment Protection Act 1975; the third stage was to have been an extension of workers' participation in the enterprise, but this did not get beyond the government policy statement on industrial democracy (1978) in response to the Report of a Committee of Inquiry under the chairmanship of Lord Bullock (1977). The government's attempts to continue some form of pay restraint after the social contract had collapsed led to a high level of industrial unrest in the winter of 1978–1979, widely regarded as a major reason for Labour's defeat in the 1979 elections. The most significant result of the incomes policies was the 'politicization' of industrial relations, the complete blurring of the distinction between economics and politics on which the traditional system was based. Government attempts to impose wage restraints and to restructure collective bargaining (*below*) forced the trade unions directly into the political arena. The traditional consensus that the state was essentially 'neutral' or 'abstentionist' could not survive. The boundaries between 'legitimate' economic 'trade disputes' and political action came under stress in a way which had not occurred since the abortive General Strike of 1926.

60. The second strategy which signalled the breakdown of the traditional voluntary system was that of direct legal intervention. Here policies both of reform and of the restriction of collective bargaining have been adopted and these have not always been consistent. On the side of reform, the first legislation on the contract of employment since 1875 had been introduced by a Conservative administration in 1963 and received 'without enthusiasm' by the unions. The Contracts of Employment Act 1963 laid down minimum periods of notice to terminate employment (these have been progressively increased since then but are still low by European standards), and to require employers to provide employees with written statements of their main terms of employment, largely in the hope that this would remove the causes of some disputes. The Redundancy Payments Act 1965, introduced by a Labour government, provided for lump sum payments based on age and length of service for those dismissed on grounds of redundancy after a minimum of two years' employment. The Conservative's Industrial Relations Act 1971 implemented the recommendation of the Royal Commission on Trade Unions and Employers' Associations (1965–1968) (chaired by Lord Donovan) that there should be a statutory right for employees not to be unfairly dismissed. This was re-enacted, with improvements, in Labour's Trade Union and Labour Relations Act 1974, and, as already mentioned, the Employment Protection Act 1975, as part of the 'social contract', created a number of other rights for individual employees, such as maternity pay and the right to return to work after pregnancy and confinement, guarantee payments by the employer when work is not available, and protection of wages on the insolvency of the employer. As already mentioned, a comprehensive Health and Safety at Work etc. Act was enacted in 1974. Starting with the Equal Pay Act 1970 and complemented by the Sex Discrimination Act 1975, action has been taken against discrimination on grounds of sex and marital status, and the Race Relations Act 1976 (replacing the earlier Act of 1968) deals with discrimination on racial grounds. The growing volume of legislation can be seen from the fact that compared with some five general Acts of Parliament regulating employment passed between 1950 and 1959, and 16 from 1960 to 1969, there were 30 such Acts from 1970 to 1979. Most of the new individual rights were enforced through the industrial tribunals, established in 1964 (*see below*, Section V). The case law has spawned several specialist law reports and journals devoted to labour law.

61. The policy of reform has also been evident in the legislation on collective labour relations. The Donovan Commission wanted to introduce 'order' into the largely informal system of plant bargaining, in order to reduce wages drift, restrictive practices and strikes. They hoped that reform could be achieved 'if possible, without destroying the British tradition of keeping industrial relations out of the courts'.[1] However, the Conservative government, elected in 1970, saw legislation as the 'main instrument' in bringing about reform. The Industrial Relations Act 1971 contained a series of provisions designed to reform bargaining structures, to secure recognition of unions by employers, to encourage legally enforceable collective agreements and to reform union rules, in particular so as to make governing bodies responsible for controlling and disciplining their members. The immediate cause of the failure of the 1971 Act was the defeat of the Heath government in the February 1974 election which arose from the confrontation with the miners' union over incomes policy. However, the TUC's policy of non-co-operation with the Act had rendered it largely inoperable: the Act tried to bring about too drastic a change in existing institutions and behaviour by means of law, it was based on the mistaken assumption that employers would use the law, and the transplantation of legal institutions from the United States (e.g. bargaining units, cooling-off periods etc.) took insufficient account of the different economic and political climate in Britain.

1. Report of the Royal Commission on Trade Unions and Employers' Associations, Cmnd. 3623 (1968), para. 190.

62. The Labour government's 'social contract' legislation (1974–1976) returned to the path of reform by restoring the presumption that collective agreements were presumed not to be intended as legally enforceable contracts, and recreating extended immunities from legal action in respect of acts 'in contemplation or furtherance of a trade dispute'. An Advisory, Conciliation and Arbitration Service (ACAS) and a Central Arbitration Committee (CAC) were created and novel collective rights to trade union recognition and the disclosure of information for collective bargaining, as well as improved provisions for the extension of collective agreements to non-organised workers were granted. Consultation rights were enacted in respect of collective redundancies (this in response to an EEC Directive), health and safety and occupational pension schemes. The wages councils system (*above*) was strengthened and provision was made for encouraging collective bargaining in industries covered by those councils. Some 'individual' rights, such as those to time off work for trade union duties and activities and protection against victimization for trade union membership and activities, underpinned this reassertion, by legal means, of the primacy of the collective bargaining system .

63. Labour law policies, however, contained a strand of restriction of trade union power and collective bargaining. In 1969, Mr. Wilson's Labour government had unsuccessfully proposed penal sanctions against unconstitutional strikers who failed to observe a 28-day 'conciliation pause' as well as ballot requirements for certain official strikes and a power to control inter-union disputes over recognition. The Conservative's Industrial Relations Act, somewhat inconsistently with its support for collective bargaining (*above*), contained a strong element of individualist philosophy in its ban on the closed shop, with some limited exceptions, and the positive right not to belong to any trade union or to a particular union. This was an individual right capable of undermining the organisational strength and representativeness of trade unions. The Act also contained many restrictions on the right to strike, and civil liabilities for so-called 'unfair industrial practices'. These led to several confrontations between unions and the courts. The 'social contract' legislation was reformist in character, but some parts of it were restrictively interpreted by the courts and tribunals. For example, dislike of the consequences of the widening of the statutory immunities by Parliament led the Court of Appeal between 1977 and 1979 to impose novel limitations on these immunities, the statutory recognition provisions became largely inoperable because of restrictive judicial interpretations; and the protection for trade union activities proved to be very limited. For their part, employers were increasingly complaining that the new laws imposed undue burdens on them. The language and philosophy of individual rights, which had become increasingly pervasive, was also criticised from the Left on the grounds that this had strengthened managerial control over jobs giving an enormous impetus to unilateral rule-making by management, in particular through the formalization of disciplinary procedures. The factors which most severely undermined the reformist legislation were economic and political. By 1979, unemployment was mounting, inflation remained at high levels, public expenditure was being cut, and there was acute discontent with the government's policies. In May 1979, the Conservatives led by Mrs. Thatcher were elected to power.

§3. Legal Restriction and Market Individualism: the 1980s and early 1990s

64. The policies and legislation of Mrs. Thatcher's administration fundamentally shifted the parameters of labour law. The solution to the major problems of the 1970s – inflation and the politicization of the unions – was sought in the restoration of 'free' markets. The argument was that trade union 'coercion' has caused inflation and unemployment and fluctuating living standards. The unions' 'coercive powers' were said to rest upon their legal 'privileges'. Therefore, in the words of Professor F. A. Hayek, whose ideas have been extremely influential, 'there can be no salvation for Britain until the special privileges granted to trade unions three-quarters of a century ago are revoked'.[1] Trade unions and labour legislation are seen as a distortion of market relations between employer and employee. In order to make 'free' markets work, it is necessary to 'get the state off people's backs' and to 'deregulate'. It is also necessary to curb effective demand, so as to reduce inflation, and this involves weakening trade union power, and also severely reducing public expenditure. This ideology is reflected in the six main pieces of legislation introduced by the Conservative government: the Employment Acts 1980, 1982, 1988, 1989 and 1990 and the Trade Union Act 1984. This legislation has pursued four specific policies.

1. F. A. Hayek, *1980s Unemployment and the Unions*, London 1980, p. 58, and *see* generally Lord Wedderburn 'Freedom of Association and Philosophies of Labour law', *Industrial Law Journal* 18 (1989), p.1.

65. First, workers' rights of self-help through collective organisation and industrial action have been effectively restricted to their own employment units. For example, workers are now allowed to picket only outside their own place of work, and the immunity from civil action in 'trade disputes' has been narrowed to disputes between workers and their own employer. Secondary action, or solidarity action by workers in one enterprise to support fellow-workers at a different enterprise, has been progressively restricted, until the Employment Act 1990 finally made it unlawful. This prevents unions from using traditional methods of preventing the supply of goods to an employer in dispute or banning the sending of work to non-union shops. Secondly, trade union funds have been placed at the mercy of the law. Previously only union officials could be sued for acts which fell outside the boundaries of permissible 'trade disputes'. Since 1982, union funds themselves are at risk even if the action is unofficial. The increasing likelihood of confrontation with the courts has exposed the unions to the additional dangers of heavy fines for contempt of court and the sequestration of all or a substantial part of their assets to pay the fines and damages (*see* Part II, Chapters II and V, *below*). Thirdly, contrary to the public policy of the previous 100 years, in the new structure of labour law there is now a clear commitment to *restrict* collective bargaining. The government itself gave a lead by banning membership of trade unions at the Government Communications Headquarters (GCHQ) in January 1984 (*see* Part II, Chapter. I, *below*) and, in 1987, by suspending the collective bargaining rights of teachers. Statutory provisions for the recognition of trade unions by employers were repealed in 1980. The legislation since 1980 has also been calculated to weaken trade union organisation. This has been done in part by the incentive of large penal awards against employers and trade unions in favour of those who leave a trade union and are then dismissed by the employer. Unions are now required to have secret ballots before industrial action. The 1984 Act limited this duty to action which had received official sanction; but because this appeared to give union executives an incentive to disown local action, the Employment Act 1990 extended the requirement more widely unless union officials repudiate the action. The repudiation provisions are, however, so stringent as to compel union leaders, in effect, to police their members. The law also gives a remedy to individuals who are refused work on the ground of non-membership of a union (for example, where a pre-entry closed shop is in operation). It is likewise unlawful to put pressure on an employer to engage only unionists and to negotiate and consult with trade unions, while at the same time it is lawful to induce an employer *not* to negotiate with a trade union.

66. Fourthly, central to the whole strategy has been the control of labour through the market. The most striking feature of the years since 1979 has been the decline in union membership. A fall in employment by 8 per cent from 1979–1986 was accompanied by a fall in trade union membership of 17 per cent (from 13.2 million members to 11 million). Despite the upturn in employment since 1986, trade union membership continued to fall, to 10.2 million in 1989.[1] The spectre of unemployment has had a depressing effect on the labour market in general and this has been accentuated by official policies. Traditional supports for the low-paid are being removed; in 1983 the government secured the repeal of the Fair Wages Resolution (*above*); the machinery for fixing minimum wages in the road haulage industry was repealed in 1980, the provisions for extending collective agreements to unorganised sectors of a trade or industry were repealed in 1980; in 1986 the functions of wages councils (*above*) were restricted so as to exclude young people under 21 from the statutory protection and to restrict the councils to setting only a minimum hourly rate and a single overtime rate for those aged 21 and over, and to replace the 150-year old Truck Acts with less onerous provisions on deductions from wages. Indeed, under the Youth Training Scheme, employers are financially penalised if they pay workers above certain low levels. Moreover, traditional tripartite bodies are now being abolished or transformed, giving employers a majority vote. For example, the tripartite Manpower Services Commission was abolished in favour of decentralised administration by employer-dominated Training Enterprise Councils (*see below* para. 77). Job security has been diminished by Orders which first (from July 1980) increased the qualifying period for unfair dismissal rights to one year from six months, and then (from June 1986) to two years. Welfare rights have been dismantled, for example abolishing earnings-related benefits for unemployment and sickness payments in 1982, reducing many other benefits in real value, replacing sickness benefit by an inferior system of statutory sick pay from the employer for the first 28 weeks'absence and imposing charges for a number of formerly free services. These cuts not only serve to reduce public expenditure but they also act as a powerful discipline on workers to hold down their jobs.

1. *Employment Gazette*, June 1991, p. 337.

67. Measures such as these have had the effect of widening the gulf between an elite of relatively well-paid secure workers who have the good fortune to remain in full-time employment and a growing 'reserve army of labour' on the fringes of the 'core' labour market, many of these fringe workers being women, young persons and members of ethnic minorities. The trend since the 1970s has been for inequality to grow between those in full-time secure employment and the various types of marginal workers such as outworkers, part-time workers, casual workers and temporary workers, most of whom fall outside the protection of the employment legislation. In such a climate, labour law has undergone a functional transformation. On the one hand, the trade unions weakened by unemployment and the movement towards the privatization of heavily-unionised public corporations are now exposed to a wider range of common law liabilities than at any time since 1906 and they have lost most of the traditional 'auxiliary' legislation which supported collective bargaining. On the other hand, the individual employment protection legislation now applies to a diminishing 'core' of the labour market, with workers fearful of unemployment.

IV. The Role of Governmental Institutions in the Shaping and Administration of Labour Law and Industrial Relations Policy

68. The growth of legal regulation (as described *above*) has been accompanied by the development of regulatory government agencies, most of them constituted on a tripartite basis, to administer labour law and control industrial relations policy. The main institutions are surveyed in this section. In section V (para. 80, *below*) the specialised courts, known as industrial tribunals, first set up in 1964 to adjudicate on most of the new statutory employment rights, are discussed, as is the role of the ordinary courts.

69. Despite the growth of these institutions, it remains true to say that most disputes are not processed through machinery provided by the state. They are settled informally through workplace procedures and joint industrial bodies. Despite the changes since 1979, there remain some statutory provisions which support voluntary procedures. For example, employers are obliged to give every employee a note specifying disciplinary and grievance procedures applicable to each employee.[1] Another example is that statutory rights of employees in respect of unfair dismissal[2] and redundancy payments[3] and guarantee payments[4] may be replaced by procedures voluntarily agreed by the collective parties with the approval of the Secretary of State. (In practice, however, few parties have attempted to obtain approval and rigorous criteria are applied before approval is given.) A final example is the requirement that officers of the Advisory, Conciliation and Arbitration Service (*next* para.) must have regard to the desirability of using voluntary procedures before intervening in individual or collective disputes.

1. EPCA 1978, s.1(4). Since 1989 employers with less than 20 employees have been exempted: EA 1989, s.13
2. EPCA 1978, s.65: only one agreement has been approved.
3. EPCA 1978, s.96.
4. EPCA 1978, s.18.
5. EPCA 1978 ss.133(5), 134(4); SDA 1975 s.64(3); RRA 1976 s.55(3); and see generally C. Bourn, 'Statutory Exemptions for Collective Agreements' (1979) *Industrial Law Journal*, p. 85

§1. Advisory, Conciliation and Arbitration Service (ACAS)

70. This service was established from 2 September 1974[1] as an essential element in the Social Contract package of statutory aids to collective bargaining.[2] It is charged with the general duty of promoting the improvement of industrial relations, which includes the extension, development and, where necessary, reform of collective bargaining machinery. It also took over from the Department of Employment the functions of conciliation, arbitration and mediation (*see below*). In recognition of the priority of autonomous institutions, the service must have regard to the desirability of using voluntary procedures before intervening in individual or collective disputes.[3] Moreover, ACAS has no powers of compulsion – it seeks to discharge its responsibilities through the voluntary co-operation of the parties concerned. A central characteristic of ACAS is its impartiality and independence from Government. Although it is required to report annually to the Secretary of State, it is independent of Government and is not subject to the direction of Ministers. Thus during the period of operation of incomes policies, the service made it clear that it did 'not act as an interpreter or an enforcement agency' for government incomes policies.[4] ACAS is directed by a tripartite Council consisting of a full-time independent Chairman, and 9 members: three nominated by the Confederation of British Industry (CBI), three by the Trades Union Congress (TUC) and three independent members (usually academics).

1. It replaced the former Commission on Industrial Relations which had somewhat different functions and structure.
2. It was placed on a statutory basis from 1976 by EPA 1975, Part I, now TULRCA 1992, Pt IV, Chapter IV.
3. EPCA 1978, ss.133(5),134(4); SDA 1975, s.64(3); RRA, s.55(3).
4. ACAS Annual Report, 1976.

71. ACAS has eight principal functions:

(1) *Collective conciliation*: ACAS provides facilities for settling disputes by conciliation, either at the request of one or more of the parties or on its own initiative where a 'trade dispute' (*see* para. 486) exists or is apprehended. Since its establishment, there seems to have been greater willingness to accept third party intervention in disputes.[1] In 1975, ACAS completed conciliation action in 2,017 collective disputes (with a success rate of 80 per cent), a sharp contrast with conciliation in the 1960s, when the Department of Employment took action in only about 400 cases annually. The rapid rise in the number of collective conciliation cases was partly due to the search for loopholes to income policies, as is evidenced by the fact that, having peaked at 2,891 in 1977, the number of completed cases dropped sharply with the relaxation of incomes policies in 1979. These figures continued to decline in the 1980s, reaching 1,226 in 1992. However, despite the decrease in numbers, ACAS reports that cases tend to be longer, larger and more complicated with a growing number of cases concerned with changes in working practices and working time.

(2) *References to Arbitration and Mediation*: (for definition, *see* para. 48). Where a trade dispute exists or is apprehended, ACAS may appoint one or more persons (who are not officers of ACAS) to arbitrate or mediate, provided at least one party requests such a reference, both parties consent, and ACAS is satisfied that agreed procedures have been exhausted and conciliation has failed. Disputes may also be referred to the Central Arbitration Committee (*see below*). Awards of *ad hoc* arbitrators are published only if the parties consent. ACAS is also responsible for servicing a number of standing boards of arbitration in the public sector, such as the Railway

Staffs' National Tribunal, the Police Arbitration Tribunal, the Post Office Arbitration Tribunal and under the Pilotage Act 1987. As in collective conciliation, the number of cases referred to arbitration peaked in 1978 at 421, an eight-fold increase on the 54 cases dealt with by the Department of Employment in1973. The numbers then declined to 169 in 1989, and to 157 in 1991 after rising to 200 in 1990. The majority of disputes have consistently been concerned with pay and conditions of employment, dismissal and discipline and recently disputes about grading.

(3) *Conciliation in proceedings before industrial tribunals*: Conciliation officers designated by ACAS are required to promote a settlement of any complaint which has been or could be presented to an industrial tribunal (*see below*) in respect of statutory employment rights. This has proved to be a large part of ACAS's workload. From 29,100 cases received in 1975, this figure leapt to 41,930 in 1976, and has remained consistently high, peaking at 60,605 cases received in 1991. The Service has proved highly successful in its task of promoting settlements; an average of over two-thirds of cases received are cleared without reference to a tribunal. The majority of cases received concern unfair dismissal (about two-thirds in 1991).

(4) *Advice*: ACAS provides free advice to employers, employers' associations, individual workers and trade unions on a variety of subjects. It regards its advisory function as the principal means of fulfilling its statutory duty to promote the improvement of industrial relations and devotes a considerable proportion of its resources for this purpose. Advice includes both short-term assistance on specific matters and long-term, in-depth assistance which the Service considers to be more likely to lead to lasting improvements in industrial relations.

(5) *Codes of Practice*: ACAS has general power to issue codes of practice containing practical guidance to promote the improvement of industrial relations. Under this power, a Code of Practice on Disciplinary Practice and Procedures has been issued. ACAS has also issued Codes of Practice, as it is obliged to do, in respect of the disclosure of information for purposes of collective bargaining, and time off for trade union officials and members. (The effect of a Code in legal proceedings is considered in para. 96 *below.*)

(6) *Inquiry*: ACAS may inquire into any question relevant to industrial relations generally or in any particular industry. The findings may be published if ACAS considers it desirable. This power is not often used.

(7) *Disclosure of information for bargaining*: ACAS has specific duties in relation to this procedure (*see* Part II, Chapter IV *below*).

(8) *Equal pay*: ACAS has responsibility for designating independent experts to report on claims for equal pay for work of equal value when required to do so by an industrial tribunal (*see* Part I, Chapter VIII *below*)

1. All statistics are derived from ACAS Annual Reports, 1976–91.

§2. CENTRAL ARBITRATION COMMITTEE (CAC)

72. The Central Arbitration Committee was established in 1975 as a permanent tripartite arbitration committee maintained at state expense.[1] It consists of a Chairman and members with experience as employers' and workers' representatives respectively. For hearings, the Chairman (or Deputy) sits with two other members, one drawn from each side. It is independent of ACAS and is not subject to governmental directions of any kind.

1. TULRCA 1992, ss. 259–265.

73. Compulsory arbitration has never been a central feature of British industrial relations, consistent with the primacy of voluntary disputes resolution mechanisms (*see* paras. 46 and 47 *above*). Voluntary arbitration facilities have, however, been provided by the state since 1919, in the form of the Industrial Court (renamed the Industrial Arbitration Board in 1971), to which the relevant Government Minister could refer a dispute for voluntary arbitration with the consent of both parties and if all voluntary procedures had been exhausted. The CAC took over the voluntary arbitration functions of the Industrial Arbitration Board. Thus, at the request of one or more parties to a trade dispute, and with the consent of all parties, ACAS may refer a dispute to arbitration by the CAC. When created, the CAC's powers extended further, to include the power of unilateral arbitration as a sanction for failure to comply with many of the 'statutory props' introduced as part of the Social Contract legislation.[1] These included claims for the extensions of terms of employment and for the observance of fair wages in industries which receive government contracts, subsidies, loans or licences; claims arising from failure to comply with ACAS recommendations for union recognition or to disclose information for collective bargaining; disputes on statutory joint industrial councils and claims in respect of equal pay under collective agreements.

1. From 1959 to 1975, the only provision for unilateral arbitration was in cases where an employer failed to observe recognised terms and conditions (s. 8 Terms and Conditions of Employment Act 1959).

74. These facilities were widely used in the first years of the existence of the CAC, primarily because they provided a means to correct anomalies created by the operation of incomes policies. Thus, the number of references received shot up from 132 in 1976, to 1,030 in 1977 and 1,065 in 1978, dropping back to 617 in 1979. With the repeal of many of the 'statutory props' by the Conservative Government since 1979, the CAC's unilateral arbitration jurisdiction has been narrowed down to only the disclosure of information facilities (*see below* Part II, Chapter IV), under which a mere trickle of references is received each year (15 in 1989). The voluntary arbitration function remains and the CAC is anxious to develop this jurisdiction, although no references were received in 1989. The CAC determines its own procedure. Decisions under its statutory jurisdiction are published, but voluntary awards are only published with the consent of the parties. Its general practice is not to give reasons for its decision, except in the case of failure to disclose information, in which case it has a statutory duty to give reasons.

§3. Equal Opportunities Commission (EOC) and Commission for Racial Equality (CRE)

75. The EOC and CRE follow the same model and so can conveniently be dealt with together. Consisting of 8 to 15 members appointed by the Secretary of State, each Commission is charged with the general duty to work towards the elimination of discrimination, to promote equality of opportunity between men and women (EOC) or persons of different racial groups (CRE) and to review the operation of the anti-discrimination legislation.[1] The Commissions function as an important supplement to the individual right of recourse to an industrial tribunal on a discrimination complaint. Many cases of unlawful discrimination may not reach a tribunal: an individual may lack the resources or courage to initiate an action: evidence of individual detriment may be difficult to amass; or an individual remedy may be of little assistance to others affected by discriminatory practices (there are no class actions). To remedy some of these weaknesses, each Commission has the power to assist an individual complainant and to institute its own proceedings in relation to discriminatory advertisements, instructions or pressure to discriminate, and discriminatory practices.

1. SDA 1975, Part VI; RRA 1976, Part VII.

76. More significantly, each Commission has the additional power to initiate and conduct a 'formal investigation' into cases of suspected unlawful discrimination. This power, which combines investigative and judicial functions, carries with it the ability to demand written or oral evidence and the production of documents. The aim of the investigation is to secure a change in the discriminatory practices, and to this end the Commission may make recommendations for changes in policy or practice, either during or after the completion of the formal investigation. Moreover, if unlawful discrimination is revealed, each Commission has its own sanction, in the form of a 'non-discrimination notice', which (subject to the right of appeal to an industrial tribunal) may require the respondent not to commit any further unlawful discrimination and to keep the Commission informed of any changes instituted to do so. Recourse to judicial sanctions is envisaged only as a last resort – if the notice is not overturned on appeal and there is persistent discrimination within 5 years, the Commission can take the respondent to the County Court and obtain an injunction. Formal investigations have not had the impact that might have been expected, partly because the procedures are cumbersome and the courts have implied procedural requirements which have enabled some respondents to avoid or seriously delay investigation.[1] The CRE has placed more emphasis on formal investigations than the EOC, having published reports and 52 investigations between 1977 and December 1990, as against eleven by the EOC. Both Commissions also have powers to undertake and assist research or educational activities and to issue

Codes of Practice: the EOC Code was issued in February 1985 and that of the CRE in April 1984 (*see* further Part I, Chapter VII).

1. *See* C. McCrudden et al. *Racial Justice at Work: Enforcement of the Race Relations Act 1976 in Employment* (London, Policy Studies Institute, 1991), pp. 48–120.

§4. Training and Enterprise Councils (TECs)

77. In the 1970s and 1980s job creation and training activities were administered by the tripartite Manpower Services Commission (MSC). In line with the Government's retreat from tripartism, the MSC was abolished and replaced in 1988 by the Training Agency, which was part of the Department of Employment. That agency itself has now disappeared and its residual functions are carried out by a branch of the Department of Employment based in Sheffield. The centrepiece of the Government's employer-led training policy is the system of Training Enterprise Councils (TECs) in England and Wales and local Scottish agencies which have been set up since the end of 1989. At least two-thirds of the members of a TEC are employers at top management level, the other members being drawn from local education,training and development activities,voluntary bodies and trade unions which support the aims of the TEC. The TECs are intended to 'place ownership of the training and enterprise system with employers,'[1] often being based on local Chambers of Commerce or the CBI. The key functions of a TEC are to plan local training schemes, manage training programmes for young people, unemployed people and adults requiring new knowledge and technical retraining and to support small businesses. The Government provides some funding for TECs and staff are made available on secondment from the Department of Employment. The TECs usually sub-contract training activities to local providers. There is also a National Training Task Force (two-thirds of the members being employers) to assist the Secretary of State in carrying out his training functions. The National Council for Vocational Qualifications (NCVQ), set up in 1986, works with examining, validating, testing and professional bodies, with the aim of developing a flexible qualification system.

1. *Employment for the 1990s*, Cm. 540 (1988), para. 5.7.

§5. Certification Officer (CO)

78. The CO is an independent statutory officer, appointed under EPA TULRCA 1992, ss. 254–258, who is responsible for supervising several aspects of the internal affairs of trade unions. The powers of the CO, although less interventionist than his immediate predecessor, have been progressively augmented by the legislation of the 1980s. The CO was originally established with the primary function of scrutinising trade unions to decide whether they were truly independent of employers and issuing certificates of independence (*see* Part II, Chapter II). In addition, he or she has been responsible for monitoring the annual returns and accounts of unions and employers' associations, and supervising political funds and mergers between unions. To these have been added some of the central functions of the legislation of the 1980s, such as reimbursing expenditure by unions in conducting secret postal ballots, and dealing with complaints by union members that their union has failed to comply with balloting requirements in respect of elections, political funds and industrial action (*see below* paras. 493–495)

§6. Commissioner for the Rights of Trade Union Members (CROTUM)

78bis. The office of Commissioner was introduced by the EA 1988 (now TURCA 1992, ss. 266–271) in order to assist individual union members to bring legal action against their unions. The Commissioner may assist members in a wide range of complaints, including that the union has failed to comply with balloting requirements in respect of industrial action, political funds or trade union elections. In addition, members may seek assistance to assert rights established by the Employment Act 1988, such as to inspect the union's accounts, to complain that property has been used unlawfully by trustees, or that union funds have been used to indemnify unlawful conduct. These powers were further expanded by the Employment Act 1990, to include assistance for proceedings arising, not out of statutory provisions, but out of breach or threatened breach of certain union rules. The establishment of the Commissioner is unprecedented. No similar office exists for the protection of employees' rights against their employers; to the contrary, legal aid is not available for proceedings in industrial tribunals. By contrast, the Commissioner is fully funded by the State, and such assistance is available regardless of the means of the applicant. This is justified by Government policy-makers on the grounds that the applicant is pursuing 'public' rights and not simply private interests. In her first year of activity, the Commissioner received relatively few complaints. Although 324 enquiries were received, there were only 29 formal applications for assistance. Very few of these resulted in legal action: for example of six applications received in respect of ballots before industrial action, assistance was granted to two to seek interlocutory injunctions, but in both cases the court refused to issue the order.[1]

1. *Commissioner for the Rights of Trade Union Members* Annual Report 1989/90.

§7. Department of Employment (DE)

79. It is clear from the above that many functions exercised in other countries by Labour Ministries are, in Britain, entrusted to independent or semi-independent Government agencies. In fact, these functions were originally developed by the Department of Employment and its predecessors. The Labour Department of the Board of Trade was set up in 1886 mainly to collect information on trade unions, strikes and other matters. During World War I, a separate Ministry of Labour was established, exercising various functions in relation to conciliation and arbitration, functions which were retained by its successors, the Department of Employment and Productivity and finally the Department of Employment, until they were transferred to ACAS in September 1974 (*see above*). During the 1980s, the Department has in fact regained some of these functions. For example, since 1985, it has been responsible for government policy on deregulation; and in 1989 it regained training functions from the Manpower Services Commission and its successors, the Training Commission and the Training Agency. The Department has always retained a central role in the co-ordination and formulation of policy, research and consultation with employers' associations and trade unions, as well as having specific functions such as the promotion of equal opportunities, and the collection of labour statistics. It is also responsible for wages councils, industrial tribunals, the Employment Appeal Tribunal and Courts of Inquiry (on the latter *see* para. 505, *below*).

V. Industrial Tribunals and Courts

§1. Jurisdiction of Tribunals

80. A specialised system of labour courts, known as industrial tribunals, has only existed in the UK since 1964. They were first created, under the Industrial Training Act 1964, to deal with the relatively minor question of appeals by employers against levies imposed on them by industrial training boards. Since then, the jurisdiction has been expanded enormously, to cover almost all the statutory individual employment rights, including for example, unfair dismissal, redundancy compensation, equal pay, and sex and race discrimination in employment. The Donovan Commission suggested that industrial tribunals should be concerned with individual rights only, and not in collective matters, 'since these are matters which must be settled by procedures of, or agreed through, collective bargaining' (para. 576). While this is broadly the case (*see*, for example, the provision excluding claims for unfair dismissal during industrial action, para. 477, *below*), the distinction has not always proved easy to draw, as with the right not to be dismissed for trade union activities, and the right to have one's trade union consulted about impending redundancies. Since 1980, industrial tribunals have been given additional powers which have clear collective ramifications, particularly in closed shop cases.[1] Nor have industrial tribunals been given jurisdiction over all claims concerned with employment. An awkward separation of jurisdictions between tribunals and the ordinary civil courts remains. Jurisdiction for claims arising out of breach of contract, including the contract of employment, remains with the ordinary civil courts, as do actions for damages in tort, particularly for personal injury or death. Similarly, collective disputes, insofar as they give rise to civil action, are dealt with by the ordinary courts. This is not to say that tribunals never have to decide questions of breach of contract, for example, in the case of 'constructive dismissal', an unfair dismissal claim is premissed on the tribunal making a preliminary finding of breach of contract (*see* Part I, Chapter VII). The tribunals have power under the Wages Act 1986 to make awards in respect of 'deductions' from pay. This covers non-payment of wages or holiday pay, but not the failure to pay wages in lieu of notice.[2] The Lord Chancellor (for England) and the Secretary of State (for Scotland) have the power, not yet exercised, to confer jurisdiction on industrial tribunals to deal with claims for damages for breach of the contract of employment and other related contracts, in limited circumstances, such as contractual claims arising or outstanding on the termination of employment.

1. For example, the right not to be unreasonably excluded or expelled from one's trade union, and the right to join a trade union as a defendant in unfair dismissal proceedings in closed shop cases (*see* further Part II, Chapter I, *below*).
2. *Delaney* v. *Staples* [1992] IRLR 191, HL.

§2. Jurisdiction of Courts

81. The ordinary courts have exclusive jurisdiction in respect of (1) actions for damages and other remedies arising out of breach of contract; (2) actions in tort (delict), the most important of which are for injunctions and damages in connection with industrial action (*see* Part II, Chapter V, *below*); (3) actions for damages for personal injuries in respect of a person's death. In England and Wales these actions may be brought in either the county court or the High Court. Since 1 July 1991, there has been a new system of allocation of business between these courts. There is a presumption that actions whose value is less than £25,000 are to be tried in the county court, and those with a value of over £50,000 in the High Court (but personal injury actions whose value is less than £50,000 must be tried in the county court). These presumptive limits are rebuttable by various other considerations, namely financial substance, importance, complexity and speed. In Scotland, the action may be brought in either the sheriff court or in the Court of Session. There are special speedy and relatively cheap procedures for small claims in the county court and sheriff court. There is an appeal to the Court of Appeal (Civil Division) in England and Wales, or to the Sheriff Principal and then to the Inner House of the Court of Session in Scotland. Other cases, in particular those for injunctions arising out of industrial action, are brought before a single judge in the High Court in England and Wales (in either the Queen's Bench or Chancery Division) and the Court of Session (Outer House) in Scotland. There is an appeal to the Court of Appeal and the Inner House of the Court of Session respectively. The House of Lords is the final appellate court for both England and Wales and Scotland; appeals to this body require either leave of itself or of the court below. The High Court and the Court of Session also have a general supervisory jurisdiction over inferior tribunals. The ordinary courts have also been given jurisdiction to adjudicate on some of the new rights given to trade union members by the Employment Act 1988. In addition, the High Court has an inherent jurisdiction to review certain decisions and actions of public employers.

§3. Composition of Tribunals

82. Industrial tribunals have a tripartite structure, consisting of a legal chairman (a barrister[1] or solicitor of at least 7 years' standing drawn from a panel of chairmen appointed by the Lord Chancellor[2]) and two lay members with industrial experience, drawn from panels appointed by the Secretary of State for Employment, one after consultation with the trades unions, the other after consultation with employers' organizations. This structure made industrial tribunals more acceptable to trade unions than the ordinary courts, which, as we have seen, had frequently been hostile to trade union interests. The lay members have full voting rights and it is not unknown for them to outvote the lawyer chairman, although they are generally reluctant to do so on points of law. The lay members are not intended to act as representatives of trade unions or employers' associations. Instead, they are expected to act as neutral arbiters, drawing on their experience of industrial relations to enhance the quality of their decision-making. Indeed, about 96 per cent of decisions are unanimous.

1. Advocate in Scotland.
2. Secretary of State for Scotland in Scottish tribunals.

83. As at November 1990, there were 60 full-time (permanent) chairmen and 81.5 part-time chairmen in England and Wales.[1] There is no professional civil service-type judiciary in Britain: chairmen usually come from the ranks of private practitioners in the ordinary courts and may have no special expertise in labour law when first appointed. At May 1990, there were 1,860 lay members for England and Wales. They are all part-time, and are usually practising trade union officials or personnel managers of companies.

1. All statistics in this section are derived from the Central Office of the Industrial Tribunals (England and Wales), Fact Sheet November 1990.

84. There are three separate Central Offices of Industrial Tribunals: one in London, for England and Wales, one in Glasgow, for Scotland, and one in Belfast, for Northern Ireland, each with its own President. In addition, there are 11 regional offices in England and Wales, each with a Regional Chairman. Permanent accommodation for hearing applications is provided at 24 centres in England and Wales, dealing with approximately 12,500 hearings per annum.

§4. Procedure

84bis. Despite their structure, industrial tribunals retain many of the characteristics of ordinary courts. The adversarial system prevails, with each party responsible for presenting and proving its case and the tribunal having no investigative powers of its own. Furthermore, the tribunal itself has no power to promote or order a compromise, the function of conciliation being given instead to ACAS (*see above*, para. 70) at the pre-hearing stage. On the other hand, their enforcement powers are not as strong as those of ordinary courts. The ultimate sanction for breach of an order made by an industrial tribunal is payment of a sum of money; it has no power to issue injunctions or to fine or imprison for contempt of court. Instead, the county courts in England and Wales and the sheriff's court in Scotland have jurisdiction to enforce tribunal orders in the same way as other orders.

85. Nevertheless, tribunals have several advantages over the ordinary courts They are much quicker – 80 per cent of all applications reach a first hearing in under 26 weeks, whereas a case in the civil courts can take years rather than months. Furthermore, tribunals are more accessible, sitting, as we have seen, all over the country. Although the basic adversarial procedure remains, tribunals are more informal than courts: there are no complicated pleadings and tribunals are not bound by the strict rules of evidence. It was initially envisaged that legal representation would normally be avoided in tribunals. A party can choose any representative or be unrepresented. State-funded legal aid is not available. Each party bears his or her own expenses and legal costs will only be awarded against a party who acts frivolously or vexatiously or otherwise unreasonably. In practice, legal representation has become common, particularly on the parts of employers. In 1988–89, 47.1 per cent of all respondents had legal representatives at the hearing, as against 32.4 per cent of all applicants. Applicants were represented by trade union officials in a further 15 per cent of cases. About 37 per cent of applicants and 43 per cent of respondents appeared in person. With respect to costs, a discretionary provision for a pre-hearing assessment was introduced in October 1980, to function as a filter for worthless claims, and a party who insists on pursuing a case despite a warning at the pre-hearing assessment may have costs awarded against him or her. The figures demonstrate, however, that the use of this procedure declined rapidly after the first few years. In 1988–1989, assessments were arranged for 517 cases, as compared with 3,000 in the year ending September 1984. Moreover, only a small proportion of these led to awards of costs: of the 47 per cent warned in 1988–1989, only 13 eventually had costs awarded against them. Partly because of the ineffectiveness of this procedure, provision was made in the Employment Act 1989 for the Secretary of State to make regulations providing for a new pre-hearing review at which a party to the proceedings may be required to pay a deposit of up to £150 if he or she wishes to continue to participate in the proceedings. This would replace the existing system of pre-hearing assessments. This has been criticised as an unprecedented obstacle to the pursuance of a legal claim by the poorest applicants.

86. Tribunals have come to occupy a central position in labour law, as is evidenced by their workload. The number of applications registered jumped from 13,555 in 1972 to 43,066 in 1976 as the number and scope of tribunal jurisdictions increased. The intake declined thereafter until 1981 (as a result of the removal of certain short-service workers from protection: *see* Part I, Chapter VII *below*), when the numbers again increased to 40,042. Thereafter numbers declined. There was an increase in 1986 caused by some very large multiple applications; this made even more dramatic the decline in 1987 following legislative changes relating to unfair dismissal. Since then, the numbers of applications have started to increase once more. In 1988–1989 26,127 applications were registered. Almost 60 per cent of these were complaints of unfair dismissal. This percentage has dropped from the 1987 figure, which was over 70 per cent. The principal cause of the increase in the number of complaints is the Wages Act 1986 (deductions from pay) which accounted for 15 per cent of applications in 1988–1989. In 1989–1990 there were 34,697 applications to tribunals, 58 per cent of them about unfair dismissal.

§5. Employment Appeal Tribunal (EAT)

87. The EAT was established by the Employment Protection Act 1975, replacing the National Industries Relations Court which had been established to administer the unpopular Industrial Relations Act 1971 (*see* Introduction, § III). The EAT adjudicates on appeals on questions of law from decisions of industrial tribunals in most of their jurisdictions,[1] and on questions of fact and law in appeals on decisions relating to exclusion or expulsion from a trade union (*see* Part II, Chapter I *below*); and has original jurisdiction to assess compensation in some of the latter cases. The EAT can entertain appeals on questions of both fact and law from certain decisions of the Certification Officer (e.g. listing and independence) (*see above*, para. 78). In its earlier years, the EAT went to some lengths to establish guidelines and standard criteria for application by tribunals, but in recent years, it has been more inclined to refuse appellate jurisdiction by classifying issues as questions of fact, on which no appeal lies, rather than questions of law. The rationale for thus limiting possible points of appeal has been to discourage legalism and technicality, retaining the tribunals' character as quick, cheap and accessible means of resolving disputes. This stance has, however, been criticised as leading to inconsistencies in the application of legislative provisions by different tribunals. There is a further appeal on questions of law from the EAT to the Court of Appeal (CA) in England and Wales and to the Court of Session (Inner House) in Scotland, but the leave of either the EAT or the higher court must first be obtained. From these courts, there is a final appeal, with leave, on questions of law to the House of Lords, the highest court. In practice, most appeals do not go beyond the EAT.

1. Appeals on a few question of law, such as under compensation schemes for displaced local authority employees and industrial training levies, go from industrial tribunals to the High Court in England and the Court of Session in Scotland.

88. Unusually for an appellate body, the EAT has a tripartite composition, consisting of a judge, drawn from a panel of High Court and Court of Session judges, and either two or four lay members, drawn from a panel of persons appointed because of their special knowledge and experience of industrial relations. As in the case of industrial tribunal proceedings, in any case there is an equal number of persons with experience as representatives of employers and workers respectively, again the aim being to draw on industrial relations expertise, rather than to adopt a partisan approach. In the period 1988–1989, the EAT registered 642 appeals from decisions of industrial tribunals in England and Wales, approximately 5.5 per cent of cases determined at a tribunal hearing. Of the cases that were heard on appeal during this period, the EAT dismissed 36.18 per cent, allowed or remitted 24.8 per cent to the tribunal for rehearing. A further 39.02 per cent were withdrawn. The majority of these appeals (51.63 per cent) were lodged by employees.

89. The doctrine of precedent, by which lower courts and tribunals are bound by the *ratio decidendi* (or grounds) of decisions of higher courts, applies equally to the industrial tribunals and the EAT. Thus, industrial tribunals are bound by the decisions of the EAT and of all the higher courts. The EAT is in turn bound by decisions of the Court of Appeal and the Court of Session (Inner House), and, at the top of the pyramid, the House of Lords. The EAT is considered to be of equal jurisdiction to the Queen's Bench Division of the

High Court and the Court of Session (Outer House); therefore decisions of these latter courts will have persuasive but not binding force in the EAT. This system of precedent means that law reporting is a matter of some importance. Since tribunal decisions are binding only on the parties, reports of these decisions are of interest only as illustrations of the practice of tribunals. Reports of decisions of the EAT and superior courts are, however, potential precedents. The main series of reports are listed at the end of this book.

VI. Sources of Labour Law

90. Legal norms regulating employment relationships are derived from a variety of sources, including the common law, legislation, codes of practice and voluntary or autonomous sources.

§1. Common Law

91. At common law, the focus of legal analysis is the relationship between the employer and each individual employee. This relationship is characterised as a contract, the assumption being, as in other contractual relationships, that there is a personal and voluntary exchange of freely bargained promises between two parties [employer and employee] equally protected by the civil law alone. In practice, however, the terms and conditions of employment of most employees are not negotiated individually and on an equal basis with the employer. In the vast majority of cases, terms and conditions are either unilaterally imposed by the employer, or are laid down in a collective agreement between the employer or employers' organization and the relevant trade unions. Nevertheless, industrial relations continues to be characterised by lawyers as a mass of individual contracts of employment and it is through the mechanism of contract that most rights and obligations take effect. For example, terms and conditions laid down in a collective agreement are only given legal effect if they can be shown to be incorporated into an individual contract (*see* Part I, Chapter II).

92. The common law has also been a source of legal norms regulating collective relationships. A series of civil wrongs regulating industrial action was developed by the courts (for example, the tort of inducing breach of contract) and although these have been overlaid by a complex system of statutory immunities (*see* Part II, Chapter V), the foundation remains the common law. The relationship between trade unions and their members is construed as one of contract (*see* Part II, Chapter II).

§2. Legislation

93. In the absence of a written constitution (para. 11, *above*), the major legislative impetus comes from Parliament. Although voluntary collective bargaining was the primary source of protection for employees until the 1960s, certain aspects of industrial relations have been regulated by the State since the nineteenth century. This included legislation protecting children and women, regulating some aspects of health and safety and establishing mechanisms for setting minimum wages in certain industries. More recently, there has been a rapid increase in employment legislation, with 60 general Acts of Parliament regulating employment being passed between 1960 and 1991 (*see* section III, *above*). To these must be added numerous statutes applying to specific sectors of employment.

94. In addition to Parliament, other bodies such as Ministers, Departments of State, public corporations and local authorities have limited law-making powers, subject to repeal or alteration by Parliament. There are several hundred pieces of subordinate legislation of this kind, covering matters as diverse as the employment of children, levies for industrial training, minimum wages orders, the licensing of employment agencies and the procedure of industrial tribunals. There is also a large number of regulations applying to specific employments. A peculiar feature of law-making in the UK is that regulations governing the terms and conditions of employment of civil servants (in central government) are made by the Minister for the Civil Service under the ancient prerogative powers of the Crown. It was only in 1984 that it was established, for the first time, that the exercise of these powers is subject to judicial review on grounds of illegality, irrationality or procedural impropriety.[1]

1. *Council of Civil Service Unions* v. *Minister of the Civil Service* [1984] 3 All ER 935 HL; *see* Part II, Chapter I.

§3. Relation between Legislation and Common Law

95. Because legislative intervention developed in parallel and often independently of the common law concept of the contract of employment, the relationship between statutes and the contract is complex:

(1) Some statutory rights operate wholly outside of the contract of employment. For example, a breach of an employer's statutory safety duties may be the subject of criminal prosecution or administrative enforcement under the Health and Safety at Work Act 1974 or, in some cases, a civil action for damages by an injured employee in tort.
(2) In some cases, both statutory and contractual rights exist, as in the case of statutory rights to guarantee payments for employees who are laid off work, maternity pay and payment for time-off (*see* Part I, Chapters IV and V). In such cases, overlap is avoided by express provision in the statute either for the set-off of sums of money awarded under the statute against amounts due under the contract, or vice versa, or by the creation of 'composite' rights enabling the employee to claim those features of the contractual and statutory rights which are most favourable.
(3) Some recent legislation expressly provides that the duties they impose are to take effect as terms of the individual contract. An example is the Equal Pay Act 1970 which provides that an 'equality clause' is deemed to be included in the contract of every man and woman employed at an establishment in Great Britain.
(4) Other statutes are silent on this point, leaving the courts and tribunals free to decide whether or not rights arise under the contract. This has on occasion led to the employee being deprived of statutory protection (e.g.

protection against unfair dismissal is lost if the contract is illegal because of an agreement to defraud the Revenue of PAYE tax).

(5) Arbitration awards made by the CAC under its statutory jurisdiction take effect as compulsory terms of the contracts of employment of the employees concerned (*see* Part II, Chapter IV).

§4. Codes of Practice

96. Codes of Practice are issued under statutory powers to provide guidance to industrial relations practitioners on the application of various statutory provisions. The Codes do not have the same status as statute or subordinate legislation: failure to observe the provisions of a Code does not of itself render a person liable to legal proceedings. But a Code is admissible in evidence in proceedings before an industrial tribunal or the CAC or court and any provision of the Code which appears to be relevant to any question arising in the proceedings must be taken into account by the tribunal or CAC or court in determining that question.[1] Several bodies now have powers to issue Codes which have to be approved by both Houses of Parliament.

1. TULRCA 1992, s. 207.

97. The Industrial Relations Code of Practice (1972), remained in force until revoked from 1 June 1991. Thus far, ACAS has issued 3 Codes, dealing with: (i) disclosure of information for collective bargaining (1977); (ii) time off for trade union duties and activities (1977, revised 1991), and (iii) disciplinary practice and procedures (1977).[1] The Commission for Racial Equality and the Equal Opportunities Commission have issued Codes for the elimination of race and sex discrimination respectively,[2] while the Health and Safety Commission has issued a Code in respect of safety representatives and safety committees.[3] In 1980, the Secretary of State for Employment was given power to issue Codes[4] and has issued three: one on Picketing (17 December 1980) one on Closed Shop Agreements and Arrangements (18 May 1983, now revoked as from 1 June 1991), and one on Trade Union Ballots and Industrial Action (1990, revised 1991). The latter have proved contentious, and some critics have argued that since they do not reflect a consensus view of industrial relations practice, these Codes should have obtained full Parliamentary approval through the legislative process. This is particularly so since the Code on picketing appears to have influenced both police conduct with respect to picketing and the common law.

1. A draft revised Code was circulated for consultation by ACAS in October 1985 but rejected by the Secretary of State
2. RRA 1976, s. 47(1); SDA 1975, s. 56A.
3. Health and Safety at Work etc. Act 1974, s. 16.
4. Now consolidated in TULRCA 1992, ss. 203–206. The EA 1980, s. 12 made it easier to revise or revoke Codes.

§5. VOLUNTARY SOURCES

98. As we have seen, it is a distinctive characteristic of British labour law that the parties themselves have wide scope for creating norms which in practice govern working relationships. These norms are not always given legal effect even if they function in practice as a code governing important aspects of behaviour, the preference being for non-legal means of enforcement (such as disciplinary or industrial action). Where such norms are given legal effect, it is generally at the individual rather than collective level, via incorporation into the individual contract of employment. The most important 'voluntary' sources of terms and conditions of employment are: (i) works' rules, notices and other documents issued by management to employees; (ii) collective agreements; and (iii) 'custom and practice', a more informal source of regulation, whereby working conditions are determined by force of tradition or by informal arrangements between workers and employees. Custom and practice is also an important source of norms supplementing the rulebook which governs the relationship between trade unions and their members.[1] These norms may be emanations of either unilateral management decision-making or joint regulation, or even unilateral worker action. Thus works' rules are examples of unilateral government by management of the workplace. Collective agreements are important examples of joint regulation, as are resolutions of joint negotiating bodies such as the Whitley Councils (*see* Part II, Chapter IV). While custom and practice is frequently an example of joint regulation, albeit informal, it may also be a result of unilateral management decision-making which has become the accepted status quo. The methods of incorporation of these sources into the individual contract of employment are considered in Part I, Chapter II.

1. *Heatons Transport (St. Helens) Ltd.* v. *TGWU* [1972] ICR 308 (HL).

VII. Private International Labour Law

§1. Scope and Sources

99. The increasing international migration of labour gives rise to three distinct problems. (1) The limits of the jurisdiction (i.e. the power to hear and determine issues) of national courts and tribunals. (2) The choice of the system of law to be applied in determining cases with a foreign element. (3) The law as to nationality and the minimum standards to be applied to workers of foreign nationality. In England and Scotland, the terms 'private international law' and 'conflict of laws' are synonymously applied to the first two of these problems. Rules as to nationality and the treatment of foreign workers are considered as part of constitutional and administrative law, and in this monograph are dealt with briefly in paras. 143–145. Since England and Wales, Scotland, and Northern Ireland have separate legal systems, it follows that English private international law rules are distinct from those of each of the other law-countries within the United Kingdom: thus Scots law and the law of Northern Ireland are as 'foreign' in England as the law of Italy or France. Scottish private international law rules are markedly similar to those of the English and Northern Irish legal systems, and the following brief account of the English rules may be taken to be generally similar to the Scottish and Northern Irish rules.

100. Judge-made case law is the most important source of the law in this field. The rules have been developed piecemeal by the judges on the basis of principles of justice, comity and convenience. The 'choice of jurisdiction' question is treated entirely as a question of procedure. Whether or not a court or tribunal is competent to try an issue depends solely upon procedure, and not upon nationality, domicile or residence. So far as proceedings in the High Court are concerned so long as a writ of summons has been served upon a person, who is present within the jurisdiction, in accordance with the rules of procedure he or she is subject to the power of the court even though he or she is a foreigner and the cause of action has no factual connection with England. This basic common law rule has been modified by Acts of Parliament and rules of court, which give a discretionary power to a judge to authorise service of a writ of summons upon a defendant abroad in a limited number of cases. For example, where a contract was made within the jurisdiction or a breach of contract was committed within the jurisdiction it may be possible to obtain leave to serve process abroad in an action affecting that contract and by so doing create an 'assumed jurisdiction'. The details fall outside the scope of this monograph. The scope of the jurisdiction of the industrial tribunals, which deal with various statutory employment rights, is dealt with in para. 80, *above*.

101 . The problem as to which national labour law to apply depends upon (1) the English and Scottish private international law rules, as developed by the judges, which determine whether a contract or tort (delict) is governed by a particular system, and (2) the express or implied territorial scope of Acts of the

United Kingdom Parliament and of subordinate legislation. These are matters which have received little attention from the courts and legal writers.[1] These problems are particularly important in the context of the freedom of movement guaranteed by Article 48 and the freedom of establishment guaranteed by Article 51 of the Treaty of Rome. The EC Convention on the Law Applicable to Contractual Obligations (1980) which seeks to harmonise the rules applying to all cases having a foreign element, whether or not they have any connection with the EC, makes special provisions in Article 6 for the choice of law in the case of employment contracts. This has been implemented in the UK by the Contracts (Applicable Law) Act 1990.

1. For a more detailed treatment than is possible here *see* B.A. Hepple in Sweet and Maxwell's *Encyclopedia of Employment Law*, Part I, I; Dicey and Morris on *The Conflict of Laws*, 11th ed. (London, 1987) with supplements, Chapter 33, Part 6.

§2. Choice of Law Rules

102. One must distinguish three questions: (a) which is the law that applies to the contract or tort (delict)? (b) if English (or Scottish) law is the applicable law, is there a statute which, within that law, restricts its application in space, i.e. is there a self-limiting statute such as a statute restricted to the contracts of employees who ordinarily work under the contract in Great Britain, or excluding those who under an English or Scottish contract ordinarily work abroad? (c) is there a statute which by its terms applies irrespective of what is the law applicable to the contract or tort in question, for example on the ground that the employee ordinarily works under the contract in Great Britain, thus including those who do so under a contract governed by foreign law i.e. 'is there a true *loi d'application immédiate* which, on proper analysis, is a crystallised rule of *ordre public*'?[1] In regard to question (a) the English and Scottish courts apply the 'proper law of the contract', by which is meant the law that the parties intended to govern the contract. Where their intention has not been expressed and cannot be implied from the circumstances, the 'proper law' is the legal system with which the contract is most closely connected. In this latter case the judge puts himself in the position of the 'reasonable person' in order to discover the law with which the contract has the 'closest and most real connection'. There is no rigid rule as to which connecting factors must be applied. In the case of high-level management, advisory staff and specialists it is likely that the proper law (in the absence of express or implied choice by the parties) will be the law of the place where the undertaking has its centre of control and management because such employees are an integral part of the organization's management. Lower-level employees are usually engaged in the State where they reside and where they are required to work and so the proper law (in the absence of express or implied choice by the parties) is likely to be the law of the place of residence of the employee or the law of the place where the contract is to be performed. However, the rules are flexible and other factors such as the connection with the place of contracting may also be relevant. Some issues arising out of the employment relationship are classified as questions of tort (delict) and not of contract. A work accident may be classified either as a breach of contract or as a tort (delict).[2] If it is treated as a tort and the accident occurred in a foreign country it will be actionable in England only if it satisfies the so-called double actionability rule: the act must be both (a) actionable as a tort according to English law, had the act occurred in England, and (b) actionable according to the law of the foreign country where it was done. The second limb of this rule appears to mean that if the injured employee is entitled only to social security or analogous state benefits by way of compensation for injuries received under the foreign law it will not be possible for the employee to succeed in a tort action in England.[3] Where there is an exception clause in the contract of employment limiting or excluding the employer's liability, it is first necessary to ask whether the law governing the tort would regard the defence as admissible, and then whether the clause is valid by the proper law of the contract.[4] The EC Convention on the law applicable to contractual conventions (implemented from 1 April 1991 by the Contracts (Applicable Law) Act 1990) permits free choice of law as a general rule, and where there has been no such choice the contract is governed by the law of the country with which it is most closely connected.[5] Article 6(1) of the Convention, by way of derogation from this general principle, provides that in the case of individual employment contracts a choice of law made by the parties 'shall not have the result of depriving the employee of the protection afforded by the mandatory rules of the law that would be applicable under paragraph 2 [of Art.6] in the absence of choice.' These mandatory rules would include not only those relating to the contract itself but also other legal rules such as those on health and safety. Article 6(2) says that where there has been no valid choice contracts of employment shall be governed by the law of the country in which the employee habitually carried out his work even if he is temporarily employed in another country, or if he does not habitually work in any one country by the law of the country in which the place of business through which he is engaged is situated. To this there is a proviso allowing the application of some other country's law if it appears from the circumstances as a whole that the contract as a whole is more closely connected with that country. The concept of 'habitual' place of work appears to be similar to that of 'ordinary place of work' under British employment legislation (*see* para.104 *below*).

1. O. Kahn-Freund, *Selected Writings* (London, 1978), p. 271.
2. *Matthews* v. *Kuwait Bechtel Corp.* [1959] 2 QB 57 (an English contract with a Panamanian company to work in Kuwait: held claim arising out of work accident in Kuwait could be pleaded in contract or tort for purposes of obtaining leave to serve a writ of summons out of the jurisdiction).
3. *See* comment on *Coupland* v. *Arabian Gulf Petroleum Co.* [1983] 3 All ER 226, CA, by C. G. J. Morse (1984) 33 *International and Comparative Law Quarterly* 449.
4. *Ibid,*; *see* too, *Sayers* v. *International Drilling Co. NV* [1971] 1 WLR 1176, criticised by L. Collins (1972) 21 *International and Comparative Law Quarterly* 320.
5. *See* generally, C.J.G. Morse, in *Contract Conflicts* (ed. P.M.North) (London,1982), pp. 143–173, and in (1982) *2 Yearbook of European Law 107.*

§3. Application of Statutes

103. An important feature of judicial interpretation of statutes in Britain is that the courts have refused to apply to statutes the ordinary criteria of private international law. In other words, instead of regarding the territorial scope of statutes as being co-terminous with the proper law of the contract, labour legislation has generally been confined in its operation to work done within the territorial boundaries of Great Britain. (In this connection, it is to be noted that most labour legislation extends to the whole of Great Britain, including Scotland; in a few exceptional cases, such as agricultural wages and teachers' remuneration, there is separate Scottish legislation.) For example, the Factories Acts have been judicially interpreted as applying only to work within Great Britain,[1] and most modern employment protection legislation is expressed to apply only to those employees who under their contracts of employment 'ordinarily work' within Great Britain. This is the case, for example, with the right to complain of unfair dismissal, various other rights arising in the course of employment, maternity rights, rights upon the insolvency of the employer,[2] and the protection of wages.[3] The criteria for applying the Equal Pay Act 1970, the Sex Discrimination Act 1975 and the Race Relations Act 1976 are that the work must be 'at an establishment' in Great Britain and, subject to a number of exceptions, this covers all those who are not proved to do their work 'wholly or mainly' outside Great Britain.[4] With regard to redundancy payments, an employee who ordinarily works outside Great Britain is not entitled to a redundancy payment unless on the 'relevant date' (i.e., the date when the dismissal takes effect) he is in Great Britain in accordance with instructions given to him by his employer. An employee who is outside Great Britain on the 'relevant date' is entitled to a redundancy payment only if he ordinarily works inside Great Britain.[5]

1. *Yorke* v. *British & Continental Steamship Co.* (1945) 78 LILR 181 (accident in Gibraltar to employee under contract governed by English law: held dock regulations made under Factories Act 1937 did not apply), *Tomalin* v. *S. Pearson Ltd.* [1909] 2 KB 61 (Workmen's Compensation Acts applied only to accidents arising out of and in the course of employment in Great Britain); see now Social Security Act 1975, s.131 and regulations thereunder.
2. EPCA 1978, s. 141(2).
3. Wages Act 1986, s. 30(1).
4. Equal Pay Act 1970, s.1(1); SDA, ss. 6,10; RRA, ss. 4, 6, 8, 9, 37.
5. EPCA 1978, s.141(3) (4) (5). Generally speaking, for the purposes of calculating a person's period of continuous employment (upon which eligibility and the amount of payment depends) no account may be taken of weeks during which he was employed outside Great Britain and no social security contributions were being made.

104. The criterion used to determine the territorial application of legislation is usually whether the employee 'ordinarily works' outside Great Britain. The Court of Appeal has held[1] that the correct approach is to examine the relevant terms of the contract of employment, express or implied, over the whole period of the contract. If the contract expressly or impliedly requires the work to be wholly or substantially done outside Great Britain, no problem arises. Similarly, there is no problem if the contract expressly or impliedly requires the work to be wholly or substantially done inside Great Britain. The difficulty arises where the contract leaves it to the employer's discretion where the work shall be carried out. In such a case, the Court of Appeal has said[2] that it must be asked where the employee's base was to be, and in the absence of special factors leading to the contrary conclusion the country where his base was to be is likely to be the place where he is to be treated as 'ordinarily' working. This is so, even if he spends a considerable amount of time working abroad. In ascertaining the 'base' all the relevant express and implied terms of the contract must be considered, including those which define where the employee's headquarters were to be, indicating where his travels would begin and end, where his orders came from, where his residence was and in what currency he was to be paid. It seems that an employee cannot have a 'moving' base and cannot during the whole period of his contract be ordinarily working both inside and outside Great Britain.[3] In general, British labour legislation affords an example of *loi d'application immédiate*, or crystallised *ordre public*. For example, The Trade Union and Labour Relations (Consolidation) Act 1992, the Employment Protection (Consolidation) Act 1978 and the Equal Pay Act 1970, apply irrespective of the proper law of the contract.[4] A similar result has been achieved by judicial interpretation in respect of the Truck Acts which regulate deductions from wages of manual employees.[5] An English or Scottish court will, in these cases, apply the British statute, insofar as the statute has territorial application (e.g., to a person ordinarily working inside Great Britain), to a person working under a contract governed by foreign law. This approach may be justified on the ground that labour legislation is part of the public policy of the *lex fori* (Great Britain), and employers should be prevented from abusing their superior bargaining power by obtaining the employee's agreement to apply a less socially advanced system of law.

1. *Wilson* v. *Maynard Shipbuilding Consultants A. B.* [1978] ICR 376; *Todd* v. *British Midland Airways Ltd.* [1978] ICR 959; *Janata Bank* v. *Ahmed* [1981] ICR 791, CA.
2. *Wilson's* case at p. 387, *Todd's* case at pp. 964, 967.
3. *Wilson's* case at p. 384, overruling *Portect (UK) Ltd.* v. *Mogensen* [1976] ICR 396.
4. TULRCA 1992, s. 289; EPCA 1978, s.153(5); Equal Pay Act 1970, s.1(11).
5. *Duncan* v. *Motherwell Bridge & Engineering Co. Ltd.* 1952 SC 131 (held by Inner House of Court of Session that Truck Act 1831 applied if deductions made from wages paid in Scotland irrespective of proper law).

§4. Collective Labour Relations

105. A collective agreement is conclusively presumed by Section 179 of the Trade Union and Labour Relations (Consolidation) Act 1992 not to have been intended by the parties to be a legally enforceable contract unless the parties expressly agree in writing that it shall be enforceable (*see* Part II, Chapter IV). The Court of Appeal has held that this provision is not a material consideration in determining the proper law of the collective agreement.[1] This was in the context of a case in which Maltese shipowners claimed damages from the International Transport Workers' Federation (ITF), based in London, on grounds *inter alia* of their failure to issue a certificate, that the crew of a ship flying a Maltese flag and manned by a Spanish crew were engaged on terms acceptable to the ITF. The undertaking to issue the certificate was contained in a 'special agreement' on a printed form issued by ITF in London, but executed in Bilbao, Spain. It contained no statement of enforceability under Section 18 of the British Act. On a preliminary point, it was held that the proper law of the 'special agreement' was Spanish law and not English law. This was because the agreement, intended to be used worldwide, had been entered into in Spain and affected the recruitment of Spanish crews and so had its 'closest and most real connection' with Spanish law. Section 18 of the British Act was treated as substantive and not merely procedural in effect: hence it was the proper law, rather than the *lex fori* which should govern the issue.

1. *Monterosso Shipping Co. Ltd.* v. *ITF* [1982] ICR 675, CA. No reference was made in this case to TULRA 1974, s. 30(6) (now TULRCA 1992, s. 289) which provides that for purposes of the Act 'it is immaterial whether the law which (apart from this Act) governs any person's employment is the law of the United Kingdom, or of a part of the United Kingdom, or not'.

106. So far as industrial action is concerned, trade unions and others who take international solidarity action with workers in other countries risk legal liability in tort (delict) in British courts. There have been several instances of such action leading to the grant of injunctions. This has been because the statutory immunity afforded to any person who commits certain torts 'in contemplation or furtherance of a trade dispute' (Part IV, Chapter V), has been held not to apply.[1] The re-definition of a 'trade dispute' in the Employment Acts 1980 and 1982 and the illegality of secondary action now make it likely that most types of action will fall foul of the law (Part II, Chapter V). Moreover, the territorial scope of the immunity was specifically narrowed by the Employment Act 1982. There is a 'trade dispute' only so long as the person whose actions in the UK are said to be in contemplation or furtherance of a trade dispute relating to matters occurring outside the UK are likely to be affected in respect of one or more of a list of specified subjects by the outcome of the dispute.[2] Even where the industrial action is lawful where committed, the courts have allowed the recovery of money paid as a result of that action on grounds of economic duress because the relevant contracts were governed by English law.[3]

1. In particular on a variety of grounds in a series of cases involving action by the ITF against 'flags of convenience', and also solidarity action by communications workers against apartheid in South Africa.
2. TULRCA 1992, s. 244(3). The subjects are those which fall within the permitted scope of a 'trade dispute' so presumably excluding a strike over the investment plans of a multinational enterprise.
3. *Dimskal Shipping Co. SA* v. *ITWF* [1992] IRLR 78, HL.

Part I. The Individual Employment Relationship

Chapter I. Formation of the Relationship

§1. Categories of Workers

A. Introduction

107. The coverage *ratione personae* of British labour law is not consistent. As we have seen (para. 50, *above*) the contract of 'service' was slow in overtaking the pre-industrial characterisation of the employment relationship according to status and the nature of the employment (e.g. 'servant in husbandry', 'artificer', 'labourer'). In the nineteenth century the law struggled to develop a general notion of a contract of service regardless of the type of work. Unlike the civil law systems of Continental Europe which moved from a general theory of contract towards a specific concept of an autonomous contract of employment, British labour law only slowly conceptualised the contract of employment on a case by case basis utilising pre-industrial conceptions of 'service'. The common law developed a distinction between those under a contract for services (self-employed workers) and those under a contract of service (employees), which does not correspond exactly to the civil law distinction between *locatio conductio operis* and *locatio conductio operarum*. The English common law category of 'employee' is frequently narrower than the range of persons under a contract of employment in a civil law system. Scots law, despite its civil law roots, has broadly speaking the English approach. Statute law, since the nineteenth century, has usually been limited in coverage to those under contracts of service, but the tests for determining whether the contract is one of service has been left to the common law. By 1951, Kahn-Freund could say that the common law had 'fallen into a maze of casuistry'.[1] This tendency has become even more pronounced in the past 40 years. The changes in the labour force,[2] from the pattern of full-time employment in the core of the labour market, towards part-time, temporary and homework (including the expanding 'cottage' technological industry), and the expansion of self-employment and of employment in the twilight area between employment and self-employment, have highlighted the uncertain inconsistent and inadequate coverage of the common law concepts. There are many workers who in reality fall within the category of dependent labour, such as those on the 'lump' in the building industry, who are not always regarded as working under contracts of service. There is ample scope for the avoidance of labour legislation. Quite apart from the inadequacies of the common law tests of the contract of employment, legislation is sometimes confined to employees in specific employments (e.g.) merchant seamen, teachers, agricultural workers) or to certain types of contract of service, with complex exclusions in particular statutes of different categories such as part-time workers, casuals and domestic servants in private households.

1. (1951) 14 *Modern Law Review* 504.
2. See generally P. Leighton, *Contractual Arrangements in Selected Industries*, DE Research Paper No. 39, February 1983; 'Employment contracts: a choice of relationships' (1982) 90 *Employment Gazette* 433; 'Employment and self-employment' (1983) 91 *Employment Gazette* 197; S. Deakin (1986) 10 *Cambridge Journal of Economics* 225; B. Wood and T. Smith, *Employers' Labour Use Strategies*, DE Research Paper No. 63.

B. Contract of Service or Contract for Services

108. The criteria for distinguishing between a contract of service and a contract for services have been developed by the courts on a casuistic basis. For this purpose, several tests have been expounded. The early cases, emphasising the elements of command and subordination inherent in the employment relationship, established a test based on the employer's power to control the manner in which the work is done.[1] A contract of service, on this test, is one under which an employer 'can not only order or require what is to be done, but how it shall be done'.[2] The test yields straightforward answers in some cases, but is difficult to apply where the employee's skills surpass those of the employer and the employer is a corporate entity. Thus more recent cases have held that control cannot be the determining test when dealing with a professional person or a person with skill and experience.[3] The greater the skill, the less significant is control in determing whether the employee is under a contract of service'.[4]

1. *Performing Rights Society Ltd.* v. *Mitchell and Baker Ltd.* [1925]1 KB 762, *Mersey Docks and Harbour Board* v. *Coggins and Griffiths Ltd.* [1947] AC 1.
2. *Collins* v. *Hertfordshire County Council* [1947] KB 598 at 615, *per* Hilberry J.
3. *Cassidy* v. *Ministry of Health* [1951] 2 KB 343 at 579; *Morren* v. *Swinton and Pendlebury Borough Council* [1965] 2 All ER 349; *Market Investigations* v. *Minister of Social Security* [1969] 2 Q B 173.
4. *Beloff* v. *Pressdram Ltd.*[1973] 1 All E R 241 at 250.

109. A second test, which has been applied in only a few situations, is whether the person forms part of the employer's organisation. Denning L.J. (as he then was) explained this as follows: 'Under a contract of service, a man is employed as part of the business, and his work is done as an integral part of the business; whereas under a contract for services, his work, although done for the business, is not integrated into it but is only accessory to it.'[1] This test has been applied, for example, to determine whether a regular contributor to a newspaper is an employee,[2] but it has failed to provide a comprehensive test, particularly in cases where the worker provides some equipment or is paid on a piece-rate basis.

1. *Stevenson, Jordan & Harrison Ltd.* v. *Macdonald & Evans* (1925) 1 TLR 101.
2. *Beloff* v. *Pressdram Ltd.* [1973]1 All ER 241.

110. The courts have therefore moved to a more complex test, the so-called multiple or mixed test, in which a multiplicity of factors are considered, none of which is necessarily determinative. The starting point of this approach is to ask whether there is a sufficient degree of control to make the worker an employee, and then to ask whether the provisions of the contract are consistent with its being a contract of service. This is a somewhat question-begging approach, because if it were asked whether the contract is consistent with a contract for services, precisely the opposite result could be achieved. Moreover, everything depends upon the weight which is given to a particular 'inconsistency'. A series of recent cases have emphasised, as the most significant 'inconsistency' with a contract of employment, the entrepreneurial character of self-employment, asking the question: Is the person in business on his or her own behalf?[1] Factors to be considered in this context include the extent to which the person takes the chance of profit or risk of loss by investing money or equipment in the business.[2] This test has been referred to as the 'fundamental test'[3], but the Court of Appeal has rejected the notion that any single test is fundamental.[4] Thus, in any case, consideration should be given to all the factors, including degree of control, the risk of loss and the chance of profit, the provision of equipment, the methods of tax and national insurance payment, and the parties' intentions. The industrial tribunal should 'consider all aspects of the relationship, no single feature being in itself decisive and each of which may vary in weight and direction'.[5]

1. *Ready-Mixed Concrete (SE) Ltd.* v. *Minister of Pensions* [1968] 2 QB 497.
2. *Market Investigations Ltd.* v. *Minister of Social Security* [1968] 3 All ER 732.
3. *Per* Cook, J. in *Market Investigations Ltd.* v. *Minister for Social Security*, [1969] 2 QB 173 approved in *Ferguson* v. *John Dawson* [1976]1 WLR 1213, *Young & Woods* v. *West.* [1980] IRLR 201; and *Lee* v. *Chung* [1990] IRLR 236.
4. *Addison* v. *London Philharmonic Orchestra Ltd.* [1981] ICR 261; *Midland Sinfonia Concert Society Ltd.* v. *Secretary of State for Social Services* [1981]) ICR 454; *Warner Holidays Ltd.* v. *Secretary of State for Social Services* [1983] ICR 440.
5. *O'Kelly* v. *Trusthouse Forte (plc)* [1983] ICR 728 at 743.

111. There has been much debate as to whether the classification of a contract is a question of fact or law, appeals to the higher courts only being available on points of law. The most recent authorities include dicta which differ on the extent to which a non-interventionist approach should be adopted by the higher courts. In *O'Kelly* v. *Trusthouse Forte*,[1] Ackner Ltd held that it is a question of law whether the parties must have intended a contract of service or for services, and some support for this view is found in the later House of Lords case of *Davies* v. *Presbyterian Church of Wales*.[2] However, the majority of the Court of Appeal in *O'Kelly* took a less interventionist view, stating that the issue required judgements on questions of degree and fact which the tribunal of first instance should determine. 'The precise quality to be attributed to various individual facts is so much a matter of degree that it is unrealistic to regard the issue as attracting a clear legal answer'.[3] Appellate courts only interfere with a first instance decision if there has been a misdirection in law or if the decision is one which no tribunal properly conducting itself on the relevant facts could have reached.[4] More recent cases have attempted to reconcile these two methods by holding that the question-of-law approach in *Davies* applies only where the case turns entirely upon the construction of a document. Where the issue has to be determined by an investigation and evaluation of the factual circumstances in which the work was performed, the question whether the contract is one of service or for services is one of fact to be determined by the tribunal of first instance.[5] An implication of this is that each decision tends to depend upon its own balance of factors and the outcomes of cases are difficult to predict.

1. [1983] IRLR 369.
2. [1986] IRLR 194 *per* Lord Templeman.
3. *O'Kelly* v. *Trusthouse Forte plc* [1983] IRLR 369 *per* Fox LJ.
4. *Edwards* v. *Bairstow* [1956] AC 14.
5. *McCleod* v. *Hellyer Brothers Ltd.* [1987] IRLR 232 at 237–38; *Lee* v. *Chung* [1990] IRLR 236 at 238.

112. One of the major sources of difficulty concerns marginal workers, such as homeworkers, casual workers and agency workers. None of these could be said to be entrepreneurs and yet they do not fit comfortably in the traditional categories of workers employed under a contract of service. In this connection, it is important to determine not only the nature of the contract, but whether or not there is a contract at all. Almost all employment, however transient, constitutes a simple wage-work bargain; but where there is a series of such contracts over time between the same parties, the question arises whether there is a continuing overriding or 'global' contract which governs the whole of the relationship. Recent case-law has used the concept of 'mutuality of obligation' to determine whether a global contract exists; indeed, such mutuality, whereby an employee is obliged to work and an employer to continue to provide work or remuneration, has been held to be the 'irreducible minimum' of a contract of service. Where the worker has the option of declining to work on any specific occasion, then he or she cannot be said to be employed under a contract of service. This is so even if, in practice, economic need obliges the worker to accept the work. Thus it has been held that regular casual waiters,[1] trawlermen engaged to work for the duration of a specific voyage,[2] or secretaries working as temporary workers for an employment agency,[3] were not employed under a global contract because they were not contractually obliged to work, between specific engagements. Since many employment protection rights depend on being employed under a contract of service, the consequence is that some of the most vulnerable workers remain unprotected. However, in one important case, the Appeal Court was willing to imply the existence of such a contractual obligation on the basis of a course of dealing, so that a homeworker who had regularly worked for an employer was held to be working under a contract of service.[4]

1. *O'Kelly* v. *Trusthouse Forte plc.* above.
2. *McCleod* v. *Hellyer Brothers Ltd* [1987] IRLR 232. *See* generally, B. Hepple (1986) 15 ILJ at 75.

3. *Wickens* v. *Champion Employment* [1984] ICR 365. *See* Employment Agencies Act 1973; Hepple and Napier, 'Temporary Workers and the Law' (1978) 7 *Industrial Law Journal* 84.
4. *Nethermere (St. Neots) Ltd.* v. *Gardiner* [1984] ICR 612 (CA); *see also Airfix Footwear (Ltd.)* v. *Cope* [1978] ICR 1210.

113. Another area of difficulty concerns cases where one or both parties to the employment relationship choose to place themselves in one category rather than another in order to reap the benefits of a particular tax or social security regime. In strict contract theory, the parties' agreement should be conclusive. However, the courts have been willing to look beyond the label given by the parties to the substance of the relationship. For example, an employer could not escape liability for breach of a statutory safety duty owed to a building worker by pleading that the worker had agreed to be self-employed simply in order to mislead the Inland Revenue.[1] But where there is a detailed written contract which explicitly carries out the genuine intentions of the parties to create a status of self-employment, that contract has been regarded as 'the best material from which to gather the true relationship between them'.[2]

1. *Ferguson* v. *John Dawson & Partners (Contracts) Ltd.* [1976]1 WLR 1213.
2. *Massey* v. *Crown Life Insurance Co.* [1978] ICR 590 at p. 594.

C. Specific Categories of Worker

I. Employees

114. The statutory definition of employee is based on the common law contract of service. Thus an employee is defined as 'an individual who has entered into or works under (or where the employment has ceased, worked under) a contract of employment, otherwise than in the police service'. A contract of employment, in turn, means 'a contract of service or apprenticeship, whether it is express or implied and (if it is express) whether it is oral or in writing'.[1]

1. EPCA 1978, s. 153(1); *see below* for apprenticeship; TULRCA 1992, s. 295 (1), subject to s. 235 which gives a wider definition in relation to ballots before industrial action.

115. Most employment rights are limited to employees. For example, rights to complain of unfair dismissal,[1] to claim compensation for redundancy,[2] to be given a written statement of employment terms,[3] and a variety of other individual employment protection measures are confined to employees. Similarly, some collective rights, such as legally binding recommendations by ACAS for disclosure of information to trade unions, may be enforced only through the contracts of employment of employees.[4]

1. EPCA 1978, s. 54(1).
2. EPCA 1978, s. 81(1).
3. EPCA 1978, s. 1(1).
4. TULRCA 1992, s. 185.

II. Workers

116. Some statutes extend beyond employees to those who work under contracts personally to execute work or labour. In the Trade Union and Labour Relations (Consolidation) Act 1992, a 'worker' is defined to include those who normally work or seek work under a contract of employment or under any other contract whereby the worker undertakes to do or to perform personally any work or services for another party to the contract who is not a professional client.[1] This definition is wide enough to cover all employees, those who are temporarily unemployed and workseekers, as well as those under contracts of services to personally perform work. It excludes the contract for the sale of a completed work (e.g. by an author[2]) and those such as solicitors who work for a 'professional client'.[3] Parliament has, however, expressly provided that individuals providing general medical, pharmaceutical, dental or ophthalmic services under the National Health Services are to be treated as workers.[4] Inclusion in the category of 'workers' is important to secure certain collective rights, such as listing as a trade union (which must consist of workers). Similarly, the Race Relations Act and Sex Discrimination Act[5] apply to those employed under a contract of service or apprenticeship as well as those employed under a contract personally to execute any work or labour. A contract which entitles a person to delegate all the contractual duties to others to perform does not qualify as a contract personally to execute work.[6]

1. TULRCA 1992, s. 296; SDA 1975, s. 82(1). RRA 1976, s. 78(1) Wages Act 1986, s.8.
2. *Writers' Guild of Great Britain* v. *BBC* [1974] ICR 234.
3. *Carter* v. *Law Society* [1973] ICR 113.
4. TULRCA 1992, s. 279.
5. RRA 1976, s. 78(1); SDA 1975, s. 82(1).
6. *Mirror Group Newspapers Ltd.* v. *Gunning* [1986] IRLR 27; *Tanna* v. *Post Office* [1981] ICR 374; cf. *Hitchcock* v. *Post Office* [1980] ICR 100.

III. Public Employees

117. Although this monograph is primarily concerned with workers in the private sector, the fact that 6.1 million people, or 23 per cent of the total employed labour force in 1989 were employed in the public sector makes it important to give a brief account of their legal status. Public sector employment includes: (i) those who are employed by public corporations such as the Post Office, British Rail and the National Coal Board (0.8 million in 1989); (ii) those employed by local authorities, including education, the social services, fire services, and police (2.9 million); and (iii) central government employees, including the National Health Service and the armed forces (2.3 million).[1] In some respects, public employees are treated in the same way as their private sector counterparts. In particular, employees in local government, the National Health Service and public corporations are all employed under contracts of employment and fall within the scope of most employment protection rights. However, the availability of public law remedies to employees in these sectors is controversial and a complex case-law exists.[2] Two sectors, the police and the civil service, are subject to different treatment from private sector employees. Police are not employed under contracts of employment but are considered to be 'independent' officers, exercising 'original authority' derived directly from the legal powers inherent in their office.[3] Police constables are paid by local police authorities and are under the 'direction and control' of the chief constable.[4] In the important area of natural justice, police constables have been held to be 'office-holders' (*see* para. 119 *below*) and thus have more extensive rights than civil servants. Basic terms and conditions are specified in statutory regulations and they are subject to statutory disciplinary codes.

1. *See* generally S. Fredman and G. Morris, *The State as Employer*, London, Mansell 1989; and (up to 1970) Hepple and O'Higgins, *Public Employee Trade Unionism in the UK*, Ann Arbor, Michigan, 1971.
2. Fredman and Morris, *The State as Employer*, pp. 251–275.
3. *Fisher* v. *Oldham Corporation* [1930] 2 KB 364, *Attorney-General for New South Wales* v. *Perpetual Trustee Co.* [1955] AC 477.
4. Police Act 1964, s. 5 (1).

118. The most important distinct group of public sector employees are civil servants, or 'Crown Servants'. The legal framework governing Crown servants harks back to the personal retinue of the monarch rather than the complex bureaucratic structure of the modern civil service. Crown servants may be dismissed at will, and it is debatable whether they have contracts of employment. The source of the power of the State as employer is the Royal Prerogative, 'the residue of the discretionary power left at any moment in the hands of the Crown'.[1] This power has been delegated by the Sovereign on the advice of Ministers by successive Orders in Council, by virtue of which the Minister for the Civil Service may determine the terms and conditions of employment of civil servants.[2] In contrast to their tenuous legal position, civil servants have traditionally enjoyed a relatively protected *de facto* status. A formalised collective bargaining system, the Whitley Councils, has been in operation since 1919; trade unionism was actively encouraged until 1979 and established civil servants have greater security of tenure than most private employees.[3] Government policy in this respect has changed since 1979: trade unionism is no longer encouraged, and many parts of the civil service are being hived off into semi-independent agencies, which will not necessarily comply with national collective agreements. In an important judicial development the House of Lords has held, on the basis of the tradition of negotiation and consultation between Government and Civil Service trade unions, that the Minister should consult trade unions before making important changes to terms and conditions of employment, unless the Minister considers that national security would thereby be imperilled.[4] Failure to do so may result in a ministerial decision being set aside by the High Court on procedural grounds, but there is no judicial review of the substance of Civil Service regulations. Legislation does not bind the Crown unless there is a specific provision to that effect. For example, the Crown is not bound to supply Crown employees with written statements of terms of employment. However, the unfair dismissal provisions do apply to civil servants, unless the Minister certifies that such protection is withdrawn in the interests of national security. This power was exercised in 1984 when trade union rights were withdrawn from civil servants employed at Government Communications Headquarters (*see* para. 375, *below*).

1. Dicey, *Law of the Constitution* (8th ed.), p. 421.
2. The most recent is the Civil Service Order in Council of 1982.
3. D. Winchester in *Industrial Relations in Britain* (G. S. Bain ed.), London, 1983, pp. 155–178.
4. *Council of the Civil Service Unions* v. *Minister for the Civil Service* [1984] 3 All ER 935 (HL).

IV. Office-holders

119. The concept of an 'office' is sometimes applied to those in positions of authority in various public and private institutions. For example, there are the Fellows of Oxford and Cambridge Colleges and the steward and bailiff appointed by the Lord of a manor. Historically, offices such as these were distinguished from the 'contract of service', and the proprietary interests attaching to these offices were specially protected by the common law. In modern times tax legislation specifically applies to 'office-holders'. In other cases the mere fact that an individual holds an 'office' does not preclude him or her from belonging to the category of *workers* or that of *employees*.[1] In these cases it all depends on factors such as whether he or she is a member of the corporate body in question, whether the office is a permanent one created by an enactment, whether the office continues to exist whether or not it is occupied at any particular time, and how the office-holder can be removed. The most important example of an office-holder in modern law is the director of a limited liability company. If he or she is also a working (i.e. executive) director then he or she will have a service contract with the company. There is also an important category of elective and other offices, such as those in a trade union, where special protection (e.g. in respect of natural justice) is granted by the courts.[2]

1. *Miles* v. *Wakefield* [1987] IRLR 193 at p.197.
2. e.g. *Taylor* v. *NUS* [1967] 1 WLR 532; *Ridge* v. *Baldwin* [1964] AC 40.

V. Manual Workers

120. In general labour legislation applies equally to manual (or 'blue-collar') workers and non-manual (or 'white-collar') employees. However, some 19th-century legislation was limited in coverage to those engaged in manual labour. The last of this legislation, the Truck Acts (*see* Chapter IV, *below*) was repealed by the Wages Act 1986.

VI. Domestic Servants

121. In the 19th century, special rules applied to those 'whose main or general function is to be about their employer's person, or establishments, residential or quasi-residential, for the purposes of ministering to their employer's needs or wants, or to the needs or wants of those who are members of such establishments or those resorting to such establishments'.[1] The Truck Acts excluded such employees from their coverage. This pattern has been continued by some modern legislation, despite the fact that such employees tend to be particularly vulnerable. The most important example is the Race Relations Act 1976 which does not apply to employment in a private household except where the discrimination is by way of victimisation.[2] The Sex Discrimination Act 1975 contained a similar exclusion, but after the European Court held that this constituted a breach by the UK Government of its obligations under the EC Treaty,[3] the Act was amended. It now includes domestic and other workers in a private household, unless objection is likely to be taken to a worker of a particular sex because the job involves a degree of social or physical contact with the employer or a knowledge of intimate details of the employers life.[4]

1. *Re Junior Carlton Club* [1922] 1 KB 166.
2. RRA, s. 4(3).
3. *Commission of the European Communities* v. *UK* [1984] IRLR 29 ECJ.
4. SDA 1975, s. 7(2) (*6a*) as inserted by SDA 1986, s. 1.

VII. Specific Employments

122. Among the groups of workers to whom specific legislation applies are: agricultural workers, bakers and confectioners, building and engineering workers, hotels and catering workers, civil aviation employees, docks and harbours employees, drivers, teachers, electricity and gas workers, firemen, hairdressers, laundry workers, court officials, local government officers, merchant seamen, national health service employees, oil-rig workers, shop and office workers, postal workers, railway workers, share fishermen and some transport workers.[1]

1. For further details *see Sweet and Maxwell's Encyclopedia of Employment Law, Part 12.*

VIII. Apprentices and Trainees

123. Until recently, apprenticeship was a major source of training for skilled craft workers. However, the annual intake of apprentices has dropped from about 142,000 in 1962 to only 5,000 in 1989 and the apprenticeship system is near collapse. Many of the cases and legal rules on apprenticeship were decided in different social conditions, and appear anachronistic in modern conditions. A contract of apprenticeship is one under which the employer agrees to instruct and teach the apprentice his or her trade, profession or business and to maintain him or her during the existence of that relationship. The apprentice in turn agrees to serve and to learn from the employer. The apprentice may leave only if the employer's conduct indicates that the employer is unwilling to teach the apprentice and the employer may only dismiss the apprentice if the latter's conduct makes it impossible to instruct him or her. A wrongfully dismissed apprentice may claim damages not only in respect of loss of earnings but also for the value of lost future prospects. Employment protection legislation usually applies to apprentices,[1] but an apprentice who comes to the end of a fixed term apprenticeship cannot claim a redundancy payment or complain of unfair dismissal if he or she is not kept on as a journeyman.[2] A far more important source of employment-related training is found in Government-sponsored schemes. These date back to the Industrial Training Act 1964 but have proliferated during the 1980s. The nature and scope of training programmes are subject to frequent changes. Until 1990, the two major schemes were Employment Training (ET), which was targeted at workers who had been unemployed for more than two months, and the Youth Training Scheme, (YTS), which was open to all 16– and 17–year old school leavers. An element of compulsion was built into these schemes by denying certain social security benefits to anyone who refused to accept a training place, or lost such a place through misconduct or voluntary resignation. Responsibility for training now lies with Training Enterprise Councils (TECs), which are permitted to establish their own local schemes. The employment status of trainees on all such schemes is unclear, but on balance it appears that the trainee does not have a contract of employment with either the person supplying the work and training or the TEC.[3] (Police cadets are in a similar position.[4]) The Secretary of State has the power to specify whether or not trainees are to be treated as 'employees' for specific purposes[5] and designation orders have been made under the Race Relations and Sex Discrimination Acts making it unlawful to discriminate against trainees on grounds of race or sex.[6]

1. For example, EPCA 1978, s.153(1).
2. *Northeast Coast Shiprepairers Ltd.* v. *Secretary of State for Employment* [1975] ICR 755.
3. For a case decided under an earlier work experience programmes, *see Daley* v. *Allied Suppliers Ltd* [1980] ICR 649.
4. *Wiltshire Police Authority* v. *Wynn* [1980] ICR 649.
5. EA 1988, s. 26.
6. SDA 1975, s. 14, RRA 1976 s. 13, and *see also* Health and Safety (Youth Training) Regulations 1983 (SI 1983 No. 1919).

IX. Casual or Short-term Workers

124. There is no separate legal category of casual workers. Until 1979 there was important progress towards the decasualisation of labour, notably through a special regime of job and income security for registered dockworkers.[1] However during the 1980s this policy was reversed, as illustrated by the repeal of the dockworkers' scheme in 1989. Until 1977 there was a significant part of the workforce, particularly in seasonal trades and services, work for relatively short periods of time, or with frequent breaks in continuity of service, for a particular employer. The effect of this is usually to deprive them of employment protection rights. First, their freedom to choose whether or not to work on a particular occasion, and the employer's freedom to deny them work may lead to a finding that there is insufficient 'mutuality of obligation' to constitute a contract of employment.[2] Secondly, even if they are employees, they may have insufficient continuity of employment to qualify for particular statutory rights.[3]

1. Under the Dock Workers Employment Scheme 1967 (SI 1967, No. 1252) repealed by the Dockworkers Act 1989.
2. *O'Kelly* v. *Trusthouse Forte plc, supra.*
3. *See* para. 279, *below* on continuity of employment. *See* generally B. Casey, *Temporary Employment: Practice and Policy in Britain* London, PSI, 19888, N. Meager, *Temporary Employment in Britain*, IMS Report No. 106 University of Sussex, 1985.

X. Temporary Workers Supplied by an Intermediary

125. Distinct from casual workers of the kind just described are those commonly known as 'temporary' workers because their services are supplied by an intermediary (the employment agency or business) for the benefit of a third party (the hirer) for a limited period of time. The activities of fee-charging employment agencies and businesses are regulated under the Employment Agencies Act 1973. A distinction is drawn between the 'employment agency' which supplies workers for placement with employers, and the 'employment business' which supplies the services of workers it itself employs. The system of regulation applies to both, and is not limited to those supplied on short-term assignments, although in practice this is a major part of their activities. It is a criminal offence to carry on an employment business or agency without a licence. Detailed regulations[1] lay down standards for the conduct of employment businesses and agencies and provide, as a sanction, for the withdrawal of the licence. Workers may not be charged fees by an employment business or agency, save in exceptional circumstances, but there is no regulation of the fees charged to hirers. The workers supplied by an employment business or agency have relationships with both supplier and hirer. The legal nature of these relationships is ambiguous. It has been held that 'where A contracts with B to render services exclusively to C, the contract is not a contract for services (or of service) but a contract *sui generis*, a different type of contract from either of the familiar two'.[2] More recently, the absence of an obligation on the part of the worker to accept any particular assignment has been held to indicate the absence of a contract of service between the supplier and the worker.[3] The temporary worker almost certainly also has no contract of service with the hirer, and probably does not have a contract of any kind with the hirer.[4] The relationship between the worker and the supplier is to a limited extent governed by the regulations (e.g. the employment business must supply a written statement of employment terms to the worker, and the supplier is responsible for deducting social security contributions). The hirer may be responsible, under health and safety legislation, for work accidents to the worker. A proposed EEC Directive in 1982 which would have enhanced the protection of temporary workers, was opposed by the UK Government, on the ground that employment agencies and businesses in the UK are significantly different from their counterparts elsewhere in the Member States and would be severely handicapped if the

Directive were given effect.[5] The UK government also rejected directives proposed under the EEC's Action Programme in 1990, except one relating to the health and safety of temporary workers.

1. Conduct of Employment Agencies and Employment Businesses Regulations 1976 (SI 1976, No. 715), and related regulations; for further discussion *see* B. Hepple and B. Napier, 'Temporary Workers and the Law' (1978) 7 ILJ 84
2. *Construction Industry Training Board* v. *Labour Force Ltd.* [1970] 3 All ER 220, per Cooke J; *Ironmonger* v. *Movefield* [1988] IRLR 461.
3. *Wickens* v. *Champion Employment* [1984] ICR 365.
4. *O'Sullivan* v. *Thompson-Croom* (1973)14 KIR 108.
5. House of Lords Select Committee on the European Communities Session 1982–83, 6th Report (HMSO, January 1983).

XI. Homeworkers

126. A further important category of workers is that of outworkers, usually working at home rather than at the employer's establishment, or working from home as a base (e.g. market research). These are well established working practices, dating back to the times of 'sweated labour' in the early twentieth century. Recent estimates suggest that the number of home-based workers is increasing. As many as 229,800 people in England and Wales work at home and a further 400,800 work from home as a base, together accounting for 4 per cent of the workforce.[1] Homeworking has traditionally been common in the manual trades, such as sewing, and it is popularly considered to consist largely of manufacturing done at home. In fact, by 1981, less than one-tenth of those who worked at home (58,750 people) were engaged in manufacturing homework. Instead, white-collar and service work now form the predominant type of home-based work, with further additions in the areas of new technology, such as punch card operation and word processing. Homeworkers tend to fare less well than their counterparts working at the workplace. Even if the rate paid for the job is similar, allowances for overheads are the exception rather than the rule and holiday pay is a rarity.[2] The vast majority are employed by non-unionised establishments. Despite their vulnerability, homeworkers do not form a separate legal category. There are some statutory protective measures relevant to homeworking, such as the requirement that the employer observes minimum safety requirements,[3] while some types of homeworking fall into the jurisdiction of Wages Councils[4] which set a single hourly rate for adult workers. However, these regulations are inadequate and often unenforced. Furthermore, employment protection rights, as we have seen, depend on being able to establish both a contract of service and the necessary continuity of service. The employment status of homeworkers is ambiguous: some recent cases have held that homeworkers may be employed under a contract of service[5] but these are confined to their own facts. A recent survey found that while 57 per cent of home-based workers believed themselves to be self-employed, as many as 20 per cent had doubts about their correct employment status.[6]

1. All figures in this paragraph are to be found in C. Hakim, *Home-Based work in Britain*, DE Research Paper No. 60 (1987) and (1987) 95 *Employment Gazette*, 92–104 and 221–225.
2. C. Hakim, 'Employers' Use of Homework and Outwork and Freelances' (1984) 92 *Employment Gazette* 146.
3. Factories Act 1961, s. 133.
4. Wages Act 1986, s. 26(1).
5. *Airfix Footwear Ltd* v. *Cope* [1978] ICR 1210; *Nethermere (St. Neots) Ltd.* v. *Gardiner* [1984] ICR 365.
6. Hakim, *op. cit.* (note 2).

XII. Part-time Workers

127. Part-time workers form an increasingly important sector of the workforce. By 1990 just over 5.5 million employees worked part-time, forming 21 per cent of the workforce the largest proportion in the EC, apart from Denmark and the Netherlands.[1] Of these 4.5 million were women, constituting about 43 per cent of all women in employment, as against 8 per cent of all employed men. Indeed, part-time work has been the only source of increase in the overall level of employment in Great Britain since 1951.[2] Part-time work is heavily concentrated in the service industries, particularly distribution, hotels and catering, although a significant number of part-timers work in manufacturing.

1. New Earnings Survey, *Employment Gazette*, December 1990 and April 1991.
2. O. Robinson and J. Wallace, *Part-time employment and sex discrimination legislation in Great Britain*. Department of Employment Research Paper No. 43, 1984.

128. Part-time work is associated with relatively low levels of pay and the absence of important fringe benefits. In 1990 about 48 per cent of part-time workers in the distributive trades earned less than £2.80 per hour. Although this is in some cases due to part-timers being paid less per hour than full-timers in the same job, the main reason for the earnings differential between full-time and part-time workers is the fact that part-time working is concentrated in the lowest paying occupations, with fewer opportunities to supplement earnings with overtime premia. In fact, recent years have witnessed a deterioration in the relative position of part-timers, especially since 1977. For example, hourly earnings of women in part-time manual work fell from 65.4 per cent of that of full-time male manual employees in 1977 to only 59 per cent in 1990.

129. There is no statutory definition of part-time work, but many employment protection rights depend on the number of hours worked per week. Thus a minimum working week of 8 hours is a prerequisite for eligibility for rights relating to redundancy, unfair dismissal (except if the dismissal is due to trade union activities), guarantee pay, maternity pay and the right to return to work after confinement. For those who work at least 8 but less than 16 hours per week, the qualifying period for most of these rights is 5 years rather than two, as is the case for full-time employees. Although the definition of part-time work in official statistics usually applies to those who work less than 30 hours a week, a growing number of part-timers fall outside of the statutory limits. Thus,

14 per cent of female part-timers worked fewer than 8 hours in 1990 compared with 3.9 per cent in 1975, while the numbers working between 8 and 16 hours per week increased to 29.7 per cent in the same period.

130. The most important rights for which hours of work are irrelevant concern sex and race discrimination, with the result that these Acts are the primary source of protection for part-time women. It has been established that payment of lower hourly wages to part-timers may indirectly discriminate against women and so contravene the Equal Pay Act 1970 unless the employer can justify the discrepancy.[1] In addition, the European Court has recently held that the exclusion of part-timers from other employment benefits, such as access to occupational pension schemes, may contravene article 119 of the EC Treaty and give rise to rights in the UK.[2] It may also be discriminatory to make part-timers redundant before full-timers, regardless of length of service,[3] and to refuse to allow a woman to return to work in a part-time capacity after maternity leave.[4] In each of these cases, however, it is open to the employer to argue that his or her action is justifiable on reasonable commercial grounds.

1. *Jenkins* v. *Kingsgate (Clothing Productions) Ltd.* [1981] ICR 715 and *see* Part I, Chapter VIII below.
2. *Bilka-Kaufhaus GmbH* v. *Weber von Harz* [1986] IRLR 317.
3. *Clarke* v. *Eley (IMI) Kynoch Ltd.* [1983] ICR 165, but *see Kidd* v. *DRG* [1985] ICR 405.
4. *Home Office* v. *Holmes* [1984] ICR 678.

131. Collective bargaining practice in relation to part-timers is not consistent.[1] Some agreements apply differential hourly rates of pay to fulltimers and part-timers,[2] but most pay the full-time rate *pro rata*. Many agreements give full-timers and part-timers the same leave entitlement, while some reduce the part-timers' entitlement according to days normally worked. Few agreements appear to provide sick pay for part-timers. Part-timers may be denied access to occupational pension schemes solely because they work part-time, and even where they have access the benefits may be less favourable than for full-time workers. Such restrictions may now infringe Article 119 of the EC Treaty (see above).[2] Some agreements provide that part-timers should be declared redundant before full-timers, but in a recent case, this practice was held to amount to sexual discrimination.[3] The UK Government opposed a draft EC Directive in the 1982, which sought to apply the principle of equal treatment between full-time and part-time workers.[4] It has also opposed draft directives in 1990 under the EEC's Action Programme on this subject.

1. A full survey will be found in Income Data Services Part-time Work Study No.118, London, March 1976.
2. Para. 130.
3. *Clark* v. *Eley Kynoch (supra)*.
4. House of Lords Select Committee on the European Communities Voluntary Part-time Work Session 1981–1982, 19th report (1982).

131bis. Job-sharing is a variant of part-time working which is becoming increasingly popular, particularly for women who need to combine parenting with work outside the home.[1] This is an arrangement whereby two employees co-ordinate and collaborate within a single job, and both have responsibility for the whole. For legal purposes, each person has a separate contract with the employer, and if this falls below the requisite weekly hours, he or she will not be eligible for a range of employment protection rights, either at all, or before 5 years. In addition, an arrangement whereby each party works one week on and one week off may break employment continuity, so that neither is ever in a position to acquire employment protection rights (paras. 279–282 *below*). Like other part-timers, job-sharers may nevertheless seek the protection of sex discrimination law; but a recent case has held that a refusal by an employer to allow a woman to job share her post on her return to work after maternity leave, was not, in the circumstances of that case, unlawful.[2]

1. *See* EOC *Job Sharing* (1986); P. Leighton (1986) 15 ILJ 173.
2. *Clymo* v. *Wandsworth KBC* [1990] IRLR 241; cf *Briggs* v. *North Eastern Education and Library Board* [1990] IRLR 181.

§2. Written Statement of Employment Terms

132. The employer is obliged to provide every employee (with some exceptions) with a written statement reflecting the main terms of employment.[1] The aim of this provision is to 'ensure for the benefit of an employee that the terms of his (or her) contract of employment are set out in writing so that the employee knows his legal rights in terms of the contract and can, if need be, insist upon them by legal action against the employer'.[2]

1. EPCA 1978, s. 1.
2. *Owens* v. *Multilux Ltd.* [1974] IRLR 113 at p. 114.

133. The statement must be given to the employee not later than 13 weeks after the beginning of his or her employment with the employer and must reflect the terms of employment at a specified date not more than one week before the statement is given. The statement should identify the parties, specify the date on which the employment began and state the date on which the employee's period of continuous employment began (taking into-account any employment with a previous employer which counts towards that period). It should also give particulars of the following terms of employment:

(i) The scale or rate of remuneration, or the method of calculating remuneration (including for example, any terms on piece-rates, or overtime pay).
(ii) The intervals at which remuneration is paid (that is, whether weekly or monthly or some other period).
(iii) Any terms and conditions relating to hours of work (including any terms and conditions relating to normal working hours).
(iv) Any terms and conditions relating to:
  (a) entitlement to holidays, including public holidays, and holiday pay (sufficient to enable the employee's entitlement, including any entitlement to accrued holiday pay on the termination of employment, to be precisely calculated);

(b) incapacity for work due to sickness or injury, including any provisions for sick pay;
(c) pensions and pension schemes (employees who are covered by special statutory pensions schemes and whose employers are already obliged by law to provide information about them are excepted).

(v) The length of notice of termination which the employee is obliged to give and entitled to receive, stating the date when the contract expires if the contract is for a fixed term.
(vi) The title of the job which the employee is to do.

The statement may refer to some other document, in which these particulars are to be found but the employee must have reasonable opportunities for reading that document in the course of his employment, or it must be made reasonably accessible to him in some other way.

134. In addition the Act of 1978 requires the statement given to the employee to include a note which must:

(i) specify any disciplinary rules (other than those relating to health and safety at work) which apply to the employee or refer to a document, reasonably accessible to the employee, which specifies the rules;
(ii) specify by description or name the person to whom the employee can apply and the manner in which such applications should be made:
(a) if he is dissatisfied with any disciplinary decision relating to him, or
(b) for the purposes of seeking redress of any grievance relating to his employment; and
(iii) where there are further steps which follow from an application under (ii)(a) or (ii)(b), explain those steps or refer to a document which explains them and is reasonably accessible to the employee;
(iv) whether the employer has an occupational pension scheme which has a certificate that it is 'contracted-out' of the state pension scheme under the Social Security Pensions Act 1975.

135–136. The obligation to provide a written statement under the 1978 Act does not apply to certain categories of employees, *viz*. (i) employees whose normal hours are less than 16 (and, in some cases, 8) weekly, (ii) masters and seamen on certain British ships; (iii) Crown servants; (iv) employees who ordinarily work for their employers abroad during any period when these employees are engaged in work wholly or mainly outside Great Britain; (v) an employee who is re-engaged by the same employer within 6 months of the ending of the last period of employment; (vi) an employee who has a written contract of employment covering each of the particulars listed in section 1 of the 1978 Act. The note specifying disciplinary rules need not be given if the number of employees employed by the employer and any associated employer was less than twenty on the day when the employment began.[1]

1. EA 1989, s. 13(3).

137. It is essential to note that the statement is not the contract itself, and may be an inaccurate reflection of the terms to which the parties actually agreed. 'The document is a unilateral one merely stating the employer's view of what those terms are . . . In the absence of an acknowledgement by the parties that the statement is itself a contract and that the terms are correct, the statutory statement does not itself constitute a contract in writing.'[1] While the statement is strong *prima facie* evidence of the terms of the contract, it is by no means conclusive.[2] Nor does the fact that an employee has signed acknowledgement of receipt necessarily mean that she or he has signed a contract or accepted the accuracy of the terms in it. It is only a contract if the parties acknowledge it as such.[3]

1. *System Floors Ltd.* v. *Daniel* 11982] ICR 54 at 58.
2. *Ibid.*, approved in *Robertson* v. *British Gas Corporation* [1983] ICR 351.
3. *Gascol Conversions Ltd* v. *Mercer* [1974] ICR 420.

138. Any changes in the listed particulars must be given to the employee not more than one month after the change. A statement of change does not in itself vary the terms of the contract; at most, it may provide evidence of an agreed variation. Nor does the fact that an employee continues working without objection mean that he or she has impliedly agreed to the change, especially where the variation relates to a matter which has no immediate practical application.[1] The statutory obligation to notify all changes can be avoided in cases in which the particulars refer to another document (such as a collective agreement), provided that, in the original statement, the employer indicates that future changes will be entered up in that document.

1. *Jones* v. *Associated Tunnelling Company Ltd.* [1981] IRLR 477.

139. Where no statement has been given, or a statement is incomplete or its accuracy is in doubt, the employee may complain to an industrial tribunal, which will determine any missing particulars or confirm, amend or substitute for inaccurate particulars.[1] The tribunal should attempt to discover what the parties have in fact agreed, 'taking into account all the circumstances, including the parties' subsequent conduct. In this exercise, the tribunal is not confined to the tests applicable in deciding the terms to be implied in a commercial contract. If the tribunal cannot ascertain the agreed terms, it may imply a reasonable term. 'Section 11 would seem to impose upon the tribunals a statutory duty to find the specified terms and in the last resort to invent them for the purpose of literally writing them into the contract.'[2] Although this appears to be an important departure from the traditional means of discovering contractual terms, recent cases have stressed that the function of the tribunal is to establish the accuracy of the statutory statement, not to recast the contract, nor to adjudicate on the fairness or unfairness of the employment relationship.[3] (*See* Part I, Chapter II, *below*). The effect of this determination is that the employer is deemed to have supplied a statement in the corrected form. However, the tribunal cannot enforce the terms of the contract; the employee's remedy for breach of contract is in the County Court or High Court (*see* para. 80, *above*).

1. EPCA 1978, s. 11.
2. *Mears* v. *Safecar Security Ltd.* [1982] ICR 626, CA.
3. *England* v. *British Telecommunications* [1990] IRLR 330 at 331.

§3. Capacity to Contract and Restrictions on Employment

A. Children and Young Persons

140. Persons under the age of 18 have limited capacity to contract. A minor may obtain benefits under an employment contract, but the general rule is that he or she is bound only if the obligations are on the whole beneficial to him or her. It seems that simple financial advantages are enough to make the contract 'beneficial'.[1]

1. *Chaplin* v. *Leslie Frewin (Publishers) Ltd.* [1966] Ch. 71.

141. There are statutory restrictions on the employment of children under the school-leaving age of 16.[1] The minimum age at which a child may be employed is 13, and between the ages of 13 and 16 children may not be employed at all in any factory, mine, transport undertakings or United Kingdom registered ship. They may be employed in industrial undertakings only if members of the same family are employed there. Previously, local authorities had the power to regulate the employment of children under 16, but this was replaced in 1973 by an enlarged power for the Secretary of State to restrict their employment. There is specific control over the employment of children during the last year of compulsory schooling in work experience schemes and special regulations apply to the employment of children in the entertainment industry. Until 1989, a wide variety of legislation regulated the employment of 'young persons', i.e. persons over 16 but under 18 years of age. However, such regulations were repealed by the Employment Act 1989, on the grounds that they imposed an 'administrative burden' on employers, and that long hours did not have a different effect on young persons from those on adults. This in turn involved the denunciation of certain provisions of the European Social Charger. The few restrictions which remain are considered necessary on health and safety grounds.

1. The principal Acts are: Employment of Women, Young Persons and Children Act 1920, s. 1; Children and Young Persons Act 1933; Mines & Quarries Act 1954, s. 124; Factories Act 1961, s. 167; Children & Young Persons Act 1963, ss. 37–44; Employment of Children Act 1973; Merchant Shipping Act 1970, s. 51.

B. Women

142. Both single and married women have the same capacity to contract as men, and sex discrimination on grounds of marriage has been outlawed since 1975 (*below*, Chapter VIII). Protective legislation, restricting women's employment on night and shift work, and prescribing other differential treatment, has now largely been repealed.[1]

1. SDA 1986, s.7; EA 1989, s.9.

C. Foreign Workers

143. In the face of rising unemployment, British governments have imposed increasingly stringent limitations on the rights of foreigners to work in the United Kingdom. Immigration controls are for the most part found in a complex set of non-statutory regulations administered with a large measure of discretion.[1] Only a very brief description is possible here.[2]

1. The main statutory source is the Immigration Act 1971, and a large body of EC rules, based on Articles 48 to 58 of the EC Treaty. *See* generally, I.A. MacDonald, *Immigration Law and Practice*, 2nd ed., London, 1987.
2. These paragraphs have been compiled with the assistance of Philip Trott, solicitor.

144. Only British citizens[1] have the unrestricted right to work in the United Kingdom. Anyone else may only work in the United Kingdom in accordance with the immigration rules. The principal categories are as follows: (i) Commonwealth citizens between the ages of 17 and 27 on holiday may work in the UK provided that such work is incidental to their holiday. They may be admitted in that capacity for an aggregate period of two years. (ii) No permission is needed to engage in certain occupations ('permit-free' occupations). These include ministers of religion; representatives of overseas firms which have no branch, subsidiary or representative in the UK; and representatives of overseas newspapers, news agencies and broadcasting organisations on long-term assignments to the UK. Doctors and dentists were removed from this category in March 1985.[2] (iii) Permission may be granted to establish a business provided certain criteria are met, including a minimum investment and the ability to demonstrate that the business will be successful and will create jobs. (iv) A work permit may be issued by the Department of Employment on application by the prospective employer. The permit is issued for a specific job and a named worker only. In recent years, very strict criteria have been applied to the issue of work permits. (v) Writers and artists may work in that capacity provided that they can maintain themselves without recourse to public funds from their earnings as writers or artists (or their savings in their first year of being in the country in this capacity). (vi) Indefinite leave to remain and work without restriction may be granted to anyone who has been in categories (ii), (iii), (iv) and (v) above for 4 years. Spouses and dependants are similarly eligible. In addition, indefinite leave to remain may be granted to anyone who has been admitted as a person of independent means and has remained for 4 years. (vii) Nationals of other Member States of the European Economic Community have the right to seek or take up employment or set up in business.[3] (viii) Students and dependants may also work in limited circumstances.

1. The British Nationality Act 1981 contains the definition of a 'British citizen'.
2. *See* House of Commons Paper 293, 26 March 1985.
3. This category is governed by the provisions of the EC Treaty, Title III, Chapter 1 on the free movement of persons and the regulations and directions of the EC.

145. There are some further restrictions including the prohibition on employment of non-British subjects in the civil service without a certificate[1] and as regards military employment. The recruitment of workers from outside the United Kingdom by private employment agencies and businesses is regulated, for example to ensure that the worker obtains full written details of the employment in a language he or she can understand.[2] Discrimination against EC workers is prohibited by Article 48 of the EC Treaty and EC regulations which are directly applicable in the United Kingdom,[3] and discrimination against any person on grounds of race, colour, ethnic or national origins or nationality is prohibited by the Race Relations Act 1976, insofar as this is not specifically authorised by legislation.[4]

1. Aliens Employment Act 1955.
2. Conduct of Employment Agencies and Employment Businesses Regulations 1976, SI 1976 No. 715, reg. 6.
3. In particular, Council Regulation 1612/68 of 15 October 1968, Articles 7, 8, 9 as amended.
4. *See* Part I, Chapter VIII, *below*. An example of specific statutory authority for discrimination is the Race Relations (Prescribed Public Bodies) Regulations 1984, SI 1984, No. 218, which allows certain public bodies to discriminate on grounds of birth, nationality, descent or residence when making appointments.

Chapter II. The Sources of Terms of the Contract of Employment

§1. Express and Implied Terms

146. The reciprocal rights and duties of employer and employee depend upon the express and implied terms of the contract of employment. Where the parties have not expressly dealt with any matter, the courts are willing to imply terms in order to make the contract a workable one. These terms are sometimes treated as resting upon the presumed intentions of the parties (terms *implied in fact*), sometimes as based on *custom and practice* (*see* para. 157, *below*) and sometimes as a legal incident of the relationship or status of employer and employee (terms *implied in law*). Two particular approaches from the law of commercial contracts have traditionally been adopted by the courts in deciding whether to imply terms in accordance with the presumed intentions of the parties. The first is 'to give such business efficacy to the transaction as must have been intended'.[1] The second is to imply 'something so obvious that it goes without saying; so that if, while the parties were making their bargain, an officious bystander were to suggest some express provision for it in their agreement they would testily suppress him with a cry of "Oh, of course!"'.[2] More recently, the courts have acknowledged that implied terms may involve judicial norm-making rather than reflecting the actual intentions of the parties. According to this approach, the relationship of employer and employee requires that there should be some kind of agreed term on certain matters, such as sick pay or the place of employment. Where that term has not been agreed and the parties would not have agreed had they been asked at the time of contracting what that term should be, the court has to imply the term.[3] In this type of case, all the facts and circumstances of the relationship, including the way in which the parties have worked the contract since it was made, must be considered. Recent decisions differ as to whether such a term should be upheld as a legal incident only if 'necessary' to the relationship,[4] or whether the more flexible 'reasonableness' test is appropriate.[5] The most important terms which have been implied in law as 'necessary' incidents of the relationship are (i) the reciprocal duty of *co-operation*; (2) the employee's duty of *faithful service*; and (3) the employer's duty to take *reasonable care* for the health and safety of his employees, and the employee's duty to take reasonable care about his employer's business. These are discussed in Chapter III, *below*.

1. *The Moorcock* (1889)14 PD 64 at 68.
2. *Shirlaw* v. *Southern Foundries Ltd.* [1939] 2 KB 206 at p. 227.
3. *Lister* v. *Romford Ice and Cold Storage Co. Ltd* [1957] AC 555 (House of Lords); *Mears* v. *Safecar Security Ltd.* [1982] ICR 626 (Court of Appeal).
4. *Mears* v. *Safecar Security Ltd.* at pp. 650–651 per Stephenson L. J.; *Courtaulds Northern Spinning* v. *Gibson* [1988] IRLR 305 at p. 309.
5. *Howman & Son* v. *Blyth* [1983] ICR 416 (EAT) at p. 420; *Jones* v. *Associated Tunnelling Co. Ltd.* [1981] IRLR 477 (EAT)

147. The scope of implied terms is important for several reasons. Many of them were developed in the context of the employer's right at common law to dismiss an employee without notice. Where the breach of the term is sufficiently serious, the employee may be said to have repudiated the contract so entitling the employer to dismiss him or her without notice. Conversely, the employee may be able to claim damages for breach of contract where the employer repudiates a contractual obligation (*see* para. 298, *below*). Legislation on redundancy payments and on unfair dismissal has incorporated the contractual notions into the statutory definition of 'dismissal'. This is particularly important in the context of 'constructive dismissal' where the employer's repudiation may entitle the employee to terminate the contract without notice (*see* para. 299, *below*). Moreover, in determining the reasonableness of an employer's actions, tribunals are strongly influenced by the express and implied contractual obligations of the parties. The legislation has therefore spawned an important body of case law on implied terms, particularly those implied in law. We must next examine the judicial techniques for incorporating collective agreements, works rules and notices and custom and practice into individual contracts. The use of statutory provisions as terms of contract is discussed in the Introduction, para. 95, *above*.

148. Two preliminary points must be stressed. The first is the optional nature of implied terms (including custom). A term will not be implied if it is contrary to an express term; and a custom may not be proved if it is contrary to an express or implied term. These principles of the common law distinguish it sharply from the civil law systems: there are no imperative norms in the legal relationship between employer and employee. In particular, implied terms can always be replaced by express ones, even if these are less favourable to the employee. This is particularly important in relation to collective agreements (para. 149, *below*). The second preliminary point is that the written statement of particulars of terms of employment (para. 132, *above*) may facilitate proof of the express and implied terms of the contract, although this is not conclusive evidence of those terms.

§2. Terms Incorporated from Collective Agreements

149. In practice, the main terms and conditions of employment of the majority of employees in Britain are determined by collective bargaining rather than by individual negotiation. A recent survey indicated that in 1984 pay increases for 62 per cent of manual and 54 per cent of non-manual workers were the direct result of collective agreements.[1] The pay and conditions of (probably) another 25 per cent of employees are indirectly influenced by collective bargaining. Nevertheless, British labour law remains rooted in the notion that terms and conditions are a matter of contract between individuals. Collective agreements are presumed not to be intended to be enforceable as contracts between the trade union and employer parties unless an intention to be so bound is expressed in writing.[2] However, the terms of collective agreements may achieve legal effect if they are incorporated into individual contracts of employment. Incorporation is not automatic, not even as minimum terms, and express agreement always takes precedence. In this respect, British labour law stands in sharp contrast to that of other countries, such as France, where the clauses of collective agreements apply to employment contracts except where there are provisions more favourable to the worker. The seriousness of this gap in British labour law has become apparent in times of recession when employers have been able to cut wages by the simple expedient of terminating contracts of employment and offering re-employment on revised terms and conditions less favourable than those laid down in the collective agreement.

1. Milward and Steven, *Workplace Industrial Relations In Britain*, London 1986, p. 226.
2. TULRCA 1992, s. 179. *See* Part II, Chapter IV, *below*.

150. Under what circumstances will a term of a collective agreement become legally enforceable as a term of the individual contract? Unfortunately, attempts to construct a theory of incorporation which is both consistent with contractual principle and reflects reality have not been wholly successful. There are several difficulties. First, collective agreements usually apply to all workers of a particular category, whether or not they are members of a trade union which is party to the agreement, and even if they subsequently join or leave the union. Many workers may not even know of the existence of the agreement. This is difficult to reconcile with the contractual principle that parties should consent to the terms of their contract. Secondly, collective agreements contain procedural terms which may not be amenable to individual enforcement, or may not have been intended to create individual rights. Thirdly, collective bargaining may take place on several different levels at once, with a national or industry-wide agreement being supplemented by local or plant level agreements. The courts have to decide which of these should be incorporated. It should be noted that a worker cannot sue directly on the collective agreement, since he or she was not a party to it.[1]

1. But this may be possible in Scots law: J. Casey, *Juridical Review* (1973) p. 22 at p. 39.

151. The first major issue in any attempt at incorporation is that of 'bridging' the gap between the collective agreement and the individual contract. Several principles of incorporation have emerged:

(a) *Express Incorporation*: This will occur where employer and employee expressly agree that the individual contract is subject to a particular collective agreement or agreements. Proof that such agreement has been reached may be facilitated by express reference to the collective agreement in the written statement of employment terms which the employer is obliged to provide.[1]
(b) *Incorporation by Custom*: It is a well-recognised contractual principle that a contract can be taken to include terms which are sanctioned by custom unless the parties clearly specified otherwise. To become a term of a contract, a custom must be certain, reasonable and well-known, although the individual worker may be ignorant of its existence. Kahn-Freund characterised collective agreements as 'crystallised custom', arguing that this was the basis of incorporation.[2] This explains much of the reality of employment conditions, particularly the fact that collective agreements refer to all workers, regardless of their knowledge or approval. But it does not explain how new or varied collective agreements come to be incorporated.

(c) *Implied Incorporation:* In practice industrial tribunals and courts are very willing to find even in the absence of express agreement or proof of custom, that the terms of collective agreements have become impliedly incorporated into contracts of employment, almost to the point of a presumption of fact that such agreements apply unless the contrary is shown.[3] The principles used are those described in para. 146, above.

1. EPCA 1978, s. l; *see above*, para. 132.
2. Kahn-Freund, *System of Industrial Relations in Great Britain* (ed. Flanders and Clegg), Oxford 1954, pp. 58–59; *see* e.g. *Donelan* v. *Kirby* [1983] 1 IRLR 191 (EAT).
3. *Marley* v. *Forward Trust* [1986] IRLR 369 (CA).

152. The 'bridging' problem is resolved by these techniques of express or implied terms or custom and practice. In general, the trade union negotiating a collective agreement is not treated as the agent of its members even if it purports to act as their 'representative'. The only exceptions to this might be where the number of workers involved is very small and the issues are local or are personal to those workers. English law has not favoured the agency approach because, in Wedderburn's words, 'many puzzles would then arise.'[1] For example, the fact that collective agreements are generally regarded as applicable to non-unionists as well as trade union members is incompatible with the concept of the union as agent only for its own members. Another problem would arise with workers who joined the enterprise after the agreement was concluded. By the doctrines of the English law of agency, only those who were themselves capable of contracting at the time the agent made the contract may subsequently ratify the agent's action. This would mean that workers below the contractual capacity (18 years) at the time the collective agreement was made could not be bound by it. The most difficult question of all would be whether a member may revoke an agent's authority at any time in the same way as a principal may revoke an agent's authority. If this were possible, stable bargaining arrangements could be upset by individual withdrawals of authority.[2]

1. Wedderburn, *The Worker and the Law*, 3rd ed., London, 1986, p. 327.
2. *Land* v. *West Yorks CC* [1979] ICR 452; *Singh* v. *British Steel Corporation* [1974] IRLR 131.

153. Several problems remain, common to all the above theories. Firstly, not all terms of a collective agreement may be incorporated into individual contracts. The courts have distinguished between terms which are appropriate for individual enforcement and those which are not,[1]; but the classification of any particular term must be determined on a case by case basis depending on the presumed intention of the parties.[2] Thus a collective agreement regarding hours of work,[3] dismissal procedure[4] and a redundancy selection procedure[5] has been held to be capable of individual incorporation, since such terms affect workers individually. However, a collective agreement between an employer and a union providing machinery for collective bargaining and for resolving industrial disputes has been held not be individually incorporated, even though it is of great importance to individual employees because 'it is almost inconceivable . . . that it could have been intended to become legally enforceable at the suit of an individual worker.'[6] Instead such procedures are to be operated by the union and employers party to the agreement. Nor have the courts developed clear-cut principles to deal with collective bargaining at both national and local level.[7] Some collective agreements do, however, make specific provision by their own terms as to what is to happen in case of conflict with other agreements. A further complication arises if an employer or union unilaterally withdraws from a collective agreement. Contractual theory requires consent by both parties to a variation; it has thus been held that, once a collective agreement has been incorporated into the individual contract, its terms cannot be removed by the employer's or union's unilateral withdrawal from the collective agreement.[8] The employee's consent may however be implied if he or she continues to work without objection. Moreover, it remains open to the employer to terminate the conditions incorporated from the collective agreement by terminating the individual contracts and offering to re-employ the relevant workers on the new terms.[9] If the collective agreement is varied with the consent of the trade union, individual contracts will usually be varied accordingly, on the basis of an express or implied term that the individual contract is subject to collective agreements *for the time being in force*.

1. *National Coal Board* v. *National Union of Mineworkers* [1986] IRLR 439 at p. 454.
2. *Alexander* v. *Standard Telephones & Cables Ltd* [1990] IRLR 55.
3. *National Coal Board* v. *Galley* [1958] 1 WLR 16.
4. *Barber* v. *Manchester Regional Hospital Board* [1958] 1 WLR 181, *Irani* v. *Southampton and South West Hampshire Health Authority* [1985] IRLR 203,
5. *Alexander* v. *Standard Telephones* [1990] IRLR 55.
6. *National Coal Board* v. *National Union of Mineworkers* [1986] IRLR 439 at p. 454. Contrast *City and Hackney Health Authority* v. *National Union of Public Employees* [1985] IRLR 263 (CA), where a shop-steward's recognition procedure was held to have been incorporated into an individual's contract.
7. Compare *Clift* v. *West Riding CC, The Times* 10 April 1964 (local agreement prevailed) with *Gascol Conversions Ltd.* v. *Mercer* [1974] ICR 420 (national agreement prevailed).
8. *Robertson* v. *British Gas Corporation* [1983] ICR 351; *Gibbons* v. *Associated British Ports* [1985] IRLR 376.
9. *Burdett Coutts* v. *Hertfordshire CC* [1984] IRLR 91 (QBD).

§3. Terms Incorporated from Works Rules and Notices

154. The terms of individual contracts of employment may also be found in rules, notices and other documents issued by management to employees either at the time of engagement or subsequently. In some cases, such rules are collectively agreed, in which case the methods of incorporation are as set out above. Frequently, however, they are unilaterally imposed. In that case, they become terms of the contract in one of the following ways.

155. Unilaterally imposed rules may become part of the contract of employment:

(1) By *express* incorporation, for example by the worker signing an acknowledgement, at the time of making the contract or subsequently, that the rules are binding upon him, or if reasonable notice is given to the worker of the existence of the rules and he works under them without objection.

(2) By *implied* incorporation, for example where the worker has accepted employment on the 'usual conditions', which would be taken to include the works rules.
(3) By proof that the rules were recognised by *custom and practice* (*see below*, para. 157).

Express rules take precedence over the second and third categories.

156. Works rules in British industry are of so many different kinds that no general statement can be made about their function as contractual terms. But it needs to be stressed that not all works rules are contractual in character. For example, the Court of Appeal[1] decided in 1972 that the British Railways Rules Book setting out the duties of railway employees were not terms of the contracts of employment of those employees. They were simply 'instructions to a man as to how he is to do his work'. This meant that they could be unilaterally altered by the employer without the employee's consent, at any time. The employee, on the other hand, was obliged to obey the rules, as altered from time to time, because of his duty of obedience to the lawful instructions of the employer. In cases like this therefore, works rules will be treated simply as instances of lawful managerial commands. In other cases, they may be construed as being contractually binding on both parties.

1. *Secretary of State for Employment* v. *ASLEF* [1972] 2 QB 443.

§4. Terms Incorporated from Custom and Practice

157. The custom and practice of a trade or industry has traditionally been an important source of terms and conditions of employment, although this form of regulation has become less frequent with the greater formalization of conditions of work, encouraged by the obligation to supply a statutory statement of terms (see para. 132, above). A somewhat different type of custom and practice developed in manufacturing industry during the 1950s, in the form of informal workplace bargaining, displacing national agreements. This was increasingly recognised as an important source of terms of the contract. In the past decade, however, workplace bargaining has itself become increasingly formalised, and informal workplace bargaining is less prevalent. To become a term of a contract, a custom or practice must be certain, reasonable and well-known. Even if an individual worker is ignorant of the particular custom, he or she may be taken to know of local customs.[1]

1. The classic example is *Sagar* v. *Ridehalgh* [1931] 1 Ch. 310. But *see* now *Bond* v. *CAV Ltd.* [1983] IRLR 360, where the requirement of notoriety was more strictly applied.

Chapter III. The Duties of Co-operation, Fidelity and Care

158. Three of the most important duties implied in law into every contract of employment (*see* para. 146, *above*) are discussed in this Chapter. These are (1) the duty of mutual co-operation; (2) the duty of faithful service; and (3) the duty of reasonable care.

§1. The Duty of Mutual Co-operation

A. The Employee's Duty to Obey Lawful and Reasonable Orders

159. One of the most important terms implied by the common law into the contract of employment is the employee's duty to obey lawful and reasonable orders. This reflects a judicial endorsement of the employer's 'managerial prerogative' and of the notions of command and subordination inherent in the employment relationship. This has sometimes been treated as an aspect of the duty of faithful service (*see below*, para. 166). But case law suggests that the rationale of such an implied term lies in the duty not to frustrate the commercial objectives of the employer,[1] a perspective which assumes a unity of purpose between employer and employee in contrast with the pluralist premise of an intrinsic conflict of interest between the two sides. Thus it has been held to be an implied term that 'each employee will not, in obeying lawful instructions, seek to obey them in a wholly unreasonable way, which has the effect of disrupting the system, the efficient running of which he is employed to ensure'.[2]

1. *Secretary of State for Employment* v. *ASLEF* [1972] 2 All ER, 949 at pp. 971–972, *per* Buckley L. J.; and see *Ticehurst* v. *British Telecommunications plc.* [1992] IRLR 219, CA.
2. *Ibid.*, at p. 980 *per* Roskill L. J.; *see* too Lord Denning MR at p. 965.

160. The scope of this implied term is of particular importance in determining the extent of the employer's common law right of summary dismissal. In the l9th century, a single act of disobedience was treated as entitling the employer summarily to dismiss an employee, provided the order was 'lawful'. Thus a refusal to allow an employee to visit her sick mother was held to be lawful,[1] as was an order to remain in a zone of danger so long as there was no *immediate* threat of violence or disease to the employee. More recent cases have held that one act of disobedience can only justify a dismissal if it in effect amounts to a repudiation by the employee of the contract.[2] It was judicially stated in 1974 that 'many of the decisions which are customarily cited date from the last century and may be wholly out of accord with current social conditions. . . . We have by now come to realise that a contract of service imposes upon the parties a duty of mutual respect'.[3]

1. *Turner* v. *Mason* (1845)14 M&W 112
2. *Laws* v. *London Chronicle (Indicator Newspapers) Ltd.* [1958] 1 WLR 698 (CA).
3. *Wilson* v. *Racher* [1974] ICR 428 at 430.

161. Several recent cases have concerned the reasonableness of an order that the employee transfer to a new place of work. Where there is no express obligation to transfer, the courts have been willing to imply a reasonable term, taking into account such factors as the nature of the employer's business and whether the employee had been moved before.[1] Even where there is an express mobility clause which requires the employee to transfer to another location, an industrial tribunal may imply a term that reasonable notice will be given to the employee when the employer decides to exercise its powers to require the employee to move.[2] Although the Court of Appeal has refused to imply a term that the employer's exercise of an express or implied right to require mobility should be exercised only for 'genuine operational reasons' (such a term being too uncertain in scope),[3] the EAT has recently utilised the implied term that the employer must not behave in a manner calculated to undermine the relationship of trust and confidence when exercising an express power to require mobility.[4]

1. *Jones* v. *Associated Tunnelling Co. Ltd.* [1981] IRLR 477 (EAT).
2. *Prestwick Circuits Ltd* v. *McAndrew* [1990] IRLR 191, Ct of Session; *United Bank Ltd* v. *Akhtar* [1989] IRLR 507, EAT.
3. *Murco Petroleum Ltd* v. *Forge* [1987] ICR 282.
4. *United Bank Ltd.* v. *Akhtiar* [1989] IRLR 507, EAT.

B. The Employer's Duty to Take Steps to Achieve the Purposes of the Employment Relationship

162. In contrast to the extensive nature of the employee's implied duties, the employer's implied obligations have traditionally been limited to the duty not to prevent or hinder the occurrence of an express condition upon which the performance of the contract by the employee depends (e.g. the provision of piecework to a worker paid on piece rates). Under the influence of the law of unfair dismissal (*see below*, Chapter VII), this duty has been developed into an implied duty of mutual trust and confidence.[1] Although this does not extend to a requirement that the employer should treat employees reasonably,[2] it does require that the employer should not behave in a manner calculated to damage the relationship of trust and confidence[3] and should be good and considerate to employees.[4] The employer should take positive steps to achieve the purposes of the employment relationship, not only with regard to the material conditions of employment such as pay and safety, but also in respect of the psychological conditions which are essential to the employee's performance. For example, it has been held that the employer is under a positive duty to protect the employee from harassment by fellow employees,[5] to refrain from severely criticizing a supervisor in the presence of subordinates,[6] to investigate the employee's genuine grievances,[7] and generally to treat the employee with dignity and respect.[8] The employer must not falsely accuse the employee of serious misconduct on the basis of scanty evidence[9] nor may he give unjustified warnings with a view to disheartening the employee.[10] Nor may he require an employee to submit to a medical examination or search (in the absence of an express term) and to suspend the employee when he or she refuses.[11] Although an isolated action by the employer may not amount to a breach of this term, a course of conduct may be established which does so.[12] This extended duty of co-operation is particularly important in the context of unfair dismissal, since an employee is entitled to resign and claim to have been 'constructively dismissed' if the employer breaches this duty.

1. E.g. *Woods* v. *W. M. Car Services (Peterborough) Ltd.* [1982] ICR 693 (CA).
2. *Post Office* v. *Roberts* [1980] IRLR 347 (EAT).
3. *Courtaulds Northern Textiles Ltd* v. *Andrew* [1979] IRLR 84.
4. *Woods* v. *W. M. Car Services (Peterborough) Ltd., supra.*
5. *Wigan Borough Council* v. *Davies* [1979] IRLR 1278; *Bracebridge Engineering Ltd* v. *Darby* [1990] IRLR 3, EAT.
6. *Courtaulds Northern Textiles Ltd* v. *Andrew, supra.*
7. *British Aircraft Corporation* v. *Austin* [1978] IRLR 332.
8. *Garner* v. *Grange Furnishing Ltd.* [1977]. IRLR 206; *Palmanor Ltd.* v. *Cedron* [1978] ICR 1008.
9. *Robinson* v. *Crompton Parkinson Ltd.* [1978] ICR 401.
10. *Walker* v. *Josiah Wedgwood & Sons Ltd.* [1978] ICR 744 at 754.
11. *Bliss* v. *South East Thames Regional Health Authority* [1987] ICR 700.
12. *Lewis* v. *Motorworld Garages Ltd* [1986] ICR 157.

C. The Provision of Work

163. It is the duty of employer and employee to co-operate in fulfilling their obligations under the contract. From the employer's point of view however this generally means no more than a duty to pay remuneration. Failure to pay wages over a period of time is regarded as a breach of the employer's fundamental obligations, so entitling the employee to terminate the contract without notice. However, in general, the employer is under no obligation to provide work so long as he goes on providing remuneration.

164. There are *three* exceptional situations[1] in which the employer must provide work:

(1) in contracts in which the bargain is that the employer will provide a salary plus the opportunity of becoming better known, such as in the case of an actor or artist:
(2) in contracts with commission or piece-workers in which the employer promises to pay an agreed rate and impliedly promises to provide a reasonable amount of work;
(3) in contracts with skilled workers in which the employer promises to pay a salary and impliedly promises to provide a reasonable amount of work to maintain or develop skills.

1. *Langston* v. *AUEW* (No. 2) [1974] ICR 510, per Sir John Donaldson at p. 521.

165. It has been suggested by Lord Denning[1] that there is a general right to be provided with work, but this view is not generally accepted. In the exceptional situations mentioned where the employer is under a duty to provide work his failure to do so may entitle the employee to terminate the contract without notice. Occasionally the failure to provide work may be due to some supervening event, without the fault on either side, and so may be treated as a *frustration* of the contract bringing it to an end automatically (e.g. a fire burning down the place of work) (*see* para. 289, *below*).

1. *Langston* v. *AUEW* [1974] ICR 180 at p. 190.

§2. The Employee's Duty of Faithful Service

166. The employee must serve his employer faithfully and honestly. This basic duty may be amplified by express terms but even if nothing is said it will be implied as a matter of law that the employee is not to misappropriate his employer's property or misuse his trade secrets or confidential information. (Restraints against competition by ex-employees are discussed in Chapter IX *below*.)

A. Misappropriation of Property

167. The employee is obliged to keep proper accounts, and if he or she receives any secret profit or bribe this belongs to his employer and he can be made to account for it.[1] Misappropriation of property is a ground for summary dismissal at common law, even if the facts come to light only after the dismissal.[2] The dismissal will be lawful under the unfair dismissals legislation provided that the employer had reasonable grounds for his belief at the time of dismissal, and carried out as much investigation as was reasonable in the circumstances.[3] Where misappropriation is discovered only after the contract has been terminated with due notice, the employee is still entitled to the contractual remuneration for the period after the breach during which normal services were rendered.[4]

1. *Reading* v. *Attorney-General* [1951] AC 507, HL.
2. *Boston* v. *Ansell* (1888) 39 Ch. D. 339 (CA).
3. *British Home Stores Ltd.* v. *Burchell* [1980] ICR 303; approved in *Weddell & Co. Ltd.* v. *Tepper* [1980] ICR 286 (CA).
4. *Horcal* v. *Gatland* [1984] IRLR 291 (CA).

B. Spare-time Work

168. Unless the parties have expressly agreed to the contrary, there is generally no restriction on a worker taking spare-time work. However, he or she cannot take a job which might inflict harm on his principal employer. So an injunction may be granted to restrain an employee from working for a rival employer during his spare-time, and competitive work would normally justify dismissal by the employer. It is probably not enough that the spare-time work is in the same field of activity as that of the principal employer. There must be substantial drain on the employee's time or energies or some clear danger causing loss to the employer.[1]

1. *Hivac Ltd.* v. *Park Royal Scientific Instruments Ltd.* [1946] Ch. 169; *Nova Plastics Ltd.* v. *Froggett* 11982] IRLR 146.

C. Trade Secrets and Confidential Information

169. An employee must not disclose the employer's trade secrets to a third party, nor misuse confidential information acquired in the course of employment. In some situations, this obligation may continue even after the employment has ended (on which *see* para. 365, *below*). In the absence of an express term on these matters, the obligations of the employee are the subject of implied terms. While the employee remains in the employment of the employer, the extent of the duty of fidelity will vary according to the nature of the contract. The duty will be broken if an employee makes or copies a list of the customers of the employer for use after his employment ends or deliberately memorises such a list. The obligation not to use or disclose information clearly covers secret processes of manufacture, such as chemical formulae, or designs and other information which is of a sufficiently high degree of confidentiality to amount to a trade secret.[1] In *Thomas Marshall (Exports) Ltd.* v. *Guinle*[2] a general test of the class of protected information was suggested, namely if (i) the owner reasonably believed that its release would be injurious to him or her; (ii) the owner reasonably believed that it was not yet in the public domain, and (iii) the information could be judged confidential in the light of the usage and practices of the particular industry or trade. However, in *Faccenda (Chickens) Ltd* v. *Fowler*,[3] a distinction was drawn between information amounting to a trade secret and less sensitive information. During employment, both types of information, which the employee 'could only acquire as a result of and in the course of his employment', fall within the scope of the implied term. But the Court of Appeal held that after the employment has ended, the implied term protects only information which is sufficiently confidential to amount to a trade secret. All the circumstances have to be taken into account, including the nature of the employment (a higher obligation being imposed where the employee habitually handles sensitive material because the employee can be expected to understand its nature), the nature of the information, whether the employer impressed upon the employee the confidentiality of the information, and whether the information can be easily isolated from other information which the employee is free to use or disclose. The employer may, of course, supplement the implied duty against disclosure by an express covenant (*see* para. 365, *below*). Employees who deliberately copy or memorise information for their use after leaving the employment, obviously break the implied duty of good faith and fidelity, and as long ago as 1895 the Court of Appeal said that there was no need in such a case for the employer to show that the information was confidential.[4] This has been recently reaffirmed by the Court of Appeal, when rejecting an argument by an employee who had taken with him his employer's card index containing the names and addresses of customers that he could have compiled a comparable list from trade journals and telephone directories.[5] Former employees who obtain the information from legitimate sources are as free as any other competitor to do so, but they may not make unlawful use of the employers' own list.

1. *Faccenda (Chickens) Ltd.* v. *Fowler*, [1986] ICR 297 CA; *Herbert Morris Ltd.* v. *Saxelby* [1916] AC 688 at 704.
2. [1978] ICR 905.
3. [1986] ICR 297.
4. *Robb* v. *Green* [1895] 2 QB 315, CA
5. *Roger Bullivant Ltd* v. *Ellis* [1989] ICR 464, CA.

170. It is not a breach of the employee's duty of confidentiality if he disclosed 'any misconduct of such a nature that it ought in the public interest to be disclosed to others'.[1] This category of 'misconduct' no doubt includes the commission of a crime or other unlawful act by the employer, but it is not clear what other matters must be disclosed 'in the public interest'. It was held in one case that an employee was entitled to reveal an arrangement by his former employers to maintain prices, allegedly in contravention of fair competition legislation, on the grounds that this affected the 'public interest'.[2] In such cases the person to whom the information is disclosed must have a 'proper interest' in receiving it. It would be rare for the misconduct to be of such a nature to justify disclosure to the press.

1. *Initial Services Ltd.* v. *Putterill* [1968] 1 QB 396.
2. *Initial Services Ltd.* v. *Putterill* [1968] 1 QB 396.

171. The employer who alleges that his trade secrets or confidences have been betrayed may seek remedies in the ordinary civil courts. An injunction may be granted restraining the employee or ex-employee from acting in breach of his duties, and he may be ordered to account for the profits made through their use, and also to pay damages for breach of contract. The employer may be able to dismiss the employee without notice provided proper procedures are followed (*below*, Chapter VII).

172. A consequence of the rules about confidential information is that individual employees are not at liberty to disclose information which may be relevant to collective bargaining to trade unions, and workers' representatives on company organs are likewise bound by the ordinary rules as to breach of confidence. A trade union official who induces an employee to disclose information for collective bargaining purposes before a claim has been prepared may be restrained by injunction and ordered to pay damages.[1] However if a dispute with an employer exists or is in immediate contemplation, the trade union official inducing the employee to disclose information would be immune from civil proceedings by reason of the statutory protection given to any person inducing a breach of contract 'in contemplation or furtherance of a trade dispute'.[2] The employee who disclosed such confidential information to a trade union may nevertheless be in breach of contract even during a trade dispute.[3]

1. *Bent's Brewery Co. Ltd.* v. *Hogan* [1945] 2 All ER 570.
2. TULRCA 1992, s. 219, *see* Part II, Chapter V.
3. *Norbrook Laboratories* v. *Sands* [1984] IRLR 201. (Northern Ireland CA).

173. An employer is under a *duty* to disclose information to trade unions for collective bargaining purposes in certain circumstances, which are discussed in Part II, Chapter IV.

174. The duty of fidelity does not, however, oblige the employee to disclose his or her own misconduct. In the leading case, Lord Atkin said: 'The servant owes a duty not to steal, but having stolen, is there a superadded duty to confess that he has stolen? I am satisfied that to imply such a duty would be a departure from the well-established usage of mankind and would be to create obligations entirely outside the normal contemplation of the parties'.[1] This decision of the House of Lords seems to rest upon the general idea of the right not to incriminate oneself, and serves to protect the right to retain wages already paid, before the misconduct is discovered.[2] However, the principle of fidelity dictates that the employee, particularly if he or she is in a managerial or supervisory position, may be obliged to disclose the misconduct of fellow employees.[3]

1. *Bell* v. *Lever Bros. Ltd.* [1932] AC 161 at p. 813.
2. Mark Freedland in (1984) 13 *Industrial Law Journal* 25 at p. 30.
3. *Sybron Corporation* v. *Rochem Ltd.* [1983] ICR 801 (CA); *Swain* v. *West (Butchers) Ltd.* [1936] 3 All ER 261.

§3. The Duty of Reasonable Care

A. The Employee's Duty

175. An employee is under a duty to exercise reasonable skill and care in the exercise of his or her duties. What is reasonable depends upon all the circumstances, and different standards may apply according to whether (1) the employer seeks damages or an indemnity from the employee for the financial loss to the employer resulting from the negligence, or (2) the employer seeks to dismiss the negligent employee.

I. The Employer's Claim for Damages or an Indemnity

176. There are two legal bases upon which an employer may seek damages or an indemnity. The first arises under the Civil Liability (Contribution) Act 1978, which allows a joint tortfeasor (i.e., wrongdoer) who is liable to a third party in respect of any damage to recover a contribution (which may be a full indemnity) from any other tortfeasor who is, or would if sued have been liable in respect of that same damage. The usual situation in which this applies is where an employee in the course of the employment negligently injures a fellow-employee, who then claims damages from their common employer. The employer may then join the negligent employee as a third party to the proceedings, if he is not already a co-defendant, and seek a contribution. The second basis for an indemnity rests on a controversial decision of the House of Lords in the case *Lister* v. *Romford Ice and Cold Storage Co. Ltd.* (1957)[1] in which it was decided, as a matter of law, that there was an implied duty in a lorry-driver's employment contract to exercise reasonable care about his employer's business.

1. [1957] 1 All ER 125.

177. In practice, these rights are not often enforced against employees.[1] The reason is that usually the employer does not suffer any loss because it is insured in respect of liability to its own employees (such insurance has been compulsory since 1 January 1972)[2] and for liability to third parties suffering injuries in road accidents (such insurance is also compulsory). Only if the employer's insurance company chooses to exercise its rights of subrogation under the contract of insurance will an attempt be made to claim an indemnity from an employee. In fact, as a result of a threat of nationalization after *Lister's* case (*above*), most insurance companies are now parties to a 'gentlemen's agreement' not to enforce their rights of subrogation against employees. Recently, the Court of Appeal has refused to allow the right of subrogation to be enforced in an industrial setting, because of the potential disruption to labour relations, in circumstances where the 'gentlemen's agreement' did not apply.[3]

1. An example of the (rare) use of the right of action is *Janata Bank* v. *Ahmed* [1981] ICR 791 (CA) where the damages exceeded £36,000.
2. Employers Liability (Compulsory Insurance) Act 1969.
3. *Morris* v. *Ford Motor Co. Ltd.* [1973] QB 792.

II. The Power of Dismissal

178. In general, a single act of negligence will not justify termination of the employment contract without notice.[1] Under the law of unfair dismissal it is only gross negligence which would justify dismissal without a warning and an opportunity to improve performance. It has been recognised, however, that there are certain occupations (such as the pilot of an aircraft and the driver of an express train) where a single act of negligence in a matter central to the employee's duties might render the dismissal fair although there has been no previous misconduct, and the employee has rendered long service (*see* Chapter VII, *below*).[2]

1. *Jupiter General Insurance Co. Ltd.* v. *Shroff* [1937] 3 All ER 67.
2. *Turner* v. *Pleasurama Casinos* [1976] IRLR 151.

B. The Employer's Duty

179. An employee who is injured at work may seek to hold his employer responsible on two possible grounds: (1) the breach of a common law duty to exercise reasonable care for the safety of employees in the course of their employment, or a statutory duty to take specified precautions for the employee's safety; or (2) the breach of a common law or statutory duty owed by a fellow-employee to the injured employee, the employer being vicariously liable for the torts (delicts) of its employees. The first of these duties may be classified either as an implied term of the contract of employment or as arising in tort (*ex delicto*). The second is normally classified as a duty in tort alone. (Before 1948,[1] an action against the employer on the second ground was barred by the doctrine of common employment.) This subject of compensation for work accidents, which in part rests on the employer's liability, and in part on Social Security law, lies beyond the scope of this monograph. It must, however, be mentioned that, under section 2(1) of the Unfair Contract Terms Act 1977 (in force since 1 February 1978) any term of a contract or notice which excludes or restricts liability for death or personal injury resulting from negligence is void. Section 2(2) of the Act of 1977 prohibits exclusion or restriction of liability for negligence in the case of 'other loss or damage' (e.g. to property or economic interests) unless the term or notice satisfies a test of 'reasonableness'. These provisions extend to the contract of employment, but only in favour of the employee not the employer. These provisions do not appear to affect the kind of indemnity clause in *Lister's* case (*above* para. 176).

1. Law Reform (Personal Injuries) Act 1948, s.l.

Chapter IV. Working Time and Holidays

§1. The Importance of Collective Agreements

180. It is a distinctive feature of British labour law that there is no general legislation laying down minimum standards for the length of the working day or the number of rest days and holidays. Indeed, the United Kingdom Government has declined to accept the obligations in ILO Recommendation No. 116 and Article 2(1) of the European Social Charter, concerning reduction of hours of work, on the grounds that these are 'not consistent with the methods by which conditions of employment are normally determined in the United Kingdom'.[1] Instead, the substantial gains which have been achieved in most industries in this respect are largely the result of collective agreements. Where trade unions are recognised for collective bargaining purposes, both the length of the working week and holiday entitlement are subjects of negotiation.[2] Particularly important gains have been made in the early 1980s, with a general reduction in the average basic hours per week from 40 in 1979 to 39 in 1984.[3] For the rest of the decade, the basic working week for most employees remained largely unchanged: at the end of 1990, the average basic working week in nationally negotiated agreements covering manual employees remained at just under 39 hours.[4] Among Western European countries, West Germany enjoys the lowest annual working hours in manufacturing, while Greece, Ireland and Portugal have the highest. The UK is around the middle of the table.[5]

Recently, trade unions in some industries have appeared more determined to secure a reduction in working hours, and in 1989/1990 this issue led to major industrial action in the engineering industry. At the same time, there has been growing interest in moves towards more flexible patterns of hours, including, for example, annualised hours contracts in which employees agree to work a certain number of hours each year rather than fixed hours each week.[6] Similarly, entitlements to paid holidays (in addition to public or customary holidays) have increased since 1979. By the end of 1989, more than 91 per cent of manual workers subject to national collective agreements had a minimum entitlement of four weeks or more and over 27 per cent had a minimum entitlement of five weeks or more. The average was almost 23 days. In many cases, actual holiday entitlements are higher than minima because of additions for seniority and local arrangements.[7] It should nevertheless be stressed that the absence of statutory minimum standards means that it is always possible for individual employers and employees to override collectively agreed minima by expressly agreeing a longer working week or fewer holidays.

1. Cmnd. 1993, London, HMSO, 1963.
2. Daniel and Millward, *op. cit.*, p. 197.
3. *Employment Gazette*, April 1985, p. 154.
4. *Employment Gazette*, April 1991 p. 167.
5. IDS Study 444 October 1989 p. 5.
6. ACAS Annual Report 1989, pp. 5, 11; *see* generally, B. Hepple, *Working Time: a New Legal Framework?* London, Institute for Public Policy Research, 1990.
7. *Employment Gazette*, April 1990, p. 228.

181. Proof that a collective agreement has been incorporated into the individual contract is facilitated by the requirement in Section 1 of the Employment Protection (Consolidation) Act 1978 that the employer must give the employee particulars relating to hours of work, and entitlement to holidays and holiday pay (*above* para. 133). The statement of particulars may refer to a collective agreement.

§2. Statutory Restrictions on the Working Day

182. There are a number of Acts of Parliament, a legacy of 19th Century social reforms, which limit the working hours of children (para. 141 *above*). These are enforced by the Health and Safety Executive. The complex network of provisions restricting the working hours of women and young persons were repealed in 1986[1] and 1989[2] entailing the denunciation of two ILO conventions[3] and two provisions of the European Social Charter.[4] The Secretary of State also has wide powers to amend or repeal statutory provisions which deal with the employment of persons under the age of 18.[5]

1. SDA 1986, s. 7.
2. EA 1989, s. 10.
3. ILO Convention No. 451 (1937); ILO Convention 1935 (No. 45).
4. Articles 8(4)(a) and 7(8).
5. EA 1989, s. 10 (3).

183. The absence of statutory controls has recently led some employees to seek the protection of the employer's common law duty of care (para.179 *above*). In *Johnstone* v. *Bloomsbury Health Authority*[1] junior hospital doctors were employed under a contract providing for a standard working week of 40 hours and the doctor was also required to be available for a further 48 hours 'on average'. The doctors claimed that the employers had acted unlawfully in requiring them to work for so many hours as would foreseeably injure their health. The Court of Appeal (by a majority) allowed the claim to go forward to trial. The decision indicates that the employer's power to require overtime working has to be exercised in the light of their duty to take care of the employee's health and if they should have known that they were exposing the employee to the risk of injury to his health by requiring him to work the hours they did, then they should not have required him or her to work more than the number of hours they could safely have done.

1. [1991] IRLR 118, CA.

184. Reserved.

185. It is rare for there to be any statutory limits on the hours of work of adult men. Among the few instances are (1) The Hours of Employment (Conventions) Act 1936 restricts the hours of sheet glass-workers; (2) Part VI of the Transport Act 1968 limits the hours of work of drivers of certain classes of vehicles to 10 hours a day, or exceptionally 14, with a maximum of 60 hours per week, and lays down rest periods and limits continuous driving. EEC Regulation 543/69 on the harmonisation of legislation on road transport applied to international transport operations from 1 April 1973 and Community rules in respect of national operations since 31 December 1980.[1] The Coal Industry Act 1992, s. 2, repealed legislation which had been in force since 1908 restricting the hours of work below ground.

1. Commission Decision 78/85 of 21 December 1977 (OJ 1978, L33/78 of 3 February 1978). For the detailed regulations *see Sweet and Maxwell's Encyclopedia of Employment Law*, Part 3.

§3. Statutory Provisions Relating to Holidays

186. There is no general legislation on holidays.[1] Bank Holidays apply as of right only to those men and women working in financial institutions, but they are not infrequently applied (by collective agreement or managerial discretion) to other employees, or alternative days off in lieu of these holidays are granted. However, for such employees these holidays are not enjoyed as of statutory right. The current Bank Holidays are – New Year's Day, Easter Monday, the first and last Mondays in May, the last Monday in August, 26 December (if not a Sunday), 27 December (in a year in which 25 or 26 December is a Sunday).

1. There is regulation of holidays in agriculture.
2. Banking and Financial Dealings Act 1971, which confers a power to suspend financial and other dealings on bank holidays. In Scotland 2 January is also a bank holiday.

§4. Time Off Work

187. Employees have the statutory right to take time off during working hours in six situations.

A. Union Officials

188. Employees who are officials of independent trade unions recognised by the employer for purposes of collective bargaining are entitled to reasonable time off with pay.[1] (An official includes a shop steward.) The scope of this right was significantly narrowed in 1989. Previously, an official could claim paid time off to carry out all duties concerned with industrial relations between his or her employer or an associated employer and its employees, and the courts generally construed this phrase broadly. The Employment Act 1989, however, removed the right to paid time off for matters in respect of which the union is not recognised by the employer. Thus a union official is only entitled to paid time off for duties concerned with negotiations with the employer over those matters in relation to which the union is recognised by the employer, or for duties in relation to which the employer has agreed that the union may perform functions on behalf of his or her employees. Time off for training is restricted to training relevant to such duties, and there is no longer a right to time off for duties involving industrial relations with an associated employer.

1. EPCA 1978, s. 27, as amended by EA 1989, s. 14.
2. TULRCA 1992, s. 168.

B. Union Members

189. Members of independent trade unions recognised by the employer are entitled to reasonable time off for activities of their union and in order to represent the union.[1] This does not include time off for industrial action. It is time off without pay. An ACAS Code of Practice gives guidelines.

1. EPCA 1978, s. 28

C. Public Duties

190. An employee must be allowed reasonable time off for certain specified public duties (such as justice of the peace, member of a tribunal, or member of a local authority or the governing body of any educational establishment).[1] This time off may be used only for attending meetings and for executive functions. This is time off without pay. No Code of Practice is to be issued. Since 1989, local authority employees (excluding the chairman of the council) have been limited to 208 hours of time off for local authority duties.[2]

1. EPCA 1978, s. 29.
2. Local Government and Housing Act 1989, s. 10.

D. Redundant Employees

191. An employee who has been given notice of dismissal by reason of redundancy has the right to reasonable time off during the notice period to seek new employment or to make arrangements for training.[1] The employee must have been continuously employed for 2 years or more.

1. EPCA 1978, s. 31.

E. Ante-natal Care

192. An employee who is pregnant has the right not to be unreasonably refused time off with pay during her working hours to enable her to keep an appointment to attend at any place for the purpose of receiving ante-natal care.[1] This has to be on the advice of a medical practitioner, midwife or health visitor and a certificate or appointment card must be produced for a second or subsequent appointment.

1. EPCA 1978, s. 31A.

F. Safety Representatives

193. The Safety Representatives and Safety Committees Regulations 1977[1] require employers to permit safety representatives[2] appointed by an independent trade union to take such time off with pay as is necessary for the purposes of performing his or her statutory safety functions and undergoing reasonable training in relation to those functions having regard to the Health and Safety Commission's Code in regard to training.

1. S.I. 177 No. 500, reg. 3(1).
2. *See* Part 11, Chapter III below for the structure and functions of these committees and representatives

G. Claims for Breach of Rights

194. In each of the above cases, the employees may complain to an industrial tribunal within 3 months of the failure to give time off. If the complaint is well-founded, the tribunal may make a declaration. In the case of trade union officials and safety representatives, the tribunal may award the remuneration due as well as compensation, having regard to the employer's default and the employee's loss. Union members and employees with public duties may be awarded compensation but no remuneration is due to them. A redundant employee may claim up to two-fifths of a week's pay and a pregnant woman may claim the remuneration due in respect of time off for ante-natal care.

H. Excluded Classes of Employees

195. The most important exclusion from the above rights concerns part-time workers. Those normally working less than 16 hours weekly (or 8 hours in some situations) are excluded from the first three rights set out above, and the requirement of two years' continuous service in the case of redundant employees makes it difficult for part-timers to qualify. Part-timers are, however, eligible for time off for ante-natal care, as are all other employees. Employees normally working outside Great Britain are excluded from all the remaining rights as are share fishermen. Merchant seamen may not claim time off for public duties or workseeking when redundant.

Chapter V. Remuneration and Benefits

§1. Regulation of Remuneration

196. Apart from periods of incomes policy (*see* Introduction, paras. 57–63, above), there has been little state intervention into levels of pay. The main examples of pay regulation are the minimum wage legislation, which only operates in small pockets of industry (*see* paras. 205–212, *below*) and the Equal Pay Act 1970, which obliges employers to pay men and women at the same rates for like work or work of equal value (*see* Part I, Chapter III, *below*). Pay determination is largely left to collective bargaining, individual negotiation or unilateral management decision-making. The pattern of wage differentials between industries has remained remarkably stable over time, with industries such as newspaper printing, oil refining and air transport consistently among the best paid industries and catering, agriculture and retail distribution among the worst paid.[1] However, during the 1980s, the first post-war decade in which Government made no attempt to regulate pay by formal pay policies, wage differentials widened significantly. In particular, non-manual workers fared better than their manual counterparts. Whereas the real earnings of non-manual workers increased by 38 per cent, those of manual workers increased by only 13 per cent. More problematic was the fact that the earnings of low paid workers increased far less than those of workers with higher pay. Thus the real earnings of the lowest decile of manual workers improved by only 4 per cent, whereas the highest decile of non-manuals increased by 46 per cent.[2]

1. *See* generally D. Marsden, Ch. 11, *Industrial Relations in Britain* (ed. G. S. Bain), Oxford 1983, pp. 264–265.
2. ACAS Annual Report, 1989, p. 11.

§2. Payment Systems

197. Methods of remuneration are a central feature of workplace industrial relations. They have an important influence on the opportunities available for bargaining and the extent of management control.[1] In addition, they reflect crucial distinctions within the workforce, particularly the differences between manual and non-manual workers. Manual workers are more likely to be subject to payment systems based on direct sanctions and incentives than non-manual workers. On the other hand, incentive-based payment systems tend to present more opportunities for bargaining than the fixed remuneration paid to most non-manual workers.[2]

1. W. Brown (ed.), *The Changing Contours of Industrial Relations*, p. 110.
2. W. W. Daniel and N. Millward, *Workplace Industrial Relations*, p. 200.

198. There is a wide variety of pay systems in Britain. One common form of payment is based on units of *Time* (monthly, weekly, daily or hourly). Monthly payment is an indication of high ('staff') status and is usually associated with non-manual workers. *Overtime*, which is generally remunerated at a higher (premium) rate (e.g. time-and-a-half) constitutes an important element in the pay of manual employees. In 1990 for example, employees in manufacturing industries worked an average of 9.5 hours per week overtime.[1] It remains true to say, as the Donovan Royal Commission did in 1968, that 'overtime is widely used in Britain to give adult males levels of pay which they and those who arrange the overtime regard as acceptable'.[2] The statutory definition of a 'week's pay' for the purposes of compensation in the event of redundancy, unfair dismissal and other statutory rights does not, however, include overtime pay unless overtime is obligatory on both the employer and the employee.[3] Problems arising out of uneven distribution of overtime have been a frequent source of shop floor conflict, and there are many informal and formal rules enforced by unions to ensure equality of overtime.

1. *Employment Gazette*, July 1990, p. 517.
2. Report of the Royal Commission on Trade Unions and Employers' Associations, Cmnd. 3623, para. 92.
3. EPCA 1978, Schedule 14. *Tarmac Roadstone Holdings Ltd.* v. *Peacock* [1973] 1 WLR 594 (CA); *c.f. Lotus Cars Ltd.* v. *Sutcliffe & Stratton* [1982] IRLR 381 (CA). *See below*, para. 214.

199. Also important is the payment system known as Payment By Results (PBR), whereby pay is related to effort and output. Although the traditional aim of PBR is to encourage workers to raise their output, it has increasingly become an instrument of management control designed to ensure consistency of output. There is a wide variety of PBR systems, ranging from long established piece-working to complex systems of commission and bonus payments. PBR has, however, declined in popularity. Whereas in 1982, as many as 44.5 per cent of full-time men aged 21 or over were in receipt of PBR by April 1990 this proportion had decreased to 27.1 per cent for male manual workers.[1] PBR is most common among male manual workers in the private sector and is relatively rare among non-manual workers.

1. New Earning Survey, 1990.

200. Payment by results systems have been a fertile source of dispute over such matters as price fixing, inequality of earnings of different members of a work group and shortage of work. This gives many opportunities for informal plant level bargaining and the establishment of customary arrangements. For example, workers themselves may set limits on earnings to equalise benefits, or institute various forms of 'fiddling the system' to help members of a group over fluctuations in output. Recently, however, there has been a tendency to base schemes on relatively rigorous work study techniques rather than the traditional intuitive methods of rate fixing, decreasing the scope for informal and fragmented pay bargaining.[1] Moreover, some bonus schemes, such as that operated by the National Coal Board, are assessed on a plant to plant basis, rather than considering individual output, leading, as in the coal-mining industry, to conflicts of interest between workers at pits with more productive potential and those at less productive pits. Unlike overtime, PBR is included in the statutory calculation of a week's pay.[2]

1. K. Sisson and W. Brown, Ch. 6 in Bain (ed.), *op. cit.*, p. 141.
2. EPCA 1978, Schedule 14 Part II, paras. 3(3), (4), (6).

201. One system which enjoyed a brief period of popularity was called *Measured Day Work*. according to which workers were paid at time rates higher than those usual in the industry in return for maintaining a specified level of work performance. Measured day work schemes spread rapidly in the late 1960s in response to the pay policy of 1965–1969 (*above*, paras. 57–63), under which improved productivity was a justification for exceptional pay increases. With the demise of incomes policies, this system has been of declining significance.

202. Great emphasis is placed in pay bargaining on comparisons between different grades of workers, and disagreements over differentials are a common cause of dispute. One way of rationalizing grading systems is to use a *Job Evaluation Scheme*, defined by the Trades Union Congress as a method to 'determine the relationship between jobs and to establish a systematic structure of wage rates for them'.[1] Several methods of job evaluation are in use. Some are based on a simple ranking of jobs, while others use a more complex system whereby jobs are awarded points according to characteristics such as skill, responsibility and physical effort. Job evaluation is used in relation both to time payments and payments by results. In the 1980s there was a significant increase in the use of job evaluation. In 1984, about 21 per cent of establishments reported that some employees at the establishment were covered by job evaluation schemes, and such schemes were particularly prevalent in larger establishments, in the private sector and in manufacturing industry.[2] In many cases, employee representatives sit on review bodies. Job evaluation is also significant in relation to claims for equal pay under the Equal Pay Act 1970 (*see* para. 357, *below*).

1. TUC, *An Outline of Job Evaluation and Merit Rating*, London 1964, p. 1.
2. Millward and Stevens, *British Workplace Industrial Relations 1980–84*, pp. 253–259.

§3. Fringe Benefits

203. Fringe benefits, which may be defined as payments in cash or kind additional to salary, bonus and commission, are an increasingly significant form of remuneration, particularly among high-income earners and high-status occupations. Examples of such benefits among higher-paid employees are company cars, subsidised lunches, medical insurance and share acquisition schemes (interest free or at a reduced rate). In order to prevent tax avoidance on non-cash benefits, the Income and Corporation Taxes Act 1988 (Part V. Chapter II), provides a complex system of taxation, the broad effect being to tax as many benefits as possible. The Act provides that directors (with some exceptions) and higher paid employees are to be charged tax at the 'cash equivalent' of all benefits (normally the cost to the employer of providing the benefit). Special rules apply to provision of cars, petrol, beneficial loan arrangements and share purchase schemes. Although employees who are not directors or who earn less than the prescribed amount are generally in a more favourable position, special rules apply to living accommodation, credit cards and vouchers.

§4. Occupational Pensions

204. The structure of occupational and state pension schemes set up by the Social Security Pensions Act 1975 aimed to encourage the provision of pensions. Men over 65 and women over 60 who had retired from regular employment were entitled both to the basic state pension, depending on their record of national insurance contributions over their working life and an additional earnings-related pension (SERPS). Partial contracting-out of the State scheme was permitted, but only if the occupational scheme satisfied certain minimum standards and secured a 'guaranteed minimum pension' (GMP) which broadly matched the state additional pension. However, a series of Acts since 1985 have radically altered the statutory framework on pensions, sharply reducing the responsibility of both the state and employers for providing pensions.[1] The Social Security Act 1986, while leaving the basic state pension unchanged, reduced the value of benefits payable under the earnings-related pension. Instead of calculating benefits on the basis of the best 20 years of an employee's earnings, the 1986 Act used an average of all years in a working lifetime, to the detriment of those with periods of low earnings. By 2010, the maximum pension SERPS contributors will receive is one-fifth rather than a quarter of average revalued earnings. From 2000, spouses will inherit one half of their partner's SERPS pension, rather than all of it. In addition, the 1986 Act provided legislative encouragement for those wishing to contract out of SERPS. From 1988, it became possible to contract out of SERPS on a 'defined contributions' basis, instead of, as previously, a 'defined benefits' basis. Rebates of national insurance can now be used as minimum payments to set up a contracted-out money purchase scheme, subject to certain conditions. A two per cent incentive is also payable for five years by the Government to be invested on behalf of employees in new contracted-out occupational schemes. Moreover from April 1988, employees could no longer be required to join their employer's occupational pension scheme as a condition of employment. Individuals can leave their occupational schemes and contract out of SERPS by taking out an appropriate personal pension; and certain incentives are available here too. In addition, scheme members must be permitted to pay further contributions voluntarily into at least one of their employer's occupational schemes, or to separate schemes, but any additional contributions must remain within the overall limit of 15 per cent of remuneration. Finally, the 1985 Act improved the position of those who leave before normal retirement age.

204bis. Occupational pensions have also been affected, from a different direction, by EC sex discrimination law. Until recently, retirement and pensions were excluded from the scope of sex discrimination law in Britain. However, EC law has followed a different route.

Article 119 of the Treaty of Rome provides that men and women should receive 'equal pay for equal work' and defines 'pay' as 'the ordinary basic minimum wage or salary or any other consideration, whether in cash or in kind, which the worker receives directly or indirectly, in respect of his employment from his employer.' This article has been held to be directly enforceable in the

Member States (*see* para.19 *above*). After a considerable amount of litigation, the ECJ has reached the conclusion that employers' contributions to occupational pension schemes and the pensions paid by such schemes are 'pay' within the meaning of Article 119.[1] The most important decision to date is that in *Barber* v. *Guardian Royal Exchange Assurance Group*[2] in which it was confirmed that British supplementary occupational pension schemes (i.e contracted-in schemes) come within the scope of Article 119 and have done so since that article has had direct effect (8 April 1976). Contracted-out occupational schemes also come within Article 119 from the date of the *Barber* judgment (17 May 1990). It is however, uncertain whether the *Barber* judgment only applies to such pensions so far as they are based on *service* after 17 May 1990, or also applies to pensions which started to be paid after that date although based on earlier service.[3] The scheme in *Barber* was a final salary (defined benefit) scheme, and it is clear that schemes in which the employer contributes are covered by Article 119 but not additional voluntary contribution schemes to which only the employee makes a contribution unless possibly the employer pays a significant contribution to administration costs. It appears that contracted-out money purchase schemes, to which the employer must contribute to contract-out, and also schemes where the employer makes a contribution to the employee's personal pension are covered by Article 119. In the public sector, the Pensions (Miscellaneous Provisions) Act 1990 (purporting to implement EEC Directive 86/378) removes, from 1 January 1993 an entitlement previously enjoyed by women, but not by men, under 55. It may be that this 'levelling down' is not in accordance with the *Barber* judgment, but the point has not yet been tested. As a result of *Barber*, it is now clear that different ages for men and women for entitlement to benefits, or eligibility for membership, are unlawful, even if different pensionable ages are based upon the discrimination in the national social security scheme. Many difficult questions arise as to the application of *Barber* to various other rules which produce different levels of benefit for men and women. In relation to indirect discrimination (e.g. in relation to the treatment of part-time workers) the key issue is likely to be whether the discrimination can be objectively justified (*see* generally para. 359 *below*). A Protocol to the Maastricht Treaty (February 1982), which (if ratified) will apply from 1 January 1993, has added to the uncertainties in this area with an ambiguous provision that benefits are not to be considered as 'remuneration' if and insofar as they are 'attributable' to periods of employment prior to 17 May 1990.

1. Among the landmarks were *Defrenne* v. *Sabena* (Defrenne II) [1976] ECR 455, which opened the possibility that most forms of occupational pensions were 'pay'; *Worringham and Humphreys* v. *Lloyds Bank Ltd* [1981] ECR 767, holding that an employers' contribution was 'pay'; *Bilka-Kaufhaus GmbH* v. *Weber von Hartz* [1986] ECR 1607,where exclusion of part-time workers from an employers' non-contributory scheme was held to constitute 'pay'; cf. *Newstead* v. *Department of Employment* [1987] ECR 4753, in which it was held that compulsory deduction of an employer's contribution to a substitute scheme does not lead to disparate treatment.
2. [1990] ICR 616.
3. The rival arguments are analysed by J. Mesher in *Sweet and Maxwell's Encyclopedia of Employment Law*, Part 1, G, paras. IB–2618–2622; and compare R. Ellison, *Pensions Law and Practice*, para. 22–094B.

§5. Minimum Wage Legislation

205. There is no general minimum wage legislation in Britain. In the words of Kahn-Freund:

'Ever since its inception in the [Trade Boards] Act of 1909, British minimum wage law (as distinct for example from French and American legislation) has had the characteristic of being selective. Minimum remuneration is not fixed for the whole of the economy, but for carefully chosen categories of workers. It is one example of the *ad hoc* nature of much of British labour legislation. Minimum remuneration is fixed only for workers in need of a statutory "floor" of wages and this was subsequently extended first to holidays and holiday remuneration and then to all other terms and conditions of employment. Criteria for selecting these workers have changed as one minimum wage statute followed another, and this has enabled the legislation to be adjusted to changing social conditions.'[1]

1. O. Kahn-Freund, Labour and the Law, 3rd ed., London 1983, pp. 46–47.

206. The approach of successive governments prior to 1980 is best understood in the context of two parallel policy objectives, namely, the prevention of low pay and the encouragement of collective bargaining. The earliest minimum wage legislation, instituted in 1909, concentrated on combating low pay, particularly in relation to 'sweated labour', employment characterised by starvation wages and inhuman working conditions. Later legislation also embodied the policy of encouraging collective bargaining, in the belief that low pay was closely associated with the absence of adequate collective bargaining machinery and correspondingly, that the development of such machinery was the best way of counteracting low pay. This was reflected in legislation, which provided that minimum wage-fixing machinery could be established for a category of workers if the Secretary of State considered that no adequate machinery existed for the effective regulation of the remuneration of those workers. However, since 1980, both policy objectives have been set aside in favour of permitting employers to develop pay systems 'wholly in accordance with the best interests of their businesses'[1] even if this leads to lower pay. Indeed, it is argued that minimum wage-fixing machinery in the form of wages councils causes poverty by reducing jobs and increasing unemployment. According to a Department of Employment Consultative Paper in 1985, 'wages councils interfere with the freedom of employers to offer and job seekers to accept jobs at wages that would otherwise be acceptable.'[2] This approach has led to legislation severely restricting the operation of wages councils, and to repeated calls that they be abolished altogether. To facilitate the new legislation, the Government withdrew from ILO Convention No. 26, which requires the creation and maintenance of wage-fixing machinery.

1. Department of Employment Wages Councils: 1988 Consultation Document, p. 5.
2. DE Consultative Paper 1985, para.7.

207. The policy of encouraging collective bargaining also helps to explain the structure of the wage-fixing machinery. Minimum wages are not determined centrally, but by wages councils, which set wages and other terms and conditions of employment for particular categories of workers. Wages councils consist of equal numbers of representatives of employers and employees (usually nominated by relevant employers' associations and trade unions), together with up to three independent persons (usually lawyers, university teachers or social workers) nominated by the Secretary of State, one of whom acts as chairman. The function of the independent members is to conciliate between the two sides, but if no agreement can be reached, the independent members may vote with either side. Ministers have no power to veto or amend decisions of wages councils. Interested persons are entitled to make representations. Agricultural Wages Boards regulate the wages of agricultural workers.[1]

1. Agricultural Wages Act 1948 and Agricultural Wages (Scotland) Act 1949.

207 bis. The antipathy of the Thatcher government to minimum wage-fixing machinery was given legal expression in the Wages Act 1986. Although the Act stopped short of outright abolition, it severely curtailed the operation of wages councils. The Act removed all workers under 21 from the remit of wages councils, thus giving the green light to very low pay for young workers. In addition, wages councils may only set a single minimum hourly rate and a single overtime rate as well as a limit to the amount which may be charged for accommodation. The reason given for this was that Wages Councils orders tended to be inordinately complex. However, anomalies can arise due to the very narrowness of their powers: for example, wages councils no longer have the power to set separate rates for different occupations within their sphere of operation, or premium rates for anti-social working time or difficult shift work. The Act makes abolition of wages councils easier than in the past, and prevents new councils from being established. Wages councils also have a statutory duty to have regard, when setting a rate, to the effect that rate will have on the level of employment among the workers to whom it will apply. This reflects the belief that minimum pay may increase unemployment.

208. Orders laying down minimum levels of pay and other terms of employment made by Wages Councils and the Agricultural Wages Boards are legally binding. Hence, unlike collective agreements, wages councils orders operate as compulsory minimum standards replacing any less favourable terms in the express or implied contracts of employees to whom they apply. Thus workers who are under-paid have a claim for breach of contract, subject to the usual limitation period of six years. In addition to the civil remedy, there are two further methods of enforcement. Firstly, an employer who fails to comply with an order commits a criminal offence, triable before magistrates, and is liable on conviction to a fine of up to £400. There is provision for the magistrates to order a guilty employer to pay up to two years' arrears of remuneration to the relevant employees. The function of policing these provisions is entrusted to the Wages Inspectorate (and Agricultural Wages Inspectorate). The inspectors have powers to obtain information from employers and to bring legal proceedings in the name of and for the benefit of underpaid employees. But these powers are little used in practice (*see below* para. 210). The final method of enforcing wages councils orders is by complaint to an industrial tribunal, a new right of redress created by the 1986 Act. Workers who are paid less than the minimum laid down by a Wages Council Order may claim that the employer has made an unlawful deduction, and thus bring themselves within the provisions on deductions. (*see* paras. 219–221 *below*).

209. The system of wages councils has undergone several waves of expansion and contraction. It grew rapidly at the outset, and by 1921 there were 42 trade boards (as wages councils were then called) covering about 3 million workers mainly in manufacturing industry.[1] A peak of 66 wages councils concerned with 3.5 million workers was reached in 1953. Since then, abolitions and mergers have proceeded apace, so that in 1985 there were 26 wages councils covering about 2.75 million workers.By 1988, these 26 councils covered fewer (2.5 million) workers. Whereas the earlier wages councils were concentrated in manufacturing, the present system is largely concerned with service trades, with 1.2 million of all wages council workers in retailing, almost 1 million in catering and 64,000 in hairdressing. The most important manufacturing wages council is in clothing manufacture (147,000). The remaining wages councils are concerned with a patchwork of occupations, ranging from button manufacture to ostrich and fancy feather and artificial flowers to coffin furniture and cement making. About two-thirds of wages councils employees work part-time and the majority of workers are women.

1. See generally on the background, F. J. Bayliss, *British Wages Councils*, Oxford 1962. All figures are from the Department of Employment's Consultative Papers on Wages Councils, 1985 and 1988.

210. Even before 1986, the system of wages councils was the object of much controversy. Neither of its dual aims has been wholly achieved. Low pay is an increasing problem in the economic recession and few wages councils have been successfully substituted by collective bargaining machinery. There are several reasons for the lack of success in counteracting low pay. First, wages councils tend to set low minimum rates. In 1988–89, most minimum hourly rates set by wages councils ranged from £1.96 to £2.49. This is well below the average; in 1988, manual workers in wages council areas earned only 62 per cent of the average national earnings. About 1 million wages council workers are paid little or no more than the statutory minimum. Secondly, the Wages Inspectorate lacks the resources for effective enforcement. The number of inspectors has been cut from 120 in 1984 to only 71 in 1988, a reduction of 41 per cent in four years. This meant that in 1988 only 8.6 per cent of establishments were checked, and much reliance was placed on checking by methods other than visits. Even where establishments are found to be underpaying, very few prosecutions are carried out. In 1988, 5,597 establishments were found to be underpaying, but there were only 10 prosecutions, leading to fines of only £348 on average. In 1987, 9,129 workers were found to be underpaid, amounting to a debt of over £1.25 million. As much as 35 per cent of this debt remained unpaid. Finally, substantial pockets of low paid employees are found within high paying sectors,such as the civil service, where wages councils do not operate. Similarly, the lack of success in establishing adequate collective bargaining machinery has several explanations. In particular, wages councils industries have certain characteristics which make unionization difficult. Most establishments tend to be small, with the result that it is difficult to achieve a collective identity and to shield employees from direct employer pressure, whether patronizing or oppressive. Furthermore, almost two-thirds of wages council employees are part-timers (compared with about one-fifth in the economy generally) who are particularly difficult to recruit into unions.[1]

1. C. Pond, Ch. 8 in Bain (ed.), *op. cit.*, p. 196; D.E. Consultative Paper on Wages Councils, 1985; *Employment Gazette*, September 1985, Vol. 93, p. 355; Low Pay Unit, *Undervalued, Underpaid and Undercut*, London, 1989.

211. The economic crisis of the 1980s brought about a marked change in the flavour of the debate about wages councils. In the years of full employment of the 1950s and 1960s, it was argued that wages councils were no longer necessary, since a reasonable level of wages was maintained by market conditions. Indeed, it was thought that wages councils merely inhibited the establishment of effective bargaining. Councils could only be abolished on a joint application by employees and employers and the latter tended to oppose abolition in order to avoid direct bargaining.[1]

1. E.g. Report of the Royal Commission on Trade Unions and Employers' Associations, Cmnd. 3623.

212. As noted earlier, Government policies towards wages councils favour abolition for very different reasons, the argument being that wages councils restrict job opportunities and thus aggravate high unemployment, particularly among young people. However, the evidence for this belief is controversial. Indeed, employment in service sectors covered by wages councils, such as hotel, catering and retailing, has grown faster than in most other sectors in recent years. For example, the numbers employed in the sector covered by the Retail Trades (Non-Food) Wages Council rose from 512,800 in 1982 to 745,000 in 1987.[2]

1. DE Consultative Paper 1985, para.7.
2. *Hansard*, 1 March 1989, cols 201–202; Low Pay Unit, *No Return to the Sweatshops*, Pamphlet No. 37, pp. 10–13.

§6. Payment and Calculation of Wages

A. A question of Contract

213. Outside the Wages Councils industries, pay rates are fixed entirely as a matter of contract. As has been indicated above, pay is central to collective bargaining. In such cases, the relevant collective agreements will usually be incorporated into the individual's contract of employment, either expressly or impliedly (*see above*, para. 149). In a few isolated cases (e.g. where an employer has failed to comply with an operative order to disclose information to a trade union), there may be a binding arbitration award of the CAC which is incorporated into the contract. The determination of wages is therefore a matter of agreement, and this may involve questions of interpretation. As explained earlier (*above*, para. 44) these questions of interpretation are often themselves resolved through a dynamic ongoing bargaining process and are generally not seen as disputes of rights. Only rarely will such questions reach the courts, for interpretation. The CAC has power to interpret its own awards.

B. The Concept of a 'Week's Pay'

214. Special rules exist for the calculation of a 'week's pay' for statutory purposes. This precise calculation needs to be made, for example, to determine the amount of redundancy payment, and guaranteed payments during periods of lay-off and during the minimum periods of notice to determine the contract. These rules are set out in Schedule 14 to the Employment Protection (Consolidation) Act 1978. This makes it necessary to determine whether there are 'normal working hours' (these exclude overtime unless the employee is required to work overtime and the employer is required to provide it). If there are, the amount of a 'week's pay' depends on whether or not the amount of pay varies with the amount of work done. If it does not, a 'week's pay' is the amount payable under the contract on the 'calculation date' (this date differs according to the statutory rights in question). If it does vary, the amount of the 'week's pay' is then usually the amount of pay for the number of normal working hours in a week calculated at an hourly rate of remuneration payable in respect of a 12-week period. In cases where there are no 'normal working hours' a week's pay is the amount of the employee's average weekly remuneration over a 12-week period. In calculating pay for these purposes, benefits in kind (such as travelling allowances) are disregarded. The maximum amount of a week's pay for various statutory purposes is varied from time to time.

1. From 1 April 1992 this has been raised to £205.

C. No Agreement as to Amount

215. If there is no express or implied provision in the contract of employment regarding the rate of remuneration the employee may claim a reasonable remuneration. So long as it can be shown that the work was agreed to be done on the basis that some payment was to be made, the common law implies a promise to pay what the services are worth (*quantum meruit*). However, if the circumstances show that the employer and employee did not intend an agreement to come into effect until the rate of remuneration was agreed then such a term cannot be implied. For example, a promise to pay an employee 'such remuneration as the directors may determine' will prevent the employee from claiming any remuneration unless and until the directors make a determination.[1] Similarly an arrangement that the parties will agree a future rise in salary does not oblige the employer to reach such an agreement.

1. *Re Richmond Gate Property Co. Ltd.* [1965] 1 WLR 335.

D. Payment for Incomplete Periods

216. Remuneration is payable only in arrears at the end of each period for which it is due, in the absence of an agreement between the parties to make advances on pay. The period of the employment for which payment is due depends on the express or implied agreement of the parties; for example it may be hourly, weekly, monthly or quarterly. At common law, the rule appears to have been that an employee could not recover any remuneration at all for a period which he did not complete, for any reason other than a breach of contract by the employer.[1] However, the Apportionment Act 1870, s. 2, provides that 'salaries' shall 'be considered as accruing from day to day and shall be apportioned in respect of time accordingly'. It is usually assumed that 'salaries' includes 'wages' (i.e. all remuneration) but this has not been authoritatively decided by the courts.[2] Nor is it entirely clear whether an employee who fails to complete a period because he is summarily dismissed on grounds of his own misconduct can claim wages for that part of the period for which he has worked, although the weight of academic opinion believes that he is so entitled.[3] Where the contract has come to an end by reason of 'frustration' (i.e. supervening impossibility of performance) without the fault of either party, the Law Reform (Frustrated Contracts) Act 1943 allows the court to order payment of a 'just' amount in respect of services to which the employer has had the benefit before the frustrating event (e.g. a fire burning down the workplace). In practice, employers nearly always pay for services actually performed even though the period of payment has not been completed.

1. *Cutter* v. *Powell* (1795) 6 TR 320.
2. *Moriarty* v. *Regent's Garage Co. Ltd.* [1921]1 KB 423.
3. Glanville Wilhams, *Law Quarterly Review* 57 (1941) at p. 383; but cf. Paul Matthews *Legal Studies* 2 (1982), p. 302.

E. Manner of Payment and Deductions

217. As a general rule, employer and employees are free to agree as to the manner of payment, that is whether it is to be in cash or by cheque or otherwise. Similarly, the place of payment and the periods at which payment is to be made are left to the parties' determination. Until 1986, the manner of payment of manual workers and in some cases shop assistants was regulated by the Truck Acts 1831 to 1940, which required such workers to be paid in the 'current coin of the realm.' This was initially intended to prevent abuse of workers by enforced trading and payment in kind, but with the decline of payment in kind, such protection became obsolete. These provisions were repealed by the Wages Act 1986. It is now permissible to use any modern method of payment, including payment into a bank account.

1. See *above*, para. 120.

218. The question of deductions from pay is more controversial. It is not uncommon for employers to deduct sums of money from employees' remuneration for negligent work, disciplinary offences, or cash and stock shortages, in some cases leading to a substantial reduction in wages.[1] A new framework for protecting workers in such circumstances was established by the Wages Act 1986. Unlike its predecessors, the Wages Act gives a central role to the contract of employment. Deductions are permitted if they are required or authorised by virtue of a provision in the worker's contract, or the worker has previously consented in writing to the relevant deduction. By contrast, under the previous framework, it was not sufficient for deductions to be authorised by contract; in addition, they had to be 'fair and reasonable.' In addition, deductions authorised by statutory provision (e.g. income tax or national insurance) are permitted. The Wages Act sets no general limit on the proportion of wages which may be deducted. For retail workers only, deductions or payments in respect of stock deficiencies or cash shortages are limited to ten per cent of wages payable on any pay day. However, it is permissible to make deductions by instalments, and no limit is placed on the amount deductible from the final pay packet on termination of employment. Although the 1986 Act removed some of the anomalies of the previous framework, the overall result was to decrease the protection of workers, and to reassert the 'central nature of contract', regardless of the fact that contract is of little use to workers in vulnerable positions who lack the bargaining power to resist contractual provisions.

1. Tamara Goriely, 'Arbitrary Deductions from Pay and the Proposed Repeal of the Truck Acts' (1983) 12 ILJ 236.

219. The 1986 Act also established a new method of enforcement. Whereas breach of the previous provisions was a criminal offence, and their operation was policed by an inspectorate, redress under the 1986 Act is to an industrial tribunal, which can award only what has been unlawfully deducted, with no punitive or compensatory elements. Although industrial tribunals are in some respects cheaper and more accessible than the ordinary courts, there is no legal aid and no costs may be awarded, even if the worker is successful. The scope of the tribunal's jurisdiction over claims concerning deductions has led to conflicting case-law, since jurisdiction for claims arising purely out of breach of contract remains with the ordinary courts (*see* para. 80 *above*). In some circumstances, it may be difficult to distinguish a dispute over a deduction from one concerned with the amount properly payable under a contract. In *Delaney* v. *Staples*,[1] the House of Lords held that non-payment of wages due to an employee is a deduction from wages within the meaning of the Act, so that an industrial tribunal can deal with a claim that an employer failed to pay an employee the full amount of his wages at the appropriate time. However, the

Court decided that there was no jurisdiction under the Wages Act to entertain a claim for payment in lieu of notice, since this is in effect a claim for damages for wrongful dismissal payable in connection with the termination of employment. When and if the Lord Chancellor exercises his power[2] to extend the tribunals' jurisdiction to deal with certain claims for breach of contract, it will be possible for employees to choose between the ordinary courts and the tribunals in respect of such claims. At present, the only remedy for non-payment of wages in lieu of notice is in the ordinary courts. The Wages Act 1986 is, however, an improvement on its predecessors in that it gives a right of redress to an industrial tribunal to workers in a Wages Council area who have been underpaid. This is because such underpayment counts as a 'deduction' for the purposes of the Act (*see* para. 205–212 *above*.) On the other hand, recourse to an industrial tribunal is not available in respect of any deduction made where a worker has taken part in industrial action.

1. [1992] IRLR 191, HL.
2. Under EPCA 1978, s. 131.

220. The Wages Act permits the operation of the 'checkoff', a widespread practice whereby the employer deducts trade union subscriptions from wages by the employer on behalf of a worker and pays them over to the union. Provided the worker's written consent to such an arrangement is obtained, the deduction is lawful. There is also statutory regulation of the check-off in respect of any deduction from wages of the political levy which some unions collect from members to support their political funds[1] (*see* part II, Chapter II. below).

1. TULRCA 1992, s. 86.

221. The Wages Act covers all workers, not only those under a contract of service or apprenticeship, but also those who work under any other contract to perform personally any work or services for another party to the contract, whose status is not that of a client or customer of any profession or business undertaking carried on by the individual. The Act no longer distinguishes between manual and non-manual workers, but does introduce a complex distinction between retail and non-retail workers.

222. Reserved.

F. Itemized Pay Statements

223. The Employment Protection (Consolidation) Act 1978, s. 8, gives every employee the right to be given, every time payment of wages or salary is made, a written pay statement, itemizing (1) the gross amount of wages or salary; (2) variable and fixed deductions; (3) the net amount of wages or salary payable; (4) where different parts of the net amount are paid in different ways, the amount and method of each part payment. A remedy for non-compliance with this provision may be obtained in an industrial tribunal.

§7. Rights to Remuneration on Employers' Insolvency

224. Unpaid wages or salary owed to an employee by an employer are treated as preferential debts on the insolvency of the employer. The priority over other creditors extends only to pay accrued during the four months before the date of insolvency and is limited to an amount of £800.[1] Preference is also accorded to certain statutory payments.[2]

1. Insolvency Act 1986, ss. 386–387, and Schedule 6.
2. Insolvency Act 1986, Schedule 6, para. 13.

225. The Employment Protection (Consolidation) Act 1978[1] gives an employee the right to recover certain amounts owing to him by the insolvent employer from the National Insurance Fund (*see below*, para. 323). This includes up to 8 weeks' arrears of pay, pay for the minimum legal notice period, up to 6 weeks' holiday pay; any basic award of compensation for unfair dismissal, and reimbursement of premiums paid for apprenticeship or articles of clerkship, subject to certain maximum amounts which may be varied from time to time. The trustees of an occupational pension fund may also obtain payment of unpaid contributions owing to the fund. The Secretary of State, upon making a payment from the Fund, is subrogated to the rights and remedies of the employee against the insolvent employer. Disputes are dealt with by industrial tribunals. This provides a valuable safety net for employees in the event of their employer's insolvency. However, long delays have been experienced by employees. This is to some extent mitigated by provisions of the Employment Act 1989, which permit the Secretary of State to make payments to employees before receiving a statement from the liquidator or receiver of the amount owed, if such a statement does not appear to be necessary to determine the amount due.[2]

1. EPCA 1978, s.122
2. EA 1989, s. 18 amending EPCA 1978, s. 122 and 123.

§8. Remuneration during Lay-off and Short-time

226. Workers may be 'laid-off' or put on short-time for a variety of reasons, such as temporary fluctuations in production, closure of a plant due to causes, beyond the employer's control (e.g. a failure of power supplies), or recession. The term 'lay-off' does not have a legal definition apart from the context of redundancy payments (*below*, para. 239) where it means that workers are not provided with work and, under their contracts, they are not entitled to pay. This, however, is not the meaning adopted in everyday industrial practice where the notion of 'lay-off' is taken to include any situation where the worker is not provided with work, and 'short-time' is a situation where the worker is provided with work for less than his or her normal working hours.

227. The legal rules regarding the maintenance of income during lay-offs and short-time are extremely complicated.[1] It is necessary, first of all, to appreciate that a lay-off may take one of four different legal forms depending on the circumstances. These are discussed in turn.

1. *See* generally, E. Szysczak, *Partial Unemployment: The Regulation of Short-Time Working in Britain*, London, 1990.

A. Frustration of the Contract

228. 'Frustration' means supervening impossibility of performance as by some event making the performance of the contract a physical impossibility or unlawful (e.g. the burning down of the factory). It is rare for a lay-off to occur in these circumstances, and if there is a possibility of the worker being re-employed within a short period there will be no frustration. If there is, then the worker loses any right to remuneration from the moment the event occurs.

B. The Employee is Dismissed

229. This is rare because lay-offs are generally of short duration. However, in a few exceptional cases (*above*, para. 164) failure to provide work to an employee (such as an actor) may constitute a dismissal by the employer. In that event the employee has no right to continue to receive his contractual remuneration but he may have claims in respect of unfair dismissal or for a redundancy payment (*below* Chapter VII).

C. The Employee is Dismissed but Re-engaged when Work Resumes

230. This is frequent in certain industries such as shipbuilding and construction. Since he is dismissed he is not entitled to any contractual remuneration during the period of lay-off, but he may be able to claim a redundancy payment (*below*, para. 239) or if he has been unfairly selected for dismissal on grounds of redundancy he may be able to claim a remedy for unfair dismissal (*below*, Chapter VII). If he does not claim redundancy payment and is subsequently re-engaged, the 'temporary cessation of work' due to the lay-off will not affect his continuity of employment (i.e. seniority rights) (*below*, para. 282).

D. The Employee is Suspended from Work

I. At Common Law

231. We have seen that although, at common law, an employer is under no general obligation to provide work, he must pay the employee. He cannot suspend an employee without pay, unless there is an express agreement to that effect. This means that whether the worker is paid according to time, or according to results (piece-work) he is entitled to his contractual remuneration even though there is no work for him to do.

232. There are, however, two exceptions to this general rule. First, the right to be paid may be excluded by express or implied agreement or by custom. An example of an express term was a case in 1936 where the contract provided that musicians would not be paid when they did not play, but the court interpreted this narrowly holding that the employers could refuse to pay only for those performances which it was reasonable for them to cancel.[1] Only one reported case is known to the authors in which an implied term or custom allowing the employer to refuse payment has been proved. This was where a boiler-scaler was employed whenever there was a job to be done. In between jobs he was laid-off. There was held to be an implied term, because of the casual nature of his employment, to lay him off without pay.[2] (In those circumstances he was then entitled to a redundancy payment, *see below* para. 239.) Where, however, the employer does have a contractual right to lay a worker off indefinitely without pay, there is no implied term that the duration of the lay-off should be reasonable. Thus an employee cannot claim that the employer has repudiated the contract and thus that he or she has been constructively dismissed.[3]

1. *Minnevitch* v. *Café de Paris (Londres) Ltd.* [1936] 1 All ER 884.
2. *Puttick* v. *John Wright & Sons (Blackwall) Ltd.* [19721 ICR 457. Such a term is even less likely to be implied in the case of a white-collar employee: *Namyslo* v. *Secretary of State for Employment* [1979] IRLR 450U (Industrial Tribunal). A custom would have to be reasonable, certain and notorious: *Bond* v. *C.A.V. Ltd* [1983] IRLR 360.
3. *Kenneth MacRae & Co. Ltd.* v. *Dawson* [1984] IRLR 5.

233. A second exception is where the employer's failure to provide work is due to circumstances beyond its control. For example, in a case in 1926 a colliery had to be closed to allow a dangerous state of affairs underground to be remedied. This had occurred through no fault of the employers. The court held that it was the implied intention of the parties that the risk of untoward events such as unsafe conditions or breakage of machinery should be shared.[1] It is not clear exactly how far this principle goes. What circumstances are 'outside the employer's control'? It seems likely that lay-offs caused by strikes at premises of suppliers of the employer fall within this concept. On the other hand, the court in an earlier case regarded a lay-off due to a trade recession as being within the employer's control, and so the employees laid-off remained entitled to remuneration.[2] This means that English law draws a curious distinction between lay-offs due to the fluctuations in trade, when remuneration must continue to be paid, and lay-offs due to circumstances such as mechanical failure or lack of materials, when a principle of risk-sharing is applied. Recent cases have tended to limit the scope of this exception.[3]

1. *Browning* v. *Crumlin Valley Collieries Ltd.* [1926] 1 KB 572.
2. *Devonald* v. *Rosser & Sons* [1906] 2 KB 728.
3. *Johnson* v. *Cross* [1977] ICR 872; *Bond* v. *C.A.V. Ltd.* [1983] IRLR 360.

II. Guaranteed Week Collective Agreements

234. The insecurity of workers' income during periods of lay-off has led to the negotiation of many different types of collective agreement to maintain income during the first few days or weeks or lay-off or short-time working. Most of these agreements require the employee to be willing to accept an offer of suitable alternative employment, and the amount guaranteed is normally less than a full week's pay. These agreements generally take effect as express or implied terms of the individual contract (*above*, para. 149). In general the employer cannot unilaterally 'suspend' the guaranteed agreement without the consent of the employees concerned. If the standards laid down in the agreement are less favourable than the statutory guarantee payments they are superseded by the latter (below, para. 237). Conversely, it is possible to obtain exemption from the statutory scheme where alternative collective arrangements have been made. Relatively few exemptions have been granted.

III. Guarantee Payments under the Employment Protection (Consolidation) Act 1978[1]

235. Collective bargaining has not provided adequate protection for earnings during lay-offs, and since 1 February 1977 every employee (with minor exceptions) is entitled to a guarantee payment for certain days when he is not provided with work. The maximum amount payable is £14.10 per day (1 April 1992) and in any period of 3 months an employee cannot receive guarantee payments for more than 5 days. The Secretary of State has power to raise these limits.

1. EPCA 1978, ss. 12–18

236. In order to be eligible the employee must have been continuously employed by the same employer for one month. He can claim only in respect of a day on which he is normally required to work and he must have had no work throughout the whole of the day because of a dimunition in the requirements of the employer's business for work of the kind he was employed to do, or because of any other occurrence affecting the normal working of the employer's business in relation to work of the kind which the employee was employed to do. Guarantee payments may not be claimed if the failure to provide work is the result of a strike, lock-out or other industrial action involving any employee of his or her employer or an associated employer; or if the employee unreasonably refuses an offer of suitable alternative employment for the workless day; or if the employee fails to comply with reasonable requirements imposed by his employer to ensure that his services are available.

237. Although the rights to guarantee payments under statute are separate from rights to such payments under contract (including as we have seen collective agreements), a rule of mutual set-off applies. Any contractual remuneration received by an employee in respect of a workless day goes towards discharging the employer's liability to make the statutory payment. Conversely the statutory payment is set-off against the contractual remuneration. Disputes regarding statutory guarantee payments may be referred to industrial tribunals.

IV. Social Security Benefits

238. State provision for employees affected by shortages of work has been available for much of the century. Unlike those countries which have special schemes for 'partial employment', in Britain this is dealt with by the general system of unemployment benefit, even if the employee has not been dismissed. Employees are eligible provided they have made sufficient National Insurance contributions, but, as in other areas of social security, no benefit is payable for the first three ('waiting') days. More recently, as we have seen, some of the burden has been transferred to employers, via the system of statutory guarantee payments. Unemployment benefit is not payable for days in respect of which a guarantee payment, whether statutory or collectively agreed, is payable, and the waiting days only begin to run after the period of eligibility for statutory guarantee payments has ended. This complex interrelationship may lead to difficulty where there is dispute as to whether or not an employee is eligible for statutory payments. The employer may take the view that the guarantee payment is not payable, but the social security adjudication officer may disagree, and refuse unemployment benefit. The employee's remedy as against the employer lies with an industrial tribunal, and an appeal is available within the social security system against the adjudications officer's decision, but both entail substantial delays and may lead to conflicting decisions.

V. Redundancy Payments

239. The Employment Protection (Consolidation) Act 1978 allows an employee to claim compensation for redundancy based on age and length of service for lay-offs and short-time in two situations: (1) where the employee is dismissed for redundancy, and (2) where the employee is laid-off or put on short-time within the definition of those terms in section 87 of the Act. The first situation is like any other redundancy dismissal and will be discussed in Chapter VII below. In both situations the employee must have been continuously employed for two years or more to qualify. In the second situation, to claim a redundancy payment the lay-off or short-time (or combination of the two) must have continued for 4 consecutive weeks or have occurred during 6 out of 13 weeks (weeks affected by strikes or lock-outs do not count). The employee must give notice of intention to claim a payment and give the minimum notice needed to terminate the contract. The employer must then contest liability by serving a counter-notice within 7 days of the employee's notice to claim, and by proving that there is reasonable expectation of work being provided. In order to fall under these provisions the 'lay-off' must be one in which the employee's pay depends upon being given work by the employer and the employee must not be being given this work and he must not be entitled to pay. The 'short-time' provisions apply where the dimunition of work causes the employee's earnings to drop to less than half a week's pay. These provisions are little used in practice.

Chapter VI. Incapacity for Work

§1. Statistics of Work Absence

240. About 8 per cent of workers (including both employees and the self-employed) are absent from work in any one week, a figure which has remained constant for some years. The main reason for absence is illness or injury, with about 5 per cent of workers off sick in a random week. Generally, manual workers have higher levels of sickness than non-manual workers. Women with dependent children under the age of 5 are the most likely to be absent for personal and other reasons.[1] Absence rates vary significantly between socio-economic groups and between industries.

1. *General Household Survey*, 1982.

241. Research into the reasons for absence[1] indicates that many factors contribute to absences. Among these are: (1) age structure, with 'old' labour forces having greater amounts of absence than 'young' labour forces, (2) size of firm, with smaller firms having lower absence rates; (3) length of journey to work with long journeys being associated with higher absence rates; (4) lack of supervision in the firm, this often resulting in high absence rates; (5) sick-pay schemes in firms with those providing leave with pay having higher absence rates than those which do not.

1. A review of the literature will be found in Incomes Data Services, *Absence*, Study No. 111, London, December 1975.

§2. Income Maintenance during Absence from Work due to Sickness or Injury

242. The maintenance of income of an employee who is absent from work because of sickness or injury depends on the interaction of three distinct sources. (1) The terms of the employee's contract of employment, express or implied or as a matter of custom and practice. (2) Social security benefits and statutory sick pay. (3) Lump-sum damages awarded by a court (or paid in settlement of a claim) where the sickness or injury is due to the fault of the employer or of those for whom he or she is responsible.

A. Remuneration under the Contract of Employment

243. Sick pay schemes set up either as a result of collective bargaining or unilaterally provided by management, have become widespread in the past 30 years. According to official statistics, by 1988 about 91 per cent of employees were in occupational sick pay schemes.[1] This was a significant improvement since

1974, when about 80 per cent of the full-time workforce were covered. However, these figures conceal wide discrepancies in coverage as between different employers and different working patterns.[2] Larger employers, particularly those employing over 200 workers, are far more likely to provide occupational sick pay schemes than those employing fewer than 10 workers. Moreover, in the public sector, 100 per cent of employers provided occupational sick pay, compared to only 56 per cent in the private sector. Although the position of manual workers has improved significantly, they still lag behind their non-manual counterparts. It is significant too that even where occupational sick-pay schemes exist, they may not cover all employees. In particular, part-time workers are often excluded, and half of all schemes exclude short-term workers, by requiring qualifying periods ranging from three to twelve months. Where there is a sick pay scheme this will usually be incorporated into the contract of employment either expressly or by implication. Proof of the employee's rights is aided by the employer's statutory obligation to give written particulars of any terms and conditions relating to incapacity for work due to sickness or injury, including any provisions for sick pay.

1. Department of Health and Social Security, *Occupational Sick Pay Schemes* (1988).
2. Donald Harris *et al.*, *Compensation and Support for Illness and Injury.* Oxford Socio-Legal Studies, Oxford 1984, pp. 321–323.
3. EPCA 1978, s. 1(3) (d)(ii).

244. If there is no sick pay scheme, there may be a custom relating to sick pay or a term may be implied. In some older cases, it was held that if the contract was silent as to the employee's right to sick pay, there was a presumption that the employer's obligation to pay wages continued until the contract was determined by notice.[1] However, the existence of such a presumption has been rejected in more recent cases.[2] Instead, the Court of Appeal has said that the evidence in each case should be approached with 'an open mind, unprejudiced by any precondition, presumption or assumption',[3] the aim being to discover what the agreement was. In seeking evidence of the agreement, the court is entitled to look at the subsequent conduct of the parties. Thus if an employee has never received sick pay, the court is likely to imply that he or she has no right to it.[4] Moreover, if there is a contractual right to sick pay, but the duration is not specified, there is no presumption that sick pay lasts until the contract is determined. Instead the court will imply a reasonable term as to duration, and in an industry where the normal practice is to apply sick pay for a limited period only, the reasonable term to imply is the term normally applicable in that industry.[5] The only statutory requirement is that the employee should be paid in full during the compulsory minimum period of notice.[6]

1. Marrison v. Bell 11939] 2 KB 187; *Orman* v. *Sasville Sportswear Ltd.* [1960] 1 WLR 1055.
2. *Mears* v. *Safecar Security Ltd.* [1982] ICR 626 (CA); *Howman* v. *Blyth* [1983] ICR 416
3. [1982] ICR 626 at p. 649.
4. [1982] ICR 626.
5. *Howman* v. *Blyth* [1983] ICR 416.
6. EPCA 1978, s. 50 and Schedule 3.

B. Social Security Benefits and Statutory Sick Pay

245. The principle of compulsory insurance was adopted (following the example of Germany) in the National Insurance Act 1911. In return for contributions, manual employees and certain low-earning non-manual employees were entitled to free medical treatment from doctors who agreed to participate, and the contributor also received sickness benefit which lasted for 26 weeks but could be extended for disablement. The scheme was administered by Approved Societies, including friendly societies and trade unions. The number of persons covered gradually increased between 1911 and 1946. In 1942, in his famous report on Social Insurance and Allied Services,[1] Sir William Beveridge criticised the provision for sickness and invalidism on the grounds that it was insufficiently concerned with improving health, provided too low a level of benefits, and was inadequately administered by the Approved Societies. The scheme initiated in 1946 under the inspiration of the Beveridge report retained the basic principle of social insurance conferring benefits at a flat-rate subsistence level in respect of major causes of income loss. Social insurance was made comprehensive, covering previously excluded groups and administration was unified under a Department of State. At the same time, a free and comprehensive National Health Service was established. The Beveridge scheme failed to meet its basic objective of establishing a national minimum of income support for 'normal needs' while leaving 'room and encouragement for voluntary action by each individual to provide more than that minimum for himself and his family'.[2] Successive governments kept the level of flat-rate insurance benefits below the subsistence level, so that the number of those relying on means-tested supplementary benefits (formerly called national assistance) has steadily increased. The means-tested benefit, rather than contributory social insurance, provides the minimum level of income for the poorest section of injured and disabled persons. Moreover, the Beveridge scheme failed to make adequate provision for the long-term disabled. This has led governments, in response to pressure groups, to make *ad hoc* provision for specific sections of the disabled such as workers suffering from certain dust-related diseases whose former employers are no longer in business.[3] There was a departure from the flat-rate principle when earnings-related sickness benefits were introduced in 1966 and this was extended to certain other benefits such as invalidity pensions, so bringing the British social security system closer to that on the Continent of Europe. However, there was a radical reversal in 1982 when earnings-related supplements were abolished in respect of short-term sickness benefit. This was designed to save public expenditure and to facilitate bringing the relevant benefits into taxation. The Beveridge principle of flat-rate contributions failed to generate an adequate level of benefits, and as a result there was a shift to a system of earnings-related contributions.

1. Cmnd. 6404 (1942).
2. Ibid., para. 9.
3. Pneumoconiosis etc. (Workers' Compensation) Act 1979.

246. The Beveridge scheme, as implemented in post-war legislation, improved sickness benefit and made provision for dependants' allowances. Benefit was payable for an unlimited period but the distinction between short-term and long-term benefits was retained after a year's entitlement to benefit. In 1971, an invalidity benefit was introduced for those incapable of work for more than 6 months. This supplemented the standard flat-rate benefit by an allowance graded according to the age at which the claimant became incapable of work. The invalidity benefit is available (from 6 April 1986, after 28 weeks of incapacity) with fewer contribution conditions than the standard benefit, and dependants are treated more generously. A number of other specific needs of the disabled are met with non-contributory benefits such as attendance allowance for the severely disabled who require frequent attention, an invalid care allowance for those who are unable to work because they have to care for a severely disabled relative, and a severe disablement allowance for those continuously incapable of work and disabled to the extent of 80 per cent for more than 28 weeks. There is also a disablement benefit and associated allowances, at higher rates than other benefits, for those who suffer injury due to a work-related accident or prescribed industrial disease. This is a weekly pension or lump sum for loss of mental or physical faculty according to a fixed tariff depending on the degree of disablement. The Disability Living and Working Allowance Act 1991, amalgamated attendance allowance and disability allowance, and introduced a new disability working allowance to replace invalidity benefit for those with higher earnings.

247. The major source of income support for those incapable of work for short periods owing to illness or injury since April 1983 has been statutory sick pay (SSP). Before that date a short-term industrial injury benefit was payable for work-related accidents and prescribed industrial diseases, and state sickness benefit for other illnesses. The value of these state benefits to high-earners was considerably reduced by the withdrawal of earnings-related supplements in 1982. Employers are now obliged to pay SSP to employees. From 6 April 1986, this is for a maximum of 28 weeks for any one period of incapacity for work.[1] During this period the employee has no entitlement to state sickness benefit. (The unemployed and self-employed who have paid the requisite contributions continue to be eligible for state sickness benefit.) The main justification put forward for the introduction of SSP was the reduction of administrative expenditure by placing responsibility in the employer's hands. However, it is doubtful whether the savings will be substantial because during the legislative process the government abandoned the original objective of off-loading costs on to employers without compensating them in full. The State retains ultimate financial responsibility because employers can recoup the SSP they pay by deducting it from their social security contributions. The Statutory Sick Pay Act 1991 has reduced the employer's recoupment to 80 per cent, with special provision for small employers.

1. Social Security Act 1985 which amends the Social Security and Housing Benefits Act 1982 which made the employer responsible only for the first 8 weeks in any tax year. *See* too, Statutory Sick Pay (General) Regulations 1982, SI 1982–1984.

247bis. As with unemployment benefit, SSP is not payable for the first three days of sickness, but unlike unemployment benefit, there is no requirement that the employee fulfil contribution conditions. Thus an employee may become eligible for SSP as soon as he or she begins working. Formerly, an employee was entitled to state sickness benefit even if the employer paid sick pay under the contract of employment. The new scheme, however, allows the employer to discharge contractual liability for sick pay by paying SSP (and vice versa), thus preventing double recovery and relieving the employer of some contractual obligations. SSP is not designed to replace earnings, but provides flat rate recovery on two earnings bands.[1] Many occupational sick pay schemes therefore operate by topping up the state entitlement to the level of the employee's earnings. Indeed, in 1988, 83 per cent of private sector and 74 per cent of public sector schemes topped up SSP to full basic pay.

1. From April 1992, £52.50 per week where normal weekly earnings are not less than £190 and £43.50 in any other case.

C. Lump Sum Damages

248. If the employee is able to establish that the employer was in breach of his common law duty to take reasonable care for the employee's safety, or in breach of a statutory safety duty, or that the employer is vicariously responsible for the negligence or breach of duty by a fellow-employee, then he may receive damages in the form of a lump sum payment. In assessing the amount of damages deductions will be made for remuneration received from the employer (or likely to be paid in future) since the basic principle of the damages award is compensatory. The law relating to the employers' liability for damages falls outside the scope of this monograph.

§3. Maternity Pay

249. An employee absent from work because of pregnancy or confinement may be able to receive two types of maternity benefit: (1) From her employer, under her contract of employment; (2) Statutory Maternity Pay (SMP), payable by the state, but administered by employers on lines similar to SSP above.[1]

1. Social Security Act 1986, Part IV and Schedule V, Statutory Maternity Pay (General) Regulations 1986, SI 1986 No. 1960.

A. Under the Contract of Employment

250. Some employers have schemes granting women paid leave for maternity, not infrequently on the same terms as sick leave. Prior to the introduction of statutory provisions, only 15–20 per cent of employers operated such schemes.[1] In other cases there are agreements to provide maternity leave for defined periods without pay. For example at industry level there are collective agreements for the biscuit industry, the cocoa and chocolate confectionery industry and food manufacture, allowing 26 weeks' unpaid maternity leave.

Such schemes may be expressly or impliedly incorporated into individual employment contracts. A few employers have introduced paid or unpaid paternity leave for limited periods.

1. N. Fonda, 'Statutory Maternity Leave in the UK' in P. Muss and N. Fonda, *Work and the Family*, London 1980, p. 121.

B. Statutory Maternity Pay

251. Statutory Maternity Pay (SMP), like SSP, is payable by the employer, but is recouped from national insurance contributions. There are two rates of payment, depending on the length of service of the employee. The 'higher rate', equivalent to 90 per cent of a woman's normal weekly earnings, is payable to a woman who has worked for two years (at 16 or more hours per week) continuing into the fifteenth week before the expected week of confinement.[1] The 'lower rate', which is prescribed from time to time[2], is payable to anyone who has worked for at least 26 weeks continuing into the fifteenth week before the expected week of confinement, but who does not qualify for the higher rate. The period of payment is complex. The maximum period is 18 weeks, six of which must be taken before the expected week of confinement. If an employee works during those six weeks, she forfeits a week's SMP for each week worked. The period of payment cannot start earlier than eleven weeks before the EWC, and at least seven weeks must be taken after the birth. Thus the remaining 5 weeks can be taken either before or after the birth. The higher rate, even for those eligible, is only payable for six weeks; the remaining 12 weeks are paid at the lower rate.

1. Where an employee works for between 8 and 16 hours, the qualifying period is five years.
2. From April 1992, this is £46,30 per week.

252. SMP is only payable to women whose average weekly earnings are not less than the lower earnings limit for payment of National Insurance contributions. The employee must notify her employer of her intention to be absent at least 21 days before the absence is due to begin, but the notification need not be in writing. Where an employee is also entitled to a contractual payment, she is entitled to either the contractual sum, or SNP for the relevant weeks, whichever is the greater; but not to both. The remedy for refusal to pay lies in a complaint to an adjudication officer, with appeals to the Social Security Appeals Tribunal and thence to the Social Security Commissioners.

253. Reserved.

§4. Suspension from Work on Medical Grounds[1]

254. Under health and safety legislation an employer may be required to suspend an employee from work on medical grounds, because of unsafe conditions etc. During the period of suspension under these statutory requirements the employee is entitled to be paid by his employer for not more than 26 weeks, subject to certain qualifications.

1. EPCA 1978, ss. 19–22.

§5. Right to Return to Work

A. Sickness or Injury

255. A long absence may bring the contract to an end automatically through 'frustration' (supervening impossibility of performance). The test, applied by the courts, is 'was the employee's incapacity of such a nature, or did it appear likely to continue for such a period, that further performance of [the employee's] obligations in the future would either be impossible or would be a thing radically different from that undertaken by him and accepted by the employer under the agreed terms of his employment?'.[1] Among the relevant factors will be the sick pay provisions in the contract, whether the employee is in a key position, the nature of the illness and the employee's length of service. Recent cases have tended to limit the doctrine to long-term contracts with no notice provisions.[2]

1. *Marshall* v. *Harland & Wolff Ltd.* [1972] 1 WLR 899 at pp. 902–904.
2. *Harman* v. *Flexible Lamp Ltd.* [1980] IRLR 418; cf. *Notcutt* v. *Universal Equipment Co. (London) Ltd.* [1986] ICR 414.

256. If the contract has not been frustrated, then the employer who dismisses the employee by reason of sickness or injury ('incapability') will have to satisfy an industrial tribunal, under the unfair dismissals law, that in all the circumstances (having regard to equity and the substantial merits of the case) he acted reasonably in treating the incapability as a sufficient reason for dismissal. This applies only to those who satisfy the eligibility requirements for unfair dismissal (*see* Chapter VII, *below*). The employer who acts slowly and is generous to the sick or injured employee is likely to satisfy the tribunal. There are no set rules, the only test being fairness in all the circumstances. In general it will be necessary for the employer to show that it has investigated the facts, warned the employee and heard the employee's side of the story. It will usually be found unfair to dismiss where the period of sick pay under the contract has not yet expired. The employer is not obliged to create a special job for a sick employee, suitable to his capacities, however long his service; but there may be cases, where other lighter jobs are available, that these should be offered to an employee not in good health. In some enterprises there are collective agreements which provide for sick employees to be transferred to a 'holding department' or 'inactive register' with clearly defined rights, normally after an agreed period of absence. This type of agreement does not give an automatic right to be put back in the old job but it preserves the employee's continuity of employment although he is not actually working. If the employee has not been dismissed, and the contract has not been frustrated, the employee has no automatic right to the identical job he was doing before absence from work. His right will depend on the terms of the job description in his contract of employment, which may allow flexibility. If the job has disappeared the employee may be entitled to a redundancy payment (below, Chapter VII).

B. Pregnancy and Confinement

257. An employee is automatically treated as unfairly dismissed if the principal reason for her dismissal is that she is pregnant, or is 'any other reason connected with her pregnancy'.[1] The employer may, however, show that the dismissal was fair, for one of the following reasons. (1) The woman is, because of her pregnancy, incapable of adequately doing her job. (2) Some enactment prohibits her employment because of her pregnancy. In either case, the employer must offer a suitable alternative vacancy if one exists.

1. EPCA 1978, s. 60. This applies only to those employees who satisfy the eligibility requirements (*see* Chapter VII, *below*).

258. An important part of the package of maternity rights is the right to return to work at any time up to 29 weeks from the week in which the date of confinement falls.[1] The employee who has been absent wholly or partly due to pregnancy or confinement is entitled to return to work with her original employer or successor, at her old job and on terms and conditions not less favourable than those which would have been applicable to her had she not been absent. To qualify for this right she must have continued to be employed until immediately before the eleventh week before the beginning of the expected week of confinement, and that at that date she has been continuously employed for at least 2 years (or 5 years if she works 8 to 16 hours per week) with the same employer. The notification provisions are complex: (1) At least 21 days before she begins her maternity absence (or as soon as reasonably practicable), she must inform the employer in writing that she will be absent from work wholly or partly because of pregnancy or confinement, that she intends to return to work for her employer and the date of the expected week of confinement. (2) If requested by her employer, she must produce for inspection a certificate of the expected week of confinement signed by a doctor or midwife. (3) If the employer sends a written request (not earlier than 49 days after the expected week of confinement) asking her to confirm in writing that she intends to return, she must give written notification of her intention within 14 days of receiving the request. (4) She must inform the employer in writing of the date she proposes to return at least 21 days before that date. The employee can postpone this day of return but on one occasion only, for up to 4 weeks, even if this means extending the 29 week period. The woman may do this for medical reasons only. The employer can put off the day of return, on more than one occasion, for up to 4 weeks in all, but must state his or her reasons. A woman not complying with all these formalities will lose the right to return to work.

1. EPCA 1978, ss. 33 and 45.

259. If the employer fails to permit the employee to return she may then complain that she has been unfairly dismissed. There are, however, three important restrictions on the right to return: (1) *Redundancy*. Where her former job is no longer available because of redundancy, the employee's rights depend on whether there is a suitable alternative vacancy. If there is a vacancy the employer is obliged to offer this to her, failing which the dismissal will be unfair. If there is no alternative vacancy, she is entitled to redundancy pay. The right to redundancy pay is forfeited if she unreasonably refuses a suitable offer. (2) *Small employers*. If the total number of employees employed by her employer and any associated employer immediately before the beginning of her maternity absence was 5 or fewer, the employer may refuse to take her back if he or she can show that it is not reasonably practicable to re-employ her in the same job or in suitable alternative work. In this case, the failure to permit her return will not be treated as a dismissal and she will therefore have no claim. (3) *Offer of alternative work*. In a non-redundancy situation, if any employer (irrespective of size) shows that it was not reasonably practicable to offer the employee her original job, but that she has been offered available suitable alternative work, which she has either accepted or unreasonably rejected, she will not be treated as dismissed for the purposes of an unfair dismissal claim. In all three circumstances, the alternative work must fulfil certain criteria, in particular that the terms, conditions and location are not substantially less favourable than those of her employment before her maternity absence.

260. In practice, the right of return is not used as extensively as might be expected. A survey published in 1980 found that only 10 per cent of all women employed during pregnancy gave notice of return and subsequently returned to the same employer. This low rate of return is partly attributable to the fact that many pregnant women do not qualify for the right to return. The same study found that 46 per cent of all women who worked during pregnancy did not meet the statutory conditions for reinstatement.[1] Moreover an important contributing factor to the low rate of return is the shortage of childcare facilities. The UK Government has opposed the introduction of an EEC Directive on Parental Leave (which could include rights for fathers, as is already the case in a number of other EEC Member States) on the grounds that this would impose unjustified burdens on employers and public funds.[2]

1. W. W. Daniel, *Maternity Rights: The Experience of Women*, London, Policy Studies Institute, 1980; *see* too *Maternity Rights: The Experience of Employers*, 1981.
2. Draft Directive on Parental Leave (COM (84) 63 FINAL) November 1984.

§6. Protection of Seniority Rights[1]

261. An employee will be credited with certain weeks of absence from work for purposes of calculating continuity of employment, and continuity will not be broken by those absences. These are weeks of absence: (1) during all or part of which the employee is incapable of work in consequence of sickness or injury, up to a maximum of 26 weeks; and (2) during which the employee is absent from work wholly or partly because of pregnancy or confinement.

1. EPCA 1978, Schedule 13, para. 10.

Chapter VII. Job Security

§1. Development of the Concept of Job Security

262. Since 1963 there has been a spate of legislation intended to give employees a measure of security against abrupt or unfair dismissal and to provide compensation when jobs disappear for economic reasons. A variety of imprecise concepts has been applied by commentators. One is the idea of 'property in the job' or the right to undisturbed possession of a job which cannot be taken away without due process of law.[1] This, as Professor H. A. Turner has remarked, 'is the employee's compensation for his relative lack of property in the capital that employs him'.[2] Another concept is the 'right to work' which in Britain means 'not only access to a new job after having quit or lost an old one, but also a right to continue at the old'.[3] It has, however, been argued that so far from increasing job security or job-property rights, the effect of the legislation has been to encourage British workers to abandon their 'protective' attitudes to jobs and to accept dismissals in return for cash payments.[4] It has also been suggested that the emphasis on individual rights in respect of disciplinary action by management has weakened the collective control of jobs by workers and, to some extent, strengthened managerial control.[5]

1. The classic exposition is by F. Meyers, *Ownership of Jobs: A Comparative Study*, Los Angeles, 1964, p. 1; *see* generally B . Hepple, 'A Right to Work?', *Industrial Law Journal* 10 (1981) p. 65 and H. Collins, *Justice in Dismissal* (Oxford, 1992).
2. H. A. Turner *et al.*, *Labour Relations in the Motor Industry*, London, 1967, p. 337.
3. Meyers, op. cit., p. 18.
4. R. H. Fryer, 'The Myths of the Redundancy Payments Act', *Industrial Law Journal 2* (1973) p.1.
5. M. Mellish and N. Collis-Squires, 'Legal and Social Norms in Discipline and Dismissal', *Industrial Law Journal* 5 (1976) p. 164.

263. Before 1875 the employee was, in fact, bound to his or her employer because desertion (breach of contract~ was punishable as a criminal offence and employees could also be imprisoned for debts (such as wage advances) owed to the employer. The criminal liability for desertion was modified in 1867 and abolished in 1875. 'This fundamental revolution in the law' (as Sidney and Beatrice Webb called it)[1] meant that from then on employer and employee became equal parties to a civil contract. The contractual classification of the relationship means that, in formal legal terms, the employer cannot compel the employee to continue in service – that would 'turn contracts of service into contracts of slavery'[2] – and, on the principles of reciprocity and mutual confidence, the employee cannot compel the employer to keep him or her in service. Reinstatement of a wrongfully dismissed employee is not possible.

1. S. & B. Webb, *History of Trade Unionism*, Rev. ed., London 1919, p. 291.
2. *Per* Fry L. J. in *De Francesco* v. *Barnum* (1890) 45 Ch.D. 430 at p. 438.

264. The presumption at common law was that a general hiring was for a year. This gave the employee some security during the seasons of the year, but at the same time it meant that the employee was not free to quit before the end of the period. This rule was suited to an agricultural society, but by the mid-19th century it had been replaced *de facto* by a general rule that industrial hirings for an indefinite period could be terminated by notice. The period of notice was determined by custom or, if there was no custom, was to be 'reasonable'. Before the abolition of criminal liability for desertion in 1875, trade unions pressed employers to grant 'minute contracts' (terminable at will) because this protected the right of workers to leave their employment either individually or by way of strike action. This pressure evaporated after 1875 and the rule from then until 1963 was that the contract could be terminated on either side by notice, and that the employer could summarily (i.e. abruptly) dismiss the employee for misconduct.

265. Before 1963 relatively few collective agreements contained notice periods and where they did the periods were short (e.g. in the construction industry 2 hours' notice terminating on a Friday was sufficient). Appeals against dismissal by the use of agreed procedures were rare. At the same time, unofficial ('wildcat') strikes, not authorised by a trade union, were frequent. In the words of Frederick Meyers, 'British workers are quite willing to invoke their solidarity and economic strength to protect themselves . . . and . . . their object is to secure reinstatement and not merely pay in lieu of notice.'[1]

1. Meyers, *op. cit.*, p. 29

266. There were, however, collective agreements relating to dismissals for reasons connected with the operating requirements of the enterprise, such as market fluctuations, structural reorganisation or closure of establishments. These dismissals are loosely referred to as *redundancies* in Britain, although the term 'redundancy' now has a special meaning in legislation (*see below*, para. 320). Some agreements provided for alternatives to redundancy, such as a redistribution of overtime or voluntary transfers between establishments; some laid down selection procedures to be followed when redundancies occurred, such as 'last in first out'; and some provided for severance pay, that is lump-sum cash payments to redundant workers.

267. Proposals for improving job security in the early 1960s generally took the form of a requirement that employers should give longer formal notice of dismissal. The original Contracts of Employment Bill 1963 (the first general legislation in Britain on terms of employment since 1875) placed a reciprocal obligation on employers and employees to give one another the same minimum periods of notice. The trade unions were concerned that this would restrict the right to strike after giving notice to terminate contracts, and, under pressure, the Conservative Government modified the original proposals so as to make the minimum period of notice to be given by an employee to terminate his or her contract the period of one week. The minimum period to be given by the employer, on the other hand, varied from one week (in respect of employees with between 26 weeks' and 2 years' service) to four weeks (for those with 5 years' or more service). These periods of notice by the employer have been extended in later Acts. The current legislation is the Employment Protection (Consolidation) Act 1978 (below, para. 292).

268. The Redundancy Payments Act 1965 (now included in the Employment Protection (Consolidation) Act 1978, Part VI) made employers liable to pay lump-sum compensation based on age and length of service, to redundant employees. It was originally envisaged that this cost should be shared among employers. Hence employers were entitled to recover a proportion of the redundancy payment from a Redundancy Fund made up of contributions from all employers. With the increase in redundancies after 1980, the Fund was found to be in financial difficulties, and in order to increase available resources, employee contributions were instituted in April 1982, at the rate of 0.35 per cent of earnings. The result of this was that redundancies were subsidised in part by fellow employees: indeed, since 1982, employee contributions exceeded those of employers, as a percentage both of earnings and of the Fund.[1] During the 1980s, the Redundancy Fund paid out about £200 million. In 1986 the right to a rebate was confined to employers with fewer than 10 employees, and in 1989, it was abolished entirely.[2] It has been estimated that only about one-quarter to one-fifth of employees dismissed for economic reasons has been eligible for payments under the Act, and the average lump sum payment is only about one-fifth of the median adult average wage.[3] Part of the reason for this is that there is a two-year qualifying period, and the definition of 'redundancy' is far more restrictive than the circumstances in which a worker in France can obtain severance pay or a worker in Belgium or Italy can receive payments supplementary to unemployment insurance following work-force reductions. The stated purposes of the Act included the mitigation of the economic consequences of redundancy, compensation for the loss of job property rights, and the encouragement of mobility. A survey of the main groups actually or potentially involved in redundancy[4] found that the Act has had some impact on attitudes and behaviour, increasing mobility and flexibility of labour and reducing the level of dispute activity over redundancies. One of the most important demonstrated consequences of the Act has been to increase the significance of age as a criterion for redundancy because the larger payments to older workers with long service acts as a mechanism to induce them to leave employment.[5] In this sense, the Act has facilitated movement out of the labour force.

1. *See* Paul Lewis, *Twenty Years of Statutory Redundancy Payments in Great Britain* Universities of Leeds and Nottingham, 1985 pp. 19–21.
2. Employment Act 1989, s. 17.
3. R. H. Fryer, 'Redundancy, Values and Public Policy', *Industrial Relations Journal* 4 (1973) No. 2, p. 12; *see* too *Industrial Law Journal 2* (1973), p. 1.
4. S. R. Parker *et al.*, *Effects of the Redundancy Payments Act*, London, HMSO, 1971.
5. Department of Employment, 'Age and Redundancy', *Employment Gazette* 86 (1978) 1038.

269. In 1971, as part of the Industrial Relations Act, the Conservative Government introduced unfair dismissals legislation, in large measure based on and owing its main inspiration to the ILO Recommendation No. 119 (1963) concerning termination of employment. With a number of improvements, the 1971 legislation was re-enacted in the Trade Union and Labour Relations Act 1974, Schedule 1, and this was further amended by the Employment Protection Act 1975. This legislation was consolidated in the Employment Protection (Consolidation) Act 1978, Part V. The coverage of the legislation was significantly reduced by the introduction of a one-year qualifying period of service in 1979[1] (in place of the former 6-month period), a two-year period for those employed by small employers in 1980,[2] and a two-year period for all employees in 1985.[3] The standard of proof of fairness was also weakened in 1980,[4] and important changes were made in the nature and type of remedies in 1982, discriminating in favour of those dismissed in closed shop situations.[5] In addition, levels of compensation have been kept low. The present British legislation is less extensive than that found elsewhere in Europe, and law and practice is in some respects below the standards in the ILO Termination of Employment Convention 1982, which the UK government has not ratified.

1. Unfair Dismissal (Variation of Qualifying Period) Order 1979, SI 1979 No. 959.
2. Employment Act 1980 s. 8(1) (2 year period for firms with 20 or less employees).
3. Unfair Dismissal (Variation of Qualifying Period) Order 1985. SI 1985, No. 782. There is no qualifying period for dismissal on grounds of race, sex or trade union membership or activities.
4. Employment Act 1980, s. 6 substituting a so-called 'neutral' burden or proof in place of the former burden on the employer, and requiring the industrial tribunal to pay specific regard to the size and resources of the employer's undertaking.
5. TULRCA 1992, s. 152. *See below*, para. 384.

270. The right to complain of unfair dismissal marked a major departure from the common law.[1] The employer's power to terminate employment without any reason by lawful notice or payment in lieu of notice, has been restricted. The employer has to prove the reason of dismissal (or, if more than one, the principal reason) and that this was one of a number of potentially fair reasons, namely the capability or conduct of the worker, or that he or she was redundant, or that he or she could not be employed without breach of some statutory requirement, or that there was some other substantial reason of a kind such as to justify the dismissal of an employee holding the position in question. Certain reasons are automatically unfair, such as trade union membership, or activities or non-membership of a trade union. In other cases, the tribunal has to determine whether the dismissal was fair or unfair in the circumstances, having regard to the reason shown by the employer, in 'accordance with equity and the substantial merits of the case'.[2] Control over jobs has been depersonalised in the sense that the employer can take them away from certain employees only after due process of law.[3] Moreover, there is a relatively cheap, informal and expeditious remedy for an aggrieved employee by way of complaint to an industrial tribunal (*see* Introduction, para. 80, *above*) within 3 months of the effective date of termination. Unlike the common law, the legislation (since

1976) provides that the successful employee may be granted an order of reinstatement or re-engagement (previously only a recommendation to this effect could be made).

1. See generally, B. Hepple, 'The Fall and Rise of Unfair Dismissal', in *Legal Intervention in Industrial Relations* (ed., W. McCarthy) (Oxford, 1992), pp. 79–102.
2. EPCA 1978, s. 57(3) as amended. *See below*, para. 309.
3. It was in this sense that Frederic Meyers, *op. cit.*, p. 1 spoke of the 'ownership of jobs'.

271. In reality, however, the right to be continuously employed, unless in the words of article 4 of the ILO Termination of Employment Convention 1982, 'there is a valid reason connected with the capacity or conduct of the worker or based on the operational requirements of the undertaking, establishment or service', has been far less effective than might have been expected. First, the proportion of dismissed workers utilizing the statutory remedy has been extremely modest. Although the number of unfair dismissal applications to industrial tribunals increased from 5,197 in 1972 (the first year of the legislation) to 37,000 in 1984,[1] with some fluctuations due to variations in the length of the qualifying period, the number of applications has been declining, particularly since the qualifying period was extended to two years in 1985. In 1989–1990, there were 18,098 cases of unfair dismissal brought to industrial tribunals.[2] ACAS, which has a statutory duty to promote a settlement, received 37,564 cases in 1990, only 6,376 of which went to an industrial tribunal.[3] There is also a large number of dismissed employees who make no claim at all, as indicated by a survey of manufacturing establishments employing over 50 workers by the Industrial Relations Research Unit at Warwick University who found that just under 2 per cent of the workforce had been dismissed for various reasons other than redundancy in the previous 2 years but less than 10 per cent of them had sought to challenge the unfairness of their dismissal in an industrial tribunal.[4] As Linda Dickens and her colleagues remark in their major study of unfair dismissals and the industrial tribunal system, 'claiming unfair dismissal via the industrial tribunal system is an atypical minority response'.[5] They found that 'applicants are typically male, non-union manual workers dismissed after relatively short service. Respondent employers are generally small companies, often single-establishment employers. Those industries characterised by small employment units and below average unionisation produce the most unfair dismissal claims'.[6]

1. ACAS Annual Report for 1984, London, 1985.
2. *Employment Gazette* May 1991, pp. 303 ff, and December 1991.
3. ACAS Annual Report 1990, p. 28.
4. W. Brown (ed.), *The Changing Contours of British Industrial Relations*, Oxford 1981, pp. 35–37, 115–116.
5. L. Dickens *et al.*, *Dismissed: A Study of Unfair Dismissal and the Industrial Tribunal System*, Oxford, 1985, p. 31.
6. *Ibid.*, p. 51.

272. Secondly, employees who bring claims have found themselves at a relative disadvantage vis-à-vis the employer. In 1990–91, 39.4 per cent of unfair dismissal cases proceeding to a hearing were successful.[1] One reason which has been suggested for this is the unequal representation of employees and employers before tribunals, with employers more likely than employees to have skilled lay or legal advocates.[2] However, a more important reason is the judicial interpretation which has been given to the standard of fairness in the legislation. As will be seen (*below*, paras. 305–312), the courts and tribunals have interpreted the statutory concept of unfair dismissal as resting upon the foundation of the common law contract of employment. The underlying assumption is the natural authority of management emanating from the property rights of the owners of the business. This has led to a wide interpretation of the potentially fair reasons for dismissal (in particular the residual category of 'other substantial reason'), it being sufficient for the employer to show a subjective belief in the existence of that reason, and the adoption of the view that it is not for tribunals to impose their own opinion as to whether they would have dismissed in the same circumstances but rather to decide whether the dismissal was within the range of responses which reasonable employers *might* adopt. This non-interventionist approach has been somewhat mitigated by the recent emphasis on procedural requirements regardless of the outcome of the case. This reversed the previous adherence to a 'futility' principle, namely that a procedural defect did not in itself render a dismissal unfair if the employer could reasonably have dismissed the employee had a fair procedure been followed.[3] Nevertheless, the overall approach of tribunals has reinforced traditional contractual notions that the employee's interest in job security must take second place to the employer's right to manage. The assumption has been that there are certain enlightened management styles, such as a corrective rather than a punishment-centred view of discipline. By considering how a reasonable body of employers might behave the tribunals have become, in Patrick Elias's words,[4] norm-reflecting rather than norm-setting. Not surprisingly tribunal decisions reflect conceptions of common practice rather than more radical notions of worker control of jobs.

1. *Employment Gazette* May 1991, p. 304, and December 1991.
2. Dickens, op. cit., pp. 85–93
3. *Polkey* v. *A .E. Dayton Ltd* [1988] ICR 142.
4. P. Elias, *Industrial Law Journal* 10 (1981) p. 201.

273. Thirdly, the legislation has failed to secure re-employment of unfairly dismissed employees. This remedy is rarely awarded by tribunals, although on paper it has been the primary remedy, with compensation an alternative, since 1976. In 1990–91, a mere 3 per cent of employers who lost an unfair dismissal case were ordered by the tribunal to reinstate or re-engage their former employee.[1] The remedy in all other successful cases is compensation, but levels of compensation are remarkably low. In 1990–91, the median award was only £1,733; and in a mere1.8 per cent of cases was the award more than £9,000.[2] Cases which are compromised without a hearing are settled at an average of 40 per cent of the compensation awarded by tribunals. This level of compensation cannot be said to meet the point made by the ILO Committee of Experts in 1974 that compensation is most effective as a remedy where it can act as a deterrent against unjustified termination. A number of reasons have been suggested for the small number of unfairly dismissed employees who are ordered to be re-employed. ACAS suggested in its annual report for 1983,[3] that 're-employment is neither sought by nor acceptable to many applicants'. This assumption has been strongly questioned by the Warwick study[4] which showed that a quarter of all claimants expressed a preference for re-employment when lodging their complaints. Another reason for the low level of reinstatement is employer resistance. Where the employer objects, the tribunals has to decide whether it would be 'practicable' for the employer to comply with the order. The tribunals have adopted a criterion of 'practicability' that is the employer's, namely, upon return the employee will cause no managerial problems, rather than the employee's criterion, namely that he or she will benefit from re-employment if only for a short period (*below*, para. 313). There is little incentive for management to re-employ because the sanction is only a relatively small additional award of compensation of between 13 and 26 weeks' pay.[5] The Conservative Government implicitly acknowledged that the levels of additional compensation were too low to deter employers from dismissing employees unfairly when they came in 1982 to reform the law relating to the closed shop. EA 1982 (now TULCRA 1992, ss. 157–8) introduced a new 'special award' of 156 weeks' pay, subject to a minimum of £20,100 (from April 1992) and with no maximum where an order of re-employment is made but not complied with in those relatively few cases where the dismissal is for non-membership of a union or for participation in trade union activities (*below*, paras. 376 and 384). For the vast majority of those unfairly dismissed, however, the sanction of the small additional award remains unchanged.

1. *Employment Gazette* April 1990, p. 214.
2. *Employment Gazette* May 1991, p. 305 and December 1991.
3. ACAS Annual Report 1983, London, 1984, para. 5.11.
4. Dickens, *op. cit.*, note 1 *above*; *see* too K. Williams and D. Lewis, *The Aftermath of Tribunal Reinstatement and Re-engagement*, Department of Employment Research Paper No. 23, London, 1981.
5. L. Dickens *et al.*, *Industrial and Labour Relations Review* 37 (1984) p. 507.

274. Fourthly, the legislation appears to have had relatively little success in providing a 'floor of rights' upon which collective bargaining may improve. The design of the legislation was to allow collective agreements to replace the statutory provisions with ministerial approval where the standards in the agreement were at least as high as those in the legislation. In fact, these exemption arrangements have rarely been used: only 3 exempted agreements for redundancy payments in 20 years and one for unfair dismissal in 13 years. The reasons are complex.[1] In the case of redundancy payments, it is difficult to spread the burden evenly across an industry where only one or two employees agree to an exempted scheme and it is difficult to maintain flexibility because of the practical limitations in an enterprise offering suitable alternative employment instead of a payment. In the case of unfair dismissal, the legislation has had a major impact in encouraging the growth of formal disciplinary procedures: in 1969 only about 8 per cent of private sector establishments had such procedures; in 1984 84 per cent of all establishments had a uniform procedure.[2]

However, most of these procedures are drawn up and imposed by management[3] and very few of them make provision for independent third party intervention, whether by ACAS or an arbitrator. As a result they have not qualified for exemption. Collective agreements play only a supplementary role to legislation, for example providing for 'add-on' voluntary payments over and above the statutory minima or prescribing voluntary procedures but not replacing the legislation. Such agreements show a great deal of variety.

1. C. Bourn, 'Statutory exemptions for collective agreements' *Industrial Law Journal 8* (1974) 85.
2. Millward and Stevens, *op. cit.*, p. 176; *see* too W. W. Daniel and N. Milward, *Workplace Industrial Relations in Britain*, pp. 163–170; W. Brown (ed.), *op. cit.*, pp. 35–37, 43–48; Dickens, *Dismissal: A Study of Unfair Dismissal and the Industrial Tribunal System*, pp. 232–234, 252–255.
3. S. Evans, J. Goodman, L. Hargreaves, *Unfair Dismissal Law and Employment Practice in the 1980s*, Department of Employment Research Paper No. 53, London, 1985, p. 31, found that in 80 per cent of cases in their sample in the private sector, disciplinary procedures had been introduced without consultation or negotiation with employees or unions.

275. In summary, then, it can be said that the attempts to give 'job property' or 'job security' rights to employees have proved no match for the property rights of employers. The legislation has given a boost to procedural rules made unilaterally by managers. It has supported the power of managers to buy out jobs. At the same time, however, it has given protection to individual workers against arbitrary action, where trade union organisation is ineffective or nonexistent. It has also enabled trade unions to offer better services to members in small and dispersed groups on whose behalf it is difficult to negotiate collectively, but in general British trade unions have shown relatively little willingness to use a combination of individual rights and collective procedures. Underlying trade union ambivalence about these individual rights is the feeling that individuals do not get through the tribunal procedure 'a sort of legal substitute for collective bargaining'.[1] In the future, trade union pressure is likely to be for greater recognition of the collective interest in respect of dismissals and workforce reductions. The EEC Directives on collective redundancies[2] and transfer of undertakings[3] have led to some limited statutory rights for recognised unions to information and consultation (*below*, paras. 287 and 325) but the general trend of government policy and legislation since 1979 has been to remove the traditional legal supports from collective bargaining.

1. M. Mellish and N. Collis-Squires, *Industrial Law Journal* 5 (1976) at p. 167.
2. Directive 75/129 of 17 February 1975, *OJ* 1975, L48/29, EPA 1975, Part IV.
3. Directive 77/187 of 14 February 1977, OJ 1977 L61/26; Transfer of Undertakings (Protection of Employment) Regulations 1981, SI 1981, No. 1794.

276. Those who favour deregulation argue that the legislation imposes additional costs of employment (including administrative costs of screening and supervising workers) and deters recruitment by reducing the flexibility of undertakings to respond to market changes by dismissals. It is also argued that the legislation induces inefficient use of labour because of the fear of claims for unfair dismissal. These costs are said to fall disproportionately on small firms and on those establishing new or expanded operations. Surveys of management attitudes and response[1] have shown that in practice the legislation has had only a minor impact in these respects. Few employers expressed reluctance to recruit additional labour because of the legislation. What the legislation has done is to induce greater care in the selection of recruits so as to improve quality rather than to restrict quantity.[2] This tends to support the view of those who argue that the legislation aids efficiency by achieving labour forces closer to the needs of the undertaking. There is evidence that the use of temporary contracts and casual labour is increasing, but this seems to have been prompted more by economic than legal considerations.[3] Another argument for deregulation is that the legislation has introduced greater formalism into labour relations which undermines flexible management control of the workforce. Against this, it has been strongly argued that the widespread adoption of fair procedures has made the administration of discipline more open and acceptable and has removed legitimacy from collective industrial action against dismissals.[4] A recent survey[5] indicates that the vast majority of employers now take more care in preparing for a dismissal so as to ensure that it is legally 'safe', although many small firms continue to act informally. About two-thirds of the sample of employees and trade union representatives felt that generally management dealt fairly with disciplinary matters, but some concern was expressed that procedures and unfair dismissal legislation were undermining the scope for unions to negotiate over disciplinary cases.[6]

1. W. W. Daniel and E. Stilgoe, *The Impact of Employment Protection Laws* London, Policy Studies Institute,1978; R. Clifton and C. Tatton Brown, *Impact of Employment Legislation on Small Firms*, Department of Employment Research Paper No. 6, London, 1979; S. Evans, J. Goodman, L. Hargreaves, *Unfair Dismissal Law and Employment Practice in the 1980s*, Department of Employment Research Paper No. 53, London, 1985; L. Dickens, *op. cit.*, Chap. 8.
2. This is a conclusion from all the above surveys.
3. S. Evans *et al.*, *op. cit.*, pp. 15–18.
4. S. Henry, *Private Justice*, London, 1983; K. Williams, 'Unfair dismissal, myths and statistics' *Industrial Law Journal* 12 (1983) 157. The available evidence indicates that the introduction of statutory protection has not, in fact, reduced the level of strikes over dismissal: *see* Dickens, *op. cit.*, pp. 224–232.
5. S. Evans *et al.*, *op. cit.*, pp. 33–35.
6. *Ibid.*, pp. 35–40.

§2. Job Creation Measures

277. To complete the overall picture in relation to job security, one must note that in the period of large-scale redundancies and high unemployment since 1974, there have been a number of Government measures designed first to preserve jobs and secondly to create new job opportunities. These schemes have been dubbed 'leaflet law'[1] since they are not contained in legislation, but in a series of administrative circulars from the Department of Employment. Measures designed to preserve jobs have chiefly consisted of subsidies paid by the Government to employers who were prepared to defer proposed redundancies. Some of these have been relatively successful. Thus the temporary employment subsidy scheme, introduced in 1975 and ended in March 1980, supported some 540,300 jobs in the first 3½ years. In the category of schemes designed to create new job opportunities, most attention has recently been paid to encouraging the employment of young people on low wages and to training the long-term unemployed. A series of youth training schemes were established from 1983, aiming to provide low cost training and job experience for 16 and 17 year old school leavers. (For the employment status of trainees, *see* para. 123, *above*.) During 1987/1988, there were 327,600 entrants under YTS, the total cost of grants and allowances being £1007.3 million.[2] For adults, the most important training scheme was Employment Training (ET) , which offered up to a year's training for people aged 18 to 59 who have been unemployed, available for work and signing on at an Unemployment Benefit Office for six months or more. The quality of training on these training programmes has, however, been criticised, and youth training schemes in particular have frequently been referred to as no more than a source of cheap labour. Success rates on ET have also been unsatisfactory, with as many as 42 per cent of ET trainees who completed the scheme returning to unemployment.

1. P. Davies and M. Freedland, Labour Law: Text and Materials, 2nd ed., p. 29.
2. Training Commission Annual Report, 1988.

278. The most important recent initiative with respect to training has been to devolve responsibility for training to local Training Enterprise Councils (TECs) (*see* para. 77, *above*). There are now no centrally organised training schemes; instead, it is the responsibility of the TECs to plan and manage local training schemes for young people and the unemployed. The TECs (of which there are now about 82) should follow national guidelines, but are otherwise entirely autonomous. It is therefore impossible to give a global picture of the current position with respect to training.

§3. Continuity of Employment

279. In order to qualify for statutory job security rights an employee must have a requisite period of 'continuous employment'. For example, unless the employee has been continuously employed for two years there is no right to statutory redundancy payment, and the amount of the payment depends upon age and length of continuous employment. He or she does not get the rights to statutory minimum periods of notice prescribed by the Employment Protection (Consolidation) Act 1978 unless he or she has been continuously employed for the requisite period. The employee cannot complain of unfair dismissal unless he or she has been continuously employed for 2 years, in most cases. The length of continuous employment also affects other job rights, such as maternity pay, guarantee payments and so on. Other rights, however, require no such qualifications. These include the right not to be discriminated against on grounds of race or sex. the right to time off for ante-natal care, and the right not to be dismissed for trade union reasons.

280. The method of determining whether a person has been continuously employed is set out in Schedule 13 to the Employment Protection

(Consolidation) Act 1978 as amended. These provisions are extremely complex and only the main principles are set out here. Essentially there are two elements in the concept of 'continuous employment'. The first is *continuity*, that is the existence of an employment relationship based on a contract of employment or a series of contracts with the same employer or, in some cases, successors to that employer. The second is that the employee must have continuity for a requisite *period of employment*, that is he or she must have been credited with the requisite period of weeks. For a week (which always ends on Saturday) to count it must be a week in which the employee has worked for 16 hours or more, or it must be a week for part or all of which the employment relationship is governed by a contract 'which normally involves employment for 16 or more hours weekly'. Special rules exist to protect the continuity of employment (for up to 26 weeks) of an employee whose normal hours are reduced from 16 to 8 or more a week. An employee with 5 years or more can count weeks normally involving 8 hours or more.

281. The general rule is that if a week occurs which cannot be credited to an employee then not only does that week not count as a period of employment, but also it destroys continuity of employment. If continuity is broken then any weeks credited to the employee are cancelled and the employee has to start from week one again when he or she resumes work. There is a presumption that employment is continuous and it is for the employer to produce evidence to rebut this presumption. It is necessary for the written statement of employment terms (*above*, para. 132) to include particulars of any period of continuity of employment with a previous employer which counts as a period of employment with the present employer. The effect of such a statement may be to prevent an employer contending that a change of employer had broken continuity.

282. There are two main exceptions to the general rule. First, there are certain weeks which do not count as a period of employment but which do not break continuity. These are weeks during any part of which the employee took part in a strike or was absent from work because of a lock-out. Secondly, there are weeks during which there was no contract in existence but the employee is still entitled to have such weeks counted as periods of employment and treated as not breaking continuity. These are weeks during all or part of which the employee is absent because of sickness or injury, or a temporary cessation of work[1], or by arrangement or custom he or she is regarded as continuing in the employment, or because of pregnancy or confinement.

1. E.g. where a teacher was engaged on a series of fixed-term contracts for the academic session (October to June), it was held that the interval between contracts was a 'temporary cessation of work': *Ford* v. *Warwickshire CC* [1983] 2 AC 71, House of Lords.

§4. Acquired Rights on Transfer of Undertakings

283. Changes in the control of an undertaking may have a significant effect on the job security of employees. The most common form of takeover in Britain is by transfer of share capital: shares in the company which is the formal employer become vested in an acquiring company of which it becomes a subsidiary; or the shares may be taken over by the shareholders of the acquiring company; or the undertaking may be managed by the acquiring company while the undertaking remains nominally the property of the company taken over. In these cases the identity of the employer, for purposes of the collective agreement and the contract of employment, remains the same. But the repercussions for trade unions and employees may be considerable. At present, labour law provides no protection in these circumstances. However, if the takeover, merger or amalgamation takes the less usual form of acquisition of the ownership of the undertaking in a way that there is a change of the identity of the employer, then legislation provides some protection for the acquired rights of employees. The statutory rules aim to overcome the inadequacy of the common law according to which a change of employer terminates the contract of employment and the new employer does not automatically succeed to the old employer's rights and obligations.[1]

1. *Nokes* v. *Doncaster Amalgamated Collieries Ltd.* [1940] AC 1014, House of Lords.

284. The statutory rules are extremely complex and their interpretation is controversial. There are two sets of statutory provisions, the Transfer of Undertakings (Protection of Employment) Regulations 1981,[1] and rules set out in the Employment Protection (Consolidation) Act 1978.[2] The Transfer of Undertakings Regulations (TUPE) were enacted in response to EEC Council Directive 77/1187,[3] and apply to all transfers of undertakings on or after 1 May 1982. Broadly speaking, the regulations reverse the common law principle, and provide instead for the automatic transfer of contracts of employment of anyone employed by the transferor in the undertaking (or part of it) immediately before the transfer.[4] 'All the transferor's rights, powers, duties or liabilities under or in connection with any such contract'[5] are likewise transferred. An area of particular difficulty concerns the requirement that, for the automatic transfer to take place, the employee must have been employed by the transferor 'immediately before the transfer.'[6] What if the transferor terminates the employment of some or all of the workers just an hour or two before the transfer? The authoritative House of Lords ruling in *Litster* v. *Forth Dry Dock & Engineering Co. Ltd*[7] draws a distinction between situations in which the employment has been terminated for a reason connected with the transfer, and those in which the termination is not connected with the transfer. Where the dismissal is connected with the transfer, workers are deemed to have been employed until the moment of transfer even if the dismissal has taken place prior to the transaction. This means that the transferee cannot escape his or her obligations by insisting on a 'clean slate' and requiring the transferor to dismiss the workforce before the transfer. Where, however, the dismissal is for a reason not connected with the transfer, there is no automatic transfer. For example, in *Secretary of State for Employment* v. *Spence*[8] the employee was dismissed because no work was available due to the withdrawal of the employer's major contractor. Even though the transfer took place only three hours later, there was no automatic transfer of the contract, because the dismissal was not connected with the transfer. A second difficulty has arisen because the working of the regulations makes it debatable whether or not *statutory* 'rights, powers, duties and liabilities' are included, as intended in the EEC Directive. However, the better view is that such rights are included,[9] making the transferee responsible for such statutory obligations as redundancy payment and unfair dismissal compensation. In addition, the transferee is deemed to have done anything which was done by the transferor before completion of a relevant transfer in respected of an employee. But the transferee does not incur criminal liability.[10]

1. SI 1981 No. 1794.
2. Schedule 13 para. 17.
3. OJ L61/26, 5 March 1977.
4. Reg. 5(10).
5. Reg. 5(2)(a).
6. Reg. 5(3)
7. [1989] IRLR 161.
8. [1986] IRLR 248.
9. By analogy with the reasoning in *Secretary of State* v. *Spence*, which concerned the similarly worded regulation 5 (2)(b).
10. Reg. 5(2)(b) and (4).

285. There are two specific benefits to an employee whose contract is transferred under the Regulations. Firstly, the employee's right to terminate the contract on grounds of constructive dismissal is retained[1] if a substantial change is made in his or her working conditions to his or her detriment. For example, there is a constructive dismissal where the employee resigns without notice because the transferee has imposed a reduced rate of pay in order to put the transferred employee on the same pay basis as existing employees of the transferee. (This is arguably the case even if the employee resigns with notice.) However, mere change in the identity of the employer is not in itself a ground for resignation 'unless the employee shows that in all the circumstances the change is a significant change and is to his detriment.' The second major benefit to the employee is that the dismissal of any employee of the transferor or the transferee either before of after a relevant transfer is an unfair dismissal if the principal reason for the dismissal is the transfer or a reason connected with the transfer.[2] However, there is an important exception, which could threaten to engulf the main principle. Where there is an 'economic, technical or organisational reason entailing changes in the workforce of either the transferor or the transferee before or after the relevant transfer' the dismissal is not automatically unfair, but may be found to unfair under the ordinary unfair dismissals provisions (*below* para. 305–312) . An 'economic' reason includes redundancy and a situation in which there is genuinely no work available. The case law has, however, put some limits on the scope of the exception. Thus it is not sufficient to argue that the dismissal is a result of insistence by the transferee that the workforce must be dismissed before the deal is completed or in order to obtain a higher price for the business.[3] In addition, changes in the workforce must be a necessary consequence of the social, economic or technical reason. For example, it is not sufficient to argue that the transferee intended to harmonise the terms of employment of transferred employees with those of employees already employed by the transferee undertaking.

1. Reg. 5(5).
2. Reg. 8.
3. *Litster* v. *Forth Dry Dock & Engineering Co. Ltd supra.*

286. The regulations only apply to a transfer of a commercial undertaking as a 'going concern.' The question is one of fact and degree for the tribunal.[1] This appears to exclude charities and other non-profit-making organisations, but EEC case law in other areas, such as competition law, has tended to include non-profit making bodies to the extent that they engage in economic activities. It is therefore arguable that UK courts should adopt a broad interpretation in line with the Directive.[2] This has become a significant issue in the public sector, with the growing privatisation of public services.[3] Another important exception applies to the practice of 'hiving down'. In the case of insolvency the receiver or liquidator may 'hive down' to a subsidiary that part of the business which he or she considers to be a commercial package for sale, leaving the employees in the employment of the insolvent parent company which provides their services to the potentially profitable subsidiary until it is sold. It appeared to those who drafted the regulations that their effect might be to hamper this kind of 'rescue' operation and so harm the interest of creditors including possibly the employees themselves. Accordingly, Regulation 4 provides that the transfer is deemed to be suspended until immediately before either (i) the transferee company ceases to be a wholly owned subsidiary of the transferor company or (ii) the business is sold to another person, whichever first occurs. At this point in time there is deemed to be a transfer from the insolvent company to the subsidiary company. The effect is that if the hiving-down operation is successful the employees still left in the employment of the parent company immediately before the transfer to the purchaser are automatically transferred to the subsidiary and so are acquired by the purchaser., Although this limits some of the freedom previously given by hiving-down, the purchaser can still avoid liability by insisting that the parent company dismisses those employees whom he or she does not wish to retain before he or she acquires control of the subsidiary or the business is transferred to him or her. This, of course means that the employees who are not transferred are left only with their claims against the asset-stripped parent company. It is questionable whether this is compatible with Article 3(1) of EEC Directive 77/187.

1. For case law on relevant factors, *see* Sweet and Maxwell's *Encyclopedia of Employment Law*, Part I, B, Title 5.
2. Cf. *Hadden* v. *University of Dundee Students Unions* [1985] IRLR 449.
3. *See further* Fredman and Morris *The State as Employer* (Mansell 1989) pp. 447 ff.

287. The Transfer of Undertakings Regulations operate in tandem with the pre-existing law, found in the Employment Protection (Consolidation) Act 1978, which protect continuity of employment in certain circumstances.'[1] Broadly speaking, these rules enable an employee who was re-engaged by the new employer within a week of the termination of his or her employment with the old employer to preserve his or her continuity of employment for most statutory purposes but not for contractual ones (e.g. arrears of wages or damages for breach). This includes cases where there has been a transfer to an associated employer, or a transfer of the trade, business or undertaking in which he or she was employed at the time of transfer. Obligations are also imposed on the successor of an employer in the case of re-engagement of an unfairly dismissed employee and of a woman who has exercised her statutory right to return to work after pregnancy or confinement. These provisions are most useful when the Transfer of Undertakings Regulations do not apply, namely where the undertaking is of a non-commercial nature, or where the transfer occurred before 1 May 1982.

1. Schedule 13 para. 17(2).

287bis. The regulations provide that collective agreements existing at the time of transfer shall continue in force after the transfer as if made with the transferee,[1] and also that trade union recognition is transferred provided that the undertaking retains a distinct identity under the new employer. These provisions, modelled on the EEC Directive, do not provide any *legal* safeguard in the British context because of the general presumption that collective agreements are not intended by the parties to be legally enforceable contracts (*see* para. 465, *below*). More important are the duties imposed by the regulations to inform and consult with recognised trade unions.[2] The duty to inform trade union representatives of the fact and timing of the transfer, the 'legal, economic and social implications' and the measures envisaged rests on both the transferor and the transferee in relation to any employee who may be affected by the transfer, whether or not a union member, and whether or not employed in the undertaking or the part to be transferred. The duty to consult also rests upon both the transferor and the transferee. The remedies for a breach of these obligations is by way of complaint to an industrial tribunal. Where the union's complaint is well-founded the tribunal must make a declaration and may award 'just and equitable compensation' to affected employees. If this is not paid the employee, not the union, must present a further complaint and the tribunal may then order the employer to pay the amount. The maximum award is 2 weeks' pay in respect of any employee and there is a set-off of any amounts received as damages for breach of contract. The failure to provide an effective sanction for breach of the duty to consult may mean that the UK has not fully complied with the requirements of the EEC Directive.

1. Regs. 6 and 9.
2. Regs. 10 and 11.

§5. Disciplinary Suspension from Work

288. A common sanction for misconduct of an employee is suspension from work. Since this may infringe the employee's right to be paid (above, para. 213) this sanction may be imposed only with the express or implied consent of the employee. The consent may be given in advance, and is therefore frequently found in disciplinary rules issued to employees. One of the curious consequences of the Employment Protection Act 1975 was to make it easier for employers to impose disciplinary sanctions of this kind on employees because the Act, now consolidated in the Employment Protection (Consolidation) Act 1978, s. 1(4) requires an employer to include a note of grievance and disciplinary procedures with the written statement of employment terms (*above*, para. 134). This facilitates proof that the disciplinary rules form part of the contract of employment. These rules are frequently not the product of collective bargaining, and so the Act may have widened the unilateral rule-making powers of the employer to impose disciplinary sanctions short of dismissal. Apart from suspension without pay, fines are sometimes imposed. All such deductions from wages are regulated by the Wages Act 1986 (*see* para. 219 *above*).

§6. Methods of Termination of Employment

A. Frustration

289. The contract of employment is regarded as essentially personal in nature and so some events lead automatically to its termination, for example the death of the employer, the dissolution of a partnership, or an order for the compulsory winding up of a company. There is also a broad general principle of frustration (supervening impossibility of performance). Under this principle, if a change of circumstances makes performance of the contract unlawful, or physically impossible, or its objects incapable of achievement, the contract will be automatically brought to an end, without the need for dismissal by the employer or resignation by the employee. The effect of a finding of frustration is serious: for the purposes of the unfair dismissal legislation, an employee is not treated as dismissed, and therefore cannot claim compensation regardless of the reasonableness or otherwise of the dismissal. (*see* paras. 305–312 below) Similarly, no redundancy compensation can be claimed, unless the frustrating event relates to the employer, not the employees (*see* paras. 320–324 below). The two most common instances of frustration occur in relation to illness or imprisonment of the employee. A number of important principles in this respect have been formulated by the courts.[1] Factors which may help to decide the issue include the length of previous employment, how long it had been expected that the employment would continue, the nature of the job, the nature, length and effect of the illness or disabling event, together with the prospects of recovery, the need of the employer for the work to be done, the risk to employer of acquiring obligations to the replacement employee, whether wages have continued to be paid, the acts and statements of the employer, including contractual provisions for sickness pay, and whether in all the circumstances a reasonable employer could be expected to wait any longer. In recognition of the seriousness of the consequences of a finding of frustration, the court should guard against too easy an application of the doctrine, especially in the context of redundancy. However, a suggestion that frustration should never operate where a periodic contract was terminable by short notice has been rejected by the Court of Appeal. Where the employee had become incapacitated from ever again performing his or her contract of employment, the doctrine of frustration could terminate the contract before notice of its termination, and the employer was not obliged to pay the employee in respect of any period of notice, nor to defend the dismissal on the basis of reasonableness.[2] A sentence of imprisonment may amount to a frustrating event if it renders the performance of the contract impossible or radically different from that which the parties contemplated. In this situation, the employee cannot argue that he or she has repudiated the contract, and that the employer's acceptance of that repudiation amounts to a dismissal for the purposes of the law of unfair dismissal: an employee cannot rely on his or her own fault.[3]

1. *Egg Stores (Stanford Hill) Ltd* v. *Leibovici* [1976] IRLR 376, *Notcutt* v. *Universal Equipment* [1986] ICR 414, *FC Shepherd Ltd* v. *Jerrom* [1986] ICR 802, *Williams* v. *Watsons Luxury Coaches* [1990] IRLR 164.
2. *Notcutt* v. *Universal Equipment* [1986] ICR 414.
3. FC *Shepherd* v. *Jerrom* [1986] ICR 802.

B. By Agreement

290. The parties may agree that the contract is to last (i) for a limited period of time; or (ii) until the happening of an uncertain event (e.g. until war is declared); or (iii) until the happening of a certain event, the time of which is uncertain (e.g. for the life of the Sovereign); or (iv) to perform a specific task (e.g. deliver a course of lectures, or chop down a tree). Certain statutory rights (e.g. to guarantee and medical suspension payments, paras. 235 and 254 *above*) do not apply to employment under a contract for a fixed term of 12 weeks or less, and an employee whose contract is for a fixed term of two years or more may agree in writing to exclude any right to a redundancy payment[1] or of one year or more to complain of unfair dismissal.[2] The Court of Appeal has held that a contract for a fixed term covers only category (i) above, that is for a specified stated time; this is the case even if the contract is determinable by notice within that term.[3] The statutory definition of dismissal[4] includes, where the contract is for a fixed term, the expiry of the term without its being renewed under the same contract. Since this does not cover contracts in categories (ii), (iii) and (iv) above, persons in those categories have no grounds to complain of unfair dismissal or to claim redundancy payments when the event occurs or the task is completed.[5] Some difficulty has arisen where employer and employee agree that the employment will end automatically if the employee fails to fulfil a condition (e.g. that the employee return from extended leave by a given date). A series of earlier cases held that this would be an agreed termination rather than a termination by the employer if the condition was clear and the employee could be shown to have genuinely agreed.[6] However, the courts are reluctant to uphold agreements which affect employee's statutory rights. In an important recent case, it was held that if the agreement had the effect of limiting the statutory right not to be unfairly dismissed, it fell foul of section 140 of the Employment Protection (Consolidation) Act 1978, which declares that any provision in an agreement will be void insofar as it purports to exclude or limit the operation of any provision of the Act or to preclude any person from presenting a complaint under the Act to an industrial tribunal.[7] This was an important recognition of the inequality of bargaining power of employer and employee in these contexts.

1. EPCA 1978, s. 142(2) as amended.
2. EPCA 1978, s. 142(1) as amended.
3. *Dixon* v. *BBC* [1979] ICR 282, CA.
4. EPCA 1978, ss. 55(2)(b), 83(2)(b).
5. *Wiltshire County Council* v. *NATFHE* [1980] ICR 455, *CA*.
6. *British Leyland UK Ltd.* v. *Ashraf* [1978] ICR 979 (EAT); *Midland Electrical Engineering* v. *Kanji* [1980] IRLR 185 (EAT); *Tracey* v. *Zest Equipment Co. Ltd.* [1982] ICR 481 (EAT).
7. *Igbo* v. *Johnson. Matthey Chemicals Ltd* [1986] ICR 505.

C. Dismissal by Employer With Notice

291. An employee is treated as 'dismissed' for the purposes of unfair dismissal and redundancy law, if the contract under which he or she is employed by the employer is terminated by the employer, whether it is so terminated by notice or without notice. At common law, the employer is entitled to terminate a contract for an indefinite period by giving a reasonable period of notice. The parties may expressly limit the right of either side to terminate by notice except for specified reasons. For example, the contract may be stated to be one 'until reaching the retirement age' or 'for life' or 'permanent and pensionable'. In such cases it may not be terminated by notice.

292. Where the length of notice is not specified by the contract expressly or by custom, then the length of a reasonable period of notice depends upon all the circumstances. Among relevant factors are the employee's status, the nature of the job and the general character of the services to be rendered. The frequency of payment (e.g. weekly or monthly) may be a convenient guide but this is not conclusive. These common law rules are now subject to the provisions of section 49 of the Employment Protection (Consolidation) Act 1978 which lays down the following minimum periods of notice:

1 week to a person continuously employed for between one month and 2 years
1 week for each year of continuous employment, to a person continuously employed for 2 years or more but less than 12 years.
12 weeks to a person continuously employed for 12 years or more.

The employee may accept payment of wages in lieu of notice, but the provision in a contract of employment for shorter periods of notice than those laid down in the Act is ineffective.

293. The Act of 1978 also guarantees the employee's income during the statutory minimum notice period. The detailed rules are set out in Schedule 3 to the Act.

D. Dismissal by Employer Without Notice

294. At common law, an employer is entitled to dismiss an employee summarily, that is without notice, if the employee has disregarded an essential term of the contract. This is an area of law in which old cases are of little assistance because of changing judicial attitudes. Early decisions were often not concerned with the rights of 'master' and 'servant' but with the question which arose under the Poor Laws as to whether a particular community was legally obliged to provide aid to a destitute person because he or she had acquired a settlement by virtue of having been employed there for a certain period. Other decisions, before 1867, arose under the criminal law of desertion. Modern cases have moved towards the general principles of repudiatory breach in contract law, by stressing factors such as whether an important term of the contract has been broken, whether the employee's actions have undermined mutual confidence, and whether the employee has a reasonable excuse for his or her conduct. Each case depends on its own circumstances. The contract is terminated not by the employee's repudiatory conduct, but by the employer's act in accepting that repudiation. Dismissal by the employer without notice is treated as a dismissal for the purposes of the statutory law of unfair dismissal (below para. 305). This is the case even if the employer is entitled to dismiss at common law. However, the dismissal is not necessarily unfair.

1. *London Transport Executive* v. *Clarke* [1981] ICR 334 (CA) *Rigby* v. *Ferodo* [1988] ICR 29, *Dietman* v. *London Borough of Brent* [1988] IRLR 299.

E. Variation of Contract Distinguished from Dismissal

295. In some situations the employer may introduce changes in working conditions, either with or without notice, which affect the employee adversely. If the employee consents either expressly or impliedly to such a change in terms this is called a 'consensual variation' and the employee may not then complain that he or she has been 'dismissed'. However, the courts have more than once made it clear that they dislike an attempt by an employer to make 'use of the employee's willingness to work, and to work for a lower wage' as a means of avoiding 'dismissal' and resultant liability for a redundancy payment or unfair dismissal. The courts will 'be slow to find that there has been a consensual variation where the employee has been faced with the alternative of dismissal and where the variation has been adverse to his interest'.[1] If there has been no consent, the employee may have an action for breach of contract. Employers have on occasion attempted to circumvent the need for consent by arguing that the change in working conditions was not a variation at all but notice terminating employment and offering re-employment on new terms. However, it has been held that a termination by notice will not readily be implied in such circumstances.[2] It has also been argued that consent to a variation can be implied from the fact that an employee has continued to work under the changed terms. Again, the courts have been reluctant to imply consent from conduct too readily. Provided that employees make it abundantly clear that they are not willing to accept the new terms, the fact that they have remained in their posts does not amount to consent.[3]

1. *Sheet Metal Components Ltd.* v. *Plumridge* [1974] ICR 373. Unilateral withdrawal by the employer from a collective agreement is not a variation unless the employee consents: *see* para. 153, *above*).

2. *Burdett-Coutts* v. *Hertfordshire County Council* [1984] IRLR 91.
3. *Rigby* v. *Ferodo* [1987] IRLR 516 (HL). *Burdett-Coutts supra.*

296. Because of this difficulty, employees have been given a statutory right in respect of claims for redundancy payments to a month's trial period in any changed terms of employment. But in unfair dismissal cases (and in redundancy cases where the employee has stayed in the changed job for more than one month) the old rules apply and the employees may lose the right to claim that they were 'dismissed' if they do not make it clear that they are working under protest, or if they continue for a long time in the changed job.

F. Termination by the Employee

297. At common law the employee may terminate the contract by giving the agreed notice, or where no period is specified by giving reasonable notice, depending on the circumstances. Under the Employment Protection (Consolidation) Act 1978, the statutory minimum period of notice which an employee must give is *one week*. In some employments the period required by contract is much longer.

298. At common law, the employee is entitled to terminate the contract without notice if the employer breaks a fundamental term of the contract. This is the reverse of the situation in which the employer is entitled to dismiss the employee summarily. Unilateral changes in the contract by the employer will amount to a repudiation of the employer's fundamental obligations only if they go to the basis of the contract; for example by reducing the employee's pay, suspending the employee without pay where the contract does not provide for this, making drastic changes in the working hours, forcing an employee to join a trade union, requiring an employee to work under unsafe conditions or forcing him or her to hand in his or her resignation. Sexual harassment will also amount to a repudiatory breach,[1] as will failure to pay a statutory minimum rate of remuneration as specified in a Wages Council Order.[2] Generally speaking, changes made as a result of collective agreements will not amount to a repudiation of contract by the employer unless the terms of that agreement cannot be said to have been incorporated into the individual employment contract (above, para. 149). For example, where employees have resigned from a union and have made it clear that they will not accept terms of employment negotiated after their resignation, it may be that freshly negotiated terms are not binding on them.[3]

1. *Bracebridge Engineering Ltd* v. *Derby* [1990] IRLR 3.
2. *Reid* v. *Camphill Engravers* [1990] IRLR 268.
3. *Singh* v. *British Steel Corporation* [1974] IRLR 131; cf. *Land* v. *West Yorkshire CC* [1979] ICR 452.

299. The main importance of these common law rules is that the employee may claim that he or she has been dismissed for the purposes of unfair dismissal and redundancy law if he or she terminates his or her contract, with or without notice, in circumstances such that he or she is entitled to terminate it at common law without notice. This is popularly known as 'constructive dismissal'. The test is whether the employer has repudiated the contract.[1] Strictly speaking, it is only where the employee accepts the employer's repudiation by resigning and leaving that one can speak of a 'constructive dismissal'. It should be stressed that a constructive dismissal is not necessarily unfair.

1. *Western Excavating (ECC) Ltd.* v. *Sharp* [1978] ICR 221 (CA).

§7. Reasons for Dismissal and References

300. At common law, an employer is not required to give any reason for dismissal. Moreover, if the employee brings an action for damages for wrongful dismissal the employer is entitled to justify the dismissal by proving reasons which were not known to him or her at the time of the original dismissal.[1]

1. *Boston Deep Sea Fishing Co.* v. *Ansell* (1888) 39 Ch. D. 339.

301. Both these common law rules have now been modified by legislation. An employee who has 6 months' continuous employment is entitled, under section 53 of the Employment Protection (Consolidation) Act 1978, to be provided by his or her employer within 14 days of his so requesting 'a written statement giving the particulars of the reasons for his dismissal'. If the employer 'unreasonably refuses' an industrial tribunal may award the employee a penalty equivalent to two weeks' pay. The written statement is admissible in unfair dismissal and other proceedings. The common law rule regarding subsequently discovered misconduct does not apply to proceedings for unfair dismissal, in which the employer may rely only on those facts which were known to him or her at the time of dismissal.[1] In the case of termination by notice this may include events up to the time of expiry of the notice.[2]

1. *W. Devis & Sons* v. *Atkins* [1977] ICR 662 (House of Lords).
2. *Stacey* v. *Babcock Power Ltd.* IDS Brief 315, December 1985, p. 5 (EAT).

302. There is, however, no obligation on an employer to provide an employee with a character reference. If the employer does provide a reference he or she must take care not to say anything defamatory, deceitful or without reasonable care as to its accuracy.[1] An employer may not refer to certain spent convictions of a rehabilitated offender or to any circumstances ancillary to those convictions.[2] An additional remedy is now provided by Section 22 of the Data Protection Act 1984, which gives an employee the right to claim compensation in respect of data which is factually inaccurate, provided he or she has suffered damage because of the inaccuracy of the data. This would apply to an action in respect of an inaccurate reference based on information stored on the employer's computer. The employee may also be able to have the inaccurate data rectified or deleted.

1. *Lawton* v. *BOC Transhield Ltd* [1987] ICR 7.
2. Rehabilitation of Offenders Act 1974, s. 4(4). There are detailed rules as to when a conviction becomes 'spent'.

§8. Remedies for Wrongful Dismissal

303. The concept of 'wrongful dismissal' is applied to any dismissal where the employer, not being entitled at common law to terminate the contract summarily, fails to give the period of notice required by law. The employee's sole remedy will usually be a claim for damages in the county court or the High Court. The measure of damages for wrongful dismissal will normally be the remuneration which the employee has lost by not being given the requisite period of notice. Damages are not awarded for hurt feelings, or for the manner in which the dismissal took place[1] or for the fact that dismissal made it more difficult to find alternative employment. But damages have been awarded for loss of an opportunity envisaged by the contract (such as an actor losing the chance to enhance his reputation) and for depression, anxiety and illness caused by the dismissal.[2] The damages are awarded net of tax and social security contributions and subject to deduction of certain other benefits received, such as wages earned in an alternative employment, unemployment benefit[3] and supplementary benefit.[4] The employee is under a duty to mitigate his or her loss by taking reasonable steps to find alternative employment.

1. *Addis* v. *Gramophone Co.* [1909] AC 488 (House of Lords); *Bliss* v. *South East Thames RHA* [1985] IRLR 308 (CA).
2. *Cox* v. *Phillips Industries Ltd.* [1974] IRLR 344.
3. *Westwood* v. *Secretary of State for Employment* [1984] IRLR 209 (House of Lords).
4. *Lincoln* v. *Hayman* [1984] 2 All ER 819.

304. In general, the courts will not order specific performance of a contract of employment. The accepted rationale for this is that to compel performance of a contract of employment is inconsistent with the principle that the relationship depends on mutual confidence.[1] This means that the most effective remedy for a wrongful dismissal, namely reinstatement, is in general denied to the employee. Although similar principles apply to injunctions restraining the employer from acting in breach of contract, the courts have recently evinced a greater willingness to grant injunctions.[2] This is particularly so when a dismissal has taken place in breach of a contractual disciplinary procedure, and an application is made for an interim injunction in interlocutory proceedings pending the full trial. In general, the courts will only grant an injunction if damages are inadequate and complete confidence in the relationship has been maintained. Injunctions are more likely to be granted where the employer is a large company or public authority, since it is more likely that confidence will be maintained in such a situation than in the case of a small business or partnership. The requirement that confidence be maintained may, however, be relaxed where the plaintiff does not demand full reinstatement, but merely wishes to be suspended on full pay while internal disciplinary proceedings are taking place.[3] An injunction will only be granted if the contractual relationship remains alive. This puts great emphasis on the question of when a repudiatory breach by an employer will effectively terminate the contract. On ordinary contractual principles, a breach only terminates a contract if the innocent party accepts the repudiation. This would mean that if an employer purports to dismiss an employee in breach of the contract, the contract will not end until the employee accepts the breach, making an injunction possible. Although some important cases have held that the contract of employment may be terminated by the employer without requiring acceptance by the employee,[4] effectively precluding injunctions, the predominance of recent authorities have upheld the ordinary principle that repudiation only terminates a contract if it is accepted.[5] Thus until the employee accepts a repudiatory breach, the contract remains alive, and an injunction may be granted. However, the court will readily infer that the employee has accepted the repudiation; delay in bringing proceedings will be construed as acceptance, as will seeking alternative employment. Nevertheless, the availability of injunctions entails that, in a limited class of cases, the contractual remedy may be more effective than the remedies under unfair dismissal (*below* paras. 305 ff).

1. *Hill* v. *Parsons* [1972]1 Ch. 305; *Chappell* v. *Times Newspapers Ltd* [1975] ICR 145 at pp. 173, 176, 178.
2. *Jones* v. *Lee* [1980] IRLR 67; *Irani* v. *Southampton AHA* [1985] IRLR 755; *Powell* v. *London Borough of Brent* [1987] IRLR 466 (CA); *Hughes* v. *London Borough of Southwark* [1988] IRLR 55, *Wadcock* v. *London Borough of Brent* [1990] IRLR 223
3. *Robb* v. *London Borough of Hammersmith and Fulham* [1991]
4. *London Transport Executive* v. *Clarke* [1981] IRLR 166 per Denning MR; *Gunton* v. *Richmond – on Thames LBC* [1980] IRLR 321 per Shaw LJ; *R* v. *East Berkshire AHA* [1984] IRLR 278 per May LJ.
5. *London Transport Executive* v. *Clarke* [1981] IRLR 166 per Templeman LJ; *Gunton* v. *Richmond – on Thames LBC* [1980] IRLR 321 per Buckley LJ; *Thomas Marshall* v. *Guinle* [1978] IRLR 174 per Megarry VC; *Dietman* v. *Brent LBC* [1988] IRLR 299; *Burdett Coutts* v. *Hertfordshire* [1984] IRLR 91.

§9. Unfair Dismissal

305. Every employee, with certain exceptions set out below, has the right not to be unfairly dismissed by his or her employer. At the first stage it must be established that the employee was 'dismissed'. This means either (1) termination of the contract by the employer (paras. 284 and 291 *above*); or (2) expiry without renewal of a fixed term contract (para. 290 *above*); or (3) 'constructive dismissal' (paras. 297–299 *above*). The burden of proof is then on the employer to show the reason (or if there was more than one, the principal reason) for the dismissal. In contrast to the I.L.O Termination of Employment Convention 1982, there are only four reasons which render a dismissal automatically unfair: trade union membership and activities, refusal to belong to a trade union, selection for redundancy in breach of an agreed procedure or customary arrangement, and pregnancy and confinement. All other reasons may justify dismissal, but only if the tribunal is satisfied that the employer acted reasonably in treating the nominated reason as a sufficient reason for dismissal.

A. Reasons Allowed for Dismissal

306. The employer must show a set of facts known to him or her, or beliefs held, at the time of dismissal which caused him or her to dismiss the employee. These facts must fall within one of the following categories:[1] (1) 'The capability or qualifications of the employee for performing work of the kind that he was employed by the employer to do' ('capability' is assessed by reference to skill, aptitude, health or any other physical or mental quality). (2) 'The conduct of the employee'. (3) The employee was 'redundant'. This concept is defined by reference to the redundancy payments legislation (*see below*, para. 320). (4) 'The employee could not continue to work in the position which he held without contravention (either on his part or on the part of his employer) of a duty or restriction imposed by or under any enactment' (e.g. safety legislation, or a driving disqualification imposed on a lorry driver). (5) 'Some other substantial reason of a kind such as to justify the dismissal of an employee holding the position which the employee held'. The most common examples of reasons falling within this category relate to the business needs of the employer, such as refusal to agree to changes in employment terms, pressure from an important customer to dismiss the employee, the temporary nature of the employment, and an irreconcilable conflict of personalities. This last category functions merely as a filter: according to the Court of Appeal, it is designed only to deter employers from dismissing employees for a trivial or unworthy reason.[2] By statute[3] dismissal of a temporary replacement for an employee who is absent from work because of a pregnancy or confinement or medical suspension is treated as a 'substantial reason', provided fair warning of the temporary nature of the job was given to the replacement. Moreover, dismissal for an 'economic, technical or organisational reason entailing changes in the workforce of either the transferor or transferee' on the transfer of an undertaking is deemed to be a 'substantial reason'.[4] In all these cases the tribunal still has to determine whether the employer acted reasonably in all the circumstances (*see* para. 309, *below*).

1. EPCA 1978, ss. 57(1), 57(2).
2. *Kent County Council* v. *Gilham* [1985] IRLR 18 (CA)
3. EPCA 1978, s. 61.
4. Transfer of Undertakings (Protection of Employment) Regulations 1981, SI 1981 No. 1394 (para. 286 above).

307. A dismissal is not capable of giving rise to a complaint of unfairness if a certificate is produced signed by a Minister of the Crown that the dismissal was taken 'for the purpose of safeguarding national security'.[1] Nor may an industrial tribunal entertain a complaint where at the time of dismissal the employer was instituting or conducting a lock-out, or the employee was taking part in a strike or other industrial action. (This is discussed in Part II, Chapter V.)

1. EPCA 1978, Schedule 9, para. 2. *See* para. 375, *below*.

308. It has already been indicated that certain reasons are automatically unfair. The dismissal of a pregnant employee and the right to return to work after confinement were discussed in Chapter VI above. Selection for redundancy is discussed in para. 312, below. The other automatically unfair reasons (the burden of proving which rests upon the employee) are that the employee:

> '(a) was, or proposed to become a member of an independent trade union; (b) had taken, or proposed to take, part in the activities of an independent trade union at an appropriate time, or (c) was not a member of any trade union, or of a particular trade union, or of one of a number of particular trade unions or had refused, or proposed to refuse, to become or remain a member.'[1]

The definition of an 'appropriate time' envisages that an employee may participate outside working hours off the employer's premises, or on the premises while there with the express or implied permission of the employer (e.g. during meal breaks) but while not actually at work. The right to participate during working hours depends on the employer's consent, which may be gathered from the circumstances. Enlisting the help of a trade union officer in negotiating terms of employment is an important incident of union membership.[2] ACAS has issued a Code of Practice containing guidelines. The effect of these provisions on union membership agreements (i.e. the closed shop) is discussed, in connection with trade union freedom, in Part II Chapter I.

1. TULRCA 1992, s. 152(1).
2. *Discount Tobacco & Confectionery Ltd* v. *Armitage* [1990] IRLR 15.

B. Reasonableness

309. Unless the dismissal was for a reason which was automatically unfair, the tribunal is required to decide whether the employer acted reasonably. Section 57(3) of the Employment Protection (Consolidation) Act 1978 states: 'The determination of the question whether, having regard to the reason shown by the employer, the dismissal was fair or unfair, shall depend on whether, in the circumstances (including the size and administrative resources of the employer's undertaking), the employer acted reasonably or unreasonably in treating it as a sufficient reason for dismissing the employee, and that question shall be determined in accordance with equity and the substantial merits of the case'. Since 1980, there has been no formal burden of proof in the determination of this question. The tribunal, with its tripartite composition, is expected to act as an 'industrial jury', drawing on the industrial experience of its lay members to reach a conclusion based on common sense and common fairness. The statute has, however, been interpreted to mean that the tribunal members should not substitute their own opinion for that of management. Lord Denning said that 'It must be remembered that in all these cases there is a band of reasonableness, within which one employer may reasonably take one view: another quite reasonably take a different view'.[1] Thus, the function of the industrial tribunal, 'as an industrial jury, is to determine whether in the particular circumstances of each case, the decision to dismiss the employee fell within the band of reasonable responses which a reasonable employer might have adopted'.[2]

1. *British Leyland UK Ltd* v. *Swift* [1981] IRLR 91 (CA) at p. 93.
2. *Iceland Frozen Foods* v. *Jones* [1983] ICR 17 (EAT).

310. The 'band of reasonable responses' test clearly gives the employer considerable latitude in decision-making, particularly if the concept of the reasonable employer simply reflects actual practices of most employers. One way of circumscribing this managerial prerogative without interfering too much with the ultimate substance of the decision has been to require the employer to follow certain procedures in order to ensure that a dismissal is fair. Requirements of this sort include the need to warn an employee and to give him or her the opportunity of being heard before being dismissed. The approach of tribunals and courts to procedural requirements has been transformed by the House of Lords decision in *Polkey* v. *A. E Dayton Services.*[1] Prior to this decision, procedural requirements had been considerably diluted in cases in which the tribunal considered that the employee suffered no injustice by the absence of procedure.[2] In *Polkey*, however, the House of Lords reinstated the importance of procedure, holding that the reasonableness of the dismissal could only be determined on the basis of the employer's knowledge at the time of dismissal, not in the light of facts which subsequently emerged even if they showed that no injustice had been caused.[3] This means that failure to follow a fair procedure may in itself render a dismissal unfair, even though, had the procedure been followed, it might have been fair to dismiss the employee. In such circumstances, according to *Polkey*, compensation should be reduced but the unfairness of the dismissal remains. At the same time, failure to follow a procedure does not inevitably entail an unfair dismissal. 'If the employer could reasonably have concluded in the light of the circumstances known to him at the time of dismissal that consultation or warning would be utterly useless, he might well act reasonably even if he did not observe the provisions of the [Industrial Relations Code of Practice].'[4] The width of this exception remains unclear, but it does have the potential to erode the basic principle.[5] Cases since *Polkey* have elaborated on the standards of procedure required. The most difficult area concerns disciplinary hearings. Here the guidelines set out in the early case of *British Home Stores* v. *Burchell*[6] generally apply. According to this test, in cases of alleged misconduct, it must first be established that the employer in fact believed that it had occurred. Secondly, did the employer have reasonable grounds upon which to sustain that belief? And thirdly, had the employer at the stage at which he or she formed that belief carried out as much investigation into the matter as was reasonable? There is no need for a quasi-judicial inquiry;[7] in this respect, the tribunal should take into account the business needs of the employer. Nevertheless, some basic principles apply: the employee should know the case against him or her, and where the case depends on written witness statements, these should generally be revealed to the employee.[8] An appeal can only rectify defects in the original proceeding if it is a re-hearing *de novo* rather than a mere review.[9]

1. [1988] ICR 142.
2. *British Labour Pump* v. *Byrne* [1979] ICR 347 at 353–354, *W & J Wass* v. *Binns* [1982] ICR 486 (CA).

3. *See also Devis* v. *Atkins* [1977] ICR 662 (HL); *Sillifant* v. *Powell Duffryn Timber Ltd* [1983] IRLR 91.
4. [1988] ICR 142 at p. 153, *per* Lord Mackay, and *see* Lord Bridge at p. 163.
5. *See* for example *Mathewson* v. *RB Wilson Dental Laboratory* [1988] IRLR 512; *Fuller* v. *Lloyds Bank* [1991] IRLR 336. Contrast *McLaren* v. *National Coal Board* [1988] ICR 370.
6. [1980] ICR 303.
7. *Ulsterbus Ltd* v. *Henderson* [1989] IRLR 251.
8. *Spink* v. *Express Foods Group Ltd* [1990] IRLR 320; *Louies* v. *Coventry Hood & Seating Co Ltd* [1990] IRLR 324; cf *Fuller* v. *Lloyds Bank* [1991] IRLR 336 (EAT).
9. *Whitbread & Co plc* v. *Mills* [1988] ICR 776.

311. The question of reasonableness is one of fact for the tribunal, appeals being limited to points of law. Thus an appeal is only available where either the tribunal misdirected themselves in law in that they misconstrued their function in considering the question of reasonableness, or they reached a conclusion which no reasonable tribunal, properly directed in law, could have reached.[1] This approach has been criticised for leading to inconsistent decisions as between tribunals. However, in the words of a recent Appeal Court decision:

> 'Whether or not an employer has behaved reasonably in dismissing an employee is a question of fact, and it is a question upon which different people, looking at the same set of circumstances, may reasonably come to different conclusions. It is therefore endemic in a system where there is no appeal on fact that from time to time different industrial tribunals will give different answers to broadly similar situations, and neither decision can be challenged. It is therefore important that this court should resist the temptation to seek to overturn a factual decision with which it may not agree, by searching for some shadowy point of law on which to hang its hat for the purpose of bringing uniformity to the differing decisions. If we were to take this course, it would have the very undesirable effect of encouraging innumerable appeals which raised no point of law, but depended upon comparative findings of fact.'[2]

Nevertheless, in recent cases, particularly those on procedure, the EAT has been prepared to lay down detailed guidelines for tribunals to follow.

1. *Gilham* v. *Kent County Council (No. 2)* [1985] ICR 233 (CA) at 243–244.
2. *Ibid.*, *per* Griffiths L. J. at p. 240.

312. There are two special situations in which selection for redundancy must be treated as unfair. These are where the employee shows that the principal reason for selection was trade union membership or activities or refusal to join a trade union, or that he or she was selected in contravention of a 'customary arrangement' or 'agreed procedure relating to redundancy'.[1] It is not possible for an employee to rely on a general 'custom' such as 'last in first out'; he or she must show that the custom is well-known, certain and reasonable in respect of the establishment in which he or she worked.[2] Moreover, it is not sufficient that the arrangement throws up a pool of workers from whom the final selection is made; to fall within the automatically unfair provision, the arrangement must constitute the final selection itself.[3] In other redundancy cases, normal criteria of reasonableness apply such as whether attempts were made to find suitable alternative employment for the redundant employee and whether his or her union was consulted. A clear and objective selection procedure should be used,[4] but there is no obligation to provide a right of appeal against selection for redundancy.[5]

1. TULRCA 1992, s. 153 EPCA 1978, s. 59.
2. *Sufflex Ltd* v. *Thomas* [1987] IRLR 435.
3. *Rogers* v. *Vosper Thorneycroft (UK) Ltd* [1989] IRLR 82 (CA).
4. *Williams* v. *Compair Maxam Ltd* [1982] ICR 156.
5. *Robinson* v. *Ulster Carpet Mills Ltd* [1991] IRLR 348 (NICA).

C. Remedies for unfair dismissal

313. The primary remedies available under the Employment Protection (Consolidation) Act 1978 are (1) *Reinstatement*, which means that the employer must treat the employee in all respects as if he or she had not been dismissed, restoring pay, pension and other benefits; and (2) *Re-engagement*, which differs from reinstatement in that the employee may be re-engaged in a different job from that which he or she formerly held, provided that the new job is comparable to the old or is otherwise suitable. Re-engagement may be by a successor or associated employer. In exercising its discretion whether to grant reinstatement or re-engagement the tribunal must consider the complainant's wishes, whether he or she caused or contributed to the dismissal, and whether it is practicable for the employer to comply with an order for reinstatement or re-engagement.[1] The mere fact that the employer has engaged a permanent replacement does not automatically make these remedies 'impracticable'. If the employee is reinstated, but the terms of the order are not fully complied with, the tribunal must award compensation to the extent that partial noncompliance has caused the employee's loss, with a maximum award, fixed at £10,000 (April 1992). If the order for reinstatement or re-engagement is not complied with at all, then the tribunal must award a basic and compensatory award (*see* para. 315, below) and an *additional* award of compensation. In an ordinary case, the additional award is between 13 and 26 weeks' pay; and in the case of discrimination on the grounds of race or sex, it is 26–52 weeks' pay. (The maximum week's pay from April 1992 is £205).

1. EPCA 1978, ss. 69–71

314. Since the Employment Act 1982, the tribunal must make a special award where the employer refuses to reinstate an employee who has been dismissed for being a member of a trade union, engaging in trade union activities, or refusing to be a member of a trade union.[1] The special award is 156 weeks' pay, subject to a minimum, (fixed at £20,100 from 1 April 1992) and no maximum, but where an employer shows it is impracticable to comply, this is reduced to 104 weeks' pay, with a minimum, fixed at £13,400 and a maximum of £26,800 (April 1992). Similarly, where an employee who has been dismissed for trade union membership or non-membership or trade union activities requests reinstatement or re-engagement, but the tribunal refuses this request, the special award of 104 weeks' pay should be ordered with minima and maxima as above. The special award may be reduced if the employee was partly at fault in causing the dismissal, or unreasonably prevented the order for reinstatement or re-engagement being complied with, or unreasonably refused an offer of reinstatement. (For figures on the use of reinstatement as a remedy, see above, para. 273.)

1. TULRCA 1992, s. 158.

315. If orders for reinstatement or re-engagement are not made, the tribunal must award compensation under two heads. (1) *A basic award*: This is calculated similarly to a redundancy payment (below, para. 323), on the basis of age and years of service. The employee receives one and a half week's pay for each year in employment at the age of 41 or over; one week's pay for each year from 22 to 40; and half a week's pay for each year under 22. This is reduced by one-twelfth for each calendar month over the age of 64 for all employees.[1] The maximum week's pay is £205 (from 1 April 1992), subject to a maximum of 20 years' employment. This means that the maximum basic award is £6,150 (30 weeks' pay). (For figures on actual awards see above, para. 273.) There is no minimum basic award, except in two cases. First, where the dismissal is unfair on the grounds of redundancy, but no redundancy payment is payable because the employee accepted or unreasonably refused alternative employment, a minimum award of two weeks' pay must be ordered. Secondly, where the dismissal is automatically unfair because of trade union membership or activities or non-membership of a trade union, or an automatically unfair redundancy selection, the minimum award is, £2,700 (1 April 1992), before deductions. The basic award may be reduced, to nil if necessary, in the following circumstances: (a) the employee has contributed to his or her dismissal; (b) the employee has received a redundancy payment made pursuant to legislation or otherwise; (c) the employee has received any other amount expressly or impliedly referable to the basic award; (d) the employee has unreasonably refused an offer of reinstatement; (e) the employee's conduct prior to dismissal warrants a reduction[2] (2) *A compensatory award:* This is such amount as the tribunal 'considers just and equitable in all the circumstances having regard to the loss sustained by the complainant in consequence of the dismissal insofar as that loss is attributable to action taken by the employer'[3] This is calculated according to principles laid down by the courts, and includes loss of earnings and benefits up to the date of hearing and subsequently, and loss of pension rights, expenses and statutory employment protection rights. It excludes injury to feelings, inconvenience or other non-pecuniary loss (compare sex and race discrimination and wrongful dismissal). Deductions are made in respect of the employee's failure to mitigate his or her loss, the employee's contribution to the dismissal and any other payment received from the employer or earnings elsewhere In addition, compensation can be decreased where an employer failed to follow the required procedure, but the dismissal would otherwise have been fair.[4] The maximum is fixed at £10,000 (April 1992).

1. EPCA 1978 s. 73 as amended by SDA 1986.
2. EPCA 1978, s. 73.
3. EPCA 1978, s. 74(1).
4. *Polkey* v. *AE Dayton* [1988] ICR 142, *above* para. 310.

316. A special procedure, called interim relief, is available for those who claim that they have been dismissed for trade union membership or activities, or refusal to join a trade union. This procedure enables the tribunal to order that the employee be reinstated, or if both parties agree, re-engaged in another job, or if the employer refuses to do either, suspended on full pay ('an order for the continuation of the contract of employment') until final determination of the complaint.[1] The claim has to be presented within seven days of dismissal, there must be a likelihood of the employee succeeding at the final hearing and, in the case of a trade union member, it must be supported by a certificate from an authorised official of an independent trade union. This is the only situation under the statute in which a dismissal may be suspended pending the determination of the question. (For interlocutory injunctions at common law, *see* para. 304, *above*.)

1. TULRCA 1992, ss. 161–166.

D. Relationship with Other Claims

317. Although fewer claims are brought before the ordinary courts for 3
wrongful dismissal at common law than before tribunals for unfair dismissal, the common law remedy remains important in several classes of cases. These include cases in which the worker is not eligible for statutory protection (para. 319); where the relatively short statutory limitation period for unfair dismissal has expired (*below* para. 319); where it is considered that an injunction is a likely remedy (para. 304 *above*) or where an employee was dismissed in circumstances which would be fair under the statute, but no wages have been paid in lieu of notice. It should be noted that it is not relevant to the question of unfair dismissal (in respect of which proceedings may be brought only in an industrial tribunal) whether or not the dismissal was wrongful at common law. If damages are awarded in a court in respect of loss of earnings then these would be deducted from the compensatory award for unfair dismissal. Tribunal hearings will usually be completed long before an action before the ordinary courts comes to trial. If the tribunal has awarded compensation for unfair dismissal this will include loss of pay in lieu of notice and so there is unlikely to be any loss left to compensate by an award of damages. Nevertheless, for employees in the higher earnings brackets, it may well be worth pursuing both claims if the total loss resulting from the dismissal exceeds the statutory maximum compensation awardable in an unfair dismissal claim. In such a case, the court will not set off the compensation awarded in the unfair dismissal claim against the contractual compensation.[1]

1. *O'Laoire* v. *Jackel International* [1991] IRLR 170 (CA).

318. A statutory redundancy payment (*see below*, para. 320) or a payment voluntarily made by the employer, will be deducted from the award of compensation for unfair dismissal. Double awards may not be made in respect of an act which is both an unfair dismissal and compensatable as sex or race discrimination under other legislation (*see* para. 354, *below*).

E. Exclusions from Unfair Dismissals Legislation

319. The following is a summary of those classes of employee who may not bring a complaint of unfair dismissal. (1) Employees who have been continuously employed for less than 2 years, unless the dismissal was for trade union membership or activities or non-membership of a trade union. (This qualifying period only applies to those who normally work for 16 or more hours a week. The qualification period for employees who work for 8 hours or more but less than 16 hours a week is 5 years.) (2) Unless the dismissal is for a reason related to trade union activities, employees who have reached the 'normal retirement age' for the particular job (provided that age is the same for men and women), or, if there is no normal retirement age, the age of 65.[1] The effect of this exclusion is that a woman who is retired under the age of 65 may claim that she is unfairly dismissed, unless she has reached a normal retirement age which is the same for men and women. (3) Share fishermen. (4) Persons ordinarily working outside Great Britain. (5) Persons employed on United Kingdom registered ships wholly outside Great Britain, or not ordinarily resident in Great Britain. (6) Persons employed under fixed-term contracts made before 28 February 1972, or fixed-term contracts for one year or more made after that date if they have waived their rights in writing. (7) Persons who do not present claims within 3 months of the date of termination, or such further period as the tribunal considers reasonable in a case where it is satisfied that it was not reasonably practicable for the complaint to be presented before the end of 3 months.

1. EPCA 1978, s. 64 (1) as amended by SDA 1986, s. 6 (1). *See Nothman* v. *Barnet London Borough Council* [1979] ICR 111 (HL); *Waite* v. *GCHQ* [1983] ICR 653 (HL); *Hughes and Coy* v. *DHSS* [1985] ICR 419 (HL).

§10. Redundancy

A. Meaning

320. With the enormous increase in unemployment since 1979, redundancies have been a central feature of labour relations. Advance notifications of pending redundancies reached a peak of 1.5 million in 1980, from which it has declined to 376,314, in 1990.[1] Employees have a statutory right to a redundancy payment under the provisions of the Employment Protection (Consolidation) Act 1978, Part IV. Subject to the exclusions in para. 324 below, there are two main criteria for a redundancy payment. The first is that the employee has been dismissed, and dismissal for these purposes is defined in the same way as for unfair dismissal (*above*, para. 305). Secondly, the dismissal must be by reason of 'redundancy'. This concept has a special meaning in the 1978 Act, s. 81, namely that the employee's dismissal is attributable wholly or mainly to:

> '(a) the fact that his employer has ceased or intends to cease to carry on that business in the place where the employee was so employed, or (b) the fact that the requirements of that business for employees to carry out work of a particular kind in the place where he was so employed have ceased or diminished or are expected to cease or diminish'.

There is a statutory presumption that the dismissal is by reason of redundancy. The burden therefore rests on the employer to prove otherwise.

1. Note that employers are only required to notify impending redundancies of more than 10 workers.

321. The statutory definition, stressing as it does the necessity for diminished requirements for employees to do work of a particular kind, is a narrower concept than that to be found in the ILO Termination of Employment Convention 1982 – 'the operational requirements of the enterprise'– the EEC Collective Redundancies Directive[1] which refers to 'reasons not related to the individual workers concerned' the West German Protection Against Dismissal Act which speaks of 'urgent operating requirements'. As interpreted by the courts, the definition does not include all cases in which, in order to diminish labour costs or increase productivity, the employer has changed the terms and conditions of work or re-organised the workforce. Even if the employer's actions amount to a repudiatory breach of contract, or if the dismissal is wholly a result of the employer's operational requirements rather the employee's conduct, this will not entitle the employee to redundancy compensation unless the employer's requirements for employees to do work of the particular kind the employee was employed to do have ceased or diminished. Thus, an employer was not required to pay redundancy payments to employees who could not make their own transport arrangements to and from work after the employer withdrew a free bus service. This was despite the fact that the employer was in breach of contract.[2] Similarly, a change in working arrangements and shift systems is not necessarily a redundancy situation, even if the change is a response to a fall-off in sales and leads to a substantial drop in earnings,[3] provided the employer still requires employees to do work of the particular kind. Nor will the courts question the employer's reasons for declaring employees to be redundant,[4] and conversely, if the employer honestly believes that the dismissal is justified by a reason other than redundancy, the employee is not 'redundant'.[5] As a result of the limited definition of redundancy, only straightforward cases are covered. The reference in Section 81(2)(b) to the 'place where [the employee] was so employed' has been judicially interpreted to mean the place where the employee could be required by his or her contract of employment to work. Thus an employee who had worked at one place for seven years was not redundant when his employer moved his work to another establishment, since his contract required him to work at any of the employer's establishments.[6] It has been suggested that where an employee can be required by contract to do a wide range of types of work, no redundancy compensation is payable provided the employer requires employees to do any of the work within the contractual range. Thus an employee whose contract requires him to do any work within his capabilities may not be entitled to a redundancy payment so long as the employer requires employees to do work within that range.[7]

1. OJ 1975, L.48/29.
2. *Chapman* v. *Goonvean and Rostowrack China Clay Co. Ltd.* [1973] ICR 50 (CA).
3. *Johnson* v. *Nottinghamshire Combined Police Authority* [1971] ICR 170 (CA); *Lesney Products & Co. Ltd.* v. *Nolan* [1977] ICR 235 (CA).
4. *Moon* v. *Homeworthy Furniture* [1977] ICR 117 (EAT).
5. *Hindle* v. *Percival Boats Ltd.* [1969] ITR 86 (CA).
6. *UK Atomic Energy Authority* v. *Claydon* [1974] ICR 128 (NIRC), following *Sutcliffe* v. *Hawker Siddeley Aviation Ltd.* [1973] ICR 560 (NIRC). *See also Rank Xerox* v. *Churchill* [1988] IRLR 280.
7. *Cowen* v. *Haden* [1983] ICR 1 (EAT). The case was decided on different grounds by the Appeal Court.

322. The statute provides a limited incentive to employers to attempt to redeploy redundant workers, in that an employee is not entitled to a redundancy payment if he or she unreasonably refuses an offer of suitable alternative employment, or an offer to renew the contract on the same terms immediately or within four weeks of the dismissal.[1] The employee is entitled to a trial period of four weeks before deciding to accept the new job. An employee who does not remain on beyond the end of the trial period may be entitled to a redundancy payment in the same way as if no trial period had been embarked upon.

1. EPCA 1978, s. 82.
2. EPCA 1978, s. 84.

B. Calculation of Compensation and Rebates

323. Schedule 4 to the Employment Protection (Consolidation) Act 1978 provides that for each year of employment between the ages of 18 and 21 the employee is to receive a half-week's pay; for each year of employment between 22 and 40 one week's pay; and for each year of employment between 41 and 64, one and a half week's pay. There is a scaling down for employees in their sixty-fifth year, of one-twelfth for every month by which he or she is over 64. Remuneration over £205 per week, and employment for longer than 20 years are ignored. A week's pay is calculated in accordance with Schedule 14 to the 1978 Act. In effect the maximum award for a person with 20 years' service over the age of 41 is £6,150. Until recently, employers were entitled to claim a rebate from the Redundancy Fund, but this was limited to small employers in 1986, and abolished entirely in 1989.

C. Exclusions

324. The following is a summary of the main classes of employee not entitled to receive a redundancy payment. (1) Employees who have not been continuously employed for two years or more. (2) Employees who have reached the normal retirement age applicable to their particular job, if that age is the same for men and women, and below 65; or, in other cases, employees who have reached 65. (3) Employees unreasonably refusing an offer of suitable alternative employment from the employer, or from his successor in the case of a change of ownership. (4) Employees accepting a renewal of contract or re-engagement from the employer, or from his successor in the case of a change of ownership. (5) Employees who leave their employment during the period of their notice, unless they comply with certain formal requirements to give the employer counter-notice. (6) In some cases where the employee is guilty of misconduct or where he or she takes part in a strike during the period of notice.[1]

1. *See* para. 477, below, and for other exclusions see Sweet and Maxwell's, *Encyclopedia of Labour Relations Law*, para. 1B–2303.

§11. Collective Redundancies

325. Part IV of the Employment Protection Act 1975 was enacted to give effect to the EEC Directive on Collective Redundancies.[1] The Act requires an employer contemplating the dismissal of one or more employees by reason of redundancy to consult the recognised trade union and also to notify the Department of Employment. The words 'collective redundancies' hardly seem appropriate because the obligation to consult arises even if a single employee is to be dismissed, and even though that employee is not a member of the recognised trade union or of any union. The obligation is to consult the union recognised by the employer for bargaining purposes in respect of the grade or category of employees from whose number the employer intends to select for redundancy. The obligation is to consult 'at the earliest opportunity'. If the employer is proposing to dismiss 100 or more employees at one establishment over a 90 day period, he or she must consult not less than 90 days before the first dismissal. If he or she is proposing to dismiss 10 or more employees at one establishment over a 30 day period, he or she must consult not less than 30 days before the first dismissal. There is no minimum period where the employer proposes to dismiss less than 10 employees.

1. OJ 1975, L.48/29 of 22 February 1975. See now TULRCA 1992 ss. 188–198.

326. The duty to consult is more narrowly drawn than the corresponding provisions of Article 2 of the EEC Directive, which requires the employer to consult workers' representatives 'with a view to reaching agreement'. Under the British Act it is sufficient if the employer considers the trade union representations and states why he or she chooses to reject them. Nor is there any provision in the British Act like the requirement in Article 2 of the EEC Directive that the consultations should cover 'ways and means of avoiding collective redundancies or reducing the numbers of workers affected' although this is plainly the intention of the Act. The EEC Directive left Member States to determine who the 'workers representatives' are to be: the British position is that only where the employer recognises an independent trade union does he or she have to consult anyone. The British Act does specify the information to be given to the trade union, including the detailed reasons for the proposed dismissals, the number and class of employees to be dismissed, and the total number of employees in the grade or class from whom the redundant employees are to be selected, the method of selection to be used, and the method of dismissal including the timing.

327. If the employer fails to carry out his or her duty to consult, the trade union concerned may complain to an industrial tribunal which may make a *protective award.* The effect of the award is that the employees are to be kept on the payroll for the period of the award. This means that in addition to any other claims arising out of the dismissal (such as redundancy payments) the employees are entitled to be paid their wages for this period. The length of the period is within the discretion of the tribunal subject to certain limits. Where 100 or more employees are to be dismissed, then the award can be for up to 90 days; where 10 to 99 are to be dismissed, it can be for up to 30 days; and where less than 10 workers are involved it can be for up to 28 days. An employee not paid the amount of an award due to him or her may present a complaint to an industrial tribunal.

328. The employer must notify the Department of Employment of the proposed redundancies within the same time periods as are set out in para. 325, above. There is no obligation to notify the Department where fewer than 10 employees are involved. In the notice employers must state the date on which they began consultation with any recognised union. They must also provide the Department with such other information as it may require. The penalty for failure to notify is a fine of up to £2,000 on conviction. Where the employer is a limited liability company, a director or manager who fails to notify the Department may incur personal liability if he or she is guilty of fault or neglect.

Chapter VIII. Discrimination

§1. The Development of the Legislation

329. Race Discrimination: Legal protection against discrimination on grounds of race is a relative newcomer in Britain. Judge-made common law failed to develop such protection; prior to 1965, no English or Scottish case declared racial discrimination to be against public policy. The first statutory measure, the Race Relations Act 1965, covered only a limited area and was largely ineffective. Its failure prompted a remarkable political campaign to improve the social position and employment opportunities of Britain's immigrants from the New Commonwealth and their British-born black children (*see above*, para.12). This was assisted by a report published in 1967 which revealed substantial discrimination against immigrants.[1] It was notable that this campaign was based not on the trade unions, but rather on organisations of ethnic minorities and sympathetic liberals, the Labour Party, and other left-wing political organisations.[2] The result was the Race Relations Act 1968, which was consciously modelled on anti-discrimination legislation in the United States and Canada. It was enforced, not by individual action, but by a Race Relations Board along the lines of a North American Human Rights Commission. In the employment field, a concession was made to TUC demands for autonomous enforcement by trade unions and employers by allowing voluntary industrial disputes procedures to be used as the primary means of enforcement in some 40 industries covering about one-third of the labour force. However, only a small proportion of cases were successful. Indeed, so few opinions of unlawful discrimination were formed by the voluntary industry machinery that the Race Relations Board concluded that the experiment of using industry panels had failed.[3] The Act was not, however, replaced until 1976 (*below*, para. 333.)

1. WW Daniel *Racial Discrimination in England* (1968).
2. The background is fully described in B.Hepple, *Race, Jobs and the Law in Britain,* 2nd ed. Harmondsworth, 1970.
3. Report of the Race Relations Board January 1975 to June 1976, Home Office, 1976, para. 60.

330. Sex Discrimination Law: As in race discrimination, the common law developed no protection against discrimination on grounds of sex. Indeed, the attitudes of the all-male judiciary were often openly hostile. In the notorious case of *Roberts* v. *Hopwood*,[1] the House of Lords decided that it was unlawful for a local authority to provide equal pay for women doing the same work as men. Similarly, the courts consistently upheld the policies of local education authorities in the 1920s to dispense with the services of all married women teachers.[2]

1. [19251 AC 578 (HL).
2. *Short* v. *Poole Corporation* [1926] 1 Ch. 66 (CA); *Price* v. *Rhondda UDC* [1923] 2 Ch. 372 (ChD).

331. Prior to 1970, the only legislation relating to sex discrimination was the Sex Disqualification (Removal) Act 1919, which made it unlawful to disqualify a person on the grounds of sex or marriage from the exercise of any public function or any civil office or vocation. However, this statute was too limited to have any great impact and remained largely a dead letter. Sex discrimination remained widespread; for example, it was commonplace for women to be paid less than men doing the same work. Throughout this period, the TUC had been conducting a campaign for equal pay for women workers, culminating in 1963 with the publication of a Charter for Women Workers. For the first time, the demands included a call for legislation to secure equal pay.

332. The first legis1ative fruits of the TUC's equal pay campaign came with the enactment of the Equal Pay Act 1970, which requires equal terms of employment for men and women workers. This Act did not come into force until 29 December 1975, thus giving employers a full five years to meet its requirements. By this time, both the Conservative and Labour Parties were committed to equality legislation. In 1975, the Sex Discrimination Act 1975 was passed, prohibiting discrimination on grounds of sex or marital status in matters other than terms of employment. This Act departed from the model of the Race Relations Act 1968, in particular by allowing aggrieved individuals a right of direct access to industrial tribunals (or, in cases outside the employment field, to county courts). At the same time, strategic enforcement was entrusted to an Equal Opportunities Commission (EOC), which deals with discriminatory practices by employers and encourages positive action against discrimination (*see above*, para.75).

333. This Act was used as a model for a new Race Relations Act, enacted in 1976. The new Act abolished enforcement through voluntary industry machinery, and replaced this with individual enforcement through industrial tribunals, coupled with strategic enforcement by a Commission for Racial Equality (CRE). The CRE has similar powers to the EOC (*see above*, para. 75). The Acts are supplemented by Codes of Practice, issued by the Commissions, which give practical guidance on the implementation of policies to eliminate discrimination.

334. In the meantime, the UK had entered the EEC and, by the European Communities Act 1972, agreed to be bound by Community legislation. This legislation has exerted a fundamental influence on the later development of UK anti-discrimination legislation. The main legislative provision on sex discrimination is Article 119 of the Treaty of Rome, which requires equal remuneration for men and women doing equal work. This provision is particularly powerful because it is directly applicable, both vertically (against the State) and horizontally (against private employers).[1] The practical application of Article 119 is facilitated by EEC Directive 75/117, specifying equal pay for work of equal value. This Directive is also directly applicable. There are four further directives: EEC Directive 76/207 on equal treatment as regards access to employment, training, promotion and working conditions; EEC Directive 79/7 on equal treatment in State Social Security; EEC Directive 86/378 on equal treatment in Occupational Social Security and EEC Directive 86/613 on equal treatment for the self-employed. Three further directives are still pending; relating to the burden of proof; parental and family leave and the protection at work of pregnant women before and after birth. Directives cannot in themselves be horizontally directly applicable; but they may be vertically directly applicable if they are sufficiently clear and precise.[2] Moreover, national courts are required to interpret national law so far as possible in accordance with Community law.[3] As a result of enforcement proceedings in the European Court of Justice, the Equal Pay Act was amended in 1983 (*see* para. 357 *below*), and the Sex Discrimination Act in 1986 (*see* para. 350 *below*). Recent cases in the ECJ have led to significantly wider interpretations of British law. Recommendations on sexual harassment and childcare have also recently been adopted. In respect of race relations, Article 48 of the Treaty of Rome protects Community workers from discrimination on grounds of nationality. Although there is no general EEC legislation outlawing discrimination on racial grounds, developments in the sex discrimination field have had an important impact on the UK Race Relations Act. (For further discussion of the effect of EEC law, *see* para. 18 *above*.)

1. *Defrenne* v. *Sabena* (No. 2) (Case 43/75 EEC) [1976] ECR 455.
2. *Marshall* v. *Southampton and South – West Hampshire Area Health Authority* [1986] ICR 335 (ECJ); *Integrity* v. *Rouvroy* (Case 373/89) [1991] IRLR 176 (ECJ).
3. *Von Colson and Kamen* v. *Land Nordrhein Westfalen* (Case 14/83) [1984] ECR 723; *Marleasing SA* v. *La Comercial Internacional de Alimengacion SA*, 13 November 1990, (c106/89) and *see Thomas* v. *Adjudication Officer* [1990] IRLR 436 (CA).

334bis. The UK has not ratified ILO Convention No. 111 concerning discrimination in respect of occupation and employment, but it has signed the UN International Covenant on Social and Cultural rights, which requires action in respect of a large number of discriminatory contexts. It has also ratified the European Social Charter and the European Convention for the Protection of Human Rights which list a number of rights to be secured without discrimination.

§2. The Impact of the Legislation

335. Women form an increasingly important part of the workforce. In 1989, there were 10.7 million women of working age in employment in Great Britain, constituting about 42 per cent of all those of working age in employment. In the decade since 1979, this figure had risen by 19 per cent.[1] Nevertheless, despite the Equal Pay Act 1970 and the Sex Discrimination Acts 1975 and 1986, women remain disadvantaged in British society. In particular, women as a group earn markedly less than men. Although the initial effect of the Equal Pay Act 1970 was to increase women's average gross hourly earnings from 63.1 per cent of those of men in 1970 to 75.1 per cent in 1976, progress towards equal pay has subsequently been slow and halting. In 1990, women's gross hourly earnings over all occupations were still only 76.6 per cent of those of men. When overtime and other additional payments were taken into account the gap was even wider, with women taking home a mere 68.2 per cent of men's take-home pay. In non-manual occupations, the position was worse still: in 1990, women's gross hourly pay in these occupations was only 63.5 per cent of that of their male counterparts. This gap is substantially wider than in other EC contries, such as France, Germany and the Netherlands. A central factor accounting for the continuing disadvantage of women is that the primary responsibility for childcare remains with women. As a result, women form the bulk of part-time workers: in 1989 there were 4.47 million female part-time workers (working no more than 30 hours a week) as against only 0.92 million male part-timers.[2] Part-time workers earn substantially less than their full-time counterparts (*see above*, para. 127) and than male part-timers: indeed in 1991, women part-time workers earned on average less than 60 per cent of the average hourly earnings of male full-time workers. Yet the proportion of workers who work part-time increased between 1984 and 1990.

1. Figures in this section are derived from *Employment Gazette* December 1990 p619; *Employment Gazette* April 1991 p. 175; Equal Opportunities Commission *Women and Men in Britain 1990*; Equal Opportunities Commission *Women and Men in Britain 1991*; unpublished data from the 1989 *Labour Force Survey* kindly supplied by the Equal Opportunities Commission Research Unit and EOR no. 43 p. 28.
2. *Census of Employment* September 1989.

336. The continuing differential between men's and women's pay is partly accounted for by the concentration of women in lower-paid occupations ('vertical segregation'), and in the lower-paid grades of mixed occupations ('horizontal segregation'). Thus, women workers are largely concentrated in relatively few occupations and industries, frequently those with a high demand for part-time labour. In 1989, women formed 78 per cent of all those employed in clerical and related work, 68.5 per cent of those in professional and related work in education, welfare and health, and 79.8 per cent of those in catering, cleaning, hairdressing and other personal services. By contrast, they constituted only 13 per cent of professional and related workers in science, engineering and technology. The extent of segregation was particularly marked in construction and mining occupations, where women formed a mere 0.8 per cent of the workforce, and in transport and operating occupations (9.7 per cent). Even where women work in mixed professions, there are far higher proportions of men than women in the better-paid grades. Similarly, women are seriously under-represented in senior positions. For example, in 1990 14 per cent of Labour Party Members of Parliament and Members of the European Parliament for English constitutencies were women, compared to only 5 per cent of Conservatives. This figure is even worse for Scottish and Welsh constituencies. Again, in 1988, women formed only 19 per cent of appointments to public bodies. A similar picture emerges in industry, with women forming only 26.9 per cent of those employed in managerial grades in 1989. Trade unions are scarcely better. Although in 1990, women constituted one in three trade union members, they formed only a tiny proportion of trade union leadership. Only 20 per cent of union national executive members in 1990 were women, and of a total of 75 general secretaries, only four were women.[1] The best female representation in leadership positions is found in the National Union of Public Employees (NUPE), with women comprising 75 per cent of its membership and 50 per cent of its national executive. By contrast, in COHSE (the Confederation of Health Service Employees), the membership is 79 per cent female, but women comprise a mere 31 per cent of the national executive.[2]

1. Labour Research Department *Women in Trade Unions* 1991 p. 2.
2. *Labour Research* March 1990.

337. Ethnic minorities also continue to suffer serious discrimination and disadvantage in the labour market.[1] Unemployment rates for ethnic minority groups during the period 1987–1989 were appreciably higher than those for the white population: 14 per cent compared with 9 per cent. The problem of unemployment is most marked in Pakistani/Bangladeshi and West Indian communities, and among young workers in each of the main minority groups. Even more disturbing are the figures which show that unemployment rates for ethnic minorities are generally higher than among white people with the same broad level of qualifications. There is also a significant earnings gap. A survey in 1990[2] found that white males earned an average of £209.85 per week as against £167.60 earned by Asian males. Ethnic minority women comprise the most disadvantaged group, suffering from both sex and race discrimination. The 1990 study found that Asian women earned on average only £113 per week, as against the £148 earned by white women. As many as 80 per cent of Asian women earned less than £150 per week. Job segregation too is marked among ethnic minorities: 29 per cent of ethnic minority men in employment in 1987–1989 were in distribution, hotels, catering and repairs, compared with 16 per cent of the white population. The sectoral profile of ethnic minority women is similar to that of white women, with equal problems of segregation. Thus 33 per cent of Asian women were found to be employed in plant and machinery, and only 7 per cent were in management or professional occupations. Ethnic minority workers, both male and female, are more likely than their white counterparts to be employed in the secondary labour market, in insecure, low paid and low status jobs. For example, a large proportion of Asian women in the West Midlands are employed in the clothing and footwear manufacturing sector, which is characterised by low pay, a non-unionised work-force and a relatively high dependence on home-workers.[3] Similarly, ethnic minorities tend to cluster in the lower grades of hierarchical jobs. For example, in the civil service, surveys carried out between 1984 and 1988 revealed that as many as 75 per cent of ethnic minority respondents were in relatively junior grades compared with only 45 per cent of white respondents. A similar problem is evident in the teaching profession, and in the National Health Service.[4]

1. Figures in this section are taken from *Employment Gazette* February 1991 p. 59.
2. Duffy and Lincoln *Earnings and Ethnicity* (Leicester City Council 1990).
3. Rice and Patel *The Clothes Showdown* (West Midlands Low Pay Unit 1991).
4. *See* further Fredman and Morris *The State as Employer* pp. 310–314.

338. In view of the persistence of discrimination against women and blacks, it seems surprising that little use has been made of the legislation. In 1976, the first year of operation of the Equal Pay Act there were 1,742 applications to industrial tribunals; in 1984 there were only 33 applications. This number increased somewhat after the scope of the Equal Pay Act was widened by the 1984 amendments; but in 1989/90, there were a mere 397 cases.[1] A similar picture emerges in relation to the Sex Discrimination Act: there were only 1,046 applications under that Act in 1989/1990, while under the Race Relations Act, a mere 939 applications were registered. There are many reasons for this low take-up rate of legal rights, including lack of perception of the issues as legal ones, ignorance of the rights and how to go about enforcing them, lack of adequate representation, cost, delay, inconvenience, and unwillingness to relive a humiliating experience. To these must be added the cultural and linguistic barriers faced by some members of ethnic minorities and, in the words of Lord Scarman's report on the Brixton disorders, the 'signs among black youths, despairing of an end to white discrimination, of a disturbing trend towards a rejection of white society and the development of black separatist philosophies'.[2] Even those women and blacks who are inclined to use the law may be deterred by the derisory remedies available through the legal process (*see* para. 354, *below*), and by the relative lack of success of those who have used the legal procedures. In 1989–1990, only 33 cases under the Equal Pay Act were successful (about 25 per cent of those proceeding to tribunal). In that year, there were a mere 61 successful race discrimination cases; and 86 successful sex discrimination cases. The paucity of cases has made it very difficult for tribunals to develop their expertise in this highly complex and unfamiliar field – discrimination cases make up less than 3 per cent of the tribunal's case load, and there is an absence of specialisation within the tribunals.

1. The figures in this section are based on statistics published annually in the *Employment Gazette*, the most recent being *Employment Gazette* May 1991, 303.
2. Report of an Inquiry by the Rt. Hon. Lord Scarman, November 1981, para. 6.35.

§3. Grounds of Unlawful Discrimination

339. The Sex Discrimination Act and the Equal Pay Act prohibit discrimination on the grounds of sex against men and women of any age. The Sex Discrimination Act also covers discrimination against married persons in the employment field, but it is not unlawful to discriminate against a single person on grounds of being single. Like must always be compared with like. For example the treatment of a married woman must be compared with the treatment of a married man, and not with a single person of the opposite sex.

340. The Race Relations Act 1976 applies to discrimination on the grounds of colour, race, nationality, and ethnic or national origins. Discrimination on grounds of religion is not covered in Britain, although separate legislation passed by the Westminister Parliament covers this in Northern Ireland. Nor is there legislation preventing discrimination on grounds of language, social origin or political opinion. However, 'ethnic origin' has been interpreted broadly, to mean a segment of the population distinguished from others by a sufficient number of shared customs, beliefs, traditions and characteristics derived from a common or presumed common past so as to give them an historically determined social identity, so covering groups like Jews, Sikhs and gypsies[1] but not Rastafarians.[2] There are a number of important exceptions, particularly in respect of discrimination on grounds of nationality so as to preserve immigration control (*see below*, para. 349).

1. *Mandla* v. *Dowell Lee* [1983] ICR 385 (HL); *CRE* v. *Dutton* [1989] IRLR 8 (CA).
2. *Crown Suppliers* v. *Dawkins* [1991] IRLR 326 (EAT).

§4. The Concept of Discrimination

341. The Sex Discrimination and Race Relations Acts recognise two main types of discrimination, direct and indirect. *Direct* discrimination occurs when someone treats a person less favourably than he or she treats or would treat other persons. It is a concept, as old as Aristotle, that likes must be treated alike.[1] The test of direct discrimination does not depend on the defendant's subjective reason for discriminating. Instead, the correct approach is to ask whether, but for his or her sex, the plaintiff would have been treated differently. Thus even if the defendant's motives were entirely benevolent, a finding of direct discrimination might be made.[2] For example, giving concessions to persons of 'pensionable age' (over 65 for men and over 60 for women) is discriminatory even though the defendant's aim is to help the needy. This is because, 'but for' his sex, a 61 year old man would not have been denied a concession available to a 61 year old woman. Discrimination on grounds of pregnancy has led to some conceptual difficulty for British law because of its reliance on a male comparator. An early decision held that dismissal on grounds of pregnancy did not amount to unlawful discrimination because there was no relevant male comparator.[3] More recently, the difficulty has been resolved by comparing the treatment of a pregnant woman with that of a man seeking leave of absence on the grounds of ill health.[4] By contrast, the European Court of Justice has avoided such tortuous reasoning, holding that the refusal to employ a woman on grounds of pregnancy amounts to unlawful discrimination contrary to the Equal Treatment Directive regardless of the absence of a male comparator.[5] This extends too to dismissal on grounds of pregnancy; with the effect that a period of maternity leave is obligatory. However, after the end of the maternity leave, a woman dismissed for illness arising from pregnancy or child-birth is entitled only to the same treatment as a man absent from work due to illness.[6] The direct discrimination provisions will also, in certain circumstances, render sexual or racial harassment unlawful.[7] It should be noted that where a finding of direct discrimination is made, the defendant is not permitted to argue that his or her action is 'justifiable', as is the case in indirect discrimination below.

1. SDA 1975, s. 1 (1)(a), s. 3 (1)(a); RRA 1976, s1(1)(a).
2. *James* v. *Eastleiah Borough Council* [1990] IRLR 288 (HL); *R* v. *Birmingham City Council ex p EOC* [1989] IRLR 173 (HL); *Ministry of Defence* v. *Jeremiah* [1979] IRLR 436 (CA).
3. *Turley* v. *Allders Stores* [1980] IRLR 4 (EAT).

4. *Hayes* v. *Malleable Working Men's Club* [1985] IRLR 367 (EAT), *Webb* v. *EMO Cargo Ltd* [1992] IRLR 116 (CA).
5. *Dekker* v. *Stichting Vormingscentrum voor Jonge Volwassenen* (Case 177/88) [1991] IRLR 27 (ECJ). But *see Berrisford* v. *Woodard Schools* [1991] IRLR 247.
6. *Handels – OG Kontorfunktionaerernes Forbund I Danmark (acting for Hertz)* v. *Dansk Arbejdsgiverforening (acting for Aldi Market)* (Case No. 1790/88) [1991] IRLR 30 (ECJ).
7. *Strathclyde Regional Council* v. *Porcelli* [1986] IRLR 134 (CS); cf *Balgobin* v. *London Borough of Tower Hamlets* [1987] IRLR 401 (EAT) and *De Souza* v. *Automobile Association* [1986] IRLR 103 (CA).

342. Indirect discrimination[1] is aimed at more complex forms of discrimination, sometimes called 'institutionalised' discrimination, which results from the effects of past and present disadvantage. Fewer women or blacks may be selected for a job or for promotion, not because the employer treats them less favourably, but because other factors make it more difficult for them to comply with the criteria for selection or promotion. Sexually or racially neutral rules may have a disproportionate impact on women or blacks. For example, since women have greater child care obligations than men, fewer women than men are able to comply with job specifications which include substantial overtime or mobility requirements. Similarly, educational disadvantage may make it more difficult for deprived ethnic minorities to comply with selection tests. The concept of indirect discrimination aims to make such requirements unlawful unless the employer can justify their use. The underlying theory is that in a society in which inequalities in the distribution of benefits are regarded as justifiable, the opportunities for attaining those benefits ought to be determined on a proportional basis of group entitlements. The concept was first developed in the United States. It has been translated[2] into the specific, complex and restrictive language of 'indirect' discrimination. The elements of the statutory definition are that: (i) the employer imposes a requirement or condition which is such that (ii) the proportion of persons of the complainant's group (e.g. women or blacks) who can comply is considerably smaller than the proportion of persons in the comparable group (e.g. men or whites) who can comply; (iii) the person suffers detriment because he or she cannot comply; and (iv) the condition is not justifiable irrespective of the sex, race etc. of the applicant. These elements will be examined in turn.

1. SDA s. l(1)(b), s. 3(1)(b), RRA s. l(l)(b).
2. The obstacles to this transplantation are discussed by B. Hepple, 'Judging Equal Rights' [1983] *Current Legal Problems* 71.

343. Requirement or condition. In the United States case law the concept of effects discrimination was first developed in the context of a practice of selection testing not related to the actual requirements of manual jobs which had the effect of disproportionately excluding blacks because of discrimination in school education.[1] In Britain the concept is not limited to tests or to promotion rules. For example, it has been applied to an age requirement for executive officers in the civil service,[2] to the requirement that employees work full-time[3] (both of which have a disproportionate impact on women with child-care responsibilities), and to dress and appearance requirements that have a disproportionate impact on Sikhs.[4] Unlike the American case law in which attention is focused on the employer's practices, the British legislation speaks of a 'requirement or condition'. This has placed severe restrictions on the concept of indirect discrimination, because it is often difficult to characterise practices such as unadvertised promotion procedures or word of mouth recruitment as requirements or conditions. The rigidity of these words has been further aggravated by recent cases, which have held that a flexible set of criteria which are to be weighed up in the final decision do not amount to a 'requirement or condition' because there is no absolute bar to selection.[5] The EAT has also held that where a criterion, such as that of full-time working, is part of the nature of the job, it cannot amount to a 'requirement or condition' for the purposes of the statute.[6] However, the better view is that any obligation of service, however intrinsic, can be a requirement or condition, although it is open to the employer to argue that such a condition is justifiable.[7]

1. *Griggs* v. *Duke Power Co.* 401 US 424 (1971).
2. *Price* v. *Civil Service Commission* [1978] ICR 2.
3. *Clarke* v. *Eley (IMI) Kynoch* [1983] ICR 165 (EAT); *Home Office* v. *Holmes* [1984] ICR 678 (EAT).
4. *Panesar* v. *The Nestlé Co.* (1980) IRLR 60; *Singh* v. *British Rail* Engineering,' EOR No.5, January/February 1986, p. 24.
5. *Perera* v. *Civil Service Commission (No.2)* [1983] ICR 428 (CA); *Meer* v. *London Borough of Tower Hamlets* [1988] IRLR 399 (CA).
6. *Clymo* v. *Wandsworth London Borough Council* [1989] IRLR 241.
7. *Briggs* v. *North Eastern Education and Library Board* [1990] IRLR 181 (Northern Ireland Court of Appeal).

344. The proportion who can comply is considerably smaller. This raises several questions. The first concerns the meaning of the words 'can comply'. It has been held that the test is not whether it is physically possible to comply, but whether the person can do so in practice, and consistently with his or her cultural identity.[1] Secondly, what amounts to a 'considerably lower proportion'? In particular, what is the relevant group of comparators and how much statistical evidence is required? British courts have generally been unwilling to embark on the detailed statistical exercises utilized by American courts, relying instead on a combination of elementary statistical evidence, common sense and intuition.[2] Useful guidelines have been provided by the Court of Appeal,[3] but their application in practice can be vague and unpredictable.[4]

1. *Price* v. *Civil Service Commission* [1978] ICR 2; *Mandla* v. *Dowell Lee, supra.*
2. *Price* v. *Civil Service Commission, supra; Perera* v. *Civil Service Commission, supra.*
3. *Jones* v. *Chief Adjudication Officer* [1990] IRLR 533.
4. *Kidd* v. *DRG (UK) Ltd* [1985] ICR 405 (EAT); *Greater Manchester Police Authority* v. *Lea* [1990] IRLR 372 (EAT); *Enderby* v. *Frenchay Health Authority* [1991] IRLR 44 (EAT).

345. Justification. Even if a requirement or condition has a disproportionate impact there is no unlawful discrimination if the respondent can show that it is 'justifiable' irrespective of the sex, race etc. of the complainant. In the United States the employer has to show 'business necessity', that the practice is 'necessary to the safe and efficient operation of the business' and that selection tests are 'job-related'.[1] In the early British cases the EAT decided that the term 'justifiable' required the tribunal to look at all the circumstances including necessity and the discriminatory effect of the requirement or condition.[2] But this test was weakened in a series of cases, culminating in *Ojutiko* v. *Manpower Services Commission*,[3] in which the Court of Appeal equated 'justifiable' with 'reasonable.' The employer, it was said, had to 'advance good grounds' 'acceptable to right-thinking people.' The effect was to reduce the issue to one of fact,[4] which will be decided according to the views of the particular tribunal, not always with consistent results.[5] The interplay between the unfair dismissal (above para. 309) and discrimination jurisdictions has sometimes wrongly led tribunals to respect a wide band of 'reasonable' managerial decisions, for example, in relation to dress and appearance regulations even where these could not be said to be 'necessary'. However, a change of approach was signalled by the House of Lords in the pay discrimination case of *Rainey* v. *Greater Glasgow Health Board*.[6] In applying EEC law in the equal pay field, the court held that it was necessary to demonstrate 'objectively justified grounds' for discrimination, and that the same test applied in the context of the Sex Discrimination Act. The Appeal Court has attempted to reconcile this with the *Ojutiko* case by stating that there is no significant difference between the two tests. According to Balcombe LJ, 'Justifiable requires an objective balance between the discriminatory effect of the condition and the reasonable needs of the party who applies the condition.'[7]

1. *Griggs* v. *Duke Power Co.* 401 US 424 (1971) at p. 431.
2. *Steel* v. *Union of Post Office Workers* [1978] ICR 181 at pp. 187–188.
3. [1982] ICR 661 (CA).
4. *Mandla* v. *Dowell Lee* [1983] ICR 385 (HL) at p. 395.
5. Compare *Kidd* v. *DRG* [1985] ICR 405 (EAT) with *Clarke* v. *Eley Kynoch* (supra) and *Home Office* v. *Holmes* [1984] IRLR 299.
6. [1987] IRLR 16 (HL) .
7. *Hampson* v. *Department of Education and Science* [1989] IRLR 69 (CA). The House of Lords decided the case on a different point: [1990] IRLR 302.

346. The Acts also prohibit discrimination by *victimisation*. This occurs where the respondent is shown to have treated the complainant less favourably than other persons because the complainant brought proceedings, gave evidence or information or alleged a contravention of the Race Relations Act, Equal Pay Act or Sex Discrimination Act.[1] The comparison to be made is between the complainant and a person who has not brought proceedings etc, under the relevant Acts.[2] However, victimisation can only be established if the employer's reason or motive for discriminating against the complainant was that the latter had brought proceedings etc. under the relevant Act.[3] The absence of a simple and effective form of protection against victimisation is a major defect of the anti-discrimination legislation.

1. SDA 1975, s. 4; RRA 1976 s2.
2. *Aziz* v. *Trinity Street Taxis Ltd* [1988] IRLR 204 (CA),
3. *Aziz* v. *Trinity Street Taxis* (supra); *Cornelius* v. *University College of Swansea* [1987] IRLR 141 (CA).

§5. AREAS OF UNLAWFUL DISCRIMINATION

347. The Sex Discrimination Act and the Race Relations Act make discrimination on any of the above grounds unlawful in certain defined areas of employment. These areas now cover most potential acts of discrimination but there are some loopholes. Among the main areas covered are selection arrangements, job offers, promotion, training, and other benefits. Dismissals are covered but since the burden of proof is on the complainant under this legislation, complainants are more likely to succeed under the unfair dismissals legislation (*above*, Chapter VII) where the burden of proof is on the employer. However, where the employee is dismissed before 2 years of continuous employment, the only remedy will be under the anti-discrimination statutes.

348. The Acts also outlaw discriminatory advertisements although only the Commissions can take legal action against these. Discrimination by partnerships in the admission or treatment of partners by trade unions and professional and trade associations, and by training bodies and employment agencies are covered. Those who instruct or pressurise another to discriminate or knowingly aid discrimination are themselves guilty of an unlawful act.

§6. EXCEPTIONS

349. There are relatively few exceptions, but some of these are very important. A major source of litigation has concerned provisions relating to death and retirement. The original Sex Discrimination Act excluded all provisions in relation to death or retirement, and this was broadly interpreted to include anything which was 'part and parcel of the employer's system of catering for retirement.'[1] The rationale for this exception was the fact that the retiring age for the purposes of state pensions is 65 for men and 60 for women; and similar age limits were applied in a wide variety of non-statutory schemes, particularly in respect of retirement ages. The discriminatory effects of this exception were recognised by the European Court of Justice in the important *Marshall* case,[2] which held that the dismissal of a woman solely because she had attained the qualifying age for a state pension constituted discrimination contrary to the EEC Equal Treatment Directive. This effectively outlawed differential retirement ages. In addition, the Equal Treatment Directive was held to be directly enforceable by all those employed by organs of the state, but not by private sector employees. (*see* para. 19 *above*). This finding does not in itself affect the state pension age; indeed, the EEC Social Security Directive 79/7 allows Member States to decide for themselves the age at which state pensions are payable. As a result of the *Marshall* decision, the Sex Discrimination Act was amended in 1986; but the exception was not repealed entirely.[3] In particular, provisions relating to death are still excluded from the scope of the SDA. This means that it is lawful to offer benefits to the spouse of a deceased male employee, but not the spouse of a deceased female employee: indeed the ECJ has held that survivors' benefits do not fall within the scope of Article 119 nor the Equal Treatment Directive.[4] Nor has the amendment put an end to litigation in this context. One problem concerns complaints which arose before the amendment. The House of Lords has held that the Sex Discrimination Act in its original form cannot be interpreted subject to the EEC Equal Treatment Directive, because it was enacted before the Directive.[5] This means that only State employees can complain about discriminatory retirement provisions which took effect prior to the amendment. It is therefore important to note that the European Court has defined the scope of State employment widely to include any body which has been made responsible for a public service under the control of the State and has for that purpose special powers beyond those which result from the normal rules applicable in relations between individuals.[6] A second problem concerns the status of occupational pensions and non-statutory redundancy payment schemes. The amendment was deliberately worded so as to exclude such schemes, although employers have, since 1978, been required to provide equal access to occupational pension schemes.[7] The EEC Occupational Pensions Directive 86/378 (to be implemented by 1 January 1993) provides for the elimination of discrimination in schemes designed to supplement state pensions, but it permits equalisation of access to be deferred until state pension ages are equalised. The Commission of the EEC has proposed a directive which will require equal pension ages or flexible retirement, but this is unlikely to come into force before 1993 at the earliest. Meanwhile, some of the gaps have been filled by judicial and legislative activity at domestic level. Discrimination in the statutory redundancy payment scheme was removed by the Employment Act 1989 (para. 324 *above*) and recent cases in the European Court have dealt with both pensions and redundancy payment schemes in the context of the equal pay legislation (*below* para. 362).

1. *Barber* v. *Guardian Royal Exchange Assurance Group; Roberts* v. *Tate & Lyle Food and Distribution Ltd* [1983] IRLR 240.
2. *Marshall* v. *Southampton and South West Hampshire Area Health Authority (Teaching)* [1986] IRLR 140 (ECJ).
3. SDA 1975 s. 6(4) as amended by SDA 1986, s. 2 (with effect from 7 November 1987).
4. *Newstead* v. *Department of Transport* [1988] IRLR 66(ECJ),
5. *Duke* v. *GEC Reliance* [1988] IRLR 118 (HL); *Finnegan* v. *Clowney Youth Training Programme Ltd* [1990] IRLR 299 (HL). However, *Duke* is in direct conflict with the more recent ECJ decision in *Marleasing SA* v. *La Comercial Internacional de Alimentacion SA*, 13 November 1990, Case C106/89.
6. *Foster* v. *British Gas* [1990] IRLR 353 (ECJ); [1991] IRLR 268 (HL).
7. Social Security Pensions Act 1976, ss. 53–56.

350. Other exceptions to the Sex Discrimination Act include employment as a midwife and jobs for which being a man or woman is a genuine occupational qualification, such as models, actors, toilet attendants, hospital and prison staff, and personal welfare counsellors. This exception also includes work in a private home involving close physical or social contact with a person living in the home, or knowledge of intimate details of such a person's life.

351. The Race Relations Act has a narrower list of genuine occupational qualifications, including actors, models, personal welfare counsellors and jobs involving working in a place where food and drink is provided in a particular setting for which, in that job, a person of a particular racial group is required 'for reasons of authenticity' (e.g. Chinese restaurants). It also covers jobs where 'the holder of the job provides persons of that racial group with personal services promoting their welfare and those services can most effectively be provided by a person of that racial group.' This last provision has been narrowly construed, to cover only personal services generally requiring face to face contact, or susceptibility to personal, physical contact. This means that the exception cannot be used as a way of facilitating 'positive discrimination' (*below*, para. 352).[1]

1. *London Borough of Lambeth* v. *CRE* [1990] IRLR 231 (CA); *cf Tottenham Green Under Fives Centre* v. *Marshall* [1989] IRLR 147 (EAT); *Tottenham Green Under Fives Centre* v. *Marshall* (No. 2) [1991] IRLR 162 (EAT).

§7. 'Reverse' Discrimination and Positive Action

352. Nothing in the legislation requires a 'reverse' discrimination in favour of women, married persons or blacks. Indeed, the definition of discrimination means that, apart from a few exceptions, such discrimination is itself now unlawful. One exception is in respect of discriminatory training and education, but a number of detailed conditions must be satisfied. 'Positive' action, to encourage applicants for jobs and trade union membership by women and blacks, and to provide them with training to help fit them for particular jobs, where their numbers have been disproportionately few during the past twelve months, is regarded as essential if equal employment opportunity is to be made a reality.[1] Another exception is that trade unions and similar bodies may reserve seats on elective bodies for members of one sex. In practice, the most important forms of positive action are those which follow the EOC and CRE Codes of Practice. For example, it is lawful to monitor the proportion of female or ethnic minority employees in order to identify and remove possible barriers to their recruitment and advancement. It is permissible, but not mandatory, to improve recruitment measures, for example, by removing word-of-mouth recruitment and by advertising in the minority press.

1. *See* CRE, *Positive Action and Equal Opportunity in Employment*, London, 1985.

§8. Enforcement

353. The experience under the Race Relations Act 1968 was regarded by some as proof that investigation of all individual complaints by a public agency was 'costly and wasteful' and as creating 'resentment and hostility' among those whom it was designed to assist because they were denied direct access to the courts.[1] On the other hand, it was argued that private individuals did not have the resources to find and prove discrimination, and that it was through individual casework that patterns of discrimination emerged. The new Acts try to meet these points by allowing both individual enforcement, in some cases with the assistance of the Commissions, and also action against discriminatory practices by the Commissions.

1. *Equality for Women*, Cmnd. 5724, 1974, para. 28; *Racial Discrimination*, Cmnd. 6234, 1975, paras. 40, 41.

354. An individual may complain to an industrial tribunal within three months of the alleged discriminatory act (the period may be extended) and the EOC and CRE may, in their discretion, assist individuals, for example by giving advice, procuring settlements, arranging for legal assistance or representation. Officers of ACAS have to attempt conciliation, encouraging the use, where appropriate, of voluntary industrial grievance procedures. The most serious obstacle facing the complainant is that of proving unlawful discrimination, although a procedure does exist by which the complainant may obtain information from the respondent to help him or her to decide whether or not to institute proceedings and, if he or she does, to assist in presenting a case. The remedies which the tribunal may award are less effective than those to be found in corresponding American legislation. The tribunal may (1) make an order declaring the rights of the parties; (2) award compensation (with a maximum of £10,000 including a sum in respect of hurt feelings); and (3) recommend that the respondent take within a specified period action appearing to the tribunal to be practicable for the purpose of obviating or reducing the adverse effect of the unlawful discrimination on the complainant. There is no power to order reinstatement or re-engagement or that the next job be offered to the complainant, although these measures may be recommended. If a recommendation is not complied with, without reasonable justification, the amount of compensation awarded may be increased, but not so as to exceed the overall limit of £10,000. It is arguable that these limits are inadequate and therefore contravene the obligation under Article 6 of the Equal Treatment Directive to ensure that compensation is adequate in relation to the damage sustained. However, the Court of Appeal has held that because Article 6 does not have direct effect, the obligation therein can only be achieved by legislative amendment.[1] In 1989–1990, a mere 20 awards were made in race discrimination cases, and in only 3 of those cases, was compensation of £3,000 or more awarded, while 8 were below £750. The picture for sex discrimination is only marginally better: in 1989–1990, only 55 awards were made, 24 of which were under £750, and 8 of which were over £3,000.[2] (The relationship with unfair dismissal is discussed at para. 318 above. The powers of the Commissions are discussed at paras. 75–76 above).

1. *Marshall* v. *Southampton and South West Hampshire Area Health Authority* (No. 2) [1990] IRLR 481 [CA].
2. *Employment Gazette*, May 1991 pp. 305 – 306.

§9. Equal Pay

355. The Equal Pay Act 1970 and the Sex Discrimination Act 1975 are mutually exclusive, in that the former applies only to discrimination relating to payment of money or other terms under the contract (including terms such as holidays, holiday pay, hours and sick pay), while the latter applies only to matters not included in a contract. Although the Acts are intended to be read as a code, there is a discrepancy between them, in that the Equal Pay Act requires a comparison to be made with a specific member of the opposite sex in the same employment whereas the Sex Discrimination Act covers situations where there is no comparable member of the opposite sex. i.e. a 'hypothetical' male. This has proved to be a serious limitation on the impact of the Equal Pay Act since, as has been pointed out above, many women work in predominantly female occupations or grades and are thus unable to find a suitable comparator. Moreover, the area of comparison which a woman may draw with a man's job is limited to a man in the same employment, that is employed by one employer or an associated employer at the same establishment in Great Britain. A comparison may be drawn with other establishments elsewhere in Britain only if common terms of employment are observed in those establishments. Such terms need not be identical; indeed, the House of Lords has held that the concept of 'common terms and conditions' necessarily includes terms applicable to a wide range of employees, whose individual terms could vary greatly. Terms and conditions governed by the same collective agreement 'represent the paradigm, though not necessarily the only example of common terms and conditions.'[1] The woman is entitled to choose the man or men with whom she wishes to be compared,[2] but has to be careful not to cast her net too wide. References in the Act to women apply equally to men and *vice versa*.

1. *Leverton* v. *Clwyd County Council* [1989] IRLR 28 (HL).
2. *Ainsworth* v. *Glass Tubes Ltd* [1977] IRLR 74 (EAT); *Pickstone* v. *Freemans plc* [1988] IRLR 357 (HL).

356. The Equal Pay Act entitles a woman to claim equal treatment with a man in three situations. First, it allows a woman the right to equal treatment when employed on work of the same or a broadly similar nature to that of a man in the same employment. In making the comparison, regard must be had to the frequency or otherwise with which any differences between their work occur in practice, as well as the nature and extent of the differences. This is a necessarily limited basis of comparison, and has been narrowly interpreted by tribunals and courts. Secondly, a woman is entitled to equal treatment with a man if her job and his have been given an equal value under a job evaluation study (JES). A 'job evaluation' is defined as a study undertaken with a view to evaluating jobs to be done by all or any employees in an undertaking or group of undertakings, where the evaluation is made in 'terms of the demands made on the worker under various headings (for instance effort, skill, decision)'.[1] This type of JES is known as an 'analytical' job evaluation, in contrast with more subjective evaluations based on 'whole job' or 'felt fair' comparisons. An existing JES can operate as a bar to a claim for equal pay for work of equal value (*below* para. 357), but only if it is analytical in this sense.[2] However, the employer is not obliged to undertake such a study. Even where a JES does exist, it may give disproportionate weight to traditionally 'male skills' such as physical strength or experience. However, a JES which is itself discriminatory is not a bar to an equal value claim.

1. Eq.P.A. s.1(5).
2. *Bromley* v. *H&J Quick Ltd* [1988] IRLR 249 (CA),

357. The third basis of comparison allows a woman to claim equal treatment with a man doing work of equal value.[1] This was introduced in 1983 as a result of infringement proceedings under Article 119 of the Treaty of Rome.[2] It is broader than the first two methods, since it does not require like work, nor does it rely on an employer-initiated job evaluation exercise. The equal value provisions were intended to be a residual claim, only operative if neither 'like work' nor 'work rated as equivalent' were applicable. However, the House of Lords has held that such an interpretation would conflict with European law.[3] Therefore, even if there is a man doing the same work as the complainant, she may still claim equal pay work of equal value provided that she is able to find a suitable comparator who is not himself employed on like work or work rated as equivalent. However, a claim for equal value cannot be made if a job evaluation study has been carried out unless the existing study can be shown to be discriminatory. In practice, this has proved to be a very difficult hurdle to surmount. If the tribunal is satisfied that there are reasonable grounds for determining that the work is of equal value, or that the existing JES is discriminatory, it may appoint an independent expert, one of a panel appointed by ACAS, to conduct a job evaluation exercise. The expert is given considerable discretion, the only guidelines being that the evaluation should be carried out according to the demands made on the employee, rather than using other methods of job evaluation such as market value or marginal productivity. The expert's report is only challengeable on limited grounds. The equal value provisions have been successfully used to establish entitlement to equality of pay between a female canteen worker and three skilled manual workers in a shipyard,[4] female ship packers and a male labourer[5] and a house-mother and a house-father.[6] However, the provisions are still limited in that the woman must find a comparator in the same employment doing work of the same value. There is still no redress for women in a segregated establishment, nor for a woman whose work is admittedly of lower value than a male comparator, but whose pay is disproportionately low. For example, a woman whose work is worth 75 per cent of that of a man, but who is paid only 50 per cent of his pay, has no grounds for complaint under the Act. On the other hand, European law will give redress to a woman whose work is of higher value than that of a male comparator.[7]

1. Equal Pay (Amendment) Regulations 1982, SI 1983, No. 1794.
2. *Commission of the European Communities* v. *United Kingdom* [1982] ICR 578 (ECJ).
3. *Pickstone* v. *Freemans plc* [1988] IRLR 357 (HL).
4. *Hayward* v. *Cammell Laird Shipbuilders Ltd.* [1984] IRLR 463, [1987] IRLR 257.
5. *Wells* v. *F. Smales & Son Fish Merchants* EOR, No.2, July/August 1985, p.24.
6. *Scott* v. *Beam College*, EOR, No.4, November/December 1985, p.6.
7. *Murphy* v. *Bord Telecomm Eirean* [1988] IRLR 267 (ECJ); cf *Waddington* v. *Leicester Council for Social Services* [1977] IRLR 32 (EAT).

358. Where a woman has established the relevant comparison, it is still open to the employer to argue in defence that the difference in pay was genuinely due to a material factor, other than the differences of sex.[1] The crucial question in this context is the extent to which market forces are allowed to justify a pay discrepancy. For example, could an employer argue that the reason for the difference in pay is that the male employee was in a position to demand higher pay just because he was paid more in a previous job than the female employee? In the early case of *Clay Cross* v. *Fletcher*,[2] Lord Denning recognised that such a reason could simply replicate existing discrimination within the market, and held that the employer's defence was limited to personal factors such as merit and experience. When the equal value provisions were introduced, the wording of the defence was changed, suggesting that for equal value at least, market forces should be allowed to justify a pay discrepancy. Thus in the case of 'like work' and 'work rated as equivalent', the material factor must be a 'material difference between the woman's case and the man's' whereas in the case of work of equal value, it need not be. This distinction has, however, been overtaken by the case law: the House of Lords has now expressly overruled the *Clay Cross* exclusion of market forces under the like work and work rated as equivalent provisions.[3] It is therefore permissable to justify a discrepancy in pay by reference to any economic or administrative grounds, whether the claim is based on the like work or JES provisions, or on work of equal value. The market forces defence is potentially a significant limitation on the impact of the Equal Pay Act particularly where 'women's work' is undervalued by the market due to traditional stereotypes, inferior training or responsibilities for child-care.

1. Eq.P.A. 1970, s. 1(3).
2. *Clay Cross (Quarry Services) Ltd* v. *Fletcher* [1979] ICR 1 (CA).
3. *Rainey* v. *Greater Glasgow Health Board* [1987] IRLR 26 (HL).

359. The impact of the 'market forces' defence is mitigated to some extent by the principle that it is not sufficient for the employer to show an intention to achieve an objective. Instead the difference in pay must actually achieve that objective.[1] In applying this test, there are three matters to which national courts must have regard, namely that the means chosen by the employer corresponds to a real need on the part of the undertaking, that they are appropriate to achieving the objectives pursued and are necessary to that end.[2] Although the Equal Pay Act does not explicitly include the concept of indirect discrimination (*above* para. 342–345), it has been held that the Equal Pay Act 'operates to counteract all discrimination, whether direct or indirect and whether intentional or unintentional; it looks at the effect of the contractual terms, not whether they were expressed in overtly discriminatory words or with any particular intention'.[3] Moreover there is now no difference between the defence of justification thus interpreted in the Equal Pay Act and that relating to indirect discrimination in the Sex Discrimination Act (para. 345).

1. *Jenkins* v. *Kingsgate (Clothing Productions) Ltd (No. 2)* [1981] IRLR 388 (EAT).
2. *Bilka – Kaufhaus GmbH* v. *Weber von Hartz* Case 190/84 [1986] IRLR 317 (ECJ), held applicable to domestic law by the House of Lords in *Rainey* v. *Greater Glasgow Health Board* [1987] IRLR 26.
3. *Jenkins* v. *Kingsgate (Clothing Productions) Ltd. (No. 2), supra*, at p. 724. This goes beyond the interpretation placed on Article 119 of the Treaty of Rome by the European Court of Justice: [1981] ICR 592.

360. The individual may enforce the right to equal treatment through a statutory term in the contract of employment (called the 'equality clause'). The effect is that any term of the woman's contract which is less favourable than a similar term in the comparator's contract is modified so as not to be less favourable. In making the comparison, each term is to be considered independently: thus basic pay should be compared with basic pay, sickness benefit with sickness benefit etc. An employer cannot argue that less favourable treatment in respect of one term, such as basic pay, is off-set by better treatment in respect of another term, such as holiday entitlement or sick leave, although it is possible that the defence of justification might apply.[1] The claim may be referred to the industrial tribunal either by the employee, or by the employer, and in exceptional cases (so far never used) by the Secretary of State. The tribunal may award up to two years' arrears of pay and damages for breach of an equality clause. The proceedings must be instituted within 6 months of the termination of the woman's employment. Claims in respect of like work and work rated as equivalent under a JES follow a similar procedure to the tribunal proceedings (*see above*, Introduction, para. 80), but where there is an equal value claim a much more complicated and lengthy procedure has to be followed. This includes a compulsory preliminary hearing to weed out cases where there is no reasonable prospect of success. This has meant that equal value applications have been subject to lengthy delays. For example, in one of the first cases under the new provisions, *Hayward* v. *Cammell Laird*, it took more than four years before the applicant was finally awarded her pay increase. Instead of the maximum period of 42 days envisaged by the Industrial Tribunals (Rules of Procedure), the average time for an independent expert to report to the tribunal is about 12 months. By the end of 1989, the full procedure had been completed in only 24 cases and on average each case took 17 months.[2]

1. *Hayward* v. *Cammell Laird* [1987] IRLR 257 (HL).
2. *Equal Opportunities Review* Vol. 32 (1990) p. 11.

361. There is at present no mechanism in English law for correcting discriminatory collective agreements. Until 1986, such agreements could be referred to the Central Arbitration Committee (CAC)[1] under Section 3 of the Equal Pay Act. However, because of the restrictive interpretation of its powers by the High Court, the CAC's ability to correct discrimination was limited, and references soon dried up. Its jurisdiction was abolished entirely in 1986. At the same time, the UK was required, under European law, to introduce legislation providing for any provision contrary to the principle of equal treatment in a collective agreement to be declared void or amended[2]. To this end, the Sex Discrimination Act 1986 provides that terms of collective agreements incorporated into contracts of employment are void and unenforceable if they contravene the Equal Pay Act. However, this operates only at an individual level, thus adding nothing to the existing sections of the Equal Pay Act. The more effective strategy of permitting correction of the whole collective agreement was rejected. This unsatisfactory position has now been partially remedied by an important decision of the European Court, which held that a discriminatory collective agreement could be challenged directly under Article 119.[3] The central significance of this case lies in its insistence that the offending clause in the agreement be amended to remove the discrimination rather than, as in the UK legislation, simply being avoided.

1. Para. 72, *supra*.
2. *Commission of the European Communities* v. *United Kingdom* [1984] ICR 192 (ECJ).
3. *Kowalska* v. *Freie und Hansestadt Hamburg* [1990] IRLR 447.

361bis. It is clear from the above that the Equal Pay Act must be read subject to Article 119 of the Treaty of Rome. In addition, Article 119 forms an independent cause of action. Since it is directly effective, both against the State and against private employers, an individual may bring a claim in an ordinary court or tribunal in the UK based on Article 119. The most important question in establishing a claim under Article 119 is what counts as 'pay' in this context. The direct effect of the Article can only be brought to bear if the claim concerns pay. The Treaty provision defines pay as the ordinary basic minimum wage or salary and any other consideration, whether in cash or in kind, which the worker receives, directly or indirectly, in respect of the employment from his or her employer. The area which has been the subject of most litigation has concerned the boundary between employment related benefits, which are pay within the meaning of the Article, and benefits paid by the State directly or indirectly, which are not pay. Examples of benefits which fall into a possible grey area are redundancy payments, sick pay and pensions, all of which may be voluntary, contractual, or statutory. In general, and especially in recent cases, the European Court of Justice has construed 'pay' broadly.[1] The most important recent case in this context has been *Barber* v. *Guardian Royal Exchange Assurance Group*,[2] in which the Court stated that the central question was whether the benefit arises in respect of employment, and this can be so even if it is required to be paid by statute, or is *ex gratia*. Thus statutory redundancy compensation was held to fall within the definition of 'pay', even thought it is a result of a statutory obligation. Similarly, retirement benefits count as 'pay' even though they are paid as part of a 'contracted out' scheme (*above* para. 204), because in both cases, the payment is an intrinsic part of the employment relationship. Statutory sick pay is more complex. The European Court has held that where sick pay is fully funded by the employer, it falls within Article 119.[3] This leaves open the applicability of Article 119 to statutory sick pay in Britain, where the State refunds payments administered by employers (para. 245).

1. *Worringham* v. *Lloyds Bank Ltd*, Case 69/80, [1981] IRLR 178 (ECJ); *Garland* v. *British Rail Engineering Ltd*, Case 12/81, [1982] IRLR 111 (ECJ); *Bilka-Kaufhaus Gmbh* v. *Weber von Harz* [1986] IRLR 317 (ECJ); cf *Defrenne* v. *Belgium* Case 80/70, [1971] ECR 445 (ECJ).
2. [1990] IRLR 240 (ECJ).
3. *Rinner-Kuhn* v. *FWW Spezial-Gebaudereinigung GmbH and Co. KG*, Case 171/89 [1989] IRLR 493 (ECJ); noted by Szyszczak in [1990] ILJ 114.

362. The Equal Pay Act applies to persons employed on contracts of service or contracts personally to execute any work or labour. There are several important exceptions. Firstly, the Act excludes complaints by men that women are more favourably treated by way of maternity leave or other special treatment in connection with pregnancy or childbirth. There is no statutory right to paternity leave. Secondly, provisions relating to death are excluded. This means that it is permissible to provide pensions for the spouse of a deceased male employee even if the same is not provided for the spouse of a deceased female employee.[1] Thirdly, there is a limited and extremely complex exclusion in relation to retirement. Originally, all provisions relating to retirement were excluded from the operation of the Equal Pay Act. Following the European Court's decision in the *Marshall* case,[2] (*see* para. 349) this was amended to require equal treatment in contractual provisions in connection with retirement only in so far as such terms afford access to opportunities for promotion, transfer or training, or provide for dismissal or demotion.[3] Under a separate provision, there is a right of equal access to occupational pension schemes.[4] Other provisions in connection with retirement are still excluded. It appears from this that under the British statutes, it remains lawful to exclude from the operation of the equality clause occupational pension benefits which are linked to State retiring age. However, recent caselaw suggests that this might not comply with European law. In the recent *Barber* case[5] (above, para. 361 *bis*) it was held that pensions paid under a private occupational scheme fell within Article 119. This means that it is unlawful to make access to an immediate occupational pension dependent on differential ages for men and women. In addition, the benefits themselves must be equalised. It is still lawful for States to differentiate in respect of State pension ages, but there is no similar exclusion for occupational pensions, which include all pensions which arise out of the employment relationship. It should be noted that the *Barber* decision has prospective effect only: Article 119 of the Treaty cannot be relied on to claim entitlement to a pension from a date prior to 1990, unless legal proceedings have been initiated before that date.

1. This is in compliance with European laws: *Newstead* v. *Department of Transport* [1988] IRLR 66 (ECJ).
2. *Marshall* v. *Southampton and South West Hampshire Area Health Authority* [1986] IRLR 140 (ECJ).
3. EqPA 1970, s. 6(1A)(b) as amended by SDA 1986.
4. Social Security Pensions Act 1975, ss. 53 – 6.
5. *Barber* v. *Guardian Royal Exchange Assurance Group* Case 262/88 [1990] IRLR 241 (ECJ).

§10. Reform

363. In 1985, the CRE made a number of wide-ranging proposals for the reform of the Race Relations Act.[1] These include a stronger and simpler definition of indirect discrimination, a shift to the respondent of the burden of disproving racial discrimination when less favourable treatment has been shown, a specialist division of the industrial tribunals to deal with discrimination cases, and the right to conduct formal investigations (*see* para. 76, *above*) on a more extensive basis. The CRE has also asked for powers to require ethnic record-keeping monitoring, which at present is voluntary under the Code of Practice. The EOC has presented comprehensive lists of proposed amendments to the Sex Discrimination and Equal Pay Acts on several occasions, the most recent being 1990. These included proposals for a shift in the burden of proof to the alleged discriminator, for strengthening the powers of the EOC, for specialised training of industrial tribunal and EAT members, for provisions to enable a woman to compare her work with that of a 'hypothetical' male counterpart under the Equal Pay Act and for streamlining the procedure for a claim for equal pay for work of equal value.[2] It may be that reforms of this kind could improve the effectiveness of anti-discrimination law, but the wider goal of equal opportunities can only be achieved through programmes of positive action.

1. CRE, *Review of the Race Relations Act 1976: Proposals for Change*, London 1985.
2. Equal Opportunities Commission *Equal Pay for Men and Women: Strengthening the Acts* (1990)

Chapter IX. Competition by Former Employees

364. This is a subject entirely regulated by rules of public policy formulated by the courts. Since early times restraints against competition have been regarded as void, and those who tried to control business competition were once even liable to imprisonment. It was however recognised that an employer might be unwilling to train apprentices if he could not restrain them from competing with him at the end of their time. In 1711, the rule was formulated that a restraint was *prima facie* valid if it did not extend over the whole country and was the result of a bargain between the parties. Since then, the rule has been changed in various ways and the modern doctrine is that restraints of trade are *prima facie* void but they can be justified if they are reasonable and are not contrary to the public interest. Moreover, a restraint may extend over the whole country or even the whole world, provided that this is reasonable and in the public interest.[1]

1. *Nordenfelt* v. *Maxim Nordenfelt Guns & Ammunition Co.* [1894] AC 535.

365. We have seen (above, para. 169) that the duty of faithful service obliges an employee not to disclose trade secrets of the employer or his confidential information so long as the employment lasts. The duty not to disclose secrets or information may even continue after the employment has ended, and no covenant is needed for this purpose. However, this duty is more restricted than that imposed on the employee while the employment lasts. The obligation not to use or disclose information might cover secret processes of manufacture, or designs or special methods of construction, and other information of a sufficiently high degree of confidentiality as to amount to a trade secret. The obligation, after the employment has ended, does not extend to information only 'confidential' because the employee was told to keep it confidential and it remained in the employee's head and became part of his skill and knowledge. If the employer wishes to protect this latter kind of information after the employment has ended, he must enter into a restrictive covenant.[1] Another reason for a covenant is that there is no general restriction on an ex-employee canvassing or doing his business with customers of his former employer. The doctrine of restraint of trade then becomes relevant.[2]

1. Compare *Faccenda Chicken Ltd.* v. *Fowler* [1986] ICR 297, CA, with *Balston Ltd.* v. *Headline Filters Ltd* [1987] FSR 330, *Systems Reliability Holdings plc* v. *Smith* [1990] IRLR 377, where differing views were expressed as to the permissible extent of protection by restrictive covenant.
2. This topic is extensively discussed in the *Sweet and Maxwell's Encyclopedia of Employment Law*, Part I.

366. The interests which an employer can protect by a covenant of this kind are narrowly defined. The employer cannot protect himself simply on the ground that competition by the ex-employee will harm the business in which he once worked. It has been suggested that the reasons for this are that the employer pays only for the services he receives and not for restraints against future competition, and that the employee is not an equal bargaining partner who is capable of protecting his own interests. Whatever the reasons it seems clear that an employer may expressly protect his trade secrets and confidential information (which, as we have said, might be impliedly protected anyway, but an express covenant puts it beyond doubt) and probably his 'know-how'. The employer may only restrain the employee from soliciting customers after leaving the employment if the employee's position enabled him to gain influence over them, e.g. a sales representative or hairdresser's assistant.

367. In order to be regarded as reasonable the covenant must not go beyond what is necessary to protect the employer's interests. In this regard the courts have distinguished between 'area covenants' and 'solicitation covenants'. The former prohibit *working* in a particular area, the latter prohibit *soliciting* former customers. The courts are more inclined to uphold solicitation covenants than area covenants, but an area covenant may be upheld provided that the area covered is not too large. Similarly a restraint for an excessive *length of time* will not be upheld, nor will one which restrains an activity which bears no relation directly to the business of an employer, such as a tailor being restrained from working as a seller of shoes.

368. Even if the restraint is reasonable, it may still be held to be against the public interest. This has rarely been used as a ground for invalidity and has been strongly criticised by academic writers largely because the court is unlikely to pay much attention to general economic conditions, such as whether large-scale unemployment renders restraints unreasonable and in the public interest.[1] In one case (1967)[2] a restraint contained in the rule of a pension fund to which an employee had agreed as a term of his employment was struck down as not being in the public interest. The rule which was held to be invalid stated that the employee would lose his pension if he engaged in any competitive activity. Instead of using the ground of public interest, the court could have decided that the employer had no sufficient 'interest' to protect or that the restraint was not reasonable.

1. A. L. Goodhart, *Law Quarterly Review* Vol. 49, p. 465.
2. *Bull* v. *Pitney-Bowes Ltd.* [1967] 1 WLR 273. *see* too *Sadler* v. *Imperial Life Assurance Co. of Canada Ltd.* [1988] IRLR 389.

Chapter X. Inventions by Employees

369. The law relating to inventions, patents and copyrights is a highly specialised subject which, in England, is practised by patent agents and a small number of specialist solicitors and barristers. Nevertheless, since three-quarters of all patented inventions are produced by employees in the course of their employment, the area is one of potential importance to collective bargaining and some trade unions organising research and engineering workers have been active in seeking rewards for employee inventors.[1]

1. For a fuller account, *see* W. R. Cornish, *Intellectual Property* 2nd ed. (London 1989), para. 7–003 *et seq.*

370. Before the Patents Act 1977 came into operation there were often express contractual terms requiring research workers and similar employees to assign to the employer any rights accruing to the employee from his inventions. Even if there was no express term the employee could be held by the courts to be the trustee of the invention for his employer's benefit, or, if there was no trust it could be held that there was an implied term in the contract vesting the benefit of the invention in the employer. In those circumstances the employee was not entitled to any reward, at common law. An attempt to improve the position of the employee inventor was made by the Patents Act 1949, section 56(2) of which provided that the court or Comptroller of Patents could order the apportionment of the benefit of an invention between an employer and his employee, unless satisfied that one or other was entitled to the benefit to the exclusion of the other. This section was given a narrow interpretation in *Sterling Engineering Co. Ltd.* v. *Patchett*[1] which decided in effect that the beneficial distribution of patent profits between employer and employee could take place only where *both* parties were entitled to the patent at law, a situation which has arisen in only one reported case, and that in 1905. The decision also supports the view that, at common law, it is an implied term in every contract of employment that inventions produced in the course of employment become the property of the employer. This remains the law in respect of all inventions made before the coming into operation of the Patents Act 1977, and for certain inventions where the employment was not connected with the United Kingdom at the time of making the invention.

1. [1955] AC 434.

371. The Patents Act 1977 replaces the earlier law, in respect of inventions made after the Act comes into operation, principally in respect of (1) the ownership of inventions; (2) the right of the employee to be rewarded; (3) the amount of the reward; and (4) the exclusion by express contract of the statutory rights.
(1) *Ownership of inventions.* Section 39(1) provides that, notwithstanding anything in any rule of law, an invention made by an employee belongs to the employer if

'(a) it was made in the course of normal duties of the employee or in the course of duties falling outside his normal duties, but specifically assigned to him, and the circumstances in either case were such that an invention might reasonably be expected to result from carrying out of his duties; or

(b) the invention was made in the course of the duties of the employee and at the time of making the invention, because of the nature of his duties and the particular responsibilities arising from the nature of his duties he had a special obligation to further the interests of the employer's undertaking.'

Any other inventions belong to the employee. The first limb of Section 39(1) appears to be more favourable to the employee than the old common law test of ownership, because factors such as the employee's status, the use made by him of the employer's facilities and his skills and qualifications are no longer relevant to this question, although they may affect the size of the employee's award. The relevant criteria under the first limb are (1) were the inventor's duties of employment linked to the invention? and (2) was it reasonably expected that invention would result from the performance of those duties? It has been held that an employee's 'normal duties' are those which he was actually employed to do. So the manager of a valve department, who was not employed to design and invent but only to effect sales of the company's valves and ensure after-sales service, was entitled to keep his invention of a new kind of valve.[1] The second limb of Section 39 appears to codify the common law rule that the invention belongs to the employer where the employee was employed to make inventions of that sort, as where he is a consultant of the employer company's managing director.

1. *Reiss Engineering Co. Ltd.* v. *Harris* [1985] IRLR 232, High Court.

372. (2) *The right of the employee to be rewarded.* An employee whose invention is exploited by his employer may apply to court or to the Comptroller of Patents for an award of compensation under Section 40. He is entitled to do so whether the invention belongs to employer or employee, but the requirements are different in each case.

(a) Where the invention belongs to the employer, the employee must show that (i) he made the invention; (ii) a patent has been granted; (iii) the patent is (having regard among other things to the size and nature of the employer's undertaking) of 'outstanding benefit' to the employer; and (iv) by reason of those facts it is 'just' that the employer should compensate the employee.

(b) Where the patented invention belongs to the employee, and the rights in the invention or patents or application for a patent have been assigned to the employer, or an exclusive licence granted to the employer, then all the employer need show is that (i) the benefit derived by the employee is inadequate in relation to the benefit derived by the employer from the patent; and (ii) by reason of those facts it is 'just' that the employer should compensate the employee in addition to that benefit.

However, in both these cases, the employee's statutory rights do not apply if there is a 'relevant collective agreement' i.e. made between a trade union to which the employee belongs and the employer or an association to which the employer belongs) providing for the payment of compensation 'in respect of inventions of the same description as that invention to employees of the same description as that employee'. The restrictions on contracting-out (below) do not apply to such collective agreements. While it is expected that collective agreements will improve on the statutory rights there is nothing in the Act to prevent less favourable compensation arrangements by virtue of a collective agreement. In such a case the employee could protect himself only by resigning from the union but he would need to do so *before* the invention is made.

373. (3) *The amount of the reward.* Section 41(1) provides that the employee must receive an award of compensation which secures for him ' . . . a fair share (having regard to all the circumstances) of the benefit which the employer has derived, or may reasonably expect to derive, from the patent or from the assignment, assignation or grant to a person connected with the employer . . . '

A compensation order may be varied, discharged, revised or suspended. Among the relevant criteria in determining what is a 'fair share' are (i) the mature of the employee's duties, his remuneration and other employment advantages; (ii) the effort and skill he devoted to making the invention; (iii) the effort, skill and advice contributed by others; (iv) the contribution made by the employer by the provision of advice, facilities and other assistance, by the provision of opportunities and by his managerial and commercial skills and activities.

(4) *Exclusion by express contract of the statutory rights.* Section 42(2) renders unenforceable any term in a contract which diminishes the employee's rights in inventions made after the date of the contract. This applies to Crown employees as it does to other employees, and even to contracts made with some person other than the employer e.g. a Research Council) at the request of the employer or in pursuance of the employee's contract of employment.

373 bis. In the case of literary, dramatic, musical and artistic works, Section 11 of the Copyright, Designs and Patents Act 1988 provides that the employer is the initial owner of the copyright if the work is made by his or her employee in the course of employment and in the absence of an agreement to the contrary. This means that the employee has to bargain for special arrangements.[1]

1. For further discussion, *see* Cornish, *op.cit*, para. 12-003 *et seq.*

Part II. Collective Labour Relations

Chapter I. Trade Union Freedom

§1. Government Policies

374. Until the 1980s, successive governments in the UK generally adopted policies encouraging trade union organisation and freedom of association. For most of the century, such policies were expressed primarily through the example set by the State to private employers, although after 1970, this was supplemented by legislation (*below* para. 376). From 1906, there was an official policy of encouraging public service employees to join trade unions (apart from the police, whose freedom of association is strictly limited by law[1]). In addition, the State used its vast purchasing powers as a means of influencing private sector employers. From 1946 until its repeal in 1983, the Fair Wages Resolutions of the House of Commons required government departments to include in their contracts with suppliers a clause which provided that 'the contractor shall recognise the freedom of his workpeople to be members of trade unions.' Although in practice this clause had limited effect, it was a significant gesture of support on the part of government.[2] On the international level, the UK Government expressed further official support by ratifying international treaties guaranteeing freedom of association. These include four ILO Conventions, namely, Convention No. 87 (1948) on Freedom of Association, Convention No. 98 (1949) on the Right to Organise and Collective Bargaining, Convention No. 151 (1978) on Protection of the Right to Organise in the Public Service, and Convention No. 135 (1972) Concerning Protection and Facilities to be Afforded to Workers' Representatives in the Undertaking. The UK has also accepted the obligations in Article 11 of the European Convention on Human Rights and Fundamental Freedoms, which include the right to form and join trade unions, and Article 5 of the European Social Charter on the right to organise. These obligations are not directly enforceable as part of domestic law (for the reasons explained in para. 19 above), but before the 1980s successive governments sought to comply with their obligations.

1. Police Act 1919, now the Police Act 1964, s. 47(1).
2. *See* Brian Bercusson, *Fair Wages Resolutions*, Mansell, London 1976.

375. The policy of encouragement of trade union membership changed radically when Mrs Thatcher's Conservative government came into power in 1979. A central tenet of Thatcherism has been the view that trade unions impede the operation of the 'free market' and threaten individual freedoms.

Legislation has been introduced placing increasing restrictions on trade union freedom, and the Government no longer aims by its own practices to encourage employers in the private sector to permit and recognise trade union organisation. In 1983, the Fair Wages Resolution was repealed, an action which necessitated the denunciation of ILO Convention No. 94 on labour clauses in public contracts. This policy was extended to local authorities by the Local Government Act 1988, which makes it unlawful for local authorities to require government contractors to permit trade union organisation as a condition of their contracts. Similarly, the Government has changed its policy of advocating trade union membership among civil servants. The most striking expression of the new policy direction was the Prime Minister's decision in January 1984 that trade union membership at the intelligence gathering unit, Government Communications Headquarters (GCHQ), posed a threat to national security. Without advance warning or consultation, the Government banned the trade unions which had been firmly established there since the inception of GCHQ. It is now a condition of service of all civil servants employed at the intelligence gathering unit that they will not belong to a trade union or staff association, other than the internal, management-sponsored staff association which has subsequently been established. A legal challenge to this unilateral change in conditions of service was unsuccessful.[1] The unions argued that the failure to consult them before the decision was a breach of natural justice, rendering it void. This contention was upheld by Glidewell J., but dismissed by the Court of Appeal and the House of Lords. The Law Lords unanimously held that the long history of encouragement of trade union membership and consultation over terms of employment gave rise to a duty to consult trade unions before making important changes. However, this duty was outweighed by the interests of the state in national security. The Law Lords did not require the Prime Minister to provide evidence of the alleged threat to national security beyond proving that the real reason for her action was her genuine fear of such a threat. The union's complaint to the ILO was more successful: the ILO's Committee of Experts held that the UK Government had breached Convention No. 87, which gives workers the right to join organisations of their own choosing.[2] Nevertheless, the Government took no steps to reverse the ban. As a last resort, the unions took their case to the European Court of Human Rights, complaining of a breach of Article 11 of the Convention, which gives the right to form and join trade unions. However, the European Commission of Human Rights declared their case inadmissible. Interestingly, this was not on the basis of the exception for national security, but because the Article permits the imposition of restrictions on members of 'the administration of the State'.[3] The restrictive policy on trade unions is reflected too in the removal of well established collective bargaining rights from school-teachers, an act which was held to be in breach of ILO Convention No. 98 on the right to bargain. This hostility is unlikely to be altered by EEC law. The Charter of the Fundamental Social Rights of Workers adopted in December 1989 declares that employers and workers shall have the right of association in order to constitute professional organisations or trade unions of their choice, and that every employer and every worker shall have the freedom to join or not to join such organisations.[4] Implementation, however, is left to the member states, and the Commission in its Action Programme does not propose any specific implementing measures.

1. *Council of Civil Service Unions* v. *Minister for the Civil Service* [1984] 3 All ER 935, HL; *see* too para. 94 on the basis for the judicial review of government actions in this field.
2. ILO Governing Body, 234th Report of the Committee on Freedom of Association, 1984, Case No. 1261.
3. *Council of Civil Service Unions* v. *United Kingdom* Application No. 11603/85.
4. Article 11.

§2. The Right to Belong to and Participate in the Activities of an Independent Trade Union

376. At common law, there is no prohibition against membership of trade unions. However, there is likewise no common law protection against discrimination by employers on the basis of trade union membership. It was not until the Industrial Relations Act 1971 that a statutory right to belong to a trade union of one's choice was first introduced. After the repeal of that Act there was no comprehensive legal guarantee of the right to organise. Instead three individual legal rights were introduced to protect trade union membership and activity at the workplace. These individual rights were consolidated in EPCA 1978, and are now found in TULRCA 1992. The first of these is that officials and members of independent trade unions have the right to time off to participate in union activities. (This is discussed in Part I, paras. 188 and 189.) The second is that every employee has the right not to be unfairly dismissed by reason of membership of, or activities, at an appropriate time, in an independent trade union.[1] The third is that every employee has the right 'as an individual' not to be penalised for, or deterred or prevented from joining an independent trade union or taking part in its activities at an appropriate time, by sanctions short of dismissal imposed by the employer.[2] There is no upper age limit or qualifying period of service for claiming these rights. A fourth right was introduced by the Employment Act 1990, which makes it unlawful to refuse employment to a person because he or she is a member of a trade union.[3] Although the 1990 Act was primarily aimed at preventing compulsory trade union membership (*below*, para. 381ff), the need for formal equality led to the introduction of parallel protection for union members. However, the impact of this right is likely to be limited. Most discrimination at the point of employment occurs against union activists; and the legislation was deliberately phrased so as to exclude protection for those who are refused employment on the grounds of union activities rather than merely union membership.[4]

1. TULRCA 1992, s. 152.
2. TULRCA 1992, s. 146.
3. TULRCA 1992, s. 137.
4. B. Simpson, '*The Employment Act 1990 in Context*' 1991 MLR 418.

377. A number of points may be made about these rights. The first is that they belong to *individuals*. Although they protect a *collective* freedom, they cannot be enforced by the trade union, but only by the employee against his or her employer. Although the union may be expected to support the individual in any action he or she takes, it may be a weakness of this approach that the individual is more likely than a trade union to be deterred from bringing an action against the employer, especially during the subsistence of the employment relationship. A second point is that these rights do not extend to those who are not employees, for example, 'self-employed' construction workers. A further limitation was introduced in 1977 by the Employment Appeal Tribunal, which held that an employee was not protected against dismissal for trade union activities in a previous job.[1] This left the way open to employers to blacklist trade union activists. However, in an important recent decision, the Court of Appeal has held that protection extends to dismissal on the basis of the employee's previous union activities[2], since the real reason for the dismissal must be the likelihood of activism in the present job. However, if the real reason for the dismissal was that the employee deceitfully failed to reveal relevant factors, then the section does not apply.

1. *City of Birmingham District Council* v. *Beyer* [1977] IRLR 210, (EAT).
2. *Fitzpatrick* v. *British Railways Board* [1991] IRLR 376 (CA).

378. A third point is that the right to belong is not unlimited. It is a right to belong to an *independent trade union* (*see* para. 416, *below*) and so properly excludes employer-dominated 'company unions'. Nevertheless, the employee may belong to any union and not necessarily the union which the employer recognises for collective bargaining purposes. (For situations in which there is a closed shop, *see below* paras. 390ff.)

379. A fourth point is that the ambit of legitimate trade union activities has been severely limited by judicial interpretation. The House of Lords has held that the protected activities are only those not requiring the employer's assistance or those normally available to employees or those requiring him or her to submit to no more than trifling inconvenience. So use of a canteen outside working hours while the employees are permitted to be on the premises is protected but not necessarily use of a notice board.[1] Moreover, the Court of Appeal has decided that the employee is protected only if the employer's action is a response to the individual's activities as part of a trade union and not in respect of a general reprisal against the union itself. So a management decision to dismiss employees as a direct response to a union's request for recognition, after the employees had joined the union, was not unlawful.[2] At the same time the EAT has excluded an employer's action against employees who presented a petition about safety at work on the grounds that they were acting as individual members of a trade union rather than as part of the activities of the trade union.[3] In other words, only where the employer's action is taken against employees for their *individual* participation in the *collective* activity does the legislation provide any remedy. Finally it is to be noted that the right to participate is confined to activities at 'an appropriate time'. This in effect means times outside working hours, or times when the employee is on the employer's premises with permission but is not required to be at work (e.g. during meal breaks). While the employee is at work the employer's permission is required.[4]

1. *Post Office* v. *Union of Post Office Workers* [1974] ICR 378, HL.
2. *Carrington* v. *Therm-a-Stor Ltd.* [1983] ICR 208, CA.
3. *Chant* v. *Aquaboats Ltd.* [1978] ICR 643, EAT.
4. TULRCA 1992, s. 146 (1), s. 152 (1).

380. The employee's remedy for breach of these rights is to make a complaint to an industrial tribunal within three months of the act complained of. In the case of unfair dismissal, the special procedure of 'interim relief' is available to continue the employee's contract of employment until his or her rights are determined (*see* Part I, para. 316, *above*). Where reinstatement or re-engagement is not ordered, there is a minimum *basic* award of compensation, and also a *special* award (*see* Part I, paras. 314 and 315 *above*). These relatively high levels of compensation were introduced by the Employment Act 1982, and were mainly intended to deter closed shop dismissals (*see* para. 392, *below*). In the case of action short of dismissal, the tribunal may grant a declaration as to the employee's rights and may award compensation for the loss sustained (e.g. loss of earnings) and also in respect of 'the infringement of the complainant's rights' (a statutory penalty not limited in amount). In cases of refusal to employ on grounds of trade union membership, the tribunal may, in addition to a declaration to that effect, make an order requiring payment of compensation and a recommendation that the respondent take appropriate action.

§3. The Right Not to Belong

381. The right not to belong to a trade union has frequently been treated differently from the right to belong. The question is of particular relevance where membership of a trade union is a precondition for obtaining or retaining employment (the 'closed shop'). (The closed shop is dealt with *below*, para. 386.) It has been argued that whereas freedom of association is essential to the protection of workers in a pluralist society, the right not to belong is of a different character and may lead to disruption of orderly industrial relations. The Donovan Commission, for example, argued that 'the two are not truly comparable. The former condition [the right not to belong] is designed to frustrate the development of collective bargaining, which it is public policy to promote, whereas no such objection applies to the latter'.[1]

1. Report of the Royal Commission on Trade Unions and Employers' Associations Cmnd. 3623, 1968, para. 599, and *see* generally R. Lewis and B. Simpson (1982) 11 *Industrial Law Journal* 227; cf. Industrial Relations Act 1971, s. 5.

382. A persistent argument against the closed shop centres around the alleged threat to individual freedom. The debate about whether the right to freedom of association is infringed by the closed shop depends to some extent on whether freedom of association is seen as an aspect of individual autonomy, or as a social right, to which exclusively individual interests are to some extent subordinate. One question which arises is whether the closed shop infringes Article 11 of the European Convention on Human Rights and Fundamental Freedoms, which states that freedom of association should not be subject to any restrictions except such as are prescribed by law and are necessary in a democratic society for the protection of the rights and freedoms of others. In the discussions leading up to the formulation of Article 11, it was explicitly agreed that it would be undesirable to include a right not to be compelled to join a union parallel to the right to join a union. In 1981, this question was raised directly before the European Court of Human Rights.[1] Three former employees of British Rail complained that their rights under Article 11 had been infringed when they were dismissed for refusal to belong to the unions with which British Rail had concluded a union membership agreement. Although the Court refused to review the closed shop system as such, it upheld the applicants' complaint in the particular circumstances of the case. The fact that the closed shop had been imposed on the applicants after their employment had begun and under the threat of dismissal was held to be an unacceptable infringement of their freedom of association. In addition, the Court held that the applicants' freedom of association had been infringed by the limitation on their choice of which union to join. The implications of the judgment are ambiguous.[2] Since the majority of the Court declined to find a general 'negative right to dissociate' it is difficult to see what right the compulsion to join violated. Moreover, 'freedom of choice' is meaningless where, as in this case, there was effectively only one union the men could join. Freedom to choose does not logically imply a freedom not to join *any* union.[3]

1. *Young, James and Webster v. United Kingdom* [1981] IRLR 408 (ECHR).
2. M. Forde, (1982) *Industrial Law Journal* Vol. 11, p. 1 at pp. 4–5.
3. *See* F. Prondzynski (1982) *Cambridge Law Journal* 256.

383. The Industrial Relations Act 1971, reflected an individualist philosophy by conferring a general right not to associate, in parallel with the new right to associate. This clashed with the collectivist aims of trade unions, most of whom had in any case refused to register as required by the Act. Competition for members developed between unregistered TUC unions and new or splinter unions who utilised the new rights as a platform to organise. As a result stable bargaining arrangements were threatened with disruption. After the repeal of the 1971 Act, the right not to belong to a union was recognised in only two specific instances, by legislation enacted between 1974–1976. First, there was a right not to be compelled to be a member of a non-independent (employer-dominated) trade union. Secondly, where a closed shop existed, an employee who genuinely objected on grounds of religious belief to being a member of any trade union whatsoever was protected from dismissal on grounds of non-membership.

384. The Conservative Government elected in 1979 took the view that the right not to belong to a trade union was equivalent to the right to belong. This was reinforced by the view that the closed shop was an unwarranted restriction on individual freedom of choice, and an unnecessary fortification of trade union power, distorting the free market (*see* Introduction, para. 64). The statutory protections of the right to belong have therefore been expanded to include similar protections for the right not to belong. Thus the right not to be unfairly dismissed for membership of a trade union has been extended, so that it is automatically unfair to dismiss an employee where the principal reason for dismissal was his or her non-membership of or refusal to belong to a particular or any trade union.[1] As in the case of trade union membership, dismissal for non-membership attracts very high levels of compensation, particularly where reinstatement has been ordered and not complied with (*see* Part I, paras. 314 and 315, *above*). Similarly, employees are protected from action short of dismissal compelling them to be or become a member of any trade union or a particular trade union, or to enforce a requirement to make a payment as an alternative to joining a trade union.[2] In addition, interim relief is available to those dismissed for non-membership in the same way as for membership (*see* para. 316, *above*).

1. TULRCA 1992, s. 152(1)(c) and see *above*, para. 305 (automatically unfair reasons for dismissal).
2. TULRCA 1992, s. 146. For closed shop provisions see *below*, para. 390.

385. A further significant innovation of the Employment Acts 1980 and 1982 was the introduction of a right to include the trade union as a third party or co-defendant in proceedings against the employer for unfair dismissal or action short of dismissal.[1] Both the employer and the employee have the right to join the trade union as a party to the proceedings if it is claimed that the union took industrial action or threatened to do so in order to put pressure on the employer to dismiss the employee or take action short of dismissal. The tribunal may then make an award against the union only, or against both the employer and the union.

1. TULRCA 1992, ss. 150, 160.

§4. The Closed Shop

386. The closed shop has been defined as a 'situation in which employees come to realise that a particular job is only to be obtained and retained if they become and remain members of one of a specified number of trade unions'.[1] The closed shop is normally maintained by unions threatening to take industrial action unless the employer dismisses or refuses to employ non-members. The phenomenon takes many different forms. A distinction is sometimes drawn between the *pre-entry closed shop*, in which a worker cannot apply for a job unless he or she is a union member, and the *post-entry closed shop* (called the 'union shop' in America), in which the worker is required to join a union within a stated period after having taken up the job. In Britain, the line between these two is often blurred in practice. Another distinction is between the requirement that the worker should become a member of any union or that he or she should belong to a specified union, or even a section of a specified union. Closed shops of all these varieties are found in Britain.

1. W.E.J. McCarthy, *The Closed Shop in Britain*, Oxford, 1964. This definition was followed by the Royal Commission on Trade Unions & Employers' Associations, Cmnd. 3623, 1968, para. 588.

387. The function of the closed shop has changed over the years. In a major study published in 1964, McCarthy found that the closed shop was a response by unions and workers to certain organisational problems, such as high turnover, scattered workforces, inter-union competition and the existence of an alternative workforce which might undermine industrial action. The closed shop assisted unions in establishing and maintaining membership, in disciplining the members, and (in the case of a pre-entry closed shop only) in controlling an alternative workforce.[1] Recent studies show, however, that in the 1970s the closed shop became less an instrument of employee control and more an instance of joint trade union and employer regulation in the interests of orderly industrial relations.[2] Employers not infrequently regarded the closed shop as a useful means of preventing inter-union disputes, of ensuring that collective bargaining arrangements cover all workers, and of maintaining effective discipline by union officials over the workforce. Indeed, during the period 1971–1974 when the closed shop was prohibited by law, it appears that employers and trade unions colluded to maintain closed shops in existence. Moreover, closed shop agreements are now more likely to be formal and in writing than they were 20 years ago.

1. McCarthy, *op. cit.*
2. S. Dunn and J. Gennard, *The Closed Shop in British Industry*, London, 1984; and Ch.4 in *Industrial Relations and the Law in the 1980s: Issues and future Trends* (eds. P. Fosh and C.R. Littler), London, 1985.

388. By the end of the 1970s, closed shop arrangements covered about a quarter of the workforce, more than 5.2 million people.[1] About 800,000 of these (4 per cent of the workforce) were in pre-entry closed shops, nearly all of these having been established in the era of craft unionism and in industries, such as merchant shipping, dock work and acting, in order to counteract the employers' use of a plentiful supply of casual non-union labour.[2] In the early 1960s post-entry closed shops covered 3 million people (12 per cent of the workforce), and were concentrated in a few industries, in particular engineering and coal-mining.[3] By the end of the 1970s, the number in post-entry closed shops had grown to at least 4.5 million, an increase of over 50 per cent since the early 1960s. Post-entry closed shops had emerged in industries where they were little known previously, such as food, drink, clothing, footwear and chemical manufacture, local authorities and the nationalised industries.[4] However, even before the Conservative Government's Employment Acts of 1980, 1982, 1988 and 1990 (below) had begun to take effect, the closed shop had reached a point of stagnation and decline. By mid-1982, it had fallen by 13 per cent to approximately 4.5 million in both pre- and post-entry closed shops.[5] The shrinking of industries such as coalmining, steel, shipbuilding, clothing, footwear, vehicles and railways where the closed shop was widespread, has not been compensated by extension in other industries. The continuation in these economic trends, with an overall decline in union membership, coupled with the impact of the Employment Acts means that the closed shop has continued to decline since 1982. A recent survey of 558 UK companies, largely in the private sector, found that the coverage of the closed shop had substantially declined during the

1980s, and the decline was most marked after 1985. However, it also found that the closed shop remained widespread: nearly a quarter of firms in the survey that recognized trade unions were still operating some form of closed shop arrangement in 1990.[6] Nevertheless, Government estimates that there were as many as 1.3 million employees in pre-entry closed shops in 1989[7] were treated with widespread scepticism, the better view being that there were no more than 150,000.[8]

1. J. Gennard *et al.*, (1980) 88 *Employment Gazette* 16.
2. *Ibid.*
3. McCarthy, *op cit.*, pp. 14–22.
4. Gennard *et al.*, *op cit.*, p. 147.
5. Dunn and Gennard, *op cit.*, p. 147.
6. P. Gregg and A. Yates, 'Changes in Wage-setting Arrangements and Trade Union Presence in the 1980s' 1991 *British Journal of Industrial Relations* p. 361 at p. 366.
7. Department of Employment *Removing Barriers to Employment* (Cm 655, March 1989) para 2.6 and 2.7
8. B. Simpson (1991) MLR 418 at p. 423.

389. Successive governments have displayed differing attitudes to the closed shop. It remained outside the scope of legal regulation until the Industrial Relations Act 1971 directly challenged the practice by making all pre-entry closed shop agreements void and allowing the post-entry closed shop only in two exceptional situations (the 'agency' shop and the 'approved closed shop'). The legitimacy of the closed shop was subsequently recognised by the Trade Union and Labour Relations Acts 1974–1976 in that a dismissal for refusing to belong to a union was deemed fair if there was a 'union membership agreement' made with an independent trade union, under which employees had to belong to a trade union. A limited exception was provided in the case of employees who genuinely objected to union membership 'on grounds of religious belief'. With some amendments, this remained the legal framework until 1980. The Conservative Government of the 1980s, by contrast, repeatedly avowed to put an end to the closed shop. Initially, there was a perceived need to compromise. Hence the Employment Acts 1980 and 1982 amended the legal framework in order to undermine the closed shop as far as possible without outlawing it directly. Union membership agreements or closed shops were given limited protection, but only if they received exceptionally high levels of support. Where there was such support, dismissal of a non-member remained possible, but so many exceptions were introduced that in most cases dismissal was in fact unlawful.

390. The incremental approach to restriction of the closed shop was finally abandoned by the Employment Act 1988, which effectively outlawed the post-entry closed shop. It is now automatically unfair to dismiss an employee for non-membership of a trade union, even if a closed shop is in operation.[1] This deprives unions and employers of their main sanction against non-members. The prohibition was further extended by the Employment Act 1990, which was aimed at the pre-entry closed shop. The new Act provided a right of complaint to an industrial tribunal for any individual whom an employer refuses to engage on the ground of non-membership of a trade union, or on the ground of refusal to agree to become a member after the employment begins. Protection extends widely, to include situations in which an employer refuses or deliberately omits to entertain and process an application, or makes an offer of employment the terms of which are such as no reasonable employer would offer, or places an advertisement which might reasonably be understood as indicating that a job is open only to union members.[2] Other avenues for securing employment to union members are similarly barred: employment agencies may no longer refuse to provide services to job seekers who do not belong to a union;[3] and employers may no longer enter into arrangements with unions whereby employment is offered only to persons put forward or approved by the union.

1. TULRCA 1992, s. 152.
2. TULRCA 1992, s. 137.
3. TULRCA 1992, s. 138.

391. The impact of the new provisions on the coverage of the closed shop is difficult to assess. The most recent study, cited above, found that most of the changes in the closed shop took place in 1988 or 1989, probably due to the introduction of the 1988 Act. However, despite the fact that legally a closed shop can no longer be enforced by dismissals, the study found that some three-quarters of companies with a closed shop in 1984 still had some arrangement in 1990.[1] The impact of the 1990 Act is likely to be similarly limited. However, there remain areas, such as theatre and broadcasting, where the need to maintain professional skills and the excess of supply over demand for labour have meant that pre-entry closed shops have provided a valuable stabilising influence, which may well be lost if the closed shop is prohibited. It is noteworthy that the Government refused to bring professional associations within the scope of these provisions.

1. P. Gregg and A. Yates *op cit*.

392. The restrictive effect of the above provisions is further reinforced by the very high levels of compensation available in cases in which a dismissal is unfair by virtue of these provisions (*see* Part I, paras. 314 and 315, above), and the possibility of using the interim relief procedure (above, para. 316) to continue the contract of employment until a tribunal has resolved a complaint. In cases of refusal to engage a person because of non-membership of a union, the tribunal may order the employer to pay compensation up to the maximum limit in an ordinary unfair dismissal case (£10,000 from April 1991), assessing compensation on the same basis as damages for breach of statutory duty. In addition, the tribunal may make a recommendation that the respondent take action to obviate or reduce the adverse effect on the complainant. This could include a recommendation that the employer consider the complainant for the next available job vacancy. If the respondent refuses to comply with such a recommendation, the tribunal may increase compensation, up to the maximum above.[1] As described above (para. 385), it is possible for either the applicant or the employer to join the trade union as a respondent or third party in the proceedings, where the dismissal or refusal to engage is a result of pressure by the union. Clearly, it will not be infrequent for the union to make direct or indirect threats of industrial action where necessary to preserve the closed shop. In such cases, the tribunal may award compensation against the union, or against both the union and the employer.

1. TULRCA 1992, s. 149.

§5. Exclusion or Expulsion from the Union

393. In a further important innovation, the Employment Act 1980 provided a right not to be unreasonably excluded or expelled from a trade union where a union membership agreement is in operation.[1] An employee who has been excluded or expelled from a union in these circumstances has the right to complain to an industrial tribunal, which may declare that the exclusion or expulsion was unreasonable. The statutory provisions give little credence to the union's interest in autonomy in respect of its internal procedures. Thus there is no requirement that workers first exhaust internal complaints or appeals procedures before applying to a tribunal. Nor is it sufficient for the expulsion or exclusion to be consistent with the union's own rules; such an exclusion or expulsion may nevertheless be considered unreasonable by the tribunal. Conversely, the union's actions are not necessarily unreasonable simply because they contravened the union's rules. (This may be contrasted with the strict common law requirements that a trade union abide by its own rules – below, para. 424.) It has been held that it is not necessary for the applicant to show that he or she was denied a particular job; it is sufficient to be seeking work in the particular field of industry to which the closed shop relates.[2]

1. TULRCA 1992, ss. 174–7.
2. *Clark* v. *NATSOPA (Sogat'82)* [1985] IRLR 494 (EAT).

394. If the union does not admit or re-admit the person after a tribunal has declared his or her complaint to be well-founded, he or she may apply for compensation to the Employment Appeal Tribunal, which must award such compensation as it considers just and equitable in the circumstances. This includes loss of earnings, loss of earning opportunity in the industry where the closed shop operates, and non-pecuniary loss, such as injury to feelings and upset in the person's personal life resulting from the refusal of membership.[1] The award may be reduced if the applicant caused or contributed to the refusal or exclusion and the applicant has the duty to mitigate his or her loss. If the person has been admitted or re-admitted, he or she may apply to an industrial tribunal for compensation for any loss sustained in consequence of the refusal or expulsion complained of. (The common law controls on the relationship between unions and their members are described below, para. 424). The right not to be unreasonably excluded or expelled has been exercised very infrequently; indeed, in 1990, only four such cases were heard by an industrial tribunal.[2]

1. *Howard* v. *NGA* [1985] ICR 101 (EAT). Compare unfair dismissal, where compensation for injury to feelings is not *per se* compensatable.
2. ACAS Annual Report 1990.

§6. The TUC's Independent Review Committee

395. In 1976, the TUC established a voluntary committee, the Independent Review Committee (IRC), as an alternative to the legal control of internal trade union affairs where a closed shop exists. Its terms of reference are 'to consider appeals from individuals who have been dismissed, or given notice of dismissal, from their jobs as a result of being expelled from, or having been refused admission to, a union in a situation where trade union membership is a condition of employment'.[1] In contrast with the statutory provisions (para. 393, *above*), the IRC will not consider a complaint before the individual has exhausted all internal procedures of his or her own union and an attempt has been made to settle the matter by agreement. If this fails, the IRC may make a recommendation to the union concerned. A majority of TUC affiliated unions have agreed to abide by the recommendations of the Committee (which consists of Professor Lord Wedderburn, Lord McCarthy and Mr. George Doughty). The IRC attaches great importance to conciliation in its work, both before and after a full hearing.[2] It has no power to award compensation, and although it has had some success in achieving admission or re-admission into membership of the union, it has had little success in securing reinstatement into employment. The Committee played an important role in the period 1976–1980, when there was a gradual extension of closed shops. Twenty cases reached a full hearing during this period. However, the Committee's work has largely been overtaken by the enactment of a statutory right to appeal to an industrial tribunal on a complaint of unreasonable exclusion or expulsion, and by the removal of legal protection for the employer who dismisses to enforce a closed shop (*above* paras. 390, 393–394). Although the Committee has the advantage of greater flexibility of procedure than the statutory remedy, the latter includes the possible remedy of compensation. In 1989, the Committee received no inquiries.

1. TUC Report, 1976, p. 94.
2. *See* K.D. Ewing and W.M. Rees, (1981) 10 *Industrial Law Journal* 84.

§7. Union-Only Practices

396. One way of supporting union membership and recognition, apart from the closed shop, is the 'union-only' or 'recognition-only' practice, whereby contracts for the supply of goods or services are made subject to the condition that the supplier's employees are trade union members, or that the supplier recognises, negotiates or consults with a union. For example, in 1982, about one in eight local authorities imposed such requirements for manual workers.[1] As part of the present government's strategy of preventing such aids to the maintenance of union membership, the Employment Act 1982 introduced provisions preventing such practices.[2] This is done in three ways. First, a clause imposing either a union-only or a recognition-only requirement in a contract for the supply of goods or services is made void. Secondly, a right to sue for breach of statutory duty is created when a person is excluded from a list of suppliers, or from those from whom tenders are invited, or when a supply contract is terminated, or when no supply contract is entered into with a person, on the grounds that that person does not recognise, bargain with or consult unions, or the work to be done under the contract is likely to be done by non-unionists. Any person adversely affected has the right to sue. These would include, for example, a sub-contractor to the supplier affected, or an employee made redundant by that supplier. Thirdly, the Act lays down certain circumstances in which industrial action intended to put pressure on employers to maintain union-only or recognition-only practices is not protected from civil liability by the immunities afforded to other types of industrial action (*see* Chapter IV, paras. 484–502, *below*). To date there have been no reported cases on this provision. This clear 'preference for non-unionism'[3] is further reinforced by the Local Government Act 1988, which prevents local authorities and several other public bodies from using unionisation of the work-force as a criterion when drawing up tender lists, selecting contractors or sub-contractors, or terminating contracts.[4] Any person suffering loss or damage as a result of an authority breaching these provisions has a right to sue the authority for damages.

1. M. Ingham and A.Thomson, *Dimensions of Industrial Relations in Local Authorities* University of Glasgow, 1982, Table 5A.
2. TULRCA 1992, s. 144–5.
3. J. Clark and Lord Wedderburn in *Labour Law and Industrial Relations: Building on Kahn-Freund* Oxford, 1983, p. 143. *See also* S. Evans and R. Lewis (1988) ILJ 209.
4. Local Government Act 1988, s. 17.

Chapter II. Trade Unions and Employers Associations

§1. Trade Union Membership

397. During the 1980s, British trade unions were confronted with a Conservative government explicitly committed to reducing trade union influence at the workplace and excluding unions from national political representation. This, combined with very high levels of unemployment, has left the unions in a far weaker position than they were in at the start of the decade. This has been especially evident in respect of membership figures; after many years of steady growth, trade union membership in Britain declined steeply during the 1980s.[1] In 1989, there were 10.2 million trade union members, compared with the 1979 peak of 13.3 million, a fall of 24 per cent. By the end of the decade, there was little sign of a reversal of the downward trend: the fall in union membership in 1989 was the tenth consecutive fall in membership since 1979, despite strenuous attempts by unions to recruit new members among 'atypical' workers such as part-time workers and women. Between 1979 and 1986, the main reason for declining trade union membership was increasing unemployment: in particular, trade union density was badly affected by the decline in manufacturing industries, where there was a traditional concentration of union members. However, while the number of employees in employment increased by 1.4 million between 1986 and 1989, trade union membership continued to fall. The decline is thus more likely to be due to an increase in employment in areas with low union density.

1. Figures in this and subsequent paragraphs come from *Annual Report of the Certification Officer 1991* and *Employment Gazette*, June 1991, p. 337. For a full discussion, see David Winchester, 'Sectoral Changes and Trade Union Organisation' in *Employment in Britain* (ed. D. Gallie) Oxford 1988, Ch. 7; P.B. Beaumont *Change in Industrial Relations*, London 1990; M.Terry, 'Annual Review Article 1990' 1991 *British Journal of Industrial Relations* 97; G. S. Bain and R. Price, Chapter 1 in *Industrial Relations in Britain* (ed. G. S. Bain) Oxford, 1983.

§2. Trade Union Structure

398. In recent years, there has been a trend towards concentration of union membership into fewer and larger unions. Whereas in 1920, there were 1,384 trade unions, this had fallen to 519 in 1973 and 309 in 1991. This reflects the continuing process of merger and transfer of membership. In 1989, as much as 60 per cent of the total membership was covered by the 10 largest unions, all of which had more than 250,000 members. The largest union was the Transport and General Workers Union, with over 1.27 million members. At the same time, there remain a large number of small unions: in 1989, almost half of all trade unions had fewer than 1,000 members, together accounting for only 0.4 per cent of the total membership of all unions. The process of concentration has been stimulated by a number of pressures including the difficulties faced by smaller unions in remaining solvent in the face of inflation and falling membership, changes in technology which have eroded traditional crafts and skills, and the active policy of expansion adopted by some unions. Hyman comments that 'two decades ago the pattern of British union membership differed little from the structure consolidated around the turn of the century: dominated by a handful of general, ex-craft and single industry sections of 19th century British capitalism. Unionism in the 1980s is far more broadly based: a reflection in part of the decline of traditional strongholds and the growth of "tertiary" employment, in part of increased density in areas of former weakness, particularly in the public sector. Occupational shifts in employment and unionisation have led to the current prominence of "white-collar" organisations.'[1] Of particular note is the change in gender composition of unions. In 1989, women constituted 37 per cent of all trade union members, as against only 20 per cent in 1960.

1. R. Hyman, Ch. 2 in *Industrial Relations in Britain* (ed. G.S. Bain), Oxford, 1983, pp. 35–36.

399. Three principal categories of trade union structure are to be found in Britain – *craft. industrial* and *general.* But these categorizations have to be used with caution because many of the larger unions spill over the categories. The *craft* unions, organising those with a particular skill, are particularly important in printing, engineering, shipbuilding and construction industries. Some unions have been regarded as *craft* unions, although skills are learned through a process of promotion from labourer to skilled worker rather than through an apprenticeship system, and the union may in fact also be an *industrial* one because it covers most workers in an industry. An example is the major steel industry union, the Iron & Steel Trades' Confederation.

400. The nearest to an *industrial* union in Britain is the National Union of Mineworkers, which until a breakaway Union of Democratic Mineworkers was formed in 1985, included the vast majority of the National Coal Board's employees, manual and clerical and some supervisory, although most of the latter belong to a separate union. Others with a claim to the description of 'industrial' include the Union of Communications Workers and the Banking, Insurance and Finance Union.

401. The *general* unions, who organise workers regardless of skill or industry, whatever the job they perform, include the Transport & General Workers' Union and the General Municipal Boilermakers and Allied Trades Union. In some industries these unions organise nearly all the workers in the industry; in some they organise only certain occupations or gradings; in some they cover white-collar employees; in some they compete with other unions. They are spread over nearly all industrial groups. The main production workers' unions, the Amalgamated Engineering Union and the Electrical, Electronic, Telecommunications and Plumbing Union (now merged) are also to be found in nearly every industrial group, including not only the majority of skilled maintenance workers but, increasingly, less well-skilled workers of all grades of skill. Consequently, there is an overlap between the avowedly general unions and these former skilled craft unions. All these large unions are showing increasing interest in technicians and white-collar employees. Indeed, in 1988, the large white-collar union, the Association of Scientific Technical and Managerial Staffs, amalgamated with the technical, administrative and supervisory section of the engineering union (AEUW-TASS) to form the MSF (the Manufacturing Science and Finance Union), which is now one of the largest unions, with 669,000 members. The greatest trend in recent years has been towards multi-industry membership: in 1989, over 4 million members belonged to unions which had multi-industry membership.

§3. Trades Union Congress

402. The Trades Union Congress (TUC), formed in 1868, lacks the power of some central trade union organisations in other countries. Nevertheless, it is almost unique in West Europe as a single trade union federation to which almost all major unions are affiliated. In 1990, there were 76 affiliated organisations, with a total membership of just over 8.4 million workers.[1] The influence and stature of the TUC suffered a major challenge in 1988, when one of the largest and most influential unions, the EETPU, refused to follow TUC guidelines and was expelled.

1. Trades Union Congress *Directory 1991*.

403. The TUC has power under its Constitution to intervene in jurisdictional disputes between affiliated unions. A set of principles for avoidance of inter-union disputes was first laid down by the TUC in 1924 (the Hull Main Principles) and revised at the annual Conference held in 1939 at Bridlington. The so-called 'Bridlington' principles (which have been subsequently revised) advise unions to reach agreement on spheres of influence, recognition of membership of other affiliated bodies, and transfers of members. The Principles prohibit a TUC-affiliated union from commencing organisational activities in any grades of workers in which another TUC union has organised a majority of the workers and negotiates on behalf of those workers. Majority membership may not, however, be required in order to protect a union where organisation has been 'exceptionally difficult'. The Principles also provide that no affiliated union should accept a member of another affiliated union into membership without inquiry. If the reply indicates that he or she is under discipline, or in arrears of subscriptions, or that there is a trade dispute (i.e. industrial action) in progress, the application should not be accepted.

404. The TUC Disputes Committee deals with complaints from affiliated unions concerning alleged breaches of the Bridlington Principles. According to revised TUC rules adopted at the 1976 Annual Conference, a fair hearing must be given. Awards of the Committee are 'binding' on affiliates and a number of sanctions, including suspension of an affiliate, are available to the General Council in cases of refusal to obey. The awards as such are probably not binding in law, because of the general view that the TUC Constitution and the Bridlington Principles are 'not intended to create legal relations.' Nevertheless, legal problems do arise when an affiliated union is required by an award to expel a member who has been recruited contrary to the Bridlington Principles. At common law a union may expel a member so long as the rules permit this. Nearly all affiliated unions now have a rule which states that the Executive Committee may by giving 6 weeks' notice in writing terminate the membership of any member if necessary to comply with a decision of the Disputes Committee of the TUC. This model rule has been strictly construed by the courts. Thus in 1975, the High Court held that if an award of the Committee was *ultra vires*, the model rule did not permit a union to expel members in pursuance of such an award.[1] This in effect gives the court jurisdiction to decide the ambit of the powers of the Disputes Committee, undermining the notion that the Principles are outside the scope of the law. The Principles have been revised on various occasions to limit the court's opportunity to intervene. For example, requirements of natural justice have been made more explicit. In the more recent case of *Cheall* v. *APEX*[2] the House of Lords took a somewhat less restrictive view. It rejected the argument that the Bridlington Principles are contrary to public policy, and held that there was no obligation to permit members who faced expulsion to appear before the Disputes Committee. Nevertheless, Lord Diplock made it clear that different considerations might apply if the effects of the expulsion were to have put a member's job in jeopardy, for example, where a closed shop was in operation. TUC Disputes Committee rulings may also come into conflict with a member's right not to be unreasonably expelled (*see* para.393 *above*).

1. *Rothwell* v. *APEX* [1976] ICR 211.
2. [1983] ICR 188.

404bis. The Bridlington Principles have come under increasing strain during the 1980s, with the arrival in Britain of Japanese and other foreign companies which invited unions to tender for the sole right to represent the workforce (ie enter into single union deals), even where this conflicted with the Bridlington Principles. The Electrical, Electronic, Telecommunications and Plumbing Union (EETPU) was expelled from the TUC in 1988 for refusing to accept Bridlington rulings that it should give up members gained in two single union deals. This union has taken advantage of the fact that it is no longer bound by Bridlington to recruit members of other unions.[1] In its most recent Green Paper, the Government proposes to introduce legislation which would give individuals the legal right not to be excluded from the union of their choice, even if another union had majority representation. This would in effect outlaw the Bridlington procedures.[2] Although the latter are in need of reform, their outright abolition would merely introduce instability.

1. *See* generally *Financial Times* 5 September 1991.
2. *Industrial Relations in the 1990s* Cm 1692, July 1991.

§4. Trade Union Amalgamations

405. Working arrangements between trade unions in order to avoid inter-union disputes, encouraged by the Bridlington Principles, is one way in which the harmful consequences of multi-unionism can be combatted. Another way is through the formation of federations of trade unions in certain industries, such as the Confederation of Shipbuilding & Engineering Unions and the Printing Trades Alliance. These federations handle negotiations in several industries and adopt joint policies. A further form of co-operation in particular industries where Joint Industrial Councils exist (*see* Chapter IV, *below*) is that achieved by the holding of joint meetings and the appointment of a joint secretariat by all the unions which sit on the 'workers' side' of such Councils.

406. Reformers have, however, tried to reduce multi-unionism by amalgamations between unions. The total number of unions has fallen and this process is likely to continue (*see* para. 398, *above*). Amalgamations have played an important role in this. Legislation has existed since 1876 to facilitate amalgamations, and the requirements were eased first in 1917 and then in 1964. The relevant provisions are now found in TULRCA 1992 (ss. 97–106). The Act provides for mergers in two ways, by amalgamation and by transfer of engagements. The first method requires the consent of the majority of those voting in each amalgamating union, while the second method requires a vote only of the members of the transferor union. Certain minimum standards are laid down for the conduct of the ballots so as to ensure that every member has a proper opportunity to vote and that he has full knowledge of the terms. Complaints may be made to the Certification Officer with a right of appeal on questions of law to the Employment Appeal Tribunal.

407. In 1991, for example, eight mergers took place, involving a total of 430,615 members. In the public services, three major unions, the Confederation of Health Service Workers (COHSE), the National and Local Government Officers' Association (NALGO) and the National Union of Public Employees (NUPE) are moving towards one of the biggest mergers ever. The result, if approved by the individual trade unions, will form the largest union in Britain, with over 1.6 million members. The result of amalgamations has not, however, been to simplify union structure. On the contrary it has helped to produce several large unions which cover nearly all industries – such as the Transport & General Workers' Union, the General Municipal Boilermakers and Allied Trades Union, and the Amalgamated Engineering Union, which has now merged with Electrical, Electronic, Telecommunications & Plumbing Union. In the words of Professor Clegg the 'consequence has not been a rationalisation of trade union structure, but increasing complexity.'[1]

1. H.A. Clegg, *The Changing System of Industrial Relations in Great Britain*, London, 1979, p.177.

§5. Definition and Objects of a Trade Union

408. For legal purposes a workers' organisation is a 'trade union' only if it satisfies the definition in section 1 of TULRCA, 1992. This lays down that the organisation (which may be temporary or permanent) must: (1) consist wholly or mainly of workers of one or more descriptions; and (2) be an organisation whose principal purposes include the regulation of relations between workers of that description or those descriptions and employers or employers' associations. It will be seen that although the definition is wide enough to cover an *ad hoc* negotiating committee, the organisation must be directly involved in negotiation with employers: a body whose sole concern is to support strike action or to exert political influence is not a 'trade union'.

409. The definition does not, however, *limit* the purposes of a trade union. A trade union may include in its rule book (constitution) any lawful purposes at all, including political objects. Many unions do in fact include the socialisation of the means of production, or support for the Labour Party, among their objects. In this respect the definition of a 'trade union', when introduced in 1974, cleared up a long-standing controversy as to whether objects other than labour-management relations could be validly pursued by a trade union.

§6. Expenditure on Political Objects

410. There is, however, one limitation on the freedom of trade unions to support political objects. In the *Osborne* case in 1909,[1] the House of Lords decided that it was beyond the powers of a trade union to levy a contribution on members to support the Labour Representation Committee, the forerunner of the Labour Party. The Trade Union Act 1913 effectively overruled this by permitting a trade union to have any lawful objects. At the same time the Act laid down a complicated set of conditions which must be observed before the union may expend funds on political objects. The purpose of these conditions is to protect political dissentients within the union. As part of the restrictive legislative programme of the Conservative Government, the conditions for the maintenance of political funds laid down in the 1913 Act were made substantially more rigorous by the Trade Union Act 1984. Further modifications were introduced by the Employment Act 1988.

1. *Amalgamated Society of Railway Servants* v. *Osborne* [1910] AC 87; *see* generally on this subject K.D. Ewing, *Trade Unions. the Labour Party and the Law*, Edinburgh, 1982.

411. If a union wishes to expend money on 'political objects' as defined by the Act, it must set up a separate fund (the 'political fund') for that purpose. Such a fund may only be set up if a majority of the members of the union vote in favour of the fund in a secret ballot. Prior to 1984, no further ballots were required to maintain the fund. TUA 1984 (now TULRCA 1992, ss. 71–96), however, required the union to win majority support for the continuation of the fund in a ballot held every 10 years. For unions which had a political fund for more than 9 years at the commencement of the Act (31 March 1985), a new ballot had to be conducted within 12 months of that date. The Act also provides for several controls over the operation of the political fund. The Certification Officer (*above* para. 78) must approve the rules governing the fund. In addition, the fund may only be financed by contributions specifically earmarked for political purposes, and it may not go into deficit.

412. If no ballot has been held, or a majority of members has voted against the formation of a political fund, the union cannot spend money on 'political objects' as defined by the Act. Thus the definition of political objects is crucial. This definition, as revised and expanded by the 1984 Act, includes the expenditure of money, directly or indirectly, on 'party political' matters such as contributions towards a political party, or provisions of a service or property for use by that political party, as well as the selection of candidates and the maintenance of holders of political office. In addition, a meeting or conference whose main purpose is the transaction of business in connection with a political party must be funded from the political fund, as must any advertising, literature, film or sound recording whose main purpose is to persuade people to vote or not to vote for a political party or candidate.[1] This last provision has led to fears that a union without a political fund would not be able to conduct campaigns which oppose Government policy even on matters which directly affect its members such as privatisation of State enterprises. Such fears were partially vindicated in *NALGO* v. *Paul and Fraser*.[2] Shortly before the local authority elections of 1987, NALGO, which at the time did not have a political fund, mounted a campaign of leaflets discussing the impact of government cut-backs and privatisation in the public services. The leaflets were distributed in marginal constituencies. Such expenditure was declared unlawful, on the basis that the timing of the campaign demonstrated that its purpose was to persuade people how to exercise their votes. Browne-Wilkinson VC stressed that disapproval of government policy at a time other than an election was not necessarily unlawful. Nevertheless, the line between criticism of government policy and persuasion is thin, and in any case, unions without a political fund cannot campaign against government policy at a time when it would be most effective. As a result, several public sector unions, including NALGO and at least four civil service unions, have voted in favour of establishing political funds.

1. TULRCA 1992, s. 72.
2. [1987] IRLR 413.

413. If a political fund has been approved, union members will usually be charged a political levy, unless they choose to 'contract out'. The Government has thus far refrained from implementing suggestions that members be required to 'contract in' to political subsidies. However, members must be notified of their right to contract out and they are protected against discrimination if they exercise their rights. A complaint of breach of the rules may be made to the Certification Officer with a right of appeal on questions of law to the EAT. In addition, the TUC has issued a Statement of Guidance which encourages trade unions to ensure that no obstacles are placed in the way of members wishing to contract out. Section 86 of TULRCA 1992 requires an employer to ensure that a political contribution is not deducted from the emoluments of a contracted-out worker who has certified that he has notified the union of his or her objection to contributing to the political fund and section 87 gives the worker a right to sue the employer in the county court or sheriff court.

414. Although the statute does not refer to any particular political party, the Labour Party has traditionally been the chief beneficiary of most political funds. Indeed, the Conservative Government expected to weaken the Labour Party by requiring periodic ballots. However, the campaigns preceding the ballots increased political awareness among union members, and all unions with an existing political fund voted by a substantial majority to retain the fund. In addition, a number of unions (eight in 1988 alone) established political funds for the first time. In 1991, there were 52 trade unions with political fund resolutions in force, and total funds at the end of 1990 were £17.3m.[1]

1. Annual Report of the Certification Officer, 1991.

§7. Legal Classifications of Trade Unions

415. A list of trade unions is maintained by the Certification Officer (*see* para. 78). This system of listing is far less intrusive than the previous system of *registration* under the Industrial Relations Act 1971, according to which registration was a pre-condition for the exercise of many collective bargaining rights and carried with it a high degree of control of internal trade union affairs. The Trade Union and Labour Relations Act 1974 abolished registration, and listing is automatically granted to any organisation which is a 'trade union' as defined in the Act, provided it complies with some simple formalities. The main advantages of listing are that a *listed* union may be able to obtain relief from tax on the income from its benefit funds, and it may seek a certificate of independence (next para.). There is a right of appeal on questions of fact and law from the Certification Officer's decision to refuse to list, or his removal from listing, of a trade union.

416. It is crucial for a trade union which is listed to obtain a *certificate of independence* in order to exercise a number of rights or to secure those rights for its members and officials. The certificate is conclusive proof that a trade union is independent. It is needed by a trade union in order to (1) enforce a right to disclosure of information; (2) be consulted in respect of collective redundancies; (3) appoint safety representatives; (4) be consulted about occupational pension schemes; (5) be consulted in respect of transfers of undertaking; (6) obtain funds for ballots from the Certification Officer and (7) to conclude a disciplinary agreement, eligible for exemption by the Secretary of State. In addition, the rights to participate in trade union membership and activities, and to claim time off for trade union activities are reserved to members of independent trade unions. The definition of 'independent trade union' in section 5 of TULRCA 1992 is one which:

'(a) is not under the domination or control of an employer or a group of employers or one or more employer associations;

(b) is not liable to interference by an employer or any such group or association (arising out of the provision of financial or material support or by any other means whatsoever) tending towards such control'. The decision whether or not a trade union falls within this definition is in the sole discretion of the Certification Officer, with a right of appeal on questions of fact or law to the Employment Appeal Tribunal.

417. A special category of organisations enjoying, broadly speaking, the same rights as trade unions are *special register bodies*. Unlike ordinary trade unions these are corporate bodies, that is, either companies registered under the legislation relating to limited liability companies or incorporated by royal charter or letters patent. Such bodies are found mainly in the public services – such as the Royal College of Nursing – and their principal purposes are to maintain professional standards, but they have become involved in recent years to an increasing extent in negotiating terms and conditions of employment with employing authorities, often in competition with ordinary trade unions. In order to protect these bodies, the Industrial Relations Act equated them with trade unions for most purposes. This special position was retained by the TULRA 1974. However, those special register bodies whose *principal* purposes do not include labour-management relations may not be listed or seek a certificate of independence. In the private sector such bodies are of relatively little importance.

§8. Legal Status of Trade Unions

418. Trade unions (with the exception of special register bodies, above) are not corporate bodies. This leads to several difficulties. For example, if a union cannot enter into contracts, who is the party to the contract of membership? How can a trade union be sued? Property ownership in unincorporated associations is complex. To resolve these difficulties, a series of cases invested trade unions with certain attributes of corporate bodies. For example, in the *Taff Vale* case,[1] the House of Lords held that a trade union registered under the Trade Union Act 1871 could be held liable in tort (delict) for the acts of its officials in the course of a strike. Similarly, in the *Osborne* case,[2] the *ultra vires* doctrine was applied to trade unions as quasi-corporate bodies. Parliament intervened in the Trade Disputes Act 1906 to give trade unions a complete immunity from actions in tort (removed from 1971–1974 and again since 1982, *below*, para. 420) and in the Trade Union Act 1913 to override the *Osborne* decision, but neither statute resolved the underlying question of the status of trade unions. Trade unions were given corporate status for the brief currency of the Industrial Relations Act 1971, but this depended on their willingness to submit to registration within the schema of the Act.

1. *Taff Vale Railway Co.* v. *ASRS* [1901] AC 426.
2. *Amalgamated Society of Railway Servants* v. *Osborne* [1910] AC 87 (HL), *above*, para. 410.

419. The present formula, introduced in 1974, restored trade unions to unincorporated status. At the same time, it resolved some of the practical problems which flow from the unincorporated character of trade unions. The 1992 Act provides that (i) trade unions are capable of making contracts; (ii) all the property belonging to a union must be vested in trustees in trust for the union; (iii) trade unions are capable of suing and being sued in their own names; (iv) trade unions are amenable to criminal prosecution in their own names, and (v) judgments, awards, and orders may be enforced against any property held in trust for the union.[1] Nevertheless, some problems remain unresolved. Trade unions are not corporate bodies for the purposes of maintaining a defamation suit,[2] but the doctrine of *ultra vires* applicable to incorporated bodies has been held applicable to trade unions (*see* further para. 430, *below*).[3] Similarly, trade unions have been held to be subject to the rule in *Foss* v. *Harbottle*,[4] by virtue of which only the association, not the individual member can sue for wrongs done to the association or for internal irregularities, unless a member's individual rights have been breached, or the acts done were fraudulent or *ultra vires*.[5]

1. TULRCA 1992, s. 10.
2. *EEPTU* v. *Times Newspapers* [1980] QB 585 (QBD).
3. *Hopkins* v. *National Union of Seamen* [1985] ICR 268 (Ch.D.); *Thomas* v. *National Union of Mineworkers* [1985] 2 All ER 1 (Ch.D.); *Taylor* v. *National Union of Mineworkers* [1985] IRLR 99 (Ch.D.); see Wedderburn (1985) 14 *Industrial Law Journal* 127.
4. (1843) 2 Hare 461.
5. *Cotter* v. *National Union of Seamen* [1929] 2 Ch. 58.

§9. Liability of Trade Unions in Tort

420. For much of the twentieth century, trade unions were given statutory immunity from liability in tort.[1] The immunity enjoyed by trade unions was broader than that afforded to individuals in respect of acts in contemplation or furtherance of a trade dispute (*below*, para. 484). The immunity of trade unions was not confined to specific torts, nor to acts taken in contemplation or furtherance of a trade dispute. Thus liability for torts committed in the course of industrial action attached to the individual organisers rather than the union, although the union generally supported its officials financially in the conduct of the case and the satisfaction of any judgment. One of the most significant changes brought about by the Employment Act 1982 was to remove this immunity, leaving trade unions, like individuals, exposed to tort action unless the more limited immunities in section 13 of TULRA 1974 now TULRCA 1992, s. 219 applied (*below*, para. 485). Further restrictions were imposed by the Trade Union Act 1984, by virtue of which Section 219 immunities would be of no avail to a union which had engaged in industrial action without conforming with the statutory balloting requirements (*below*, para. 493). The Employment Act 1990 introduced yet more stringent provisions. All these provisions have had dramatic implications for labour relations, particularly since they have meant that interlocutory injunctions are available against trade unions. Recent experience has demonstrated an increasing willingness on the part of employers to use legal remedies, both in the form of injunctions and damages.[2]

1. Trade Disputes Act 1906, s. 4, repealed by the Industrial Relations Act 1971. A more limited but still extensive immunity was contained in TULRA 1974, s. 14 (repealed in 1982).
2. Stephen Evans, 'The use of injunctions in Industrial Disputes May 1984–April 1987', *British Journal of Industrial Relations*, Vol. 25 (1987) p. 419. *Labour Research*, Vol. 77, No. 9 (1988), p. 7.

421. Since a trade union can act only through its officials and members, it is necessary to determine in what circumstances trade unions will be held liable for the tortious acts of their officials and members. At common law, a broad concept of trade union liability for actions of its members was established by the House of Lords in the famous case of *Heaton's Transport (St. Helens) Ltd.* v. *TGWU*,[1] where a trade union was held liable for the unofficial acts of shop stewards, on the basis that shop stewards have general authority and discretion to act on the trade union's behalf. The trade union could only escape liability if it had expressly forbidden its members to take particular actions, possibly by disciplining members or withdrawing shop stewards' credentials. This could put trade unions in the difficult position of having to 'police' collective agreements and the law as against its own members'.[2] Instead of relying on common law principles of vicarious liability, however, the legislation of the 1980s established a statutory scheme. Initially, only limited 'official' action sufficed to pin liability on the union. In the Employment Act 1990, this was extended more widely, the argument being that such action was a major component of industrial unrest. Industrial action is taken to have been authorised or endorsed by a trade union if it was called by (a) anyone empowered by the rules to do so; (b) the principal executive committee, the president or general secretary or (c) any other committee of the union constituted by the rules, or any other official, whether employed or not.[3] The union is liable in (b) and (c) even if the rules do not empower these committees or officials to call for industrial action. In the case of unofficial action only, the union may escape liability if the action is repudiated by the president, the general secretary or the principal executive committee. Repudiation provisions are harsh. A union must give written notice of repudiation not only to the committee or official who called the action, but also to every member of the union who the union has reason to believe is or may be participating. This extends even further: such notice must also be given to the employer of participating members, and, on request, to a party to a commercial contract whose performance is or may be interfered with as a result of the call to industrial action. In addition, repudiation may be negatived by subsequent inconsistent behaviour of the union. These provisions raise grave dilemmas for many unions. 'Can any union dependent on localised bargaining and the work of many hundred of lay activists so centralise its control procedures as to prevent all forms of potentially unlawful industrial action without effectively alienating just those lay activists on which it depends?'[4] It should be noted that the statutory formula only applies in relation to the central industrial action torts, namely, inducing breach of contract, intimidation and conspiracy. (*see below*, para. 478–483) The common law concept established in *Heaton's* continues to apply in other cases, such as nuisance or interference with business by unlawful means.

1. [1972] ICR 308, HL.
2. O. Kahn-Freund, 'The Industrial Relations Act 1971 – Some retrospective reflections' (1974) 3 *Industrial Law Journal* 186 at p. 188.
3. TULRCA 1992, s. 20.
4. Michael Terry, 'Annual Review Article 1990' (1991) *British Journal of Industrial Relations* 104 at 109.

422. In order to avoid the risk of bankruptcy, section 22 of TULRCA 1992 limits the amount of damages which may be awarded against a union in a tort action. The maximum in any single proceedings in favour of each plaintiff is £10,000 if the union has less than 5,000 members, £50,000 if it has 5,000 but less than 25,000 members, £125,000 if it has 25,000 but less than 100,000 members and £250,000 if it has 100,000 or more members. The amounts may be varied from time to time. A trade union's provident benefit funds and political fund (if it has one) are protected, as are the private property of the union's trustees, officials and members. But no property is safe, nor are there any limits in respect of the enforcement of fines imposed for contempt of court, i.e. refusal to obey a court order. Nor do the limits on damages include the legal costs which the unsuccessful union is likely to have to pay, and awards of interest need not be confined within the statutory maxima.[1] The possibility of a single strike with a small employer causing severe financial damage to a union is illustrated by the Stockport Messenger action in 1983 against the National Graphical Association as a result of which the union may have lost as much as one-tenth of its assets. The damages against the union were assessed at £131,051 plus interest (which included aggravated and exemplary damages in addition to proved losses).[2] When this was added to the £675,000 fines for contempt of court for non-compliance with an injunction, and legal costs of sequestration, it was estimated in December 1985[3] that the union had lost over £1 million. The NGA was again the subject of a stiff award of damages in 1988, when the court awarded the statutory limit of £250,000, and a further £90,000 in interest.[4]

1. *Boxfoldia Ltd* v. *NGA* [1988] IRLR 383.
2. *Messenger Newspaper Group Ltd* v. *NGA* [1984] IRLR 397.
3. *Financial Times*, 27 December 1985.
4. *Boxfoldia Ltd.* v. *NGA* [1988] IRLR 383.

423. Failure by the union to pay damages or fines for contempt of court exposes the union to the risk of sequestration of its assets, the effect being to deny the union and its officers any control over its funds and premises until the court judgments have been satisfied and the union has 'apologized' to the court or otherwise 'cleared' its contempt. Sequestration has become an increasingly common method of enforcing the law. It has been used, often with devastating effect, in most of the major recent disputes, including those of the miners in 1984–1985,[1] the printworkers who took action against News International at Wapping in 1985, and the seafarers in 1988. In the miners' strike, this was taken a step further. After the sequestration order, it was discovered that most of the union's funds had been moved abroad and the sequestrators could not get hold of them. The court therefore ordered the dispossession of the union's trustees, and their replacement by a court-appointed receiver.[2] This was the first occasion on which a receivership had been imposed on a trade union. Nevertheless, the use of receivership was reinforced and extended by the Employment Act 1988, reflecting the government's hope that the appointment of receivers would be a normal step for a court to take in an industrial dispute. Under the new provisions, a member has the right to complain to the court that union funds have been or are to be used 'unlawfully.'[3] Where trustees apply or propose to apply union funds in contravention of a court order, the court must remove all trustees, unless it is satisfied that there is good reason not to do so. This is not restricted to the trustees of the union against which a court order has been made, but may apply where one union gives financial support to another union which is in contempt.

1. The action against the NUM arose out of breach of the union's rules, below para. 430.
2. *Clarke* v. *Heathfield* [1985] ICR 203, and *see* [1985] ICR 606; Rules of the Supreme Court Order 30, rule 1; Wedderburn, *The Worker and the Law*, (3rd ed.) p. 737, Elias and Ewing, *Trade Union Democracy* (Mansell,1987) pp. 119–132.
3. TULRCA 1992, s. 16.

§10. Trade Union Rules

424. Trade union government in Britain depends in part on what is written down in the formal rules and in part on unwritten but well-understood procedures ('custom and practice'). Rule books differ widely and display varying degrees of precision. Moreover, the courts have recognised that the rules are not the constitution; they are capable of modification by the proof of custom and practice. The TUC, in words which were adopted in a leading case by the House of Lords, has said that: 'Custom and practice may operate either by modifying a union's rules as they operate in practice, or by compensating for the absence of formal rules'.[1]

1. *Heatons Transport (St Helen's) Ltd* v. *TGWU* (1972) ICR 308 (HL).

425. For most of this century, the primary means of regulating trade union rules has been by judge-made common law. In 1971, as part of its general policy of legal regulation, the Industrial Relations Act imposed detailed requirements as to the matters to be specified in trade union rules, a legislative package with which the trade unions refused to co-operate. The mandatory requirements were repealed by the Trade Union and Labour Relations Acts 1974 and 1976, except for detailed rules relating to union accounts and members' superannuation schemes. The return to 'voluntarism' so far as internal trade union affairs were concerned reflected the belief that the needs of the many types of union in Britain were not capable of fitting into a single legislative model. The reform of union rule books advocated by the Donovan Commission was left to voluntary action by the unions themselves. Many unions have improved the scope and precision of their rule books, but the differences between rule books are still enormous. No two unions have the same system of government.

426. Since 1980, little credence has been given to the value of trade union autonomy, and legislation has made significant inroads into the voluntarist approach. In particular, under the guise of instituting a greater measure of 'democracy' into trade unions, detailed legislative requirements have been imposed in a number of important areas. Trade unions are required to hold elections in the prescribed form for certain trade union posts (*below*, para. 431), and to ballot their members before taking industrial action (*below*, para. 493). Periodic ballots are also required to retain the political fund (above para. 411). In addition, a union may not discipline or expel a member who has refused to take industrial action, even if the majority of the members have supported the action in a properly conducted ballot.[1] This last provision constitutes a grave incursion into the ability of trade unions to carry out their functions of protecting their members' collective interests, and contradicts the government's assertions that its true intentions are to promote trade union democracy. Statute also lays down that where a closed shop is in operation, a trade union may not unreasonably expel or exclude a member or applicant for membership (*above* para 393). The rules relating to union accounts[2] and members' superannuation schemes[3] remain in force, but in 1988, two further rights were included. Firstly, members must be given access to the union's accounting records,[4] and secondly, a member of a union has been granted a remedy against trustees of the union who have caused or permitted an unlawful application of the union's property[5] (*see* para. 423 *above*). Finally, there are special legislative rules protecting workers from discrimination by trade unions in respect of their colour, race, nationality, ethnic or national origins,[6] or their sex or marital status.[7]

1. TULRCA 1992, ss. 64–67; *see* generally S. Fredman 'The New Rights: Labour Law and Ideology in the Thatcher Years' (1992) 12 O.J.L.S. 24.
2. TULRCA 1992, s. 28.
3. TULRCA 1992, ss. 38–42.
4. TULRCA 1992, s. 30.
5. TULRCA 1992, s. 16.
6. Race Relations Act 1976, s. 11; EEC Reg. 1612/68, Art. 8.
7. Sex Discrimination Act 1975, s.12.

427. In parallel with the statutory provisions, the judges have developed a set of principles regulating the relationship between individual members and the trade union. This common law control of internal union activities is exercised through the notion that when a worker joins a union he or she becomes a party to a contract of association. This contract is subject to the same general principles as apply to other contracts, with some important modifications. There are four principles specifically applicable to contracts of membership. Firstly, the rules are not to be construed literally or like a statute, but so as to give them a reasonable interpretation which accords with the court's view of what they must have been intended to mean, bearing in mind their authorship, their purpose and the readership to which they are addressed.[1]

1. *Heatons Transport (St. Helens) Ltd.* v. *TGWU* [1972] ICR 398 (HL); *British Actors Equity Association* v. *Goring* [1977] ICR 393 (HL); *Porter* v. *National Union of Journalists* [1980] IRLR 404 (HL).

428. The second principle relevant to a contract of membership is that the rules must be construed, in cases of ambiguity, against those who made them (*contra proferentem*). In particular, a union may not take disciplinary action against its members unless it has the express power to do so under the contract. Where it does have such power, it must act strictly in accordance with its rules: procedural requirements in the rules should be adhered to and decisions may only be taken by the body which has the power to do so under the rules. The courts have taken this further, and introduced a third principle, namely the imposition of axioms of public policy, as interpreted by the judges, to override or supplement the rules where the courts consider this to be justified. In recent years, the analogy has been drawn between union rules and a legislative code drawn up by some members to be imposed on all members, and this has enabled the courts to treat the actions of the organs and officers of a union like those of a governmental agency. Doctrines of administrative law have, in this way, infiltrated into the former contractual analysis of union rules. For example, the courts have insisted that, like administrative authorities, the so-called rules of natural justice must be followed when disciplinary action is taken, even if the rules state the contrary. (Natural justice is similar in concept to the concept of 'due process'. In essence, it means that a person accused of a serious offence must be given a fair hearing before an unbiased body.) Moreover, the administrative law analogy has led the courts to require discretions conferred on officials and committees to be exercised for proper purposes.

429. Finally, the most jealously guarded of the heads of public policy is that unions cannot oust the jurisdiction of the courts as the final arbiters on questions of law. The courts have said that even where there is an express requirement in union rules that internal remedies must be exhausted before a member can take his or her grievance to the court, the court is not bound by such a requirement. In deciding whether or not to intervene the court will consider the nature of the issue. If it is a question of legal interpretation of the rules, the court is likely to intervene even before internal appeals procedures laid down in the union rules have been exhausted.

430. These principles were particularly strictly applied in the miners' strike of 1984–1985, when several trade union members sued the union for breach of the rules in declaring a strike without balloting the members as required by the rules. In several cases, trade union officials were held to be acting *ultra vires* (i.e. beyond their powers), with the result that actions taken in pursuance of the strike, such as the expulsion of members who refused to strike, or the use of union funds for strikers' families, were declared to be unlawful. The court granted injunctions (including mandatory injunctions) requiring the union to desist from the unlawful action. The refusal to comply with such injunctions in turn led to contempt proceedings and sequestration of the union's assets.[1]

1. *Taylor* v. *National Union of Mineworkers (Derbyshire Area)* [1984] IRLR 440; *Taylor* v. *NUM* [1985] IRLR 99; *Hopkins* v. *NUS* [1985] ICR 268; *Thomas* v. *NUM* [1985] IRLR 136 (Ch.D.). *See above*, para. 423.

§11. TRADE UNION ELECTIONS

431. As we have seen, trade unions have, for most of this century, been left to determine their own methods of appointing their officials. There is therefore a wide variety of methods, ranging from direct periodic elections, to life-time appointments to indirect elections via delegates. The Trade Union Act 1984, however, introduced a statutory scheme for electing certain union officials, despite trade union opposition to what was considered an unwarranted incursion into internal affairs. These provisions were later strengthened by the Employment Act 1988. They are now found in TULRCA 1992.

432. The relevant provisions which came into effect on 1 October 1985, require the trade union to hold periodic elections for members of the 'principal executive body', defined as the principal body of the union exercising executive functions. This provision was originally confined to voting members of the principal executive committee. But the Employment Act 1988 extended the obligation to stand for periodic election to a complex network of officers. Most importantly, the Act includes the general secretary and president, even if the rules of the union deny these officers the right to vote on the executive. This gives no scope to unions who regard these officers as senior bureaucrats, employed for their professional expertise rather than their popularity among members. Also included are those who may attend and speak at some or all the committee's meetings, otherwise than to provide factual information or technical or professional advice.[1] There is no requirement that other officials, such as shop stewards or branch officials, be elected. No member of the principal executive body may hold his or her position for more than five years without being re-elected.

1. TULRCA 1992, s. 46.

433. The Act imposes a particular model of democracy on trade unions. First, elections must be *direct*, in that each relevant member must vote directly for the official, rather than electing a delegate who then has the power to cast a block vote for a particular candidate. All members must have an equal vote, but the trade union may define particular constituencies, provided no member is deprived of a vote in all relevant elections. (The union's rulebook may, however exclude unemployed members, members in arrears, and apprentices, trainees, students or new members.) Secondly, voting must be by *secret* ballot, rather than by show of hands, a method which before the Act was used by many unions. Thirdly, the primary method of voting is a *full postal* method, with the trade union being required to send ballot forms and a list of candidates to voters at their home addresses, and votes being returned by post. This slow and costly method (unions are now required to keep an up-to-date register of members) was imposed in preference to voting at workplace or branch meetings on the assumption that voters may be subject to pressure at such meetings. Unions who have traditionally conducted elections at branch or workplace meetings argue in response that it is important to hear the debate before casting a vote. Postal voting was made mandatory by the Employment Act 1988, which repealed the workplace alternative permitted by the 1984 Act. Finally, the voters must not be subject to interference from or constraint imposed by the union, its members or its officials. It is noteworthy that there is no restriction on interference by third parties, such as the employer. Government funds are available to meet the cost of ballots.[1] Initially, the TUC opposed the use by its affiliates of such money. However, in 1985, two important TUC-affiliates (the Amalgamated Engineering Union and the Electrical Electronic Telecommunication and Plumbing Union) breached the boycott by accepting government funds for conducting postal ballots. In a mood of 'new realism' in 1986, the TUC reversed the policy, and large amounts have subsequently been paid out to unions for conducting postal ballots. In 1991, the Certification Officer paid out a total of £4.08m (compared to £2.64m in 1990) in respect of 692 ballots. (The figures include payments in respect of other relevant ballots.)[2]

1. TULRCA 1992, s. 115.
2. Annual Report of the Certification Officer, 1991.

434. There are several other detailed requirements with which trade union elections must comply. Firstly, every member of the union has a *prima facie* right to stand as a candidate free from unreasonable exclusion. The union may exclude a class of members provided all members of the class are so excluded and the class is not determined by reference only to those members which the union chooses to exclude. Nor may the union require a candidate, directly or indirectly to be a member of a political party.[1] This will affect unions which have rules requiring officers, once elected, to be members of the Labour Party, or to attend the Labour Party conference. On the other hand, there is nothing to prevent a union prohibiting membership of a political party; anti-communist rules, such as that of the EETPU, are therefore unaffected. Secondly, the union must provide every candidate in the election with an opportunity of preparing an election address in his or her own words and submitting it to the union for distribution to voters together with the voting paper.[2] This provision is hedged about with extremely detailed requirements. Thirdly, before the election is held, the trade union must appoint a qualified independent person to supervise the election.[3] Finally, every union is required to compile and maintain a register of the names and proper addresses of its members.[4] Although this is subject to reasonable practicability, some unions may face considerable difficulties in fulfilling this requirement. This is particularly true for unions with a large and highly mobile membership. Enforcement of the election provisions is left to individual members of the union. Applications may be made either to the Certification Officer or the High Court for a declaration that the statutory provisions have not been complied with. The EAT has no jurisdiction. If application is made to the High Court, a declaration may be accompanied by an 'enforcement order', requiring the union to remedy the defect, unless it is considered inappropriate. These provisions have not been widely used: in 1991, a mere 2 decisions were issued by the Certification Officer, only one of which was successful.[5]

1. TULRCA 1992, s. 47.
2. TULRCA 1992, s. 48.

3. TULRCA 1992, s. 49.
4. TULRCA 1992, s. 24.
5. TULRCA 1992, ss. 54–56. Annual Report of the Certification Officer 1991.

435. A recent study showed that, prior to the 1984 Act, about 61 per cent of trade unions who were affiliated to the TUC already elected their executives by votes of the whole membership.[1] However, very few used the precise method adopted by the statute, and many unions have had to make extensive rule changes in order to comply with the legislation. Moreover, views differ as to whether periodic direct elections do in fact promote internal democracy, or whether they lead to factionalism, more militant bargaining positions, or disruptive policy changes. Available evidence suggests that postal ballots in elections for executive members have not resulted in fundamental changes to the outcome.[2]

1. R. Undy and R. Martin, *Ballots and Trade Union Democracy*, Oxford, 1984, pp. 105–106.
2. *Labour Research*, May 1990, p. 11. *See* generally S. Fredman 'The New Rights' (1992) O.J.LS 24.

§12. Employers' Associations

436. The legal definition of an 'employers' association' is identical to the definition of a 'trade union' except that the organisation must consist 'wholly or mainly of employers or individual proprietors of one or more description'.[1] The legal status of employers' associations differs from that of trade unions (other than special register bodies), however, because such an association may be either a body corporate or an unincorporated association. If it is unincorporated it possesses the same quasi-corporate attribute as a trade union (*above*, para. 419). An employers' association may have its name listed by the Certification Officer (if it fulfils the statutory definition). Whether or not listed, an employers' association is under the same duties as a trade union in respect of annual returns and accounting records. An employers' association, like a trade union, is no longer immune from actions in tort (*above*, para. 420), but there are no special rules regarding the vicarious liability of employers' associations.

1. TULRCA 1992, s. 122.

437. No general statistics are available regarding the number, size and membership of employers' associations. The Certification Officer reported that 131 associations voluntarily entered the lists in 1991 a further 146 when the Department of Employment suggested that there were 1,350 employers' organisations. The reduction is largely due to the winding-up of a number of small local organisations and the expansion of some nationally- based bodies like the Engineering Employers' Federation, the Building Employers Confederation and the British Printing Industries Federation. There has been particular growth in the private service sector. Some of the larger corporations prefer to remain non-federated, such as Ford, Imperial Chemical Industries (ICI) and the General Electric Company (GEC). It has been estimated that 70 to 75 per cent of employers in most industries among establishments with 50 or more employees belong to organisations.[1] However, the strong movement away from multi-employer industry-level bargaining to single-employer bargaining has meant that since the early 1970s, a substantial number of relatively large firms have withdrawn from employers' associations. The 1984 workplace industrial relations survey found that the use of employers' associations to settle pay and conditions disputes declined substantially in the years 1980–1984.[2] To combat this, employers' associations have attempted to broaden the range of services offered. As well as assisting members in collective bargaining over pay and conditions, the operation of disputes procedures and representation of members before tribunals and other bodies, they have begun to offer a range of advisory and consultancy services.

1. The statistics are taken from K. Sisson, Ch.5 in *Industrial Relations in Britain*, Oxford, 1983, pp. 122–125; and Certification Officer *Annual Report*, 1990; and *see* generally K. Sisson, *The Management of Collective Bargaining: an International Comparison*, Oxford, 1984.
2. N. Millward and M. Stevens *British Workplace Industrial Relations 1980–1984* p.181. *See* generally P. B. Beaumont *Change in Industrial Relations* (Routledge 1990) pp. 77–79.

438. The main national organisation is the Confederation of British Industry (CBI) which was formed in 1965 by the merger of three earlier bodies. It claims to have about 3,500 parent member companies and 4,500 subsidiaries as well as about 185 trade, employer and commercial associations. Since its most influential membership has traditionally been from the manufacturing sector, its capacity to speak for non-manufacturing establishments has been relatively limited. Moreover, the decline in manufacturing due to the recession of the 1980s has resulted in membership losses. The CBI, unlike the more right-wing Institute of Directors, tends to favour industrial relations based on collective bargaining.[1]

1. All figures have been obtained from the CBI. *See* P.B. Beaumont *Change in Industrial Relations* (Routledge 1990), p. 79.

Chapter III. Workers' Participation in the Enterprise

§1. The Concept of 'Workers' Participation'

439. Corporate enterprises in the private sector are, in law, owned and controlled by their shareholders. The result of the 'managerial revolution' has been to concentrate power in the hands of boards of directors of companies, particularly the hands of executive directors. Major decisions are taken by the directors, and as enterprises have become larger and more complex, the effective decisions have been taken by directors of parent or holding companies, sometimes overseas, remote from the working environment. An amendment to the Companies Act in 1980 required directors to have regard to the interests of employees as well as those of their shareholders when performing their duties,[1] but the employees as such cannot enforce this duty because it is owed to the company alone. It is unlikely that the company (acting through the board of directors or a majority of shareholders in general meeting) would seek to initiate legal action, and an employee or trade union with a minority shareholding would face almost insuperable barriers in proving that the directors had not acted '*bona fide* in the interests of the company'. A minor stimulus to directors was given by section 1 of the Employment Act 1982,[2] introduced by Liberal and Social Democratic peers. This requires directors of companies with more than 250 employees to state in their annual reports what they have done over the year to promote employee involvement arrangements. Surveys by the Department of Employment have shown that not all large companies fulfil this requirement; and the most recent survey concludes that about a quarter of companies appear not to be fully responding to the encouragement given by the legislation to review their existing practices.[3] However, there is also an increase in both the number and variety of employee involvement practices reported. In 1988, the most frequently reported practices were share schemes, incentive and bonus arrangements, management line communications and local consultative systems (formal and informal). It is noteworthy that trade unions and staff associations were mentioned as channels of communication or partners in joint decision-making in two-fifths of reports, despite the fact that the legislation envisages forms of participation which do *not* involve trade union channels or collective bargaining.

1. Companies Act 1980, s. 46(1), now Companies Act 1985, s. 309.
2. Now Companies Act 1985, s. 235 and schedule 7 part V.
3. *Employment Gazette* October 1988, 573 at p. 574.

440. The notion that workers' representatives should be involved to a greater extent in the decision-making process has come to be described either as *workers' participation* or *industrial democracy*. The two essential characteristics of developments in this direction in Britain are, first that trade unions have traditionally regarded *collective bargaining* as the primary way to extend collective control by workers of their work situation, and, secondly, that participation has developed without institutional devices of the kind found in some other European countries, such as works councils. Before 1974, there had been no significant attempt to establish forms of worker participation additional to collective bargaining in the private sector. There were a few schemes of 'profit-sharing' or shareholding by workers, a few 'workers' co-operatives' and the 'partnership system' of a large retail organisation. But the participation of workers in the enterprise had grown primarily through the shop steward system and collective bargaining (*see* Chapter IV, *below*). During the 1980s, with the decline in the proportion of the workforce whose pay is determined by collective bargaining (*below* Chapter IV), the question arises whether the centrality of collective bargaining is being overtaken by other structures such as joint consultative committees. Recent research has shown that consultation in some form has become more important over the past two decades. However, increases in consultation have tended to augment rather than displace collective bargaining, with trade unions playing a positive role in consultative structures. A survey conducted in 1990 of over 500 private sector companies found that nearly all managers said that they consulted their employees about some issues. It was striking that managers in workplaces where trade unions were recognised were likely to consult on more issues than those in non-union establishments. Moreover, establishments with foreign ownership tended to consult on a wider range of issues than British owned firms. Although consultation was on a wider range of issues than collective bargaining, this was not usually at the expense of collective bargaining.[1] These findings reinforce those of the 1984 workplace survey, which found that in the period 1980–1984, principal consultative committees engaged in negotiation as well as consultation in just under a third of all cases.[2] At the same time the line between consultation and negotiation was often blurred, and there was a considerable overlap between the two. There are various methods of consultation. The joint consultative committee is the best known. There was a substantial growth of such committees during the 1970s,[3] and although this was not sustained in the early 1980s, in 1984 such committees existed in over a third of work-places surveyed. In the 1990 study, managers reported joint consultative committees in about 40 per cent of workplaces, but they were more common in large workplaces and manufacturing. The 1990 study also found that such committees had grown in importance, meeting more regularly than in the past, and gaining more positive support from managers and employee representatives. Other means of consultation, such as quality circles, were used in a substantial minority of cases. However, there still remain a significant number of workplaces where important issues such as pay are determined neither by collective bargaining, nor by consultation. A 1990 survey of 588 companies found that in the 47 per cent of respondents in whose companies pay was not determined by collective agreement, management normally set wages without recourse to consultation of the work-force.[4]

1. ACAS *Consultation and Communication: The 1990 ACAS Survey* Occasional Paper 49, (1991).
2. N. Millward and M. Stevens *British Workplace Industrial Relations 1980–1984* (1986).
3. W.W. Daniel and N. Millward *Workplace Industrial Relations in Britain* (1983) pp. 129–141.
4. P. Gregg and A. Yates, 'Changes in Wage-setting Arrangements' [1991] *British Journal of Industrial Relations* 361.

441. These forms of participation, as an adjunct to collective bargaining, suffer from the weakness that they are generally confined to the level of the plant or establishment, and so are unable to influence decision-making at the *corporate* level. According to a 1981 survey,[1] almost three-quarters of manufacturing establishments of 50 or more employees are part of a multi-plant enterprise; the larger an establishment is, the less likely it is to be single and independent. Since the 1950s, there has been a striking growth of giant corporations or enterprises, much of it due to mergers and takeovers. The Bullock Report[2] noted that the degree of concentration is greater in British industry than it is elsewhere in Europe or in North America. Institutional shareholding – notably by a small number of financial institutions and pension funds – has become the dominant source of control, and this is likely to continue to grow. Foreign ownership has also increased: about a quarter of the largest companies in Britain are owned by foreign interests. The growth of multidivisional forms of organisations in large enterprises has enhanced the role of relatively few senior managers in each enterprise in developing corporate strategy and controlling subsidiary companies, particularly through budgetary policy. Corporate decisions by these managers about matters such as investment policy, product development, the closure and relocation of plants clearly lie beyond the scope of establishment-level negotiations, which is the predominant form of bargaining in British industry. Where corporate bargaining does take place, for a minority of establishments, the role of shop stewards is restricted and the possibilities of effective collective action are reduced.[3] So whether bargaining takes place at establishment or corporate level, strategic decisions by managers are unlikely to be much influenced by workers' views. With the advent of the European Common Market, this problem is likely to be exacerbated. In the EEC as a whole, as in the UK, there is a high degree of concentration. Eurostat figures show that undertakings with over 500 employees provide 28 per cent of the total number of jobs, although they constitute only 1 per cent of the total number of undertakings.[4] The process of merger and take-over across borders within Europe is likely to accelerate, thus moving the locus of control of large companies away from the country in which many of the workers are employed (*see below* para. 444).

1. W.W. Brown (ed.), *The Changing Contours of British Industrial Relations*, London, 1981, p. 68.
2. Report of the Committee of Inquiry on Industrial Democracy (Chairman: Lord Bullock). Cmnd. 6706, London, 1977, p. 4.
3. Brown *op cit*., pp. 68–69; Purcell and Sisson in *Industrial Relations in Britain* (ed. G.S. Bain), 1983, pp.108–112.
4. European Industrial Relations Review, No. 206, March 1991, p. 13.

§2. Industrial Democracy

442. During the 1970s, a movement towards a wider notion of industrial democracy appeared to be gathering steam.[1] Developments during the 1970s made it clear that collective bargaining on its own could not cope with the ultimate power of management to close down an enterprise, to shift activities to other areas, or to introduce major changes; closer forms of participation were needed. This need was recognised by the TUC, which, in 1974, adopted a policy of pressing for legislative rights to board level representation for organised workers,[2] and given impetus by proposals by the EEC Commission for worker participation in certain contexts (*see below*, para. 443). These developments led the then Labour Government to appoint a committee of inquiry, under the chairmanship of Lord Bullock, which reported in January 1977.[3] The majority made wide ranging proposals for employee representation, proposals which were only partly accepted by the then Labour Government. But the election in 1979 of the Conservative Government which remained in power throughout the 1980s effectively put an end to the possibility of legislative change. Throughout this period, the Government has remained implacably opposed to such legislation.

1. There is a vast literature on the subject. Special mention may be made of Sir Otto Kahn-Freund , 'Industrial Democracy' (1977) 6 *Industrial Law Journal* 65; P Davies and Lord Wedderburn 'The Land of Industrial Democracy' (1977) 6 *Industrial Law Journal* 197, and J. Elliott, *Conflict or Co-operation?* London, 1978.
2. TUC *Industrial Democracy* London 1974, revised 1976.
3. Cmnd. 6706, January 1977.

443. Nevertheless, industrial democracy remains a live issue at European level, and has been so for the past two decades. During the 1970s and 1980s, at least three sets of proposals have emerged from the EEC. In 1975, the Commission of the EEC drafted proposals for harmonising company law, the 'Draft Fifth Directive', including proposals for employee representation on the supervisory boards of all companies with over 500 employees in the EEC. The Draft Directive was renewed in 1983 in amended form. A second Draft Directive, the 'Vredeling' draft,[1] contained proposals on procedures for informing and consulting employees of undertakings with complex structures. Consultation would be obligatory where a decision was taken which was liable to have 'serious consequences for the interests' of employees. Thirdly, a separate set of proposals were put forward in 1970 and 1975 for a 'European Company' or *Societas Europaea*, a new type of legal entity, which included workers' participation as an integral part. However, work on all these proposals was halted during the 1980s, largely because of the hostility of the UK, which was in a position to block all progress by relying on the requirement of unanimity. As a result, the only legislation to emerge on consultation or participation has been in specific and limited areas, such as collective redundancies (*above* paras. 325–328) and transfers of undertakings (*above* paras. 283–287).

1. *Official Journal of the European Communities*, C217, 12 August 1983.

444. Renewed impetus to worker participation was given by the Social Charter adopted in December 1989. The Charter states that the rights to information, consultation and participation should be developed along 'appropriate lines'. In particular, these rights should be implemented 'in due time', especially where changes have major implications for the work force. Examples of such circumstances include technological change, restructuring operations, collective redundancy procedures, and cases in which transfrontier workers are affected by employment policies pursued by their undertaking.[1] In putting the

Charter into operation, the Commission has concentrated on the transnational element. It believes that the completion of the Single European Market in 1992 will increase the numbers of mergers, takeovers and joint ventures across borders, which in turn will mean that frequently the decision-making centre is not situated in the member state in which employees affected are employed. In order to facilitate the development of information and consultation procedures on a European level, the Commission published a Draft Directive in December 1990 on setting up European Works Councils in European-wide companies, in order to consult and inform workers.[2] The Draft Directive covers companies which have a total of at least 1,000 employees and at least two establishments in different member states with at least 100 employees each. Such companies will be required, on request by employees or on the initiative of the central management, to set up a European Works Council (EWC) or equivalent consultation mechanism. The idea is to give as much flexibility as possible to individual companies and employee representatives to negotiate the structure and remit of the consultation mechanism; but certain minimum conditions must be met if there is no agreement on an EWC or if the parties decide against establishing one. For example, there should be at least one employee representative from each relevant member state, and the body should have the right to meet central management at least once a year for information on the organisation's business and prospects. In addition, there should be timely consultation by central management about any management proposal likely to have serious consequences for employees' interests. At present, the Draft Directive is proposed under Article 100 of the Treaty, which requires unanimity. Thus unless the UK's continued hostility can be overcome, this Directive may meet the same fate as its predecessors. The European Parliament, which approved the Directive in July 1991 proposed that the legal base be changed to Article 118A (qualified majority), but the Commission's views on this remain to be seen. In the meantime, there is some evidence that transnational union-management contacts are developing voluntarily.[3]

1. *Community Charter of the Fundamental Social Rights of Workers* Articles, 17–18; *see generally* Lord Wedderburn, *The Social Charter, European Company and Employment Rights* (Institute of Employment Rights, 1989).
2. COM (90) 581 final, *Official Journal* 15 February 1991.
3. Michael Gold and Mark Hall, *Information and Consultation in European Multinational Companies* (1991).

445. Proposals for worker involvement are also contained in the draft European Company Statute Directive, published in August 1989. The draft includes three alternative models of worker participation, applicable to companies which choose to set themselves up on a European basis. These are: (i) workers' representatives may be appointed to between one third and one half of the seats on the management board or a supervisory body; (ii) workers may be represented on a separate body which must be kept informed of key developments every three months at least, and must be consulted before major decisions are taken; or (iii) a different model may be established by collective agreement, provided the same rights to consultation provided in (ii) above are included.

Further clarification is still needed as to the nature of employee representation, particularly, the role of unions, the degree of independence required, and the extent to which employers' refusal to recognise a union is permitted to undermine workers' rights.[1] The chances of adoption of these proposals are better than those of the Works Council Directive, since they have been introduced under the qualified voting provisions of Article 118A. However, the impact of the directive depends on the extent to which companies choose to set themselves up as European entities.

1. Lord Wedderburn, *The Social Charter, European Company and Employment Rights* pp. 60–61.

446. As an alternative to worker participation on a collective level, the Conservative government has favoured employee involvement on an individualised level, in the form of profit-sharing or share-ownership schemes. Although some encouragement for share-ownership schemes was given during the 1970s, these have been given greater impetus in the 1980s. In particular, tax concessions on profit-related pay were introduced in the Finance (No. 2) Act 1987. By September 1990, the Inland Revenue had approved 1,898 schemes, compared with 784 in 1988.[1] Government argues that such schemes should lead to a closer identification of employees with the companies in which they work, as well as permitting employers to adjust pay to reflect the state of the economy, without having to declare too many redundancies. The extent to which such aims can or should be achieved is, however, highly controversial.[2] A recent survey of 147 companies found that the employee participation rate was only 20 per cent. Another survey of 1,063 employees found that 51 per cent were more committed to the company, while as many as 45 per cent said shareholding made no difference.[3] It is worth noting that the proposals for the European Company above include special provision for the negotiation of profit-sharing, but this is to be done collectively, by negotiation, and should not be an alternative to worker participation.

1. *Industrial Relations Review and Report* No. 483, 1991.
2. P.P. Beaumont, *Change in Industrial Relations* pp. 244–246, C. Duncan, 'Why Profit related pay will fail' (1988) *Industrial Relations Journal* 186, G.R. Smith, 'Profit Sharing and employee share ownership in Britain', *Employment Gazette* September 1986, p. 380.
3. *Industrial Relations Review and Report* No. 483 p. 5.

§3. Safety Representatives and Safety Committees

447. There has, however, been one form of institutionalised participation which has survived the cold climate of the 1980s. Before 1975 safety and health issues were generally not regarded as matters of active 'worker participation'. However, the Health and Safety at Work etc. Act 1974, embodying the proposals of the Committee of Inquiry under the chairmanship of Lord Robens,[1] empowered the Secretary of State to make regulations for the election by employees of safety representatives from amongst the employees to represent employees in consultation with employers. The underlying philosophy was that employees and employers have a common interest in a self-regulating system of industrial accident prevention. The Employment Protection Act 1975 amended the 1974 Act by limiting to recognised trade unions the power to appoint safety representatives, so clearly embodying the philosophy of collective bargaining, namely that health and safety should be a matter for *negotiation* between trade union representatives and management. At the same time, the dependence on recognised trade unions means that employers who refuse to recognise unions are permitted to sidestep their obligations under the Act. The regulations (in force since 1 October 1978) empower a recognised trade union to appoint safety representatives from among employees in all cases where one or more employees are employed by an employer by whom it is recognised. The employer must be notified in writing of their appointment before they are entitled to exercise their statutory functions, and to make inspections of the workplace and to be provided with documents and information. Safety representatives are entitled to time off with pay during working hours to perform their statutory functions and to undergo reasonable training. If at least two safety representatives request the employer in writing to establish a safety committee he or she must do so within three months, after consulting with those representatives and with representatives of recognised trade unions whose members work in any workplace in respect of which the committee is to function. The Health and Safety Commission has issued a Code of Practice giving guidance on the establishment and duties of representatives and committees. A breach of the Code is relevant in any proceedings. A contravention of the regulations may result in the issuing of an improvement notice by the Health and Safety Executive, or criminal proceedings giving rise on conviction to a fine, or possibly to an action for civil remedies. In practice it is likely that disputes will usually be resolved through voluntary procedures. The UK provisions are augmented and strengthened by the EEC Directive on workers' representatives' rights to information, consultation and participation about health and safety in the workplace, adopted on 12 June 1989.[2] The thrust of the Directive is to require advance consultation on all safety issues, as well as 'balanced participation' in accordance with laws and practices of the Member States. However, this does not appear to include the right for safety representatives to suspend work unilaterally in the face of grave danger.[3]

1. Cmnd. 5034 (1972).
2. 89/391/EEC.
3. Lord Wedderburn, *The Social Charter, European Company and Employment Rights* p. 39, under the offshore safety (Protection against Victimisation) Act 1992, off-shore oil workers' safety representatives are protected against dismissal or action short of dismissal in pursuing safety functions.

Chapter IV. Collective Bargaining

448. Collective bargaining[1] has been a central feature of British industrial relations throughout the twentieth century. It stands out from most other collective bargaining systems because of the relative absence of legal regulation. Nevertheless, the State has taken a positive role in facilitating collective bargaining: from the end of the First World War until 1979, collective bargaining was actively encouraged by successive governments, both among State employees and in the private sector. Thus, in 1973, as many as 83.2 per cent of full-time manual men and 71.7 per cent of full-time manual women were covered by collective bargaining arrangements. By contrast, the salient feature of the 1980s has been the reversal by the Thatcher Government of the supportive policy towards collective bargaining. A striking example was the abolition in 1987 of well-established collective bargaining machinery for school teachers.[2] Nevertheless, it is remarkable how resilient collective bargaining structures have proved: although the 1980s witnessed some decline in its coverage, it remained an important feature of the industrial relations landscape. In 1985, collective bargaining still covered 70.6 per cent of full-time manual men and 61.9 per cent of full-time manual women.[3] The coverage for full-time non-manual women remained stable, although the decline for their male non-manual counterparts was more marked. A similar pattern emerges in respect of trade union derecognition. A survey conducted in 1990 of 588 companies, primarily in the private sector, found that between 1985 and 1989, 7 per cent of companies discontinued recognition in at least one establishment. Nevertheless, company wide derecognition remained rare, and the researchers concluded that the small shift away from union recognition did not represent a systematic movement towards the rejection of unionism in general.[4]

1. For a definition *see* Introduction, paras. 40 and 41 *above*.
2. Teachers' Pay and Conditions Act 1987, School Teachers' Pay and Conditions Act 1991.
3. P. B. Beaumont, *Change in Industrial Relations* (Routledge, 1990) p. 105. Note that this includes indirect coverage.
4. P. Gregg and A. Yates, 'Changes in Wage-setting Arrangements and Trade Union Presence in the 1980s' (1991) 27 *British Journal of Industrial Relations* 361.

§1. Levels and Extent of Bargaining

449. A further feature of collective bargaining in Britain is its enormous diversity. Thus the extent to which pay is influenced by collective bargaining differs markedly from establishment to establishment and between the public and private sectors and the same is true for the levels at which it takes place. Such diversity makes it difficult to present any clear or comprehensive description, and only a few trends which have been of particular importance to legal and other institutional arrangements can be highlighted.

450. There are various ways in which levels of bargaining can be categorised. Traditionally, a distinction was drawn between *industry-wide* bargaining, *regional or district level* bargaining, and *plant or workplace* bargaining. *Industry – wide* bargaining developed largely after the First World War. It was given its major impetus by the influential Whitley Committee in 1919, which recommended that industry-wide negotiating agreements should be established on a voluntary basis in all major industries. By 1965, such agreements were widespread. *Regional or district* level bargaining was historically most important before the First World War, but is now of relatively small importance. *Plant or workplace* bargaining, by contrast, is increasingly significant. More recently, analysis has tended to focus on whether the bargaining is *multi-employer* or *single employer*;[1] or, in an overlapping categorization, whether it is *national* or *local*.[2] In *multi-employer* bargaining, the most important pay agreement is usually negotiated by an employers' organisation and one or more trade unions, within a permanent body known as a joint industrial council, a conciliation board or a joint committee. These agreements could be national or regional in scope.[3] But national bargaining need not always be multi-employer: in the civil service, for example, national bargaining has been the norm until recently. *Single employer* bargaining can take place either at *plant or establishment* or at *corporate* level. Plant bargaining is likely to involve joint shop steward committees, possibly with the assistance of full time trade union officials. Corporate bargaining is only to be found among multi-establishment enterprises; here the negotiating committee is likely to involve conveners and senior shop stewards from individual establishments together with full-time trade union officials. Depending on the level of bargaining within the corporation, such bargaining could either be national or local.

1. J. Purcell and K. Sisson, in Bain (ed.) *Industrial Relations in Britain* 1983, p. 108.
2. *See* for example ACAS *Annual Report* 1990, p. 9.
3. K. Sisson and W. Brown in Bain (ed.) *Industrial Relations in Britain* 1983, p. 143.

451. The reasons why bargaining takes place at one level rather than another are complex. Multi-employer bargaining at national level is more likely in industries characterised by relatively small firm size, highly competitive product markets, and relatively labour intensive production processes. Such features make this level of bargaining useful to prevent undercutting and to rationalise specialist management functions required for bargaining.[1] In addition, it is perceived that multi-employer bargaining may neutralise the impact of trade unions on the workplace. Single employer bargaining is now more common among the larger establishments. Plant-level bargaining tends to be more common in companies with a number of geographically dispersed plants varying in size, product range and production process. Company level bargaining, on the other hand, is more likely in companies with a small number of plants in a particular area and a high degree of interdependence in production between plants.[2] Ultimately the most important factors in determining the level of bargaining are individual management strategies and tactics.[3] Whatever the reasons, the result is a bewildering diversity. There are national or industry-wide negotiations between employers' associations and trade unions; multi-employer bargaining at regional or district levels; corporate bargaining between a single employer and the recognised trade union or unions, sometimes at group level and sometimes at divisional level; workplace or plant bargaining, and also negotiations at the level of a particular shop or department. These variations have led to much discussion and analysis of the appropriateness of particular levels of bargaining.

1. P. B. Beaumont *op. cit.*, p. 114.
2. *Industrial Relations Review and Report* No. 341, 1985 p. 3.
3. Sisson and Brown *op. cit.*, p. 148.

452. The most important trend during the 1980s was the move away from national bargaining forums.[1] For example, in a highly significant development in 1990, national bargaining on terms and conditions of employment in the engineering industry was terminated. A similar picture has emerged in the newly privatised industries such as bus transport and the water industry.[2] In the public sector in general, national bargaining remains significant but this is being eroded by the antipathy of the Conservative Government to bargaining at this level. The Government has repeatedly advocated the break-up of national bargaining for local authorities. At first this yielded little change, but in 1990 a number of local authorities were reported to have withdrawn from national agreements.[3] The Government is also in the process of fragmenting the Civil Service into semi-autonomous agencies, which may eventually operate their own pay and grading structures outside of the national collective bargaining framework. Similarly in the National Health Service, Government policy is to devolve power to individual hospitals, with power to employ staff on such terms as they think fit.[4] In the non-industrial civil service, while national bargaining is still the norm, this is no longer conducted on a multi-union basis; instead the major unions negotiate individually.[5] Private sector bargaining arrangements are more varied. The 1990 survey showed a distinct move towards decentralisation in private sector bargaining between 1985 and 1989.[6] At the same time, national level bargaining remains of primary importance in industries such as footwear, construction and demolition, and food retailing.

1. ACAS *Annual Report* 1990, p. 9.
2. P. B. Beaumont, *Change in Industrial Relations* (London, 1990) p. 116.
3. ACAS *Annual Report 1990.*
4. *See* generally S. Fredman and G. Morris, *The State as Employer: Is it Unique?* [1990] 19 ILJ 142 at 146, 147.
5. *See* generally S. Fredman and G. Morris, *The State as Employer* (Mansell, 1989), pp. 142–172.
6. P. Gregg and A. Yates, 'Changes in Wage-setting Arrangements and Trade Union Presence in the 1980s' (1991) 27 *British Journal of Industrial Relations* 361.

453. While the trend away from multi-employer bargaining is clear, surveys have yielded conflicting evidence as to the relative importance of plant level bargaining as opposed to bargaining at company level. The most comprehensive evidence comes from the workplace industrial relations surveys of 1980 and 1984, which show that for non-manual workers in the private service sector, at least, company level bargaining was of growing importance between 1980 and

1984, while industry-level bargaining was on the decline. There was a similar movement towards company level bargaining for non-manual workers in the manufacturing sector, but this was generally at the expense of plant level, rather than of industry level bargaining.[1] The 1990 survey showed that between 1985 and 1989, plant or establishment level bargaining increased more than bargaining at any other level.[2]

1. N. Millward and M. Stevens (1986), *British Workplace Industrial Relations 1980–1984*, pp. 232, 238; P. B. Beaumont *op. cit.*, p. 118.
2. P. Gregg and A. Yates *op cit.*

454. The patterns of bargaining over pay, sketched out here, indicate that there have been important changes since the Donovan Commission reported in 1968 on the conflict which they found in the private sector between the formal industry-wide system of collective bargaining and the relatively informal system of workplace bargaining. The Commission said that workplace bargaining had three main characteristics: it was largely informal because of the predominance of unwritten arrangements and custom and practice; it was largely fragmented because individual shop stewards bargained for small work groups; and it was largely autonomous because it fell outside the control of employers' associations and full-time trade union officials. The Commission diagnosed the 'central defect' of British industrial relations as 'the disorder in factory and workshop relations'.[1] This defect was largely responsible for the gap between multi-employer collective agreements and actual earnings, a source of inflation under the pressure of full employment, and the relatively high incidence of unofficial (wildcat) strikes. Their solution was to formalise the informal system, by 'confining industry-wide agreements to matters which they are capable of regulating, providing guidelines for satisfactory company and factory agreements, and where appropriate granting the agreements which follow these guidelines exemption from clauses of the industry-wide agreements'.[2]

1. Report of the Royal Commission on Trade Unions and Employers' Associations, Cmnd. 3623, p.12.
2. *Ibid*, p. 46.

455. Since the late 1960s, there have been a number of major changes. In the words of Sisson and Brown,[1] 'Britain has developed a dual structure of pay bargaining which is in some respects similar to that in North America. In industries with a large number of small establishments, and with relatively low capital requirements and ease of entry, multi-employer bargaining continues to be of primary importance. . . . Elsewhere, and more generally, among the larger establishments, single employer pay bargaining has now become a formal system'. In the 1980s, there have been two further developments in the structure of collective bargaining. The first has been the introduction of *single union* bargaining. This involves a 'package deal' whereby the employer agrees to recognise a single union only, in return for a commitment from the union to refrain from taking industrial action, and to submit to final offer or pendulum arbitration (whereby the arbitrator cannot propose a compromise award, but must choose between the final offer of the employer and the final demand of the union). The number of such deals in Britain is relatively limited (in 1986, about 22 such deals, involving some 5,000 union members, were known to exist[2]). Nevertheless, they have inspired a great deal of controversy, culminating in the expulsion of the EETPU, which has been the major participant in such deals, from the TUC. The second, and more recent innovation has been the move towards *single table* bargaining, whereby an employer permits multi-unionism, but requires all bargaining to take place in the same forum.

1. K. Sisson and W. Brown in *Industrial Relations in Britain* (ed. G. S. Bain) Oxford 1983, pp. 147–148.
2. P. B. Beaumont *op cit* p. 160.

456. The scope of collective bargaining has traditionally been relatively narrow, with the principal subjects being wages and working hours. During the 1970s, the subject range of collective bargaining widened considerably as a result of factors such as health and safety legislation, the increasing incidence of redundancies, the greater role of technology and the emphasis on the shorter working week. This trend was reversed in the 1980s: the 1984 workplace survey showed that the extent of negotiation over non-pay matters declined considerably for both manual and non-manual workers in the years 1980 to 1984.[1] This was particularly marked in the private services sector and for workplace level bargaining. Nevertheless, some important negotiations have recently taken place over hours of work. A further source of joint regulation of non-pay issues takes the form of 'custom and practice' at workplace level. However, this remains largely uncodified and rarely leads to formal agreements, particularly in respect of matters such as discipline. Indeed, in respect of non-pay matters, not a great deal has changed in collective bargaining since the Donovan report. Sisson and Brown[2] comment that 'defining existing practices is often open to a great deal of argument. In these and other cases, then, one or other of the parties may refuse to enter into either a formal or an informal agreement or to recognise custom and practice. Usually, one of the parties seeks to impose a settlement on the other; it is left to the other party to react'. Managements have been reluctant to reach precise agreements on these matters for a variety of reasons including the difficulty of withdrawing concessions, the danger of 'leapfrogging' to further formal concessions and the reduction of flexibility of local management. Formalization also tends to be opposed by shop stewards who believe it would restrict the scope of bargaining and limit their freedom of action, for example, to oppose managerial decisions over discipline and redundancy.[3]

1. Millward and Stevens *op cit* pp. 249–253.
2. Sisson and Brown, *op cit*, p.151.
3. *See* Part I, para. 274, regarding disciplinary and redundancy procedures.

§2. The Role of Shop Stewards

457. Workplace bargaining is largely the responsibility of *shop stewards*. It is not easy to explain the essential character of the British shop steward. He or she is not the same, for example, as the French *délégue du personnel* or the German works council member. At one time it was unusual to describe him or her as an 'official' of the union. But since 1971, the legal definition of an 'official'[1] has included a person, elected or appointed as a representative of union members, who is an employee of the same employer as the members whom he represents. This includes a shop steward, who may go under other names such as (in the printing industry) 'father/mother of the chapel'. The steward is both an employee of the enterprise and also a representative of those other employees who hold union membership. He or she is usually elected by union members at the place of work, and is not appointed by the branch or executive committee of the union. However, in some unions the election must be ratified by a higher union authority than the members at the workplace. The courts have occasionally intervened to protect an elected shop steward whose credentials have not been issued by the union for reasons that are palpably bad, such as that the steward refuses to give an undertaking to follow all instructions of the union.[2] This highlights the 'dual authority' of the steward.[3] He or she is at one and the same time the representative of members at the workplace, which is the basis of the steward's power, and also the representative of the external union. The Conservative government's legislation of the 1980s displayed a similar ambivalence to the nature of the shop-stewards' role. The statutory provisions obliging unions to conduct secret ballots for the election of union officials, do not extend to shop stewards, (*see paras.* 431–435 *supra*). However, the Employment Act 1990 introduced provisions by virtue of which a shop steward who calls on members to take industrial action can thereby make the union liable in tort, even if the union rules do not permit shop stewards to authorise such action, (paras. 420–423 *supra*).

1. Now embodied in TULRCA, 1992, s. 119.
2. *Shotton* v. *Hammond*, *The Times*, 2 December 1976.
3. In *Heaton's Transport Ltd.* v. *TGWU* [1972] ICR 308 (HL) this analysis was used to impose vicarious liability on the union for the acts of stewards: *see* further para. 421, *above*.

458. In most places of work there is likely to be more than one shop steward (the 'shop' is defined by custom and may cover one or more departments in a plant) and a shop stewards' committee with a 'chief steward' or 'convenor' (sometimes full-time) may then exist. Because of the structure of British trade unions (*see* Chapter II above) several unions are likely to have to work together in one office or factory. In these cases the stewards' committee will be multi-union. This has the important consequence that the committees are not easily made responsible to union authority outside the workplace. The shop steward organisation at the workplace is also a far more important link between the member and the union than the trade union branch. In many unions the branch consists of small groups of members from a number of different factories and offices. The branch is therefore separate from the real business of the union at the workplace and it is left to the shop steward organisation to conduct collective bargaining.

459. Shop steward organisations grew considerably in the 1960s and 1970s. In 1961 their number was estimated at 90,000;[1] by 1978 there were thought to be more than 250,000.[2] In the manufacturing industry alone the 1978 Warwick survey suggested a total of 119,000 manual shop stewards (each representing an average of 31 workers) and 37,000 non-manual stewards (each representing on average 22 workers).[3] There was also a substantial growth in private services and in the public sector. One of the most important developments was the growth in the number of full-time stewards. The number in the manufacturing industry probably quadrupled between 1966 and 1976[4] so that they far outnumbered full-time officials employed by the union. This development was accompanied by the growing formalisation of shop steward bargaining, partly as a result of legislative measures such as the encouragement of the closed shop by legislation of the Labour Government (1974–1979) and the establishment of health and safety committees and the election of shop stewards as safety representatives (*see* para. 447, *above*), as well as encouragement by managers who found stewards 'more of a lubricant than an irritant'[5] in the conduct of workplace relations. In the 1980s, the economic recession and the policies of the Conservative Government have put shop steward organisation under great pressure. In some instances, such as British Leyland in 1981–1982, 'tough' managements have moved from plant to corporate bargaining and severely undermined the shop steward movement. Nevertheless, the shop steward system has proved to be considerably more resilient than might have been predicted, given the decline in union membership. Indeed, the total number of shop stewards in the economy as a whole increased from 317,000 in 1980 to 335,000 in 1984.[6]

1. H. Clegg, A. J. Killick, R. Andrews, *Trade Union Officers*, Oxford 1961, p. 153.
2. H. Clegg, *The Changing System of Industrial Relations in Great Britain*, Oxford 1979, pp. 51–53.
3. Brown, *op cit.*, p. 62.
4. *Ibid.*, p. 66
5. W.E.J. McCarthy and S.R. Parker, *Shop Stewards and Workshop Relations*, Royal Commission Research Paper No. 10, London 1968, p. 15.
6. Millward and Stevens *op cit* pp. 79–91, 123–37.

§3. Legal Support for Collective Bargaining

460. In the introduction (paras. 52–54, 60–67) an outline was given of the relatively few legal supports for the essentially voluntarist system of collective bargaining, and of the measures taken by the Conservative Government since 1979 to dismantle even those few statutory props for joint regulation. The repealed measures include: (1) the right to recognition for collective bargaining, first introduced in 1971, and renewed in 1975, removed by the Employment Act 1980; (2) the procedure for the extension of collective agreements, originating in war-time legislation, renewed and extended in Schedule 11 of the Employment Protection Act 1975, also removed by the Employment Act 1980; (3) the Fair Wages Resolution of the House of Commons of 1946, renewing and extending earlier Resolutions since 1891, obliging government contractors to observe terms and conditions not less favourable than those established by collective bargaining, rescinded in 1983; (4) the Road Haulage Wages Act 1938, which established tripartite machinery to fix minimum wages in that industry, repealed by the Employment Act 1980. All that remain are (1) the Wages Councils (discussed in Part I, paras. 205–212, *above*), whose coverage was severely restricted in 1986; (2) the individual employment rights to protect those belonging to unions or participating in trade union activities at the 'appropriate time' (discussed in Chapter I, paras. 376–380, *above*); (3) specific duties to consult workers' representatives over health and safety matters (Chapter III, para. 447, *above*), proposed redundancies (Part I, paras. 325–327) and over proposed transfers of undertakings (Part I, para. 287); and (4) a duty to disclose information for bargaining purposes to recognised trade unions.

461. The only one of these items not so far discussed is the *duty to disclose information*. TULRCA, 1992, ss. 181–185 obliges the employer to disclose information to an independent trade union which he or she has already recognised for collective bargaining. The information must be such that without it the union would be impeded in collective bargaining to a 'material extent' and such that the employer should disclose it in accordance with good industrial relations practice. ACAS has issued a Code containing practical guidance, which suggests that subjects which are not listed in Section 178(2) TULRCA 1992 as subjects of collective bargaining (below para. 466) can nevertheless be relevant so far as disclosure of information is concerned, such as the employer's investment plans, return for capital invested, sales and the state of the order book.

462. The enforcement procedure is complex. An independent trade union may complain to the Central Arbitration Committee (CAC) which must refer the matter to ACAS for conciliation. If this fails, the CAC must make a declaration stating whether it finds the complaint well-founded and setting out its reasons. The employer then has an opportunity to comply, and if he or she does not do so, a further complaint may be presented to the CAC. The CAC again makes a declaration stating whether the complaint is well-founded and giving its reasons. It may also determine a claim by the union regarding the terms and conditions of employment which should be observed by the employer. The award takes effect as a term of the contracts of employment of the individual employees affected. A number of statutory limitations on the duty to make disclosure are set out in Section 182 of TULRCA 1992. These include information disclosed to the employer in confidence, and information the disclosure of which would 'cause substantial injury to the employer's undertaking, for reasons other than its effect on collective bargaining'.

463. In view of the circumscribed nature of the duty to disclose, it is not surprising that relatively little use has been made of this right. Only a trickle of new complaints are brought to the CAC: 11 in 1990 and 15 in 1989. The CAC has always taken the view that the most useful avenue of approach has been to ascertain whether a complaint can be settled voluntarily. Such an approach, the Committee reports, has been very successful. To the end of 1989, the CAC had received 270 disclosure of information complaints, only 22 per cent of which had required a formal decision. The vast majority of the remainder had been withdrawn after a settlement had been reached.[1] In the 1990s, one of the greatest challenges concerns performance related pay, which, because of its individualism, in many respects excludes trade unions from their traditional role in a collective bargaining round. The disclosure provisions might be the union's only hope of retaining a role in monitoring the operation of such pay systems; provided the union can surmount the possible claim of confidentiality.

1. CAC *Annual Reports* 1989 and 1990.

464. In all these cases of a statutory duty to consult or to provide information, the legal obligations are triggered only if the employer has already decided to recognise a trade union or unions. With the repeal in 1980 of the recognition provisions of the Employment Protection Act 1975, the only remaining legal procedure for recognition is the general conciliation power of ACAS[1] (*see* para. 71 above). Recognition occupies a significant proportion of ACAS' collective conciliation caseload: one in 7 cases in 1990 concerned recognition. However, the success rate under this procedure is limited; and in 1990 ACAS acknowledged that when recognition was granted, it was usually limited to exclusive bargaining rights for one union and sometimes amounted only to rights to representation short of bargaining.[2] As mentioned above, (para. 448) in the cold climate of the 1980s, there has been an attrition of union recognition agreements. This severely limits the effectiveness of the remaining statutory consultation and information provisions; indeed, these duties can be evaded simply by the de-recognition of unions. Thus the only remaining UK provision to augment collective bargaining, namely disclosure of information, has proved to be of little practical importance, and can easily be sidestepped.[3] At European level, developments are marginally more encouraging. Adding to the existing duties in respect of redundancies and transfer of undertakings, the European Social Charter declares that workers should have the rights to information, consultation and participation (para. 444 *above*). In respect of collective bargaining, the Charter is more limited, declaring a right to negotiate and conclude collective agreements but only 'under the conditions laid down by national legislation and practice.'[4] The European Commission, in line with the *caveat*, therefore does not propose binding legislation on this topic.

1. TULRCA, 1992, s. 210.
2. ACAS *Annual Report 1990* p20.
3. For proposals on a statutory right of recognition, *see* K. D. Ewing, 'Trade Union Recognition – A Framework for Discussion' [1990] ILJ 209.
4. *Community Charter of the Fundamental Social Rights of Workers* Article 12.

§4. Collective Agreements

465. The view that a collective agreement 'is an industrial peace treaty and at the same time a source of rules for terms and conditions of employment, for the distribution of work and for the stability of jobs' is now widely accepted in Britain, largely due to the influence of Otto Kahn-Freund (*see* para. 36, *above*). This dual social function is not, however, directly reflected in the legal characteristics of collective agreements in Britain. The agreement is usually not a legally enforceable contract between the trade union and employer or employers' association. Nor is it a universally binding legal code. As we have seen, the main legal effect of the collective agreement is as an express or implied or customary term of individual contracts of employment (*above*, para. 149). To the extent that a collective agreement is so incorporated in individual contracts it may be said to have a legislative function, but only if the individual parties expressly or impliedly agree to this. In this section, the effect of the agreement between the collective parties is examined.

1. O. Kahn-Freund, *Labour and the Law*, 3rd ed., p. 154.

466. The law governing the status of collective agreements between the parties now falls into three parts. First, those which fall within the definition of a 'collective agreement' in Section 178 of TULRCA 1992, and made before 1 December 1971 and after 31 July 1974, are conclusively presumed not to have been intended by the parties to be a legally enforceable contract unless the agreement (a) is in writing, and (b) contains a provision which (however expressed) states that the parties intend the agreement to be a legally enforceable contract.[1] It does not inevitably follow that an agreement with such a provision is a contract, because it may still be expressed in language which is too uncertain to be interpreted, or it may be void as in restraint of trade or for some other reason not a contract.[2] In order to fall within the definition of a 'collective agreement' for this purpose, the agreement or 'arrangement' must be made between one or more trade unions and one or more employers or employers' associations. It must relate to one or more of the following matters:

'(a) terms and conditions of employment, or the physical conditions in which any workers are required to work;
(b) engagement or non-engagement, or termination or suspension of employment or the duties of employment, of one or more workers;
(c) allocation of work or the duties of employment as between workers or groups of workers;
(d) matters of discipline;
(e) the membership or non-membership of a trade union on the part of a worker;
(f) facilities for officials or trade unions;
(g) machinery for negotiation or consultation, and other procedures, relating to any of the foregoing matters, including the recognition by employers or employers' associations of the right of a trade union to represent workers in any such negotiations or consultation or in the carrying out of such procedures'.[3]

1. TULRCA, 1992, s. 179.
2. An agreement which is not legally enforceable is not a contract at all: *Monterosso Shipping Co. Ltd.* v. *ITF* [1982] ICR 675, CA.
3. TULRCA, 1992, s. 178(2).

467. Secondly, there are those collective agreements which were made during the period when the Industrial Relations Act 1971 was in force (i.e. 1 December 1971 and 31 July 1974). These are conclusively presumed to be intended to be enforceable as contracts unless containing an express clause to the contrary. Most agreements made during that period in fact contained such a clause, stating that the agreement was not intended to be a legally enforceable contract. (See TULRCA 1992, Sch. 3, para. 5).

468. Thirdly, there are those agreements which are not 'collective agreements' as defined above. For example, an agreement about investment plans or an occupational pension scheme which is not to operate as a term and condition of employment would not be a 'collective agreement' within the legal definition. These agreements are governed by the common law. There is considerable uncertainty about the legal status of such agreements. One view is that they are not contracts because the parties do not 'intent to create legal relations'.[1] Another view is that no general answer can be given to the question of legal enforceability. Some are contracts (e.g. some agreements in the mining industry and boot and shoe trade are expressed in a form that makes it clear that they are contracts). Others are too vague or uncertain to be capable of taking effects as contracts, but may still have a quasi-legislative function.[2]

1. This is the view of O. Kahn-Freund in *The System of Industrial Relations in Great Britain* (ed. A. Flanders and H. A. Clegg) Oxford 1954, pp. 56–58, and was applied to the facts of *Ford Motor Co. Ltd* v. *AEF* [1969] 2 QB 303.
2. This is the view of Paul O'Higgins, *Industrial Relations Review and Report* No. 12 (July 1971), pp. 3–5, and in his contribution to T. Mayer-Maly (ed.) *Kollektivvertrage in Europa*, Munich and Salzburg, 1972, a view shared by the present authors.

469. In its most recent Green Paper, the Government has revived the debate on legal enforceability of collective agreements by proposing that employers and unions be encouraged to consider making such agreements legally enforceable. The presumption would be reversed, so that collective agreements would be presumed to be binding unless otherwise stated.[1] A final point which must be noted about collective agreements in Britain is that the parties are free to include any matter they please in the agreement. The content of the agreement will be entirely within the discretion of the parties with a few exceptions such as the prohibition on racial and sex discrimination.[2] The scope and comprehensiveness of collective agreements varies from industry to industry. (For other features, see above paras. 448–456.)

1. *Industrial Relations in the l990s* Cm 1602 (1991). This proposal now appears to have been shelved.
2. *See* Sex Discrimination Act 1986, s. 6.

Chapter V. Industrial Action

§1. Patterns of Industrial Action

470. The pattern of industrial action in the United Kingdom since 1970 has changed markedly, as can be seen from Table 1.[1] In the 1970s, the annual average number of stoppages was 2,631, as contrasted with annual averages of 1,129 during the 1980s. Figures for 1990 show an even more dramatic decline, with only 630 stoppages in progress, as compared with 701 in 1989. A similar pattern emerges when we consider the number of working days lost through stoppages of work caused by industrial disputes. The annual average for the 1970s of 12.9 million fell to 7.2 million for the 1980s and then plummeted to as little as 1.9 million in 1990.

1. Table and figures in this section are taken from *Employment Gazette* July 1991 p. 379.

Table 1. Stoppages in progress 1970–1990 United Kingdom

Year	Working days lost (thousands)	Working days lost per 1,000 employees*	Workers involved (thousands)	Stoppages
1970	10,980	489	1,801	3,943
1971	13,551	612	1,178	2,263
1972	23,909	1,080	1,734	2,530
1973	7,197	317	1,528	2,902
1974	14,750	647	1,626	2,946
1975	6,012	265	809	2,332
1976	3,284	146	668	2,034
1977	10,142	448	1,166	2,737
1978	9,405	413	1,041	2,498
1979	29,474	1,273	4,608	2,125
1980	11,964	521	834	1,348
1981	4,266	195	1,513	1,344
1982	5,313	248	2,103	1,538
1983	3,754	178	574	1,364
1984	27,135	1,278	1,464	1,221
1985	6,402	299	791	903
1986	1,920	90	720	1,074
1987	3,546	164	887	1,016
1988	3,702	166	790	781
1989	4,128	182	727	701
1990	1,903	83	298	630

* Based on the latest available mid-year (June) estimates of employees in employment.

471. The reasons for such fluctuations are complex, but an important factor has always been the level of unemployment.[1] Thus, the high levels of industrial action in the 1960s and 1970s were closely associated with a low incidence of unemployment and the rise of shopfloor bargaining. The most prominent characteristic of industrial action in the 1960s, in the manufacturing industries at least, was the high incidence of small unofficial strikes (i.e. strikes not ratified by the union executive). The lower levels of industrial action since 1980 reflect in part the steep increase in unemployment rates. On the other hand, recent years have seen the re-emergence of the large official strike, particularly in the public sector, involving hitherto strike-free groups such as civil servants, teachers, health service and local authority workers. Thus a dispute in the nationalised steel industry accounted for 74 per cent of working days lost in 1980; in 1981 one dispute by civil servants contributed 0.9 million days lost; strikes in the National Health Service and by railway workers accounted for 43 per cent of the 5.3 million days lost in 1982; and the miners' strike of 1984 contributed 83 per cent of the total days lost. In 1987, teachers were involved in protracted industrial action, followed in 1988 by a large postal workers strike, and in 1989, by a highly disruptive series of strikes by railway workers, and less visible but equally important action by local government employees. The main cause of action in 1990 was the campaign for a 35 – hour week by engineering unions. It is important to note that figures on strike activity are only partial indicators of industrial action, since increasing use is being made of action short of strikes. A recent survey revealed that less than half of the establishments affected by any type of industrial action were affected by a strike which would have come within the definition used for official records. This is particularly so in local and national government.[2]

1. P. F. Edwards in *Industrial Relations in Britain* (ed. G. S. Bain), London 1983, pp. 209–234.
2. W. W. Daniel and N. Millward, *Workplace Industrial Relations in Britain*, London 1983, p. 292.

472. The pattern of industrial action internationally shows similar trends to those in the UK. Statistics for the 20 countries in the Organisation for Economic Cooperation and Development (OECD) show a general decline in the number of working days lost because of industrial disputes. In the five EEC countries for which data are available (UK, France, Germany, Italy, and the Netherlands) the level of working days lost in 1989 was less than one-third of the average for the 1970s.[1] While comparisons must be made with care, figures show that the United Kingdom tends to occupy a broadly middle ranking position when compared with other OECD countries. The UK average for 1984–1988 was exceeded by Greece, Spain, New Zealand and Finland, but was greater than Austria, Switzerland, Japan, the Netherlands, France and Germany.

1. Figures in this paragraph are taken from *Employment Gazette* December 1990, p. 609.

§2. The Freedom to Strike

473. The law regulating strike action in Britain is extremely complex, and can only be understood in the context of a century of overlapping and conflicting judicial and legislative developments. Although the 'right to strike' was described by a leading British judge in 1942 as being 'an essential element in the principle of collective bargaining',[1] there is no legally guaranteed 'right' of the individual citizen to withdraw his or her labour in combination with others; nor do trade unions have such positive rights. Nor is there a generally applicable legal definition of a 'strike' or 'lock-out' in British legislation: indeed, 'strike' is only defined for the purposes of two specific statutory provisions.[2] Instead, industrial action is regulated by a series of common law wrongs, chiefly in tort and contract, limited and circumscribed by statutory immunities for action 'in contemplation or furtherance of a trade dispute'. The criminal law ceased to be a central regulating force in 1875, but it retains an important role in respect of ordinary criminal actions such as criminal damage or breach of the peace which may take place in the course of industrial action, particularly picketing. This chapter examines the common law liabilities, the scope of the statutory immunities and the law governing picketing.

1. *Crofter Hand Woven Harris Tweed Co.* v. *Veitch* [1942] AC 435 at p. 463.
2. EPCA 1978, Sched. 13 (continuity of employment); TULRCA, 1992, s. 246 (ballot provisions).

474. It is useful to approach the question of whether industrial action is lawful in three stages:

(1) Does the act in question give rise to civil liability at common law?
(2) Is this liability removed by the immunities afforded by section 219 of TULRCA?
(3) Are these immunities in turn withdrawn because (a) the act amounts to unlawful 'secondary action' or (b) where the defendant is a trade union, the balloting provisions have not been complied with; or (c) in the course of unlawful picketing?

It is crucial to note that the withdrawal of the relevant immunity gives rise to civil liability only if the original act is tortious. None of the provisions in (3) above give rise to liability independently of the commission of a tort or other species of civil liability.

§3. Civil Liability

A. Contract and No-strike Agreements

475. An individual who takes part in industrial action almost certainly breaks his or her contract of employment. This is so even if strike notice has been given to the employer, since such notice is not generally construed as equivalent to notice to terminate the contract. At common law, this breach will usually be construed as a repudiation by the employee of the fundamental obligation to work, so entitling the employer summarily to dismiss him or her.[1] Although an attempt was made in one case to avoid this result by creating a legal right to suspend the contract by giving strike notice corresponding in length to the notice required to terminate the employee's contract,[2] this has subsequently been rejected.[3] The employer's remedies against an employee for breach of contract are, however, of limited value in this context. The courts will not grant specific performance of the employment contract, and the measure of damages has been held in the case of a non-production worker to be limited to the cost of finding a replacement for the absent worker.[4] A more effective strategy for employers is to make use of the 'self-help' remedy of withdrawal of wages. This is particularly powerful in cases of industrial action falling short of a total stoppage of work, a form of action which has become more frequent in recent years. Recent case law suggests that if a worker refuses to perform some of his or her contractual obligations, the employer may be entitled to deduct the full amount of pay, even if the worker has conscientiously performed most of his or her duties, provided the employer has made it clear that partial performance is not acceptable.[5]

1. *Simmons* v. *Hoover Ltd.* [1977] ICR 61 (EAT).
2. *Morgan* v. *Fry* [1968] 2 QB 710, CA *per* Lord Denning MR at p. 730.
3. *Simmons* v. *Hoover* Ltd. [1977] ICR 61 at pp. 70–77.
4. *National Coal Board* v. *Galley* [1958] 1 WLR 16.
5. *Miles* v. *Wakefield* [1987] IRLR 193; *Wiluszynski* v. *London Borough of Tower Hamlets* [1989] ICR 493.

476. It will be recalled that collective agreements are not legally binding unless the contrary is stated in writing.[1] Thus no action lies for breach of a peace (or 'no-strike') obligation in such an agreement unless the parties to the collective agreement expressly agree that this is to be the case and this is unusual. It is highly unusual for trade unions in Britain to conclude legally binding "no-strike" agreements. Agreements restricting strikes have been on the increase in recent years, negotiated mainly by the EETPU, and have led to fierce debate within the trade union movement. However, such agreements very rarely have legal effect. A 'no-strike' clause in the collective agreement will be incorporated in individual contracts of employment only if five conditions are satisfied. These are laid down by TULRCA 1992, s. 180 as follows: (a) the collective agreement must be in writing; (b) it must contain a provision expressly stating that such terms shall or may be incorporated into the individual contracts; (c) it must be reasonably accessible at the workplace and available during working hours; (d) each trade union party to the collective agreement must be independent; and (e) the relevant individual contract must expressly or impliedly incorporate such terms into the contract. The fifth condition is particularly important because it means that the 'translation' problem (*see above*, Part I, para. 153) must, in each case, be answered affirmatively before the term may be incorporated. The employer cannot contract out of these provisions either with the union or the individual worker. The provisions apply to any terms of a collective agreement which prohibit or restrict the right of workers to engage in a strike or other industrial action or have the effect of prohibiting or restricting that right.

1. TULRCA, 1992, s. 179, *see above*, para. 466.

B. Loss of Statutory Rights

477. In general an employee may not complain of unfair dismissal if he or she is dismissed while participating in a strike or any other industrial action. Since 1990, a distinction has been drawn between 'official' and 'unofficial' action, where action is only official if it has been authorised or endorsed by a trade union which has members participating. An employee dismissed in the course of official action will regain the right to complain of unfair dismissal if some or all the other participants are not dismissed or are allowed to return to work within three months of the dismissal.[1] In such a case, the tribunal determines the merits of the dismissal in the ordinary way (*above* Part I, para. 305). There is no claim if some of the relevant employees are reinstated after three months. However, where the action is unofficial, there is no right to complain of unfair dismissal in any circumstances.[2] This means that an employer can selectively dismiss any employee, and for any reason, provided he or she is participating in industrial action. Whether 'industrial action' has taken place is a question of fact for the industrial tribunal to decide; it probably extends even to a refusal to work by employees who believe that their health and safety are at risk. Nor are any employees entitled to redundancy payments if dismissed while undertaking any industrial action which puts them in breach of their contracts of employment, unless redundancy notice was given before the industrial action began.[3] Similarly, an employee is not entitled to a guarantee payment if the failure to provide work is due to a strike, lockout or other industrial action involving any employee of his employer or an associated employer.[4]

1. EPCA 1978, s. 62, as amended by EA 1982.
2. EPCA 1978, s. 62A, inserted by EA 1990, s. 9.
3. EPCA 1978, s. 81(2), s. 92; *Simmons* v. *Hoover* [1977] ICR 61 (EAT)
4. EPCA 1978, s. 13(3).

C. Tort

478. There are five main torts which have been developed by the judiciary with specific relevance to industrial action. Since each of these effectively removes the freedom of workers to withdraw their labour collectively, Parliament, in pursuit of the policy of tolerating industrial action has responded periodically by creating negative 'immunities' for those who commit certain specified torts 'in contemplation or furtherance of a trade dispute'. These immunities have been narrowed significantly in the 1980s, thus exposing trade unions and their officers to civil liability. In particular there is the possibility of an injunction being obtained against the organisers of industrial action, including (since 1982) the trade union itself (*see* para. 420, *above*). Each of the main torts will be considered, followed by a description of the scope of the immunities, and the use of injunctions in disputes.

479. (i) Civil conspiracy to injure. Conspiracy ceased to be of importance in trade disputes as a criminal offence after 1875 in situations where the act would not have been punishable if done by an individual,[1] and the common law crime of conspiracy was abolished (with a few exceptions not relevant here) in 1977.[2] However, civil conspiracy to injure (or 'simple' conspiracy) was developed as a major weapon against union organisers between 1901 and 1906. This tort consists of a combination of two or more persons whose predominant purpose is to inflict damage on the plaintiff rather than to serve their own *bona fide* and legitimate interests. In the early cases, trade union objectives, such as the closed shop, were not regarded as legitimate,[3] and this is why the Trade Disputes Act 1906 enacted an immunity in respect of 'simple' conspiracy in 'trade disputes' (para. 485, *below*). However, by 1942 the House of Lords had come to recognise the legitimacy of at least some trade union objectives,[4] and later others, such as opposition to a colour bar, were also held to excuse combinations.[5] Accordingly, this tort ceased to have much practical relevance.[6] In 1981, the House of Lords recognised that the tort was 'highly anomalous' but felt that it was too well-established to be discarded.[7]

1. TULRCA, 1992, ss. 242–243.
2. Criminal Law Act 1977, s. 5. This Act created a new offence of conspiracy to commit an offence, but an agreement to commit a summary offence not punishable by imprisonment in contemplation or furtherance of a trade dispute is excluded from the scope of this offence. This overcomes the main criticism of the *Shrewsbury pickets* case (*R* v. *Jones* [1974] ICR 310) decided under the old law, in which sentences of up to 3 years' imprisonment were imposed on the organisers of 'flying pickets' for conspiracy to intimidate, a substantive offence with a maximum penalty of a fine of £20 or up to 3 months' imprisonment.
3. *Quinn* v. *Leathem* [1901] AC 495, HL.
4. *Crofter Hand Woven Harris Tweed Co.* v. *Veitch* [1942] AC 435, HL.
5. *Scala Ballroom (Wolverhampton) Ltd.* v. *Ratcliffe* [1958] 3 All ER 220, CA.
6. But *see Huntley* v. *Thornton* [1957] 1 All ER 235, where district officers of a union were held liable for victimising an individual who had failed to participate in an unofficial strike.
7. *Lonrho Ltd.* v. *Shell Petroleum Co. Ltd.* [1982] AC 173, 188–189.

480. (ii) Civil conspiracy to commit an unlawful act or use unlawful means. Where an act is itself a tort, then a combination by two or more persons to do that act is a tortious conspiracy. Some confusion over the scope of this tort was created in 1981, when the House of Lords appeared to have suggested that the tort was only committed if the combiners' predominant purpose was to injure the plaintiff,[1] thus equating this tort with its anomalous 'lawful means' counterpart. However, a recent House of Lords case has clarified the situation by holding that, where unlawful means are used, it is sufficient for the conspirators to evince an intention to injure the plaintiff even if this is not the predominant propose.[2] The fact that the predominant purpose is to further the defendant's own legitimate self-interest is no defence where unlawful means are used. While this may be logical outside of industrial relations, for workers taking industrial action, it represents yet wider liability. In most industrial action, the predominant intention will be to further workers' interests, but this could not be achieved without intending to damage the interests of the employer. This is mitigated somewhat by the fact that the means will not be unlawful if protected by a statutory immunity (below para. 485). The allegation of conspiracy makes it possible to impose liability on a person who cannot personally commit the tort in question: for example, a union official who supports employees who threaten to break their contracts of employment.[3] The allegation may also make it easier to obtain exemplary and aggravated damages. What is unclear about this tort is whether it extends beyond combinations to commit a tort.[4] An unresolved issue is whether there can be an actionable conspiracy to break contracts, for example by two or more workers walking off the job.[5] As will be seen below, there is no immunity in respect of such a combination.

1. *Lonrho Ltd.* v *Shell Petroleum Co Ltd* [1982] AC 173 (HL), applied in *Metall und Rohstoff* v. *Donaldson* [1989]3 All ER 14 (CA).
2. *Lonrho plc* v. *Fayed* [1991]3 All ER 303 HL.
3. As in *Rookes* v. *Barnard* [1964] AC 1129, HL.
4. In the *Lonrho* case, the House of Lords held that there cannot be liability to commit criminal acts which did not also constitute torts; *see* too *RCA Corpn.* v. *Pollard* [1983] Ch. 135.
5. A point left open in *Rookes* v. *Barnard* (above).

481. (iii) Inducing a breach or interfering with performance of a contract. If A intentionally induces B to breach a contract between B and C, A may be liable in tort to C.[1] This tort may take place *directly*, for example where A persuades B not to fulfil the contract, or *indirectly*, as where A persuades B's employees to prevent B from fulfilling the contract.[2] *Direct* inducement gives rise to liability in tort even if the act of inducement is itself *lawful*, whereas *indirect* inducement (or procurement) is tortious only if *unlawful* means are used. As we have seen, in most cases, employees who take part in industrial action are in breach of contract. Thus the organisers of such action will generally be liable for directly inducing breach of the contract of employment. Moreover, if the employer is thereby disabled from fulfilling commercial contracts, the organisers may be liable for indirectly procuring breach of the commercial contracts, provided unlawful means are used. This last criterion will be fulfilled in most cases, since the means of procuring the breach of commercial contracts will be the unlawful act of inducing breach of the employment contracts of individual workers. Thus, apart from the statutory immunities, the effect of this tort is to undermine the freedom to organise industrial action. This is further compounded by the more recent extension of the tort to include interference with a contract short of breach, for example, preventing performance in cases where a contract contains a *force majeure* clause, exempting a party in breach from liability to pay damages.[3] So it seems that there can be liability for direct or indirect interference even without any actual *breach* of contract.

1. *Lumley* v. *Gye* [1853] 2 E&B 216; *South Wales Miners' Federation* v. *Glamorgan Coal Company Ltd.* [1905] AC 239.
2. *D.C. Thomson* v. *Deakin* [1952] Ch. 646.
3. *Torquay Hotel Co. Ltd.* v. *Cousins* [1969] 2 Ch. 106, CA *per* Lord Denning, approved in *Merkur Island Shipping Co. Ltd.* v. *Laughton* [1983] 2 AC 570, HL, which applies this as well to *indirect* interference. See also *Falconer* v. *ASLEF and NUR* [1986] IRLR 331.

482. (iv) Intimidation. This tort was developed by the House of Lords in 1964 to deal with a situation in which two shop stewards and a full-time union official threatened an employer with a strike, so causing the employer lawfully to terminate the contract of employment of a non-unionist who brought an action for damages against them.[1] It had been conceded, unusually, that a 'no-strike' clause in a collective agreement was incorporated as a term in the shop stewards' contracts of employment. It was the threat to break their own contracts which constituted the tort of intimidation. Generalising, it appears that the tort is committed where A threatens B that he will use means which are unlawful as against B with the intention of causing B to do or refrain from doing something he is at liberty to do, so causing damage either to himself (two-party intimidation) or to C (three-party intimidation). There was some attempt after 1964 to cut down the tort to threats of breach of contract which were not minor ones (e.g. an incorporated no-strike clause),[2] but its potential as a weapon in the hands of employers or third parties against *threats* of strike action, an everyday part of the collective bargaining process, are obvious. In 1982, the House of Lords applied the related doctrine of *economic duress* to an industrial action situation. Under this tort, money paid out under an agreement can be recovered on the basis that the agreement was entered into as a result of illegitimate pressure.[3] This is potentially a very wide cause of action, since most industrial action consists of coercive pressure. It enabled the owners of a ship flying a 'flag of convenience' to recover from the International Transport Workers' Federation payments which they had agreed, under threat of blacking, to make of back pay to the crew and a contribution to the ITF's welfare fund. In deciding whether pressure is legitimate, the courts will be guided by the existing scope of industrial action immunities, even where these are not directly applicable. It is likely that facts which constitute intimidation may also amount to economic duress. Duress may be even wider than intimidation covering a threat of coercive lawful action, or an *implied* threat not to perform a contract.

1. *Rookes* v. *Barnard* [1964] AC 1127, HL.
2. *Morgan* v. *Fry* [1968] 2 QB 710 *per* Russell LJ.
3. *Universe Tankships Inc of Monrovia* v. *ITF* [1983] AC 366; *Dimskal Shipping Co SA* v. *International Transport Workers Federation* [1992] IRLR 78 (H.L.).

483. (v) Interference with trade by unlawful means. This tort is committed where A intentionally uses unlawful means with the purpose and effect of causing damage to B in his or her trade or business. This category of interference by unlawful means is a 'genus' tort wide enough to cover (iii) indirect interference with contract and (iv) intimidation above, but it is of wider and more uncertain scope. One of the main uncertainties is the meaning given to 'unlawful means' for purposes of this tort. It seems that breach of a criminal statute would be sufficient only if the breach in itself could give rise to liability in tort.[1] For example, breach of local byelaws regarding demonstrations would be insufficient.[2] However, the torts of nuisance (e.g. blocking the entrance to the employer's site) or defamation (e.g. by words on placards) would be unlawful means. A threat to induce employees to breach their contracts of employment by going on strike would be unlawful means.[3] A recent case went further still, holding that it was arguable that a breach of contract of employment *per se* would be sufficient.[4] In such a case, liability would rest on striking employees themselves, even if the organisers of the action were protected by statute.[5] Equally important, particularly for public service workers, is the possibility that inducing breach of or interference with a statutory duty could amount to unlawful means for the purposes of this tort.[6] This is limited somewhat by the requirement that the statutory duty in question be independently actionable by the plaintiff.[7] Nevertheless, the scope for judicial extension of liability under this 'genus' tort is seemingly endless. The tort has also been significantly widened by the recent finding that there is no need to show that the defendant's predominant purpose was to injure the plaintiff rather than to pursue his or her own legitimate self-interest.[8]

1. *Lonrho Ltd.* v. *Shell Petroleum Co. Ltd.* [1982] AC 173, HL.
2. *Cf. Camellia Tanker Ltd.* v. *ITF* [1976] ICR 274.
3. *Hadmor Productions Ltd.* v. *Hamilton* [1983] 1 AC 191.
4. *Barratts & Baird* v. *IPCS* [1987] IRLR 3
5. No injunction could, however, be granted, since this would amount to specific performance of a contract of employment.
6. *Meade* v. *Haringey London Borough Council* [1979] ICR 494; *Barrats & Baird* v. *IPCS* (*supra*), *Associated Port Employers* v. *TGWU* [1989] IRLR 305, 399.
7. *Lonrho* v. *Shell* (*supra*).
8. *Lonhro plc* v. *Fayed* [1989] 2 All ER 65. Cf *Barratts & Baird* v. *IPCS* (*supra*).

§4. The 'Trade Disputes' Immunity

484. Until the beginning of the 1980s, the legislature responded to the judicial extensions of liability in tort for those who act in contemplation or furtherance of a trade dispute. The earliest was the Trade Disputes Act 1906 which gave immunity from action for civil conspiracy to injure and inducing breach of the contract of employment. This was supplemented in 1965, in the wake of the decision in *Rookes* v. *Barnard*[1] establishing the tort of intimidation (*above*, para. 482). The immunities were repealed during the currency of the 1971 Industrial Relations Act, and then reinstated and strengthened in the Trade Union and Labour Relations Act 1974 as amended in 1976. Since 1980, successive enactments have severely limited the applicability of the immunities.

1. [1964] AC 1129, HL.

485. The immunities are now contained in TULRCA 1992, s. 219 (formerly TULRA 1974, s. 13) which reads:

'(1) An act done by a person in contemplation or furtherance of a trade dispute shall not be actionable in tort on the ground only (a) that it induces another person to break a contract or interferes or induces any other person to interfere with its performance or (b) that it consists in his threatening that a contract (whether one to which he is a party or not) will be broken or its performance interfered with, or that he will induce another person to break a contract or interfere with its performance . . .

(2) An agreement by two or more persons to do or procure the doing of any act in contemplation or furtherance of a trade dispute shall not be actionable in tort if the act is one to which, if done without such agreement or combination, would not be actionable in tort'

It will be noted that the immunity does not extend to torts such as defamation or nuisance or breach of statutory duty.[1] Even more important is the fact that there is no immunity for the expanding tort of interference with business by unlawful means. This has allowed ingenious employers to begin proceedings for interlocutory injunctions on the basis of a wide variety of novel torts.[2] The scope of the tort is limited, however, by the principle that an act which is immune by virtue of section 219 may not constitute 'unlawful means' for the tort of interference with business by unlawful means.[3]

1. *Mersey Dock and Harbour Co.* v. *Verrinder* [1982] IRLR 152.
2. *See* for example *Falconer* v. *NUR and ASLEF*, *Baratts & Baird* v. *IPCS*, *Associated British Ports* v. *TGWU* [1989] IRLR 305 (CA), [1989] IRLR 399 (HL).
3. *Hadmor Productions Ltd* v. *Hamilton* [1982] ICR 114 (HL).

486. The scope of the freedom to organise industrial action is thus delimited by what Wedderburn dubbed the 'golden formula'.[1] 'Trade dispute' is defined by TULRCA 1992, s. 244. It is defined by reference to (i) the parties; (ii) the subject matter. In addition, section 219 of the 1992 Act requires that the action be in 'contemplation or furtherance' of the trade dispute. The elements of this formula are examined below.

(1) *The parties*. The 'golden formula' only includes disputes 'between workers and their employer'. It thus excludes industrial action in protest against government action, except where the government is the employer, or has a statutory power to control the settlement of the matters at issue, or is represented on the bargaining committee which is considering the issues.[2] However, in modern industrial society, governments are so closely involved in the economy that the line is often difficult to draw. As Kahn-Freund put it in 1954: 'The level of wages depends today only partly and perhaps only to a minor extent on decisions of private employers. In all sorts of ways it depends on governmental policies . . . How then can anyone . . . determine how far any strike is intended primarily to induce the employers to pay wages of a certain amount or the government to change its policy?'[3] Since 1982 the formula has excluded disputes between workers and other workers, such as demarcation or inter-union disputes. Also excluded are cases where the employer's own workers are not in dispute, for example, where an employer is picketed or blacked for employing non-union labour or low-paid foreign workers, where the latter themselves are not parties to the dispute.[4] It should be noted that this does not exclude all action taken by one group of workers in support of another group ('secondary' action). Whether or not secondary action is lawful depends on separate provisions (para. 490).

1. K.W. Wedderburn, *The Worker and the Law*, Harmondsworth 1965, p.222.
2. TULRCA 1992, s. 244(2).
3. O. Kahn-Freund 'Legal Framework' in A. Flanders and H.A. Clegg (eds.), *The System of Industrial Relations in Great Britain*, Oxford 1954, p. 127.
4. *Midland Cold Storage* v. *Turner* [1972] ICR 230; *Star Sea Transport Corporation of Monrovia* v. *Slater* [1978] IRLR 507; *NWL* v. *Woods* [1979] 1 WLR 1294, HL.

487. (2) *The subject matter.* Section 244(1) of TULRCA 1992 provides that the dispute should relate wholly or mainly to one of the subjects listed in that section. The phrase 'wholly or mainly' was inserted by the Employment Act 1982 in substitution for the phrase 'connected with'. The new phrase has been interpreted to mean 'predominantly about'[1] and will exclude disputes which, although connected with workers' fears for their jobs or their terms and conditions, are 'predominantly about' a subject not listed in Section 244(1), which is set out *above*, para. 466.

1. *Mercury Communications Ltd* v. *Scott Garner* (1984) ICR 74 CA.

488. Disputes which relate wholly or mainly to political or non-industrial subject-matter are thus excluded. For example, industrial action taken by a trade union in protest against apartheid in South Africa was held to be excluded from the definition.[1] Again, the line between a dispute about workers' terms and conditions and a political dispute is not always easy to draw. Thus a day of action taken by a trade union in protest against Government economic policies[2] or industrial action taken by a trade union opposed to the Government's plans to privatise their employer[3] have been held to fall outside the definition of a trade dispute. Since 1982, disputes concerning matters occurring outside the United Kingdom are only protected if the workers taking industrial action are likely to be affected in respect of one or more of the matters specified in Section 244(1) of the TULRCA 1992 (*above*, para. 466) by the outcome of that dispute.[4]

1. *BBC* v. *Hearn* [1977] ICR 685, AC.
2. *Express Newspapers Ltd.* v. *McShane* [1980] IRLR 247.
3. *Mercury Communications Ltd.* v. *Scott-Garner* [1984] ICR 74, CA.
4. TULRCA 1992, s 244(3). *See* para. 106 *above*.

489. (3) *'Contemplation or furtherance'*. Since 1906, the test of whether an act was done 'in contemplation or furtherance' of a trade dispute has generally been regarded as a subjective one turning upon the *bona fide* purpose of the person doing the act. However, dislike of the consequences of the widening of the statutory immunities by the Trade Union and Labour Relations Acts 1974–1976 led the Court of Appeal, between 1977 and 1979, to seek to add an objective element to this test in a variety of forms such as whether the act was too remote from the dispute to be protected, whether the act would help one side or another in a 'practical' way and whether the act was reasonably capable or had a reasonable prospect of achieving the honestly held objective of the person acting. These limitations were overruled by the House of Lords in a trilogy of cases[1] and the traditional subjective test was reasserted. Although the 'trade dispute' itself must exist or be imminent as an objective fact, 'contemplation' and 'furtherance' refer to states of mind and so long as the person acting honestly thought at the time that he or she might help one of the parties to a trade dispute to achieve their objectives and did it for that reason, he or she is protected. This subjective test was not altered by the Employment Acts of 1980 and 1982. Instead, its wider implications for the lawfulness of 'secondary' or 'tertiary' picketing or boycotts were limited by specific restrictions on such action. These limitations are dealt with below.

1. *NWL* v. *Woods* [1979] ICR 897; *Express Newspapers Ltd.* v. *McShane* [1980] ICR 42; *Duport Steels Ltd.* v. *Sirs* [1980] ICR 161.

§5. Restrictions on the Trade Disputes Immunity

A. Secondary Action

490. A central policy of the legislation since 1980 has been to restrict the extent to which industrial action is permitted to expand beyond the establishment concerned. There is a long tradition in Britain of 'secondary action', or action taken by workers not employed by the employer in dispute (the 'primary' employer) in support of those who are directly affected. For example, workers not employed by the primary employer may refuse to deliver raw materials to or to handle goods produced by that employer. The aim of such action is to increase the pressure on the primary employer or, where that employer is being supported by the government, to disrupt economic life more generally in order to force government concessions. The Conservative Government has always been hostile to secondary action, but in line with its step by step approach to restrictive labour legislation, it did not initially remove all protection from such action. Instead, secondary action was subject to a complex set of restrictions permitting such action only against direct customers or suppliers of the employer in dispute, associated employers to which work was diverted and lawful pickets.[1] The technical nature of this definition left wide loopholes, which were exploited by employers. Notoriously, newspaper magnate Rupert Murdoch, who had dismissed his unionised workforce in an attempt to break the union, set up nominal "buffer companies" between the primary company and suppliers or customers, thus rendering any effective secondary action unlawful. In 1990, the Government legislated to remove even the limited remaining area of lawful secondary action, with a narrow exception for picketing. Thus the Employment Act 1990 removed immunity from liability in respect of the torts in paragraphs 481 and 482 above (inducing breach of contract and intimidation) whenever there has been unlawful secondary action.[2] Secondary action occurs where the employer party to the relevant contract of employment is not party to the dispute. For example, if employees of company A are in dispute with A, and their union induces employees of company B to break their contracts of employment with B, then unlawful secondary action has occurred and the union will lose its immunity from action in tort. The 1990 Act extended the previous law in three further ways. Firstly, secondary action occurs even if the action by B's workers does not lead to a breach of or interference with a commercial contract to which B is party. This means that simple demonstrations of support, such as extended lunch hour meetings, are caught by the definition. Secondly, an employer may not be treated as party to a dispute between another employer and its workers; and where more than one employer is in dispute, the dispute between each employer and its workers is treated as a separate dispute. The effect of this is to make national industrial action impossible unless a dispute with each individual employer can be shown. It is no longer possible to take action against an employer who belongs to an employers' association merely because the association is in dispute with a union or confederation of unions. However, if employees of B are genuinely in dispute with B, then the mere fact that the action assists those in dispute with A does not turn the action against B into unlawful secondary action. Thirdly, the 1990 Act removed immunity for the first time from contracts personally to do work or perform services, in addition to contracts of employment.[3] This means that self-employed workers such as construction workers fall within the definition.

1. Employment Act 1980, s. 17.
2. TULRCA 1992, s. 224. For commentary, *see* G.S. Morris, 'The Employment Act 1990' 1991 *Journal of Business Law* 46; B. Simpson, 'The Employment Act 1990 in context' [1991] 54 MLR 418.
3. For definition of contract of employment, *see* para. 108 to 113.

491. The effect of the above provisions is that in effect almost no secondary action is protected. This is true even if A and B have identical shareholders and directors: in an earlier case, the court refused to lift the corporate veil to take into account real ownership and control.[1] Thus if A and B are two companies in a corporate group, workers employed by B cannot take action in support of workers in dispute with A even if they are indirectly affected, unless they can claim their own primary dispute with B. The union cannot call on B's workers even if A has diverted strike-bound work to B. Even more seriously, if A is a subsidiary company of B, and decisions on key industrial relations questions are in reality taken by directors of B rather than A, employees of A are restricted to ineffective industrial action against A. These provisions have particularly serious implications for the public sector, where Government policy has been to decentralise authority down to small units. For example, in education, teachers are now employed by the governors of individual schools rather than by the local education authority, and in the National Health Service, many hospitals are becoming autonomous employers. Employees in one school or hospital will not be able to call on colleagues at another school or hospital to support them in dispute unless the latter have their own primary dispute. In the private sector, the new provisions give employers an incentive to restructure their employment units in such a way as to minimise the spread of industrial action. The extent of these restrictions on the right to strike means that Britain is now out of line with other West European countries and is almost definitely in breach of its international obligations.[2]

1. *Dimbleby* v. *National Union of Journalists* [1984]1 All ER 751.
2. *See* Lord Wedderburn HL Deb Vol. 521, col 172, 10 July 1990.

492. There is only one limited exception to the above provisions, occurring in the context of picketing. Immunity from liability in tort is retained if, in the course of picketing which is lawful under Section 220 of TULRCA 1992 (*below* para. 498), a picket or union official induces an employee of an employer not party to the dispute to breach a contract of employment.[1] For example, if a lawful picket peacefully persuades a truck driver employed by a supplier of the primary employer to refuse to cross the picket line and thereby induces him or her to breach a contract of employment, the picket will not lose whatever immunity he or she would otherwise have.

1. TULRCA 1992, s 224(3).

B. Union-only Practices

492bis. A second element of the restrictive strategy of the present government is to discourage 'union-only' or 'recognition-only' practices, whereby union members attempt to spread unionism by insisting that their employers require suppliers to employ union labour, or to recognise, negotiate with or consult union officials (*see* para. 396). By Section 222(3) of TULRCA 1992, no statutory immunities are available to a person who induces or attempts to induce another to incorporate into a contract a term requiring work to be done by union or non-union members only, or requiring a party to recognise one or more trade unions, or to negotiate or consult with any trade union official. Nor is protection available to employees of one employer, A, who breach or threaten to breach or interfere with their contracts of employment, resulting in tortious interference with the supply of goods or services to B, because B uses or is likely to use union or non-union labour or refuses to recognise one or more trade unions, or to negotiate or consult with any trade union official. Protection is similarly withdrawn from the organisers of such action. It does, however, remain open to employees to put pressure on their own employer to achieve these ends.

C. Ballots Before Industrial Action

493. Even if a trade union has satisfied both Section 219 of TULRCA 1992 (para. 485, *above*) and not lost the immunity by virtue of Section 224 of the 1992 Act (para. 490, *above*) the union and any individuals involved will lose their immunity from civil action in respect of certain torts if the balloting provisions in TULRCA 1992 ss. 226–235, are not fulfilled. Originally, the remedy for breach of the provisions lay not with members of the union, but with any person who suffered harm or threatened harm as a result of acts which constituted the relevant common law torts. This meant that, although the balloting provisions were purportedly aimed at increasing membership participation, in fact, they placed a tactical weapon in the hands of employers, suppliers or customers who were affected by the industrial action. The Employment Act 1988 partially remedied this, by creating a remedy for union members who complained that a ballot had not been validly conducted. However, the 1988 Act did not remove the remedy from the hands of employers (*see* para. 495bis). The introduction of statutory ballots before industrial action has important consequences for bargaining processes.[1] Ballots tend to lengthen the bargaining process and delay tends to give time for 'cooling-off' in which both sides can assess the situation. On the other hand, ballots may increase membership commitment, especially if seen to be externally imposed. Ballots increase formality, and reduce the flexibility of negotiations because firm proposals are necessary, so reducing the possibilities of compromise by implicit undertakings. Research findings indicate[2] that ballots as such do not usually reduce the likelihood of industrial conflict; during a recession members are more likely to vote against strikes, while in times of prosperity ballots reinforce the stand of union executives with no reduction in the level of conflict. Nevertheless, the balloting provisions have influenced bargaining practice. Balloting has now become a routine part of the collective bargaining process; indeed, both ballots and the threat of legal action have been used as tactical weapons. Where, as is often the case, the ballot results in majority support for industrial action, the union is clearly in a stronger position. Paradoxically, this has led to calls by the right wing of the Conservative Party for the removal of balloting, at least in essential services, on the grounds that it provides false legitimation of industrial action.[3] More importantly, it is highly likely that the unexpected level of success in industrial action ballots prompted the government to introduce balloting requirements which are ever more complex and technical; so that a positive result in a ballot by no means guarantees that industrial action will be lawful. This has permitted employers to use the provisions as a means of delaying action, often on technical grounds. For example, in the 1989 railway strike, despite the fact that a ballot had been held and a large majority obtained in favour of industrial action, the employers sued for an interlocutory injunction on the grounds that some members had not been given the opportunity to vote. Even though the injunction was refused by both the High Court and the Court of Appeal, the proceedings caused damaging delay.[4]

1. *See* generally R. Undy and R. Martin, *Ballots and Trade Union Democracy*, London 1984.
2. *Op cit.*, p.167.
3. Charles Hanson and Graham Mather *Striking out Strikes* Hobart Paper 110 (London: Institute of Economic Affairs).
4. *British Railways Board* v. *National Union of Railwayworkers* [1989] IRLR 348. *See also Post Office* v. *Union of Communication Workers* [1990] IRLR 143 (CA).

494. Originally, the provisions only applied to 'official' industrial action, that is, action 'authorised or endorsed' by a responsible officer or committee of the union. However, the Employment Act 1990 extended this requirement (*see above*, para. 421), imposing liability on trade unions in a wide and often ill-defined set of circumstances. Moreover, the repudiation provisions described in para. 421 not only present practical problems in identifying all members involved, but place the union in the very difficult position of being forced to 'police' their own members. The 1992 Act requires the union to specify in the ballot paper the person or description of persons who are authorised to call for industrial action if the ballot yields a majority in favour.[1] The Act also extends the ballot obligation to industrial action involving self-employed workers who personally do work or perform services (s. 235).

1. TULRCA 1992, s 229(3).

495. The conditions which must be met for the ballot to be lawful are complex. A ballot is required even if the industrial action does not amount to a breach of contract. Although this will have little effect when an employer brings an action for inducing breach of contract, it may be significant if a union member complains that the ballot is unlawful. There must be no call by the union for participation in industrial action before the date of the ballot; it is unclear whether this goes so far as to even preclude the call by a union for a vote in favour of the action. Where the strike or other industrial action has not yet begun, the union's authorisation and the action itself must be within four weeks of the date when the ballot is held. Where the action has already begun the union's endorsement of it must be within that four-week period. This means that if legal action by employers delays the commencement of industrial action, the union could be forced to conduct a new ballot, even if the legal action is unsuccessful. This difficulty was mitigated somewhat by the Employment Act 1990, which permitted the union to apply to the court to extend the four week period to a maximum of twelve weeks if delay in authorisation is due to a court order against the union which has subsequently been discharged.[1] However, the court cannot make such an order if it considers that the result of the ballot no longer represents the views of those who voted, or if an event is likely to occur as a result of which those members would vote against industrial action if another ballot were to be held. This presumably refers to an offer of settlement by the employer; but the degree to which judicial speculation is required to predict voters' preferences makes this a highly uncertain provision. The ballot has to be secret, the union having the option between a postal or workplace ballot. Entitlement to vote must be accorded equally to all members whom it is reasonable to believe at the time of the ballot will be called on to break or interfere with their contracts of employment, and to no others. This poses a dilemma for unions who are contemplating action at different times by different groups of members. It needs only *one* relevant member to have been denied a vote, or one irrelevant member to have been given one for the whole ballot to be invalidated, with consequent loss of immunity.[2] This situation was made even more complex by the Employment Act 1988, which required separate balloting at individual places of work. Only in those workplaces at which a majority of workers has voted in favour of industrial action may a union call for action.[3] This was justified by the assertion (for which no evidence was produced) that a union would draw its constituency boundaries in such a way that a more militant workplace could swamp a less militant one. The statute creates one exception to the separate workplace rule. Ballot results may be aggregated across workplaces if the union reasonably believes that there is a common distinguishing factor relating to the terms and conditions or the occupational description of all the members who are given the right to vote, and that all those at a given place of work who share that common factor are given a right to vote.[4] For example, a union could aggregate results of a ballot of members in a particular occupation, such as welders, or of members covered by a common collective agreement, provided it ballots all such members. One effect of this is that a union cannot aggregate results if it only wants to call out some members of an occupational group. Every voter must be allowed to vote without 'interference' or 'constraint' from the union and any of its members, officials or employees. Employer interference does not invalidate the ballot, otherwise it would have been possible for the employer to expose the union and others to civil action simply by preventing workers from voting. Interference by another union than that conducting the ballot does not invalidate it. The content of the ballot paper is subject to detailed statutory regulation. First, the ballot paper must contain the "government health warning", namely the words: 'If you take part in a strike or other industrial action you may be in breach of your contract of employment.' This cannot be qualified or commented on by anything else on the voting paper and is required even if the industrial action will involve no breach of contract. Secondly, the voting paper must contain at least one of two questions, asking whether the person is prepared to take part or continue to take part in a strike or asking the same question in relation to action short of a strike. A union may not include other material such as a statement of the merits of the action. The High Court has made this provision even more stringent, by linking the content of the ballot-paper to the legal definition of 'trade dispute' (*above*, para. 486.) On this view, it is not permissible to ask members to vote on an issue which is not in law a trade dispute, nor to roll up some trade dispute questions with others in the same paper.[5] Even a minor and innocent transgression of these principles will lead to loss of immunity.[6] Unusually, for industrial action ballots, unions are given the choice as to whether to use postal or workplace balloting. Nevertheless, the Code of Practice on Balloting expresses a strong preference for postal balloting;[7] and the Government's most recent Green Paper proposes to introduce mandatory postal balloting except where fewer than 50 workers are involved.[8] Overall it seems clear that, far from facilitating real democracy, the Government has made the requirements for balloting before industrial action so complex and technical as to minimise the extent to which unions can use the ballot to strengthen their position.

1. TULRCA 1992, s 234.
2. An inadvertant failure to afford an opportunity to vote will not invalidate the ballot; but intentional failures will do so, even if the result would have been the same had the statute been fully complied with: *British Railways Board* v. *NUR* [1989] IRLR 348.
3. TULRCA 1992, s. 228.
4. TULRCA 1992, s. 228(3).
5. TULRCA 1992, s. 229(2); *London Underground* v. *NUR* [1989] IRLR 341, 343.
6. *Post Office* v. *Union of Communication Workers* [1990] IRLR 143 (CA); contrast *British Railways Board* v. *NUR supra*, note 2.
7. *Code of Practice on Trade Union Ballots on Industrial Action*, 1990. *See* B. Simpson [1990] ILJ 29.
8. *Industrial Relations in the 1990s* Cm. 1692; July 1991, confirmed in the Queen's Speech, May 6, 1992.

495bis. Government funds are available to cover the costs of postal ballots. Although initially, the Trades Union Congress took a policy decision that unions should not apply for such funds, this policy was reversed once it became clear that postal balloting could not be avoided. Separate figures for applications in respect of industrial action ballots are not available, but the overall number of applications is increasing significantly. In 1991, 78 unions applied for refunds as against 67 unions in 1989, and the Certification Officer paid out over £4 million in respect of 692 ballots. This compares with £1.4 million paid out in 1989.[1]

1. *Annual Report of the Certification Officer* 1991.

496. A trade union which fails to comply with the balloting requirements loses its immunity in respect of the torts of inducing breach of or interference with a contract of employment or a commercial contract. (Somewhat strangely, intimidation and conspiracy remain protected.) This means that the employer or other affected party may bring an action in tort. Union members have also given the right by Section 62 of TULRCA 1992 to complain to the court about breach of the balloting provisions. This is available to any member who was induced or was likely to be induced to take part in industrial action, even if he or she refused to comply. Application lies to the High Court, which has wide powers to make such orders as it considers appropriate to require the union to ensure that there is no further inducement of members to take part in action which was not authorised by a ballot. The Court cannot, however, directly order the union to hold a ballot, nor require that those taking industrial action return to work. The newly established Commissioner for Rights of Trade Union Members may assist a member in pursuing such an action. These provisions have scarcely been used. The Commissioner received only one application for assistance under section 62 of the 1992 Act in the year ending March 1991, as a result of which the union withdrew its proposed call for industrial action.[1]

1. Commissioner for the Rights of Trade Union Members *Annual Report* 1990/1991.

§6. Picketing

496bis. Picketing has been a traditional feature of industrial action in Britain. Striking workers gather at the gates of the workplace in order to persuade non-strikers or substitute workers not to undermine the strike by continuing to work. Picketing may also take the form of secondary action, with employees in the primary dispute picketing other places of work in an attempt to gain support from other workers, or other workers picketing their own places of work in support of the primary strikers. Large scale picketing was a favoured tactic of the National Union of Mineworkers (NUM) and was widely used in the protracted miners' strike of 1984–1985. Picketing is one area of industrial conflict in which the criminal law plays a central role. Indeed, in the 1984–1985 miners' strike, the criminal law was far more extensively used than the civil law regulating industrial action. A range of criminal laws are applicable to picketing, especially where violence takes place or is apprehended. These include: (a) conduct likely or intended to cause a breach of the peace; (b) obstructing the police; (c) criminal damage; (d) obstructing the highway. One criminal offence which relates specifically to picketing is contained in section 241 of the TULRCA 1992, which outlaws actions such as 'watching or besetting' a person's house or place of business, with a view to compelling that person to do or abstain from doing any 'act which such other person has a legal right to do or abstain from doing'. Despite its anachronistic flavour, this offence was brought back into use during the miners' strike when almost 650 such charges were laid, particularly in cases of picketing of working miners' homes.[1] During the same strike, the police made use of traffic control powers and general preventative powers to stop pickets massing at working pits, often by turning back pickets hundreds of miles from their intended destinations.[2] Subsequent legislation has given the police even more extensive powers to control public assemblies and processions. Under the Public Order Act 1986, organisers of processions (but not static assemblies) are required to give the police advance notice of such gatherings. In all cases, a senior police officer may impose conditions in advance or on the spot, if he or she reasonably believes that the gathering may result in serious public disorder, serious damage to property, or serious disruption to the life of the community. Similarly, conditions may be imposed if the police officer considers that the purpose of the organisers is to intimidate others with a view to compelling them to do an act which they have a right not to do, or vice versa.[3] This last provision could be used in cases where pickets are attempting to prevent workers from going to work. In such circumstances, the police officer may place such conditions on the place, size and maximum duration of the assembly or procession as he or she considers necessary. The attitude of police to pickets has been significantly influenced by the Code of Practice on Picketing, issued by the Secretary of State in 1980. Although the Code is no more than a guide, its suggestion that the number of pickets be limited to six has frequently been used as a working rule for controlling pickets.[4] In addition, the Act introduced five new statutory offences which may be relevant to the conduct of picketing. These are: riot, violent disorder, affray, causing fear of violence or provoking it, and (particularly relevant in the context of picketing) causing harassment, alarm or distress.[5] All may be committed in a public or private place, and all, apart from the last, carry a power of arrest.

1. (1985) 14 *Industrial Law Journal* 145 at 151.
2. *Moss* v. *McLachlan* [1985] IRLR 76.
3. Public Order Act 1986, ss. 11–16.
4. A new draft Code of Practice on Picketing was issued in July 1991.
5. Public Order Act 1986, ss. 1–5.

497. Picketing may also lead to civil liability. Thus the 'economic torts' described in paras. 479–483 above may be applicable. For example, pickets who dissuade a fellow worker from continuing to work may well commit the tort of inducing breach of contract of employment.[1] Other relevant torts include public[2] and private nuisance. In addition, it has been held in one case that it is a tort unreasonably to harass others in the exercise of their right to use the highway for the purposes of going to work.[3]

1. *Union Traffic Ltd* v. *TGWU* [1989] IRLR 127.
2. *News Group Newspapers* v. *SOGAT 82* [1986] IRLR 337.
3. *Thomas* v. *NUM* [1985] 2 All ER 1, Ch.D.

498. The freedom to picket peacefully is delimited by section 220 of TULRCA 1992. Section 220 states that 'it shall be lawful for a person in contemplation or furtherance of a trade dispute to attend (a) at or near his own place of work or (b) if he is an official of a trade union, at or near the place of work of the member of the union whom he is accompanying and whom he represents for the purpose only of peacefully obtaining information or persuading any person to work or to abstain from work'. This section differs from section 219 of the 1992 Act in that it is not limited to specific torts, but applies to all criminal and civil liability, provided the statutory conditions are observed. However, the extent of the immunity afforded for criminal liability has been limited by highly restrictive judicial interpretation, which held that the section protects only the 'attendance' at or near the workplace, and not the detention of persons or invitations to them to stop and listen to the pickets' arguments.[1] Above all, pickets generally have to follow police instructions.

1. *Broome* v. *DPP* [1974] ICR 84, HL.

499. The scope of the immunity afforded by Section 220 was substantially narrowed by the requirement introduced by the Employment Act 1980 that picketing should take place at or near the person's own place of work. Where Section 220 does not apply, neither does the usual immunity afforded by Section 219 of the TULRCA 1992.[1] Immunity is thus withdrawn not only from employees who picket premises of other employers but also from those who picket other premises of their own employer in a multi-plant group. There are only three exceptions: (i) a trade union official may accompany a member to the latter's place of work; (ii) an employee who has been dismissed in connection with the industrial action may attend at his or her former place of work; (iii) where a person does not normally work at any one place or the location of the place (e.g. an oil rig) makes it impracticable to picket that place, he or she may picket any premises from which he or she works or from which his or her work is administered. Picketing may be conducted 'near' the workers' place of work, even if this is a short distance away.[2] But the statute makes no provision for workers whose former place of work has been closed down, and who therefore wish to picket another establishment of their employer.[3]

1. TULRCA 1992, s. 219(3).
2. *Rayware Ltd* v. *TGWU* [1989] IRLR 134.
3. *Union Traffic Ltd* v. *TGWU* [1989] IRLR 127.

500. Employees picketing their own workplace may well find that they have committed secondary action (paras. 490–492 *above*). For example, if pickets induce a truck driver to breach his or her contract of employment by refusing to cross a picket line to deliver supplies to the employer in dispute, they would fall within the definition of secondary action. However, this is the only situation in which immunity from tort is specifically retained. If this were not the case, the right to picket granted by section 220 of the 1992 Act would be rendered nugatory.[1]

1. TULRCA 1992, ss. 224(1) and (3).

§7. Labour Injunctions

501. The most important intervention of the law in collective labour disputes is through the power of the High Court to issue injunctions before, during or after the trial of an action. The most common form of injunction in such disputes is interlocutory, that is pending trial of the action. This may be negative, for example restraining the union and organisers from acts of interference with trade by unlawful means, or mandatory, requiring the union executive to withdraw instructions which are alleged to constitute some tort. The interlocutory injunction is a particularly powerful tactical weapon in the hands of the employer or third party. Frequently the action is started for the sole purpose of restraining a strike or boycott, and the employer or third party has no intention of proceeding to a full trial. As a result, the substantive issues, whether torts were in fact committed, are never decided. At the interlocutory stage, the court cannot assess the evidence fully. Thus a two-stage test has been evolved to assist in deciding whether or not an injunction should be granted pending the full trial of the issue.[1] Firstly, the applicant must show that there is a serious issue to be tried. This has proved to be a relatively easy hurdle for employers to surmount: the courts have tended to accept an 'arguable case' as sufficient, and in the fluid area of economic torts, this is not difficult to show. Secondly, the courts will determine where the 'balance of convenience' lies. This again almost always favours the employer or third party, whose tangible business interests are being threatened, in contrast to the union and its officials, who can merely point to intangible industrial objectives. An attempt is made to mitigate this in cases concerning industrial disputes by section 221 of TULRCA 1992. Section 221(1) requires reasonable steps to be taken to give notice of the application and an opportunity to be heard to a party likely to claim a 'trade dispute' offence, but this has not allayed trade union criticisms that excessive speed is usual in granting such injunctions, giving the union defendants little time to prepare their evidence and denying them the opportunity to cross-examine those on whose allegations the application is based. Section 221(2) requires the court to have regard to the likelihood of the defendant establishing the 'trade dispute' defence, but despite this the courts have insisted on retaining their residual discretion to grant the injunctions where this factor is outweighed by the 'disastrous' consequences of the industrial action to the employer or the public.[2] Recent years have seen an increased willingness on the part of the courts to develop and adapt procedures which facilitate the granting of injunctions. For example, in the seafarers dispute of 1988, an injunction was granted restraining the National Union of Seamen from conducting a ballot on industrial action, even though there was nothing unlawful about conducting a ballot.[3] In addition, the court was willing to 'transfer' a sequestration order issued in contempt proceedings initiated by one company, to a different company, P&O.[4]

1. *American Cyanamid Co* v. *Ethicon Ltd* [1975] AC 396.
2. *NWL Ltd.* v. *Woods* [1979] 3 All ER 614; *Express Newspapers Ltd.* v. *McShane* [1980] 1 All ER 65; *Duport Steels Ltd.* v. *Sirs* [1980] 1 All ER, 529, HL.
3. *P & O European Ferries* v. *NUS*, *The Independent*, 28 March 1988.
4. *See* S. Auerbach 'Injunction Procedure in the Seafarers' Dispute' (1988) ILJ 227.

502. Traditionally, many British employers have been reluctant to use judicial remedies, preferring to resolve matters through the bargaining process. However, during the 1980s, this attitude has been changing, and injunctions have been sought in an increasing number of cases. This change has been particularly marked since 1982, when unions were first liable as defendants. A survey by *Labour Research* shows that between 1983 and 1990, a total of 117 injunctions have been sought.[1] The vast majority of such injunctions are granted: in the two year period 1989–1991, 18 out of 24 injunctions sought were granted unconditionally, and several others were initially granted and later withdrawn. In the early years, several injunctions were ignored by union defendants, but successful contempt of court proceedings followed by sequestration of assets in some highly publicised cases led to a greater degree of compliance with injunctions. More recently, employers have become less willing to apply for financial sanctions to be imposed on unions; there were no cases of sequestration in 1989–1991, nor any claims for damages. The aim was instead, almost exclusively to prevent industrial action. At the same time, it is clear that the threat of legal action is a significant deterrent to unions contemplating industrial action. Even if the claim is meritorious, a union might find itself unable to afford the cost of appealing against an injunction.

1. The figures in this section are taken from *Labour Research*, October 1991, pp. 19–21.

§8. Other State Intervention

503. *Emergency Powers and Regulation of Essential Services*: Under the Emergency Powers Act 1920 (as amended in 1964) the Government can make a proclamation and then govern with special powers if essential supplies are threatened for the community.[1] Parliamentary approval must be forthwith and regularly obtained. The powers are extensive, but they fall short of 'industrial conscription'. Nor may the Government use their powers to make it an offence to take part in a strike or peacefully persuade other persons to do so. The powers have been used on twelve occasions, most recently in 1973–1974. Since 1964, due to a little-noticed amendment, the Government has been able to use troops, without consultation with Parliament, for work of 'national importance'. This power has been used on several occasions, for example to remove refuse during a 'dustmen's strike' in Glasgow, thereby offsetting the impact of the strike. During the period of the Industrial Relations Act 1971 there were provisions for 'cooling-off' periods, along the lines of United States legislation, and for compulsory ballots of union members in 'emergencies'. These powers were used in only one dispute (in the railways) and failed abysmally.[2] During the 1980s, a different and less explicit tactic has been used. Buried in the legislation privatising the electricity and water industries are provisions giving ministers wide powers to issue confidential directions to the relevant operators for purposes including 'mitigating the effects of any civil emergency which may occur' where 'civil emergency' is defined in terms which could cover strike action.[3]

1. *See* generally G.S. Morris, *Strikes in Essential Services*, London 1986.
2. B. Weekes *et al.*, *Industrial Relations and the Limits of Law*, Oxford 1975, p. 213.
3. Electricity Act 1989, s. 96; Water Act 1989, s. 120; *see* generally G. Morris, 'Industrial Action in Essential Services: The New Law' [1991] ILJ 89.

504. There is no legislation in Britain which restricts industrial action in essential services as such, although some special provisions restrict the right to strike of the police, armed forces, merchant seamen and postal and telecommunications workers. Similarly, there are no special restraints on civil servants, but disciplinary sanctions may be imposed on them for individual action.[1] It remains an offence to break a contract of service with reasonable cause to believe it will result in serious bodily injury or serious property damage,[2] but there are no recorded prosecutions under this provision. During the 1970s, industrial action by workers in essential services led to calls for special restraints on such workers, but there has been no comprehensive legislation. Nevertheless, during the 1980s, a number of separate provisions have had the effect of exercising significant restraint on workers in essential services.[3] For example, restrictions on secondary action will have particular impact on workers in National Health Service hospitals which become 'self-governing' and therefore autonomous employers (*see* paras. 490–492 above). Similarly the Draft Code of Practice on Picketing issued in 1991 suggests that pickets should take particular care to ensure that the movement of essential goods and supplies and the provision of essential services should be maintained. Essential supplies, services and operations are widely defined to include activities necessary to the maintenance of plant and machinery, the proper care of livestock and the production and distribution of food and animal feeds.[4] Although the Code does not in itself engender liability, its provisions may be taken into account by a court, and this might be particularly relevant in an application for a grant of an interlocutory injunction. Also of importance in essential services is the tort of inducing breach of a statutory duty,[5] for which there is no immunity under section 219 TULRCA 1992 (*see* para. 483 above).[6] The lack of coherence and clarity in these provisions leaves the law relating to strikes in essential services in a highly unsatisfactory state.

1. On strikes in the public services, *see* S. Fredman and G. Morris, *The State as Employer* (1989), Chapter 10.
2. TULRCA 1992, s. 240.
3. *See* generally, G. Morris, 'Industrial Action in Essential Services: the New Law' 1991 [ILJ] 89.
4. *Draft Code of Practice on Picketing* Department of Employment 1991.
5. *Meade* v. *Haringey London Borough Council* [1979] ICR 494 (CA).
6. *See also* Telecommunications Act 1984, s.18(6)(a).

505. Advice, Conciliation and Arbitration. The most important form of governmental intervention in 'trade disputes' is in fact through ACAS, the Advisory, Conciliation and Arbitration Service using methods of conciliation, inquiry and arbitration with the consent of both parties. Occasionally the Government may set up a special Court of Inquiry, under the TULRCA 1992, ss. 215–6, to inform Parliament and the public about the causes of a dispute, but this too is a form of 'public conciliation'. The functions and work of ACAS are described *above*, para. 70 and the common meaning of terms such as conciliation and arbitration are discussed in para. 48.

506. Social Security Benefits: Since the turn of the century, it has been the policy of successive governments to withhold state benefits from those affected by industrial action. The rationale for this was the belief that the taxpayer should not be required to subsidise strikers. There are two relevant sources of social security benefit:

(1) Unemployment benefit: This benefit, paid out of a fund to which employees and employers make compulsory contributions, is normally available for a limited period of time to those who are involuntarily unemployed. Unemployment benefit is not payable to striking workers, on the principle that they are voluntarily unemployed. However, the disqualification is not limited to those who participate in the industrial action itself but extends to those workers who are laid off as a result of the stoppage. In such cases, workers are disqualified from receiving unemployment benefit, unless they can prove that they were not directly interested in the dispute.[1] The period of disqualification, which had been six weeks since 1911, was extended in 1986 to 13 weeks, and more recently to 26 weeks. A recent House of Lords decision has held that a person is 'directly interested' in a dispute if, despite the fact that he or she is not participating in the industrial action, the outcome of the dispute will be applied to him or her by virtue of a collective agreement or established custom and practice in the workplace.[2] This disqualification may operate extremely harshly, particularly where the stoppage is a result of a lock-out by the employer, or the dispute concerns a breach by the employer of his or her obligations. Indeed, the effect, far from State neutrality, is often to assist the employer.

1. Social Security Act 1975, s. 19(1) as amended by Social Security Act 1986, s. 44. *See* generally K. Ewing, *The Right to Strike* (1991) Chapters 5 and 6.
2. *Presho* v. *Department of Health and Social Security* [1984] ICR 463, (HL).

507. (2) *Income Support*: This is a non-contributory benefit, introduced in 1988 when supplementary benefit was abolished. It is usually payable to a claimant whose income falls below a prescribed threshold, who is unemployed but who is available for work and actively seeking employment.[1] As under the prior regime, a striker is disqualified from the receipt of income support in respect of his or her own needs. The family of the striker may continue to be entitled to income support. But the striking worker is deemed to be in receipt of strike pay (£19.90 per week in 1990) which is deducted from the family entitlement regardless of whether or not the union actually pays strike pay.[2] Moreover, if the union pays strike pay at a higher rate than the deemed strike pay, the extra amount will be taken into account to reduce the benefit otherwise payable. The effect is that single people without dependent families are entitled to no state benefits save in exceptional circumstances. Where no strike pay is in fact paid, these provisions could lead to great hardship, increasing the pressure on strikers to return to work. This clearly manifested itself in the 1984–1985 miners' strike during which the National Union of Mineworkers did not pay strike pay. As Ewing argues, 'These new punitive features of the scheme operate to deny the minimum level of subsistence to people in dispute and their families despite the fact that the individual affected may be the victim of unlawful or unreasonable conduct on the part of the employer, or may be the innocent victim of someone else's dispute . . . If the blanket disqualification of those interested in a dispute may be unjustifiable, the current treatment of strikers' families seems downright wicked and can be explained only as designed to reduce the number and length of disputes by a policy of starvation or the fear thereof.'[3]

1. Social Security Act 1986, part II, amended by the Social Security Act 1988 and the Social Security Act 1989.
2. Social Security Act 1986, s. 23(5)(b).
3. Ewing *op. cit.* p. 117.

Appendices

Appendix 1 – Selected Bibliography

§1. Bibliographical

B. A. Hepple, J. M. Neeson, and P. O'Higgins (eds.) *A Bibliography of the Literature on British and Irish Labour Law*, London, 1975; and B. A. Hepple, J. Hepple, P. O'Higgins and P. Stirling *Labour Law in Great Britain and Ireland to 1978* (companion volume), London, 1981 (a comprehensive working bibliography from the earliest times, kept up to date in regard to periodical literature, once a year, in the *Industrial Law Journal*, London).

§2. Reference Works

Butterworths' *Industrial Relations and Employment Law*, London, 1971 with supplements (2 vols.) (texts of selected legislation and commentary).

Sweet and Maxwell's *Encyclopedia of Employment Law*, London, 1972, with six supplements each year (3 vols.) (comprehensive texts and digests of all relevant case law, legislation, rules and orders, awards, reports and inquiries, precedents and EEC and international law with commentaries).

§3. Specialist Law Reports

Industrial Cases Reports, London, 1975–
Industrial Court Reports, London, 1972–1974
Industrial Relations Law Reports, London, 1972–
Industrial Tribunal Reports, London, 1966–1978

§4. Periodicals

British Journal of Industrial Relations, London, 1963–
Equal Opportunities Review, London, 1985–
European Industrial Relations Review, London, 1974–
Incomes Data Service Ltd., *Incomes Data Reports, Incomes Data Brief* and *Incomes Data Studies*, and *International Report*, London, 1971–
Industrial Law Journal, London, 1972–
Industrial Relations Journal, London, 1972–
Industrial Relations Review and Report, London, 1972– (including *Industrial Relations Legal Information Bulletin*)

§5. Official Reports etc. Published by Her Majesty's Stationery Office (HMSO)

Advisory, Conciliation and Arbitration Service, Annual Reports (1975–)
Central Arbitration Committee, Annual Reports (1975–)
Certification Officer, Annual Reports (1976–)
Commission for Racial Equality, Annual Reports (1977–)
Department of Employment, *Guides* on labour legislation (e.g. Contracts of Employment, Dismissal etc.)
Equal Opportunities Commission, Annual Reports (1976–)
Report of the Royal Commission on Trade Unions and Employers' Associations 1965–1968. Chairman: The Rt. Hon. Lord Donovan, Cmnd. 3623, and 11 research papers published by the Commission.
Report of the Committee on Safety and Health at Work. Chairman: Lord Robens, 1972, Cmnd. 5034.
Report of the Committee of Inquiry on Industrial Democracy. Chairman: Lord Bullock, Cmnd. 6706

§6. General Books

S. D. Anderman *Labour Law: Management decisions and Workers' Rights*, London, 1992.
G S. Bain (ed.), *Industrial Relations in Britain*, Oxford, 1983.
J. Bowers and S. Honeyball, *Textbook on Labour Law*, London, 1990.
P. L. Davies and M. R. Freedland, *Labour Law: Text and Materials*, 2nd ed., London, 1984.
O. Kahn-Freund, *Labour and the Law*, 3rd ed. by P. L. Davies and M. R. Freedland, London, 1983 (also available in German and Italian translations).
—, *Labour Relations: Heritage and Adjustment*, London, 1979.
—, *Selected Writings*, London, 1978.
R. Lewis (ed.) *Labour Law in Britain*, Oxford, 1986.
R.W. Rideout, *Principles of Labour Law*, 5th ed., London 1987.
I.T. Smith and J.C. Wood, *Industrial Law*, London 1989.
Lord Wedderburn, *The Worker and the Law*, 3rd ed., London 1986.
Lord Wedderburn, *Employment Rights in Britain and Europe*, London, 1991.

§7. Specialist Books

S. Auerbach, *Legislating for Conflict*, Oxford, 1991.
W. Brown (ed.), *The Changing Contours of British Industrial Relations*, Oxford, 1981.
H. Collins *Justice in Dismissal*, Oxford, 1992.
L. Dickens, M. Jones, B. Weekes and M. Hart, *A study of Unfair Dismissal and the Industrial Tribunal System*, Oxford 1985.
S. Dunn and J. Gennard, *The Closed Shop in British Industry*, London, 1984.

Appendix 1 – Selected Bibliography

P. Elias and K.D. Ewing, *Trade Unions, Democracy, Members' Rights and the Law*, London, 1987.

K.D. Ewing, *The Right to Strike*, Oxford, 1990.

K.D. Ewing, *Trade Unions, the Labour Party and the Law*, Edinburgh, 1982

S. Fredman and G.S. Morris, *The State as Employer: Labour Law in the Public Services*, London, 1986.

M.R. Freedland, *The Contract of Employment*, London 1976.

C. Grunfeld, *The Law of Redundancy*, 3rd ed., London, 1989.

Bob Hepple, *Equal Pay and the Industrial Tribunals*, London, 1984.

—, A. Jacobs, T. Ramm, B. Veneziani, E. Vogel-Polsky, *The Making of Labour Law in Europe: a comparitive study of 9 countries to 1945*, London, 1986.

P. Kahn, N. Lewis, R. Livock and P. Wiles, *Picketing: Industrial Disputes Tactics and the Law*, London, 1983.

G.S. Morris, *Strikes in Essential Services*, London, 1986.

G.S. Morris and T.J. Archer, *Trade Unions, Employers and the Law*, London, 1991.

R. Nielsen and E. Szyszczak, *The Social Dimension of the European Community*, Denmark, 1991.

K. O' Donovan and E. Szyszczak, *Equality and Sex Discrimination Law*, Oxford, 1988.

E. Szyszczak, *Partial Unemployment: The Regulation of Short-Time working in Britain*, London, 1990.

R. Townshend-Smith, *Sex Discrimination in Employment*, London, 1989.

R. Upex, *Termination of Employment*, 3rd ed., London, 1991.

Appendix 1 – Selected Bibliography

Appendix 2 – Table of Cases

Addis v. *Gramophone Co.* [1909] AC 488: 303

Addison v. *London Philharmonic Orchestra Ltd* [1981] ICR 261: 110

Ainsworth v. *Glass Tubes Ltd* [1977] IRLR 74: 355

Airfix Footwear (Ltd) v. *Cope* [1978] ICR 1210: 112, 126

Alexander v. *Standard Telephones & Cables Ltd* [1990] IRLR 55: 153

Amalgamated Society of Railway Servants v. *Osborne* [1910] AC 87: 52, 410, 418

American Cyanamid Co v. *Ethicon Ltd* [1975] AC 396: 501

Associated Port Employers v. *TGWU* [1989] IRLR 305, 399: 483, 485

Attorney-General for New South Wales v. *Perpetual Trustee Co* [1955] AC 477: 117

Aziz v. *Trinity Street Taxis Ltd* [1988] IRLR 204: 346

BBC v. *Hearn* [1977] ICR 685: 488

Balgobin v. *London Borough of Tower Hamlets* [1987] IRLR 401: 341

Barber v. *Guardian Royal Exchange Assurance Group* [1983] IRLR 240: 349

Barber v. *Guardian Royal Exchange Assurance Group* [1990] ICR 616: 204*bis*, 361*bis*, 362

Barber v. *Manchester Regional Hospital Board* [1958] 1 WLR 181: 153

Barratts & Baird v. *IPCS* [1987] 3: 483, 485

Bell v. *Lever Bros Ltd* [1932] AC 161: 174

Beloff v. *Pressdram Ltd* [1973] 1 All ER 241: 108, 109

Bent's Brewery Co Ltd v. *Hogan* [1945] 2 All ER 570: 172

Berrisford v. *Woodard Schools* [1991] IRLR 247: 341

Bilka-Kaufhaus GmBH v. *Weber von Harz* [1986] IRLR: 204*bis*, 317, 359, 361*bis*

Bliss v. *Southeast Thames Regional Health Authority* [1987] ICR 700: 162, 303

Bond v. *CAV Ltd* [1983] IRLR 360: 157, 232, 233

Bonsor v. *National Musicians Union* [1956] AC 104: 418

Boston Deep Sea Fishing Co v. *Ansell* [1888] 39 Ch. D. 399: 167, 300

Boxfoldia v. *NGA* [1988] IRLR 383: 422

Bracebridge Engineering Ltd v. *Darby* [1990] IRLR 3: 162, 298

Briggs v. *North Eastern Education and Library Board* [1990] IRLR 181: 131*bis*, 343, 344

British Actors Equity Association v. *Goring* [1977] ICR 393: 427

British Aircraft Corporation v. *Austin* [1978] IRLR 332: 162

British Home Stores v. *Burchell* [1980] ICR 303: 167, 310

British Railways Board v. *National Union of Railwaymen* [1989] IRLR 348: 493, 495

British Labour Pump v. *Byrne* [1979] ICR 347: 310

British Leyland UK Ltd v. *Ashraf* [1978] ICR 979: 290

British Leyland UK Ltd v. *Swift* [1981] IRLR 91: 309

Bromley v. *H & J Quick Ltd* [1988] IRLR 249: 356

Broome v. *DPP* [1974] ICR 84: 498

Browning v. *Crumlin Valley Collieries Ltd* [1926] 1 KB 572: 233

Bull v. *Pitney-Bowes Ltd* [1967] 1 WLR 273. 368

Burdett Coutts v. *Hertfordshire CC* [1984] IRLR 91: 153, 295, 304

Camellia Tanker Ltd v. *ITF* [1976] ICR 274: 483

Carrington v. *Therm-a-Stor Ltd* [1983] ICR 208: 379

Carter v. *Law Society* [1973] ICR 113: 116

Cassidy v. *Ministry of Health* [1951] 2 KB 343: 108

Chant v. *Aquaboats Ltd* [1978] ICR 643: 379

Chaplin v. *Leslie Frewin (Publishers) Ltd* [1966] Ch 71: 140

Chapman v. *Goonvean and Rostowrack China Clay Co. Ltd* [1973] ICR 50: 321

Appendix 2 – Table of Cases

Chappell v. *Times Newspapers* [1975] ICR 145: 304
Cheall v. *APEX* [1983] ICR 398: 404
City and Hackney Health Authority v. *National Union of Public Employees* [1985] IRLR 263: 153
City of Birmingham District Council v. *Beyer* [1977] IRLR 210: 377
Clark v. *NATSOPA (SOGAT '82)* [1985] IRLR 494: 393
Clarke v. *Eley (IMI) Kynoch Ltd* [1983] ICR 165: 130, 131, 343, 345
Clarke v. *Heathfield* [1985] ICR 203: 423
Clay Cross (Quarry Services) Ltd v. *Fletcher* [1979] ICR 1: 358
Clemens v. *Peter Richards* [1977] IRLR 332: 238
Clift v. *West Riding* CC, The Times 10 April 1964: 153
Climo v. *Wandsworth LBC* [1989] IRLR 241: 131 *bis*, 343
Coleman v. *Skyrail Oceanic Ltd* [1981] ICR 864: 341
Collins v. *Hertfordshire County Council* [1947] KB 598: 108
Commission of the European Communities v. *United Kingdom* Case 61/82 [1982] ICR 578 (ECJ): 19: 357
Commission of the European Communities v. *United Kingdom* Case 165/82 [1984] ICR 192 (ECJ): 19, 121, 361
Construction Industry Training Board v. *Labour Force* Ltd [1970] 3 All ER 220: 125
Cornelius v. *University of Swansea* [1987] IRLR 141: 346
Cotter v. *National Union of Seamen* [1929] 2 Ch. 58: 419
Council of Civil Service Unions v. *Minister of the Civil Service* [1984] 3 All ER 935: 94, 118, 375
Coupland v. *Arabian Gulf Petroleum Co.* [1983] 3 All ER 226 (CA): 102
Courtaulds Northern Spinning v. *Sibson* [1988] IRLR 305: 146
Courtaulds Northern Textiles Ltd v. *Andrew* [1979] IRLR 84: 162
Cowan v. *Haden* [1983] ICR 1: 321
Cox v. *Philips Industries Ltd* [1974] IRLR 344: 303
CRE v. *Dutton* [1989] IRLR 8: 340 IRLR 344: 304
Crofter Hand Woven Harris Tweed Co. Ltd. v. *Veitch* [1942] AC 435: 473 479
Crown Suppliers v. *Dawkins* [1991] IRLR 326: 340
Cutter v. *Powell* [1795] 6 TR 320: 216

Daley v. *Allied Suppliers Ltd* [1983] IRLR 14: 123
Davies v. *Presbyterian Church of Wales* [1986] IRLR 194: 111
De Francesco v. *Barnum* [1890] 45 Ch. D. 430: 263
Defrenne v. *Belgium Case* 80/70 [1971] ECR 445: 361*bis*
Defrenne v. *Sabena (Defrenne II)* Case 43/75 [1976] ECR 455 (ECJ): 19, 334
Defrenne v. *Sabena (Defrenne III)* Case 158/77 [1978] ECR 1365 (ECJ): 19, 204*bis*
De Souza v. *Automobile Association* [1986] IRLR 103: 341
Dekker v. *Stichting Vormingscentrum voor Jonge Volwassenen* [1991] IRLR 27: 19, 341
Delaney v. *Staples* [1991] IRLR 112: 80, 219
Devis & Sons v. *Atkins* [1977] ICR 662: 301, 310
Devonald v. *Rosser & Sons* [1906] 2 KB 728: 233
Dimbleby & Sons Ltd v. *NUJ* [1984] 1 All ER 751: 491
Dietman v. *London Borough of Brent* [1988] IRLR 299: 294, 304
Dimskal Shipping Co SA v. *ITF* [1992] IRLR 78: 106; 482
Discount Tobacco & Confectionery v. *Armitrage* [1990] IRLR 15: 308
Dixon v. *BBC* [1979] ICR 282: 290
Donelan v. *Kirby* [1983] IRLR 191: 151
Duke v *GEC Reliance plc* [1988] IRLR 118: 19, 349
Duncan v. *Motherwell Bridge & Engineering Co. Ltd* [1952] SC 131: 104
Duport Steels Ltd. v. *Sirs* [1980] ICR 161: 489, 501

Edwards v. *Bairstow* [1956] AC 14
England v. *British Telecommunications* [1990] IRLR 330: 139
Egg Stores (Stanford Hill) Ltd v. *Leibovici* [1976] IRLR 376: 289

EEPTU v. *Times Newspapers* [1980] QB 58: 419
Enderby v. *Frenchay H.A.* [1991] IRLR 44: 344
Express Newspapers Ltd. v. *McShane* [1980] IRLR 247: 488, 489, 501

Faccenda (Chickens) v. *Fowler* [1986] ICR 297: 169, 365
Factortame v. *Secretary of State for Transport* (No 2), Case 213/89, [1991] IRLR 283: 19
Falconer v. *ASLEF and NUR* [1987] IRLR 331: 481, 485
Ferguson v. *John Dawson & Partners (Contracts) Ltd.* [1976] 1 WLR 1213: 110, 113
Finnegan v. *Clowney Youth Training Programme* [1990] IRLR 299: 19, 349
Fisher v *Oldham Corporation* [1930] 2 KB 364: 117
Ford v. *Warwickshire CC* [1983] 2 AC 71: 282
Ford Motor Co. Ltd. v. *AEF* [1969] 2 QB 303: 468
Foss v. *Harbottle* (1843) 2 Hare 461: 419
Foster v *British Gas* [1990] IRLR 313, [1991] IRLR 268: 19, 349

Garland v. *British Rail Engineering* Case 12/81 [1982] IRLR 111: 361*bis*
Garner v. *Grange Furnishing Ltd.* [1977] IRLR 206: 162
Gascol Conversions Ltd. v. *Mercer* [1974] ICR 420: 137, 153
Gibbons v. *Associated British Ports* [1985] IRLR 376: 153
Gilham v. *Kent County Council* (No. 2) [1985] ICR 233: 311
Greater Manchester Police Authority v. *Lea* [1990] IRLR 372 (EAT): 344
Griggs v. *Duke Power Co.* 401 US 424 (1971): 343. 345
Grimaldi v. *Fonds des Maladies Professionelles* [1990] IRLR 400: 19
Gunton v. *Richmond-on-Thames LBC* [1980] IRLR 321: 304

Hadden v. *University of Dundee Students Unions* [1985] IRLR 449: 286
Hadmor Productions Ltd. v. *Hamilton* [1983] 1 AC 191: 483, 485
Hampson v. *Department of Education and Science* [1989] IRLR 69 (CA), [1990] IRLR 302 (HL): 345
Harman v. *Flexible Lamp Ltd* [1980] IRLR 418: 255
Harz Case 79/83 [1984] ECR 1921: 19
Hayes v. *Malleable Working Mens' Club and Institute* [1985] IRLR 367: 341
Hayward v. *Cammell Laird* [1987] IRLR 257: 357, 360
Hayward v. *Cammell Laird Shipbuilders Ltd.* [1984] IRLR 463: 357
Heatons Transport (St. Helens) Ltd. v. *TGWU* [1972] ICR 308 (HL): 98, 421, 424, 427, 457
Herbert Morris Ltd. v. *Saxelby* [1916] AC 688: 169
Hertz v. *Aldi Market* (Case 1790/88) [1991] IRLR 30: 341
Hewlett v. *Allen* [1894] AC 383: 220
Hill v. *Parsons Co. Ltd* [1972] 1 Ch 305: 304
Hindle v. *Percival Boats I.td* [1969] ITR 86: 321
Hitchcock v. *Post Office* [1980] ICR 100: 116
Hivac Ltd. v. *Park Royal Scientific Instruments Ltd.* [1946] Ch. 169: 168
Home Office v. *Holmes* [1984] ICR 678: 130, 343, 345
Hopkins v. *National Union of Seamen* [1985] ICR 268: 419, 430
Horcal v. *Gatland* [1984] IRLR 291: 167
Howard v. *NGA* [1985] ICR 101: 394
Howman & Son v. *Blyth* [1983] ICR 416: 146, 244
Hughes and Coy v. *DHSS* [1985] ICR 419: 319
Hughes v. *London Borough of Southwark* [1988] IRLR 55:304
Huntley v. *Thornton* [1957] 1 All ER 235: 479
Hurley v. *Mustoe* [1981] ICR 490: 341

Iceland Frozen Foods v. *Jones* [1983] ICR 17: 309
Igbo v. *Johnson, Matthey Chemicals Ltd* [1986] ICR 505: 290
Initial Services Ltd v. *Putterill* [1968] 1 QB 396: 170
Irani v. *Southhampton and South West Hampshire Health Authority* [1985] IRLR 203: 153, 304

Appendix 2 – Table of Cases

Ironmonger v. *Movefield* [1988] IRLR 461: 125

James v. *Eastleigh Borough Council* [1990] IRLR 288: 341
Janata Bank v. *Ahmed* [1981] ICR 791: 104, 177
Jenkins v. *Kingsgate (Clothing Productions) Ltd.* Case 96/80 [1980] ECR 911 (ECJ): 19, 359
Jenkins v. *Kingsgate (Clothing Productions) Ltd.* [1981] ICR 715(EAT): 130, 359
Johnson v. *Cross* [1977] ICR 872: 233
Johnson v. *Nottinghamshire Combined Police Aulhority* [1974] ICR 170: 321
Johnson v. *Bloomsbury Health Authority* [1991] IRLR 118: 183
Jones v. *Associated Tunnelling Company Ltd.* [1981] IRLR 477: 138, 146 161
Jones v. *Chief Adjudication Officer* [1990] IRLR 533: 344
Jones v. *Lee* [1980] IRLR 67: 304
Jupiter General Insurance Co. Ltd. v. *Shroff* [1937] 3 All ER 67 178

Kenneth MacRae & Co. Ltd v. *Dawson* [1984] IRLR 5: 232
Kent County Council v. *Gilham* [1985] IRLR 18: 306
Kidd v. *DRG* [1985] ICR 405: 130, 344, 345
Kowalska v. *Freie und Hansestadt Hamburg* [1990] IRLR 447: 19, 361

Land v. *West Yorkshire CC* [1979] ICR 452: 152, 298
Langston v. *AUEW* [1974] ICR 180: 165
Langston v. *AUEW* (No. 2) [1974] ICR 510: 164
Laws v. *London Chronicle (Indicator Newspapers) Ltd* [1958] 1 WLR 698: 160
Lawton v. *BOC Transhield Ltd* [1987] ICR 7: 302
Lee v. *Chung* [1990] IRLR 236: 110, 111
Lesney Products & Co. Ltd. v. *Nolan* [1977] ICR 235: 321
Leverton v. *Clwyd County Council* [1989] IRLR 28: 355
Lincoln v. *Hayman* [1984] 2 All ER 819: 303
Lister v. *Romford Ice and Cold Storage Co. Ltd.* [1957] AC 555: 146, 176, 177, 179
Litster v. *Forth Dry Dock & Engineering Co Ltd* [1989] IRLR 161: 19, 284, 285
London Borough of Lambeth v. *CRE* [1990] IRLR 231: 351
London Transport Executive v. *Clarke* [1981] ICR 334: 294
London Underground v. *NUR* [1989] IRLR 341, 343: 495
Lonrho plc v. *Fayed* [1989] 2 All ER 65: 483, 480
Lonrho Ltd. v. *Shell Petroleum Co. Ltd.* [1982] AC 173: 479, 480, 483
Lotus Cars Ltd. v. *Sutcliffe & Stratton* [1982] IRLR 381: 198
Louies v. *Coventry Hood & Seating Co Ltd* [1990] IRLR 324: 310
Lumley v. *Gye* [1853] 2 E. & B. 216: 481

Mandla v. *Dowell Lee* [1983] ICR 385: 340, 344, 345
Marina Shipping Ltd v. *Laughton* [1982] QB 1127: 492
Market Investigations v. *Minister of Social Security* [l969] 2 QB 173, (1968) 3 All ER 732: 108, 110
Marleasing 13 November 1990: 19, 334, 349
Marley v. *Forward Trust* [1986] IRLR 369: 151
Marrison v. *Bell* [1939] 2 KB 187: 244
Marshall v. *Harland & Wolff Ltd.* [1972]1 WLR 899: 255
Marshall v. *Southampton and South West Hampshire Area Health Authority* [1986] IRLR 140: 349, 362
Marshall v. Southampton and South West Hampshire AHA (No. 2) [1990] IRLR 481: 19, 334, 354
Massey v. *Crown Life Insurance Co.* [1978] ICR 590: 113
Mathewson v. *RB Wilson Dental Laboratory* [1988] IRLR 512: 310
Matthews v. *Kuwait Bechtel Corpn.* [1959] 2 QB 57: 102
McCleod v. *Hellyer Brothers* [1987] IRLR 232: 111, 112
McKechnie v. *UBM Building Supplies (Southern) Ltd* [1991] IRLR 283:19
McLaren v. *National Coal Board* [1988] ICR 370: 310
Meade v. *Haringey London Borough Council* [1979] ICR 494: 483, 504

Mears v. *Safecar Security Ltd.* [1982] ICR 626: 139, 146, 244
Meer v. *London Borough of Tower Hamlets* [1988] IRLR 399: 343
Mercury Communications Ltd. v. *Scott-Garner* [1984] ICR 74: 487 488
Merkur Island Shipping Co. Ltd. v. *Laughton* [1983] 2 AC 570: 481, 490, 491, 492
Mersey Docks and Harbour Board v. *Coggins and Griffiths Ltd.* [1947] AC 1: 108
Mersey Docks and Harbour Co. v. *Verrinder* [1982] IRLR 152: 485
Messenger Newspaper Group Ltd. v. *NGA* [1984] IRLR 397: 422, 423
Metall und Rohstoff v. *Donaldson* [1989] 3 All ER 14: 480
Midland Cold Storage v. *Turner* [1972] ICR 230: 486
Midland Electrical Engineering v. *Kanji* [1980] IRLR 185: 290
Midland Sinfonia Concert Sociey Ltd. v. *Secretary of State for Social Services* [1981] ICR 454: 110
Miles v. *Wakefield* [1987] IRLR 193:119, 475
Minnevitch v. *Cafe De Paris (Londres) Ltd* [1936] 1 All ER 884: 232
Minister of Defence v. *Jeremiah* [1980] ICR 13: 341
Mirror Group Newspapers Ltd. v. *Gunning* [1986] IRLR 27: 116
Monterosso Shipping Co. Ltd. v. *ITF* [1982] ICR 675: 105, 466
Moon v. *Homeworthy Furniture* [1977] ICR 117: 321
Moorcock The [1889] 14 PD 64: 146
Morgan v. *Fry* [1968] QB 710: 475, 482
Moriarty v. *Regent's Garage Co. Ltd.* [1921] 1 KB 423: 216
Morren v. *Swinton and Pendlebury Borough Council* [1965] 2 All ER 349: 108
Morris v. *Ford Motor Co. Ltd.* [1973] QB 792: 177
Moss v. *McLachlan* [1985] IRLR 76: 496
Murco Petroleum v. *Forge* [1987] ICR 282: 161
Murphy v. *Bord Telecom Eirean* [1988] IRLR 267: 357

Nalgo v. *Paul and Fraser* [1987] IRLR 413: 412
Namyslo v. *Secretary of State for Employment* [1979] IRLR 450: 232
National Coal Board v. *Galley* [1958] 1 WLR 16: 153, 475
National Coal Board v. *NUM* [1986] IRLR 439: 153
Nethermere (St. Neots) Ltd v. *Gardiner* [1984] ICR 365: 112, 126
News Group Newspapers v. *SOGAT* 82 [1986] IRLR 337: 497
Newstead v. *Department of Employment* [1988] IRLR 66: 349, 362
Nokes v. *Doncaster Amalgamated Collieries Ltd* [1940] AC 1014: 283
Norbrook Laboratories v. *Sands* [1984] IRLR 201: 172
Nordenfelt v. *Maxim Nordenfelt Guns and Ammunition Co.* [l894] AC 535: 364
Northeast Coast Shiprepairers Ltd v. *Secretary of State for Employment* [1975] ICR 755: 123
Nothman v. *Barnet London Borough Council* [1979] ICR 111: 319
Notcutt v. *Universal Equipment Co. (London) Ltd* [1986] ICR 414: 255, 289
Novac Plastics Ltd. v. *Froggett* [1982] IRLR 146: 168
NWL v. *Woods* [1979] 1 WLR 1294: 486, 489, 501

O'Kelly v. *Trusthouse Forte (plc)* [1983] ICR 728: 110, 111, 112, 124
Ojutiku v. *Manpower Services Commission* [1982] ICR 661: 345
Orman v. *Saville Sportswear Ltd.* [1960] 1 WLR 1055: 244
O'Sullivan v. *Thompson-Croom* [1973] 14 KIR 108: 125
Owens v. *Multilux Ltd* [19741 IRLR 113: 132

P & O European Ferries v. *NUS, The Independent*, 28 March 1988: 501
Palmanor Ltd. v. *Cedron* [1978] ICR 1008: 162
Panesar v. *The Nestlé Co.* [1980] IRLR 60: 343
Perera v. *Civil Service Commission* (No. 2) [1983] ICR 428: 343 344

Performing Rights Society Ltd. v. *Mitchell and Baker Ltd.* [1924] 1 KB 762: 108
Pickstone v. *Freemans plc* [1988] IRLR 357: 19, 355, 356
Polkey v. *A.E. Drayton Ltd* [1988] ICR 142: 272, 310, 315
Portect (UK) Ltd. v. *Mogensen* [1976] ICR 396: 104
Porter v. *National Union af Journalists* [1980] IRLR 404: 427
Post Office v. *Roberts* [l98O] IRLR 347: 162
Post Office v. *Union of Post Office Workers* [1974] ICR 378: 379
Post Office v. *Union of Communication Workers* [1990] IRLR 143: 493, 495
Powell v. *London Borough of Brent* [1987] IRLR 466: 304
Presho v. *Department of Health and Social Security* [1984] ICR 463: 506
Prestwick Circuits Ltd v. *McAndrew* [1990] IRLR 191: 161
Price v. *Civil Service Commission* [1978] ICR 2: 343, 344
Price v. *Rhondda UDC* [1923] 2 Ch. 372: 330
Puttick v. *John Wright & Sons (Blackwall) Ltd.* [1972] ICR 457: 232

Quinn v. *Leathem* [1901] AC 495: 52, 479

R v. *Birmingham City Council* ex p EOC [1989] IRLR 173: 341
R v. *East Berkshire AHA* [1984] IRLR 278: 304
R v. *Jones* [1974] ICR 310: 479
RCA Corpn. v. *Pollard* [1983] Ch. 135: 480
Rank Xerox v. *Churchill* [1988] IRLR 280: 321
Rainey v. *Greater Glasgow Health Board* [1987] IRLR 16: 345, 358, 359
Rayware v. *TGWU* [1989] IRLR 134: 499
Re Junior Carlton Club [1922] 1 KB 166: 121
Re Richmond Gate Property Co. Ltd. [1965] 1 WLR 335: 215
Reading v. *Attorney-General* [1951] AC 507: 167
Ready-Mixed Concrete (SE) Ltd. v. *Minister of Pensions* [1968] 2 QB 497: 110
Reid v. *Camphill Engravers* [1990] IRLR 268: 298
Reiss Engineering Co. Ltd. v. *Harris* [1985] IRLR 232: 371
Reynders v. *Belgian State,* Case 2/74 [1974] ECR 631 (ECJ): 19
Ridge v. *Baldwin* [1964] AC 40: 119
Rigby v. *Ferodo* [1988] ICR 29: 294, 295
Rinner-Kuhn v. *FWW Spezial-Gebaude-reinigung GmbH and Co. KG* Case 179/89 [1989] IRLR 493: 361*bis*, 362
Robb v. *Green* 1895 2 QB 315: l69
Roberts v. *Hopwood* [1925] AC 578: 330
Roberts v. *Tate & Lyle Food and Distributions Ltd* [1983] IRLR 240: 349
Robertson v. *Britsh Gas Corporation* [1983] ICR 351: 137, 153
Robinson v. *Crompton Parkinson Ltd.* [1978] ICR 401: 162
Roger Bullivant Ltd v. *Ellis* [1987] ICR 464: 169
Rogers v. *Vosper Thorneycroft (UK) Ltd* [1989] IRLR 82: 312
Rookes v. *Barnard* [1964] AC 1129: 52, 480, 482, 484
Rothwell v. *APEX* [1976] ICR 211: 404

Sagar v. *Ridehalgh* [1931] 1 Ch. 310: 157
Sayers v. *International Drilling Co.* NV [1971] 1 WLR 1176: 102
Scala Ballroom (Wolverhampton) Ltd. v. *Ratcliffe* [1958] 3 All ER 220: 479
Scott v. *Beam College* EOR, No. 4 November/December 1985 p. 6: 357
Secretary of State for Employment v. *ASLEF* [1972] 2 QB 443: 156, 159
Secretary of State for Employment v. *Spence* [1986] IRLR 248: 284
Secretary of State for Scotland v. *Greater Glasgow Health Board* [1991] IRLR 187: 19
Sheet Metal Components Ltd. v. *Plumridge* [1974] ICR 373: 295
Shepherd FC Ltd. v. *Jerrom* [1986] IRLR 358: 289
Shirlaw v. *Southern Foundries Ltd* [1939] 2 KB 206: 146
Short v. *Poole Corporation* [1926] I Ch. 66: 330
Shotton v. *Hammond,* The Times, 2 December 1976: 457
Sillifant v. *Powell Duffryn Timber Ltd.* [1983] IRLR 91: 310

Simmons v. *Hoover Ltd.* [1977] ICR 61: 475, 477
Singh v. *British Rail Engineering* EOR No. 5, January/February 1986, p. 24: 343
Singh v. *British Steel Corporation* [1974] IRLR 131: 152, 298
South Wales Miners' Federation v. *Glamorgan Coal Company Ltd* [1905] AC 239: 52, 481
Spink v. *Express Foods Group Ltd* [1990] IRLR 320: 310
Stacey v. *Babcock Power Ltd.* IDS Brief 315 December 1985 p. 5: 301
Star Sea Transport Corporation of Monrovia v. *Slater* [1978] IRLR 507: 486
Steel v. *Union of Post Office Workers* [l978] ICR 181: 345
Sterling Egineering Co Ltd. v. *Patchett* [1955] AC 434: 370
Stevenson Jordan & Harrison Ltd. v. *Macdonald & Evans* [1925] 1 TLR 101 109
Strathclyde Regional Council v. *Porcelli* [1986] IRLR 134: 341
Sufflex Ltd v. *Thomas* [1987] IRLR 435: 312
Sutcliffe v. *Hawker Siddeley Aviation Ltd.* [1973] ICR 560: 321
Swain v. *West (Butchers) Ltd.* [1936] 3 All ER261: 174
Sybron Corporation v. *Rochem Ltd.* [1983] ICR 801: 174
System Floors Ltd. v. *Daniel* [1982] ICR 54: 137

Taff Vale Railway Co v. *ASRS*, [1901] AC 426: 52, 418
Tanna v. *Post Office* [1981] ICR 374: 116
Tarmac Roadstone Holdings Ltd. v. *Peacock* [1973] 1 WLR 594: 198
Taylor v. *National Union of Mineworkers* [1985] IRLR 99: 419, 430
Taylor v. *National Union of Mineworkers* (Derbyshire Area) [1984] IRLR 440: 430
Taylor v. *NUS* [1967] 1 WLR 532: 119
Thomas v. *National Union of Mineworkers* [1985] IRLR 136: 419, 430, 497
Thomas v. *Adjudication Officer and Secretary of State for Social Security* [1990] IRLR 436: 19, 334
Thomas Marshall (Exports) Ltd v. *Guinle* [1978] ICR 905: 169, 304
Thomson D. C. v. *Deakin* [1952] Ch. 646: 481
Todd v. *British Midland Airways Ltd.* [1978] ICR 959: 104
Tomalin v. *S. Pearson Ltd.* [1909] 2 KB 61: 103
Torquay Hotel Co. Ltd. v. *Cousins* [1969] 2 Ch. 106.: 481
Tottenham Green Under Fives Centre v. *Marshall* [1989] IRLR 147: 351
Tottenham Green Under Fives Centre v. *Marshall* (No. 2) 1991 IRLR 162: 35
Tracey v. *Zest Equipment Co. Ltd.* [1982] ICR 481: 290
Turley v. *Allders Stores* [1980] IRLR 4: 341
Turner v. *Mason* [1845] 14 M & W 112: 160
Turner v. *Pleasurama Casinos* [1976] IRLR 151: 178

UK Atomic Energy Authority v. *Claydon* [1974] ICR 128: 321
Ulsterbus v. *Henderson* [1989] IRLR 251: 310
United Bank v. *Akhtar* [1989] IRLR 507: 161
Union Traffic v. *TGWU* [1989] IRLR 127: 497, 499
Universe Tankships Inc. of Monrovia v. *ITF* [1983] 1 AC 366: 482

Van Binsberen, Case 33/74 [1974] ECR 1299 (ECJ): 19
Van Colson and Kamann, Case 14/83 [1984] ECR 1892: 19 , 334
Van Duyn v. *Home Office* Case 41/74 [1974] ECR 1337 (ECJ): 19

Wadcock v. *London Borough of Brent* [1990] IRLR 223: 304
Waddington v. *Leicester Council for Social Services* [1977] IRLR 32: 357
Waite v. *GCHQ* [1983] ICR 653: 319
Walker v. *Josiah Wedgewood & Sons Ltd.* [1978] ICR 744: 162
Warner Holidays Ltd. v. *Secretary of State for Social Services* [1983] ICR 440: 110
W. & J. Wass v. *Binns* [1982] ICR 486: 310

Appendix 2 – Table of Cases

Webb v. *EMO Air Cargo Ltd* [1992] IRLR 116: 341
Weddell and Co. Ltd. v. *Tepper* [1980] ICR 286: 167
Wells v. *F. Smales & Son Fish Merchants* EOR No. 2 July/August 1985 p. 24: 357
Western Excavating (ECC) Ltd v. *Sharp* [1978] ICR 221: 299
Westwood v. *Secretary of State for Employment* [1984] IRLR 209: 303
Whitbread plc v. *Mills* [1988] ICR 776: 310
Wickens v. *Champion Employment* [1984] ICR 365: 112, 125
Wigan Borough Council v. *Davies* [1979] IRLR 1278: 162
Williams v. *Butlers Ltd* [1975] ICR 308: 220
Williams v. *Compair Maxam Ltd* [1982] ICR 156: 312
Williams v. *Watsons Luxury Coaches* [1990] IRLR 164: 289
Wilson v. *Maynard Shipbuilding Consultants* A. B. [1978] ICR 376: 104
Wilson v. *Racher* [1974] ICR 428: 160
Wiltshire County Council v. *NAFTHE* [1980] ICR 455: 290
Wiltshire Police Authority v. *Wynn* [1980] ICR 649: 123
Wiluszynski v. *London Borough of Tower Hamlets* [1989] ICR 493: 475
Woods v. *W. M. Car Services (Peterborough) Ltd* [1982] ICR 693: 162
Worringham v. *Lloyds Bank Ltd* Case 69/80 [1981] ICR (ECJ): 19, 204*bis*, 361*bis*, 362
Writers' Guild of Great Britain v. *BBC* [1974] ICR 234: 116

Young, James and Webster v. *United Kingdom* [1981] IRLR 408: 382
Young & Woods v. *West* [1980] IRLR 201: 110
Yorke v. *British & Continental Steamship Co.* [1945] 78 Ll. LR 181: 103

Appendix 3 – Table of Statutes

Agricultural Wages Act 1948: 207
Agricultural Wages (Scotland) Act 1949: 207
Aliens Employment Act 1955: 145
Apportionment Act 1870: 216

Banking and Financial Dealings Act 1971: 186
British Nationality Act 1981: 144

Children and Young Persons Act 1933:141
Children and Young Persons Act 1963: 141
Civil Liability (Contribution) Act 1978: 176
Companies Act 1980: 439
Companies Act 1985: 439
Conspiracy and Protection of Property Act: 50, 52
Contracts (Applicable Law) Act 1990: 101, 103
Contracts of Employment Act 1963: 60
Counter-Inflation Acts 1972, 1973: 58
Criminal Law Act 1977: 479

Data Protection Act 1984: 302
Dockworkers Act 1989:124

Education (Work Experience) Act 1973: 141
Electricity Act 1989: 503
Emergency Powers Act 1920: 503
Employers' Liability (Compulsory Insurance) Act 1969: 177
Employment Act 1980: 38, 47, 64, 106, 269, 385, 388, 389, 460, 489, 490
Employment Act 1982: 38, 64, 106, 273, 314, 380, 385, 388, 389, 390, 439, 487, 489
Employment Act 1988: 38, 64, 78bis, 81, 388, 390, 410, 431, 432, 493, 495
Employment Act 1989: 38, 64, 69, 135, 141, 142, 182, 225, 268, 349
Employment Act 1990: 38, 47, 64, 65, 78*bis*, 376, 388, 390, 420–423, 457, 494
Employment Agencies Act 1973: 112, 125
Employment of Children Act 1973: 141
Employment of Women, Young Persons and Children Act 1920: 141
Employment Protection Act 1975: 38, 47, 59, 60, 70, 87, 269, 288, 325, 447, 460, 464
Employment Protection (Consolidation) Act 1978: 38, 69, 70, 103, 104, 114, 115, 123, 132–139, 151, 181, 188–195, 198, 200, 214, 219, 223, 225, 235–237, 239, 243, 244, 254, 257, 258, 261, 267, 268, 269, 270, 279–282, 284, 287, 288, 290, 292, 293, 297, 301, 306–316, 320–324, 376, 473, 477
Equal Pay Act 1970: 60, 95, 103, 104, 130, 196, 202, 329, 332, 334, 335, 338, 339, 346, 352, 355–363
European Communities Act 1972: 19, 334

Factories Act 1833: 56, 103
Factories Act 1844: 56, 103
Factories Act 1961:103, 126, 141,
Finance (No. 2) Act 1987: 447*bis*

Health and Morals of Apprentices Act 1802: 56
Health and Safety at Work etc Act 1974: 56, 60, 95, 97, 447,
Hours of Employment (Conventions) Act 1936: 185

Immigration Act 1971: 143–144
Income and Corporation Taxes Act 1988: 203
Industrial Relations Act 1971: 4, 14, 38, 47, 59, 61, 63, 65, 87, 97, 269, 376, 381, 383, 409, 415, 417, 418, 420, 425, 461, 467, 484, 503
Industrial Training Act 1964: 80, 123
Insolvency Act 1986: 224

Law Reform (Frustrated Contracts) Act 1943: 216
Law Reform (Personal Injuries) Act 1948: 179, 248

Appendix 3 – Table of Statutes

Local Government Act 1988: 375, 396
Local Government and Housing Act 1989: 190

Merchant Shipping Act 1970: 141
Mines and Quarries Act 1954: 141
Master and Servant Act 1867: 50
National Insurance Act 1911: 245

Patent Act 1949: 370
Patent Act 1977: 370–373
Pensions (Miscellaneous Provisions) Act 1990: 204*bis*
Pilotage Act 1987: 71
Police Act 1964: 117, 374
Poor Law Act 1601: 50, 51
Pneumoconiosis etc. (Workers' Compensation) Act 1979: 245
Prices and Incomes Acts 1966, 1967: 58
Public Order Act 1986: 496

Race Relations Act 1965: 329
Race Relations Act 1968: 329, 330, 332, 333, 353
Race Relations Act 1976: 60, 69, 70, 75, 97, 103, 116, 121, 123, 145, 333, 334, 338, 339–354, 363, 426
Redundancy Payments Act 1965: 60, 268
Regulation of Chimney Sweepers Act 1788: 56
Rehabilitation of Offenders Act 1971: 302
Road Haulage Wages Act 1938: 460

School Teachers' Pay and Conditions Act 1987: 448
Sex Disqualification (Removal) Act 1919: 331
Sex Discrimination Act 1975: 19, 60, 69, 70, 75, 97, 103, 116, 121, 182, 329, 332, 334, 335, 338, 339–355, 359, 362, 363, 426
Sex Discrimination Act 1986: 121, 142, 182, 315, 319, 335, 346, 349, 361, 362, 469
Social Security Act 1975: 39,103, 506
Social Security Act 1985: 247
Social Security (No. 2) Act 1980: 507
Social Security and Housing Benefits Act 1982: 39, 247
Social Security Act 1986: 204, 249, 506, 507
Social Security Pensions Act 1975: 56, 134, 204, 349, 362
Social Security Act 1989: 507
Statute of Artificers 1563: 50, 51
Statute of Labourers 1361: 50, 51
Statutory Sick Pay Act 1991: 247

Teachers' Pay and Conditions Act 1987: 448
Telecommunication Act 1984: 504
Terms and Conditions of Employment Act 1959: 73
Trade Boards Act 1909: 52, 205, 206
Trade Disputes Act 1906: 52, 418, 420, 479, 484
Trade Disputes and Trade Union Act 1927: 53
Trade Union Act 1913: 410, 418, 426
Trade Union Act 1984: 410, 411, 431, 433, 435, 473
Trade Union Act 1871: 418
Trade Union and Labour Relations Act 1974: 38, 60, 269, 389, 415, 417, 420, 425, 485, 489
Trade Union and Labour Relations Act 1976: 38, 389, 425, 426, 484, 489
Trade Union and Labour Relations (Consolidation) Act 1992: 43, 70, 72, 78, 78*bis*, 96, 97, 104, 105, 106, 114–116, 149, 172, 188, 269, 273, 308, 314, 325–328, 376, 379, 384, 385, 390, 392, 393, 396, 406, 408, 411–413, 416, 419–423, 426, 431–434, 436, 457, 461, 462, 464, 467, 473, 474, 476, 477, 479, 485–488, 490, 492–500, 501, 504, 505
Transport Act 1968:185
Truck Act 1831–1940: 66, 104, 121, 217, 220

Unfair Contract Terms Act 1977: 179

Wages Act 1986: 80, 86, 103, 116, 126, 207*bis*, 208, 217–221, 288
Wages Councils Act 1945: 53

Young Persons (Employment) Act 1938 and 1964: 184

Appendix 4 – Table of Statutory Instruments and Orders in Council

The numbers given refer to paragraphs.

Civil Service Order in Council 1982: 118
Conditions of Employment and National Arbitration Order 1305: 53
Conditions of Employment and National Arbitration Order 1376: 53
Conduct of Employment Agencies and Employment Businesses Regulations 1976 (SI 1976, No. 715): 125, 145

Dockworkers Employment Scheme 1967 (SI 1967, No. 1252):124

Equal Pay (Amendment) Regulations 1983 (SI 1983 No.1919): 19, 357

Health and Safety (Youth Training) Regulations 1983 (SI 1983 No. 1919): 123

Race Relations (Prescribed Public Bodies) Regulations 1984 (SI 1984, No. 218): 145

Safety Representatives and Safety Committees Regulations 1977 (SI 1977 No. 500): 193
Statutory Maternity Pay (General) Regulations 1986 (SI 1986/1960): 249
Statutory Sick Pay (General) Regulations 1982 (SI 1982/1984): 247

Transfer of Undertakings (Protection of Employment) Regulations 1981 (SI 1981 No. 1794): 19, 275, 284–287, 306

Unfair Dismissal (Variation of Qualifying Period) Order 1979 (SI 1979 No. 959): 269
Unfair Dismissal (Variation of Qualifying Period) Order 1985, (SI 1985 No. 782): 269

Appendix 4 – Table of Statutory Instruments

Index

The numbers given are paragraph numbers:

Absence from work: 240–241
See Incapacity for work
'Abstention' by the law: 3, 36, 49, 52
See Voluntarism
Accident at Work: 175–179
See Injury at work, Incapacity for work
Action Short of Dismissal: 185, 376–380, 384, 404
Advisory, Conciliation and Arbitration Service: 62, 69, 70–71, 72, 73, 79, 84*bis*, 115, 271, 273, 274, 354, 357, 505
Codes of Practice: 71, 97,188,189, 308, 461
Agencies Employment *see* Employment Agencies
Agency, law of: 152
Agency Shop: 389
Agency workers: 112, 115
See Casual Workers
Agricultural Wages Boards: 207
Agricultural Wages Inspectorate: 208
Agricultural Workers: 32, 107, 122, 196, 207–208
Agriculture: 21, 32,180
Aliens: 143–145
Amalgamated Engineering Union: 401, 407, 433
Antenatal care: Time off for 192,195
Appeal: *See* Court of Appeal, Employment Appeal Tribunal
Apprentice: 123, 225, 363
Approved Closed Shop: 389
Arbitration: 35, 47, 48, 52, 53, 71, 72–74, 95, 213, 274, 455
Arbitration Awards: 213
See ACAS and CAC
Armed forces: 145, 503, 504
Articles of Clerkship: 225
Artists: 144, 164
Association of Scientific, Technical and Managerial Staffs (ASTMS): 401
Association Freedom of: See Freedom of Association
Authors: 144, 166
'Auxiliary legislation': 52–54, 67

Baking industry: 122
Ballots: 390–391, 493–495
See Industrial Action, Trade Union
ballot constituency: 495
Code of Practice: 495
postal: 78, 433, 495
remedy for union members: 493, 495*bis*
rolled up question: 495
workplace: 433

Banking: 24
Bank employees: 374
Bank Holidays: 186
Banking Insurance and Finance Union: 400
Bibliography: Appendix 1
Black Workers:
See Ethnic Minorities, Race Relations, Racial Discrimination
'Blue collar' workers:
See Manual Workers
Bridlington Principles: 403, 404
See Trade Union Congress
Breach of contract
See Contract of Employment
Britain *See* Great Britain
British Leyland: 459
See Motor Car Industry
British Printing Industries Federation: 437
British Rail: 382
railway employees: 122, 583
rule book: 156
Building Industry:
See Construction Industry
Bullock Committee Report: 442

Index

Canada: 330
Care: duty of
See Duty of Reasonable Care
Casual workers: 67, 107, 124
See Agency Workers, Temporary Workers
Catering and Hotels Industry: 122, 127
catering workers: 196
Central Arbitration Committee: 62, 71, 72–74, 95, 96, 213, 361, 462–463
Certificate of Independence: 416, 434
Certification Officer: 78, 87, 406, 411, 413, 415, 416, 433, 434, 436, 437, 495
Channel Islands: 9
'Check-off': 220, 413
Children: 55, 93, 94, 140–141
contractual capacity: 140
restrictions on employment: 141, 182
See also Factories, Young Workers
Chronology of Labour Legislation: Appendix 2
Civil Aviation Employees: 122
Civil Servants: 14, 31, 53, 94, 118, 145, 375, 481, 504
See Civil Service, Crown Servants, Public Employees
Civil Service:14, 117, 145, 210, 332, 375, 452, 471, 504
Closed Shop: 13, 63, 65, 80, 97, 269, 276, 308, 376, 378, 381, 382, 383, 384, 386–395, 416, 426, 459, 479
Coal Industry: 26, 56; 117, 200
employment of children. *See* Children
strike 1984–1985: *See* Miners Strike 1984–1985
trade unions in: 400
See also: Mine, National Coal Board, National Union of Mineworkers
Codes of Practice: 71, 76, 96–97, 189, 193, 308, 334, 363, 448, 461, 495*bis*, 496
Co-determination: 54
See Industrial Democracy
Collective agreements: 33, 40–41, 98, 213, 465–469, 506
compulsory: 47
content of: 469
contract of employment and: 91, 147, 149–153, 181, 213, 465
contractual effect of: 466, 467, 468
definition of: 40–41, 466
discriminatory: 361
dismissals: 265
disputes of rights and interests: 44–45
enforcement of: 465, 466, 467, 468, 469
equal pay and: 73–74, 361
extension of terms and conditions: 53, 62, 66, 73, 460
guaranteed week: 234
hours and holidays: 180
legal status of: 61, 62, 149
maternity rights and: 250
'no-strike' clauses in: 476
part-time workers and: 131
patents and: 372
peace obligation: 476
procedural agreements: distinction with
substantive agreements: 43, 150
private international law and: 105
redundancy: 266
sick leave: 256
statutory statement of terms and conditions: 138, 181
substantive agreements:
distinction with procedural agreements: 43
transfer of: 287
variation: 153, 208
Collective Bargaining: 15, 33, 36, 40–41, 93, 448–469, 470, 493
definition of: 40–41
disclosure of information for: *See* Dis–closure of Information for Collective Bargaining
discipline and: 288, 456
disputes of rights and interests: 44–45
dynamic method of: 43, 44, 213
encouragement of: 70
extent of: 149, 449–456
formal and informal: 33, 61,157
health and safety: 447
historical: 15, 51–67
job security: 274
lay-off and: 234, 235
legal support for: 52–54, 460–464
levels of: 150, 153, 450–455
low pay and: 206, 210, 211
pay: 196,197, 213
recognition of trade unions for: 47, 52, 61, 62, 287, 326, 448, 464
restriction: 65–67

school-teachers: 448
scope of: 213, 456
sick pay: 243
single union: 455
Single table: 455
voluntary and compulsory: 46
See Industrial Democracy
Collective Redundancies: *See* Redundancy
Commission for Racial Equality (CRE): 75–76, 97, 333, 348, 353, 354, 363
Commissioner for the Rights of Trade Unionist Members 78*bis*, 496
Committee of Inquiry on Industrial Democracy (Bullock Report): 442
Common Employment: Doctrine of: 179
Common Law: 1, 17, 91–92, 475
dismissal at: 270, 300
suspension from work at: 231–233, 288
termination at: 289–299
wrongful dismissal at: 263, 264, 303, 304, 323
See Contract of Employment, Duty of Reasonable Care, Restraint of Trade, Summary Dismissal, Trade Union: rules
Community (EEC) Law
See European Economic Community
Company: 283, 285, 441, 442, 443–447
Company Directors: 119, 203, 328, 439, 443–447
Compensation: 273, 310, 313, 314, 315, 317, 380, 384, 392, 394, 395
See Unfair Dismissal
Competition by Former Employees: 364–368
See Restraint of Trade
Comptroller of Patents: *See* Patents
Conciliation: 35, 48, 52, 71, 354, 505
See Advisory, Conciliation and Arbitration Service
Confederation of British Industries (CBI): 70, 438
Confederation of Health Service Employees: 336, 407
Confederation of Shipbuilding and Engineering Unions: 405
Confidential Information: 166, 169–174, 365, 366, 462
Conflict of Laws
See Private International Law
Conservative Party: 5, 13, 26, 27, 53, 375, 384, 447, 459
Conspiracy
criminal: 479
civil: 479, 480, 484, 485
See Industrial Action
Constitution: 13, 18, 93
Construction Industry: 107, 122, 133, 230, 451
Constructive Dismissal: 147, 162, 232, 299
See Redundancy, Unfair Dismissal
Consultation: 42, 54, 62, 118, 275, 375, 416, 440, 447
See Workers Participation
Contempt of Court: 84*bis*
Continuity of Employment: 124, 126, 129, 230, 236, 239, 261, 279–282, 284
Contract: collective agreement as: 466, 467, 468
Contract: trade union rules as: *See* Trade Union: rules
Contract of Employment: 50–51, 80, 91, 100, 107, 108–113, 114–116, 288, 321
breach: 81, 137, 160, 163, 167, 172
collective agreement, relation to: 91, 147, 149–153, 213
constructive dismissal and: 147
continuity of *See* Continuity of Employment
contract of apprenticeship: *See* Apprenticeship
contract of service: *See* Contract of Service
contract for services (self employment):
See Contract for Services
contractual capacity: 140–142
crown servants and: *See* Crown Servants
custom and practice and: 157
damages: 171, 176
duration: 290
duties of employer and employee: *See* Duty of Mutual Co-operation, Duty of Reasonable Care, Duty of Faithful Service, Duty to Provide Work, Duty to pay
equality clause: 360
fixed term contract: 290, 319

frustration: 165, 216, 228, 255, 256, 289
fundamental breach: 147
history: 50–51,107, 263–264
implied terms: 138,146, 147, 148, 154–156, 158–179, 215, 231–233
inventions: 370
lay-off and: 231–233, 234, 237
maternity and: 249, 250
pay and: 213, 215, 231–233
private international law: *See* Private International Law
place of work: 146
purpose contract: 290
repudiation of contract: 147, 289, 294, 298, 299, 321
sickness and: 242, 243, 247*bis*
sources of terms of contract: 146–157
specific performance of: 263, 475
statute: relation to: 95
strike: effect of: 475–483
terms of: 98, 146–179
termination of: 153, 160, 270, 289–299
transfer of: 285
unfair dismissal and: *See* Unfair Dismissal
variation of contract: 138, 153, 295–296
works' rules and: 154–156
Contractors Independent
See Contract for Services
Contract for Services: 107, 108–113, 494
Contract of Service: 107, 108–113, 114–115, 116, 362
Co-operation Duty of
See Duty of Mutual Co-operation
Corporatist Industrial Democracy: 59
See Industrial Democracy
Court System: 68, 80, 81, 84*bis*, 85
Court of Appeal: 81, 87, 89
Courts of Inquiry: *See* Inquiry
Court of Session: 79, 81, 87
Criminal Law: 50–51, 496
See Industrial Action
Crown Prerogative: 94, 118
Crown Servants: 118, 135, 375
See Civil Servants, Civil Service, Public Employees
'Custom and Practice': 33, 51, 57, 98, 146, 147, 151, 155–157, 232, 242, 243, 456
Damages: 171, 176, 303
Declaration: 303
Deductions: *see* Wages
Defamation: 483, 485
Demarcation disputes: 393
Denmark: 4
Department of Employment (DE): 71, 79, 144, 277, 328
Director: *See* Company Directors
Disablement: 246
Discipline: 133, 219, 262
Codes of Practice: 71
collective bargaining and: 288, 456
disciplinary suspension from work: *See* Suspension from Work
fines: 219
procedures to deal with: 69, 97, 274, 276, 288
Discipline by Trade Unions: *see* Trade Union
Disclosure of Information for Collective Bargaining: 47, 62, 71, 73–74, 97, 115, 172, 173, 213, 460–463
Discrimination: 75–76, 145, 329–363, 426
See Racial Discrimination, Sex Discrimination
Dismissal: 123, 147, 160, 162, 167, 171 175, 178, 216, 232, 263, 264, 265, 270, 289–299, 300, 303, 304, 323, 475
reasons for: 300–302
See Closed Shop, Compensation, Constructive Dismissal, Notice Terminating Employment, Redundancy, Summary Dismissal, Termination of Employment, Transfer of Undertakings, Unfair Dismissal, Wrongful Dismissal
Disputes of interest: 44–45
Disputes of rights: 44–45
Disputes Procedures: 97, 153
Distributive Trades: 122, 196
See Shop assistants
Docks 122, 124
registered dockworkers: 124
Domestic workers: 107, 121, 124, 350
Donovan Report: See Royal Commission on Trade Unions and Employers' Associations
Drivers: 122, 185
See Road Transport Industry
Duress: 482
See Industrial Action

Duty of Faithful Service: 146, 158, 166–174, 365
Duty of Mutual Co-operation: 146, 158, 159–162
Duty of Reasonable Care: 146, 158, 175–179, 183, 248
Duty to Pay: 231–233
Duty to Provide Work: 163–165, 231

Earnings
See Remuneration, Wages
Economy: 20–32
Electrical, Electronic, Telecommunications and Plumbing Union (EETPU) 401, 402, 407, 433, 434, 476
Electricity workers: 451, 504
Emergency Powers: 503, 504
Employee: 114–115, 119, 135, 377
See Agency Workers, Casual Workers Contract of Service, Contract for Services, Part-time Workers, Temporary Workers, Worker
Employer
insolvency of: *See* Insolvency
rights and duties of: *See* Duty of Faithful Service, Duty of Mutual Co-operation, Duty of Reasonable Care, Duty to Pay, Duty to Provide Work
Employers' Associations: 436–438
Employment:
continuity of: *See* Continuity of Employment
termination of: *See* Termination of Employment
Employment Agencies: 94, 112, 125, 145, 348
Employment Business: 125
Employment Appeal Tribunal (EAT): 79, 87–89, 111, 394, 406, 413, 416
Employment Law: 34
Employment Training: 123, 278
Engineering Employers' Federation (EEF): 437
Engineering Workers: 122, 459
England: 7–9
Equal Opportunities Commission (EOC): 75–76, 97, 332, 333, 348, 352–354, 363
Equal Pay: 4, 19, 60, 71, 73–74, 86, 95, 103, 104, 130, 196, 202, 204, 204*bis*, 257, 329, 332, 334, 335, 338, 346, 349, 355–362, 363
Essential Services: 503, 504
Ethnic minorities: 12, 67, 329, 337, 338
See Race Relations, Racial Discrimination
European Commission on Human Rights: 375
European Convention for the Protection of Human Rights and Fundamental Freedoms: 13, 334*bis*, 374, 375, 382
European Court of Human Rights: 375, 382
European Court of Justice: 18, 19, 204, 249, 329, 334, 349, 361, 362, 374
European Economic Community (EEC): 4, 5, 18–19, 121, 144–145, 204, 260, 349
Action Programme: 5, 18, 125, 131
Charter of Fundamental Social Rights of Workers: 5, 18, 334*bis*, 375, 444, 464
collective redundancies: 18, 19, 321, 325–328, 464
Convention on the Law Applicable to Contractual Obligations: 101, 103
Draft Fifth Directive: 443
equal pay and equal treatment: 18, 204*bis*, 334, 335, 345, 349, 357, 361, 361*bis*, 362, 375
European Company: 443, 445
European Works Council: 5, 18, 444
free movement of labour: 18, 101, 143, 144, 145
freedom of association: 375
Industrial democracy: 443–445
Health and Safety: 447
Occupational Pensions Directive: 349
part-time workers: 127, 131
Regulation 543/69: 185
Regulation for European Company Statute: 5
Social Security Directive: 349
temporary workers: 121
Transfer of Undertakings: 18, 19, 275, 284–287, 464
Vredeling Draft Directive: 447
European Social Charter:141,182, 334*bis*, 374
Extension of Collective Agreements
See Collective Agreements

Factories Acts: 56, 103
children: 141
Fair Wages Policy: 375

Index

Fair Wages Resolutions: 52, 53, 66, 73, 374, 375, 460
Faithful Service
See Duty of Faithful Service
Fidelity
See Duty of Faithful Service
Firemen: 117, 122
Fixed Term Contracts: 290, 319
See Contracts of Employment
Flanders, Allan: 33, 41
Ford Motor Company: 437
Foreign workers: 143–145
Formal Investigation: 76, 363
See Commission for Racial Equality, Equal Opportunities Commission
France: 2, 4, 20–26, 149, 205, 472
Freedom of Association: 374–396
Fringe Benefits: 128, 203
Frustration of Contract: 165, 216, 228, 255, 256, 289

Gas Workers: 122, 504
General Electric Company (GEC); 437,
General, Municipal, Boilermakers and Allied Trades Union (GMBATU): 401, 407
Geography: 7–9
Germany: 321, 444, 472
'Golden formula': 486
See Trade Disputes
Government
Parliamentary Government: 13–14
role of governmental institutions: 68–79
See Historical Background
Government Communications Headquarters (GCHQ): 13, 65, 118, 375
Great Britain: 1
economy: 20–32
geography: 7–9
political and legal system: 13–17
Greece: 180, 472
Grievance Procedures: 69, 97
Guarantee Payments: 69, 95, 129, 214, 235–237, 238, 279, 290, 477
Guaranteed week collective agreements: 234
See Collective Agreements

Health and Safety at Work: 3, 34, 42, 55–56, 60, 62, 93, 95, 97, 125, 126, 183, 248, 254, 448
Health and Safety Commission: 97, 193, 352, 448
Health and Safety Executive: 182, 448
Historical Background: 1–6, 15, 49–67, 263–264
Holidays: 55–56, 80, 81, 133, 180–186, 205, 224, 225
Homeworkers: 107, 112, 126
Hotels and catering: 122, 127
Hours of Work: 55–56, 133, 180–185
See Time Off Work, Overtime
House of Commons: 13, 14
See Parliament
House of Lords
judicial function: 19, 81, 87, 89
legislative function: *See* Parliament

Immigration controls: 143–145
Immunity, statutory
See Industrial Action, Strike, Trade Dispute
Imperial Chemical Industries (ICI): 437,
Implied terms
See Contracts of Employment
Incapacity for Work: 240–261, 282
Income Tax: 113
See Tax
Incomes Policies: 5, 58–59, 61, 70, 74, 196
Incorporation of Collective Agreement:
See Collective Agreement, Contracts of Employment
Independent contractor
See Contract for Services
Independent Labour Party: 15
Independent Review Committee of the TUC: 395
See Trades Union Council
Inducing Breach of Contract: 52, 481, 483, 484, 485, 494
See Industrial Action
Industrial Action: 52, 61, 63, 92, 470–507
authorisation by trade union: 420, 421, 495
ballots: 47, 63, 65, 78, 78*bis*, 97, 493–496, 503
conspiracy: civil: 52, 479, 480, 484, 485
conspiracy: criminal: 52, 479
contract and: 264, 473, 475–476
continuity of employment and: 282
'cooling off' period: 503

criminal sanctions: 473, 496, 498, 504
damages for: 475
definition: 473
dismissal for: 307, 477, 499
duress: 482
emergency powers and: 503
Government intervention in: 52–54, 503
history: 50–54
immunity statutory: 47, 52, 62, 63, 65, 92, 473, 474, 478, 479, 484–489, 490–492, 498, 499
inducing breach of contract: 52, 481, 483, 484, 485, 494
inducing breach of statutory duty: 483
injunction to restrain: 81, 478, 501–502
interference with business by unlawful means: 52, 483, 485
intimidation: 52, 482, 483, 484, 485, 494
lay-off: 233, 236, 239
lock-out: 473, 477
notice of: 267, 475
nuisance and: 483
patterns of: 470–472
peace obligation: 476
picketing: 65, 97, 473, 490, 492, 496–500, 502
'right to strike': 3, 13, 52–54, 63, 473–474
secondary: *See* Secondary Action
sit-ins: 442
state intervention: 503–507
strikes – *See* Strikes
social security benefits during: 506–507
tortious liability for: 52, 473, 474, 478–483
unconstitutional: 63
unfair dismissal and: 307, 324, 477, 499
unofficial: 420, 421, 477, 494
withdrawal of wages: 475
work-in: 442
See Trade Dispute
Industrial Arbitration Board (IAB): 73
Industrial Conflict – *see* Industrial Action
Industrial Court: 73
Industrial Democracy: 439–448
See Corporatist Industrial Democracy, Workers Participation
Industrial Injury Benefit: 247*bis*
Industrial Relations: 33, 97
Industrial Relations Research Unit, Warwick University: 271, 273
Industrial Tribunals: 4, 38, 68, 75, 76, 79, 80–86, 94, 96, 110, 111, 139, 194, 333, 338, 354, 357, 360, 390
ACAS and: 71
appeals from: 87–89
composition of: 82–84
jurisdiction:19, 80, 194, 219, 223, 237, 238, 270–273, 287, 373, 393, 394
precedent: 89
procedure in: 84*bis*–86
See Employment Appeal Tribunal
Inflation: 57–67
Information – Disclosure of *See* Disclosure of Information
Injunctions: 81, 84*bis*, 171, 172, 304, 420, 430, 478, 501–502
See Industrial Action
Injury at work: 448
See Incapacity for Work
Inquiry: 48, 71, 79, 505
Insolvency: 103, 224–225
Insurance: 177
Interference with Trade: 483, 485
See Industrial Action
Interim Relief: 380, 384
International Labour Organisation (ILO): 2, 5,180, 182, 374, 375, 377
ILO Convention No. 26: 206
ILO Convention No. 41 (1937): 182
ILO Convention No. 45 (1935): 182
ILO Convention No. 87 (1948) on Freedom of Association: 374, 375
ILO Convention No. 94 on Labour Clauses in Public Contracts: 375
ILO Convention No. 98 (1949) on the Right to Organise and Collective Bargaining: 374
ILO Convention No. 111 (1951) on Equal Pay: 334*bis*
ILO Convention No. 135 (1972) concerning Protection and Facilities to be Afforded to Workers' Representatives in the Undertaking: 374
ILO Convention No. 151 (1978) on Protection of the Right to Organise in the Public Service: 374
ILO Recommendation No. 119 (1982) concerning Termination of Employment: 269, 271, 273, 305, 321

Index

International Transport Federation (ITF) 105, 482
Intimidation: 52, 482, 483, 484, 485, 494
See Industrial Action
Invalidity Benefit: 246
Inventions by Employees: 369–373
Ireland 7–9, 180, 472
Iron and Steel Trades' Confederation: 400
Isle of Man: 9
Itemised Pay Statement: 223

Japan: 20–26, 472, 476
Job creation: 277–278
Job evaluation: 202, 356, 357, 360
Job security: 262–328
Job-sharing: 131*bis*
Joinder of trade union: 385
Joint Industrial Councils: 44, 73, 405, 451
Joint Shop Stewards Committee. 458
Judicial Review: 375

Kahn-Freund, Professor Sir Otto: 3, 15, 36–37, 44, 47, 151, 205

Labour Courts: *See* Industrial Tribunals
Labour Force, Structure of: 27–32, 335
Labour Law
definition of: 34–38
sources of: 90–98
Labour Legislation, a Chronology to: Appendix 2
Labour Minister
See Department of Employment
Labour Party: 4, 13, 15, 16, 26, 53, 409, 410, 414, 434, 446, 459
Labour Representation Committee: 15, 410
Laissez-Faire: 1, 56
See Historical Background
Language: 11
'Last in first out': 266
Lay-off: 226–239
Legal system: 17
Legislation, as a Source of Labour Law: 93–95
Liberal Party: 14
Local Authorities: 396, 451
employees: 117, 122, 190, 471
Local Government Officers: 122
Low Pay: 206, 210, 211
See Women Workers

Manpower Services Commission (MSC): 66, 77
Manual workers: 27, 120, 126, 196, 197, 199, 217, 218, 219, 220, 221, 240, 245, 271, 450–453, 456, 458, 459, 464
Manufacturing Industry: 21–26, 28, 198, 202, 209, 271, 453, 459, 471
Manufacturing Science and Finance Union :401
Marital Status: 142, 339
See Sex Discrimination
Marx: 36
'Master and Servant' Law of: 34, 50–51
Maternity Rights: 103, 129, 130, 192, 249–253, 257–260, 362
pay: 95, 249–253, 279
right to return: 257–260
See Pregnancy, Sexual Discrimination, Women
Measured Day Work: 201
Mediation: 48, 71
Merchant Seamen: 107, 122, 135, 195, 221, 504
Midwives: 350
Military Employment:
See Armed Forces
Mine: 141, 184,185
See Coal Industry, National Coal Board, National Union of Mineworkers
Miners' Strike: 61
miners' strike 1984–1985: 5, 24, 423, 430, 470, 471, 496, 507
See Coal Industry, National Union of Mineworkers, National Coal Board
Minimum Wage Legislation: 52, 55, 66, 93, 94, 196, 205–212, 460
See Wages Councils
Mining
See Coal Industry
Minister of Labour: 53
See Department of Employment
Minors
See Children
Mobility: 146, 161
Monetarism: 64–67
Motor Car Industry: 25
See British Leyland

National and Local Government Officers Association: 407, 412
National Coal Board (NCB): 117, 200, 400

See Coal Industry, Miners Strike, National Union of Mineworkers
National Graphical Association: 422,
National Health Service (NHS): 116, 117, 122, 245, 337, 452, 471
National Federation of Building Trade Employers: 437
National Industrial Relations Court: 87
National Insurance 204, 238, 247*bis*
National Insurance Fund: 225
National Security: 307, 375
National Union of Mineworkers: 204, 400, 423, 496, 507
See Coal Industry, Miners Strike, National Coat Board
National Union of Public Employees: 336, 407
National Union of Seamen: 501
Nationalised industries: 54
See Public Corporations
Natural Justice: 404, 428
Negligence: 175–179
See Duty of Reasonable Care
Negotiation: 42
See Collective Bargaining
Netherlands: 127, 472
'New Commonwealth' countries: 12, 331
See Ethnic Minorities
Northern Ireland: 7–9, 10
See Ireland
Notice Terminating Employment: 133, 147, 214, 225, 239, 244, 264, 265, 267, 279, 290, 291, 292, 297, 317, 324, 475
common law provisions: 147
statutory minimum period of: 4, 60
Nuisance: 483, 485, 497

Occupational Pensions
See Pensions
Office workers: 122
Office-holders: 119
Oil: 22, 196
Oil Rig Workers: 122, 499
Overtime: 128,183, 212, 214, 266
See Hours of Work, Time Off Work

Parliament: 13, 14, 93, 94, 96
Participation
See Workers' Participation
Part-time Work: 29, 67, 107, 127–131, 135, 195, 210, 243, 280, 336
Patents: 369–373
Paternity leave: 250, 362
Pay
See Remuneration, Wages
Pay As You Earn Tax (PAYE): 95, 221
Pay Statement: 223
Payment By Results: 199–200, 202, 231
Payment of Wages
manner of payment: 217–221
payment by weight: 222
payment in kind: 218
Payment Systems: 197–202
Peace Obligation: 476
See Collective Agreement, Industrial Action
Pendulum arbitration: 455
Pensions: 42, 133, 134, 204, 204*bis*, 349, 361 *bis*, 368
occupational pension schemes 62, 130, 131, 204, 225, 349, 362, 416
State Earnings Related Pension Scheme (SERPS): 204
Picketing: 65, 97, 473, 490, 492, 496*bis*, 500, 502
See Industrial Action
Piece-work: 109, 164, 199, 231
'Pluralism': 33, 159
Police: 71, 117, 123, 375, 471, 496, 504
Political system: 13–19
Population: 10–12
Post Office: 71
postal workers: 117, 122, 504
Precedent: 89
Pregnancy: 249–253, 257–260, 261, 341, 362
continuity of employment: 282, 284
right to return to work: 257–260
right not to be dismissed: 252, 305, 306, 308
time off for antenatal care: 192, 194
See Maternity Rights, Sexual Discrimination, Women
Prerogative
See Crown Prerogative
Printing Trades Alliance: 405
Printing Industry: 5, 196, 422, 476, 502
Prison Officers: 503
Private International Labour Law: 99–106
Productivity: 21–26
productivity agreements: 201
Profit-sharing: 440, 447*bis*
Public Corporation: 5, 31, 67, 450–451

Index

Public Duties: Time Off for: 190, 195
Public Employees: 31, 117–118, 374, 375, 449, 453, 459, 464, 504
See Civil Servants, Civil Service, Crown Employees
Public Sector 26, 31, 285, 451, 470

Race Relations: 12, 30, 329
Racial Discrimination: 60, 75–76, 80, 86, 103, 116, 121, 130, 145, 313, 315, 318, 329–354, 426
See Ethnic Minorities
Railways: 71, 471, 504
See British Rail
Receivership: 423
Recognition of Trade Unions: 47, 52, 61, 62, 287, 326, 449, 460, 464
See Collective Bargaining, Trade Union
Redundancy: 60, 80, 86, 115, 123, 147, 226, 229, 256, 259, 266, 268, 274, 320–328, 349
collective bargaining and: 456, 477
collective redundancy: 4, 19, 62, 323, 325–328, 416
eligibility: 279–282
exemption from: 69
lay-off and: 239
part-time workers and: 129, 130
Redundancy Fund: 268, 323
redundancy payments: 80, 318, 320 328
selection for: 153, 312
time off work for redundant employees 191, 194, 195
transfer of undertaking: 285
trial period: 296
'voluntary redundancy': 318
Registration: 415
Regulatory legislation: 55–56, 93–95
Remedies for Wrongful Dismissal: 303
Remuneration: 126, 128, 133, 196–239, 288
See Wages
Restraint of Trade: 364–368
Retail Trade: 196, 209
See Shop Assistants
Retirement: 349, 362
'Right to Return to Work': 255–260, 262
'Right to Strike': 3, 13, 52–54, 63, 473–474
'Right to Work'
See Duty to Provide Work, Job Security
Road transport industry: 185, 452, 460
See Drivers
Robens Lord Committee of Inquiry into Health and Safety at Work: 56, 448
Royal College of Nursing: 417
Royal Commission on the Trade Unions and Employers' Associations (Donovan Report): 33, 61, 198, 381, 425, 453, 454
Royal Prerogative: 94, 118

Safety at Work: 34
See Health and Safety at Work
Safety Representatives and Safety Committees: 56, 193, 194, 416, 447, 459
Scotland: 7–9, 17, 99, 103
Seaman
See Merchant Seamen
Secondary Action: 65, 474, 486, 489, 490–492, 499, 502
See Industrial Action, Strike
Self-employment: 107, 494
See Contract for Services
Seniority Rights, Protection of: 261
See Continuity of Employment
Sequestration: 423
Service, Contract of:
See Contract of Service
Service Industries: 28, 127, 209
Services, Contract for:
See Contract for Services
Sex discrimination: 19, 60, 75–76, 80, 86, 103, 116, 121, 130, 131*bis*, 142, 145, 313, 315, 318, 329–354, 355, 359, 363
See Women Workers
Share Fishermen: 122, 195, 319
Share ownership schemes: 439, 446
Shipbuilding: 230, 319, 442
Shop assistants: 122, 185, 288
Shop stewards: 57, 188, 432, 440, 441, 444, 450, 454, 457–459
Short-term Workers: 124
Sick Pay: 131, 133, 146, 224, 240–247*bis*, 282, 289, 362
See Incapacity for Work
Sickness Benefit: 66
See Statutory Sick Pay
Sinzheimer, Hugo: 36

Social Charter: *see* EEC – Charter of Fundamental Social Rights and European Social Charter (Council of Europe)
'Social Contract': 4, 58, 59, 60, 62–63, 70, 73, 74, 470
Social Democratic Party (SDP): 14
Social Law. definition of: 39
Social Security: 39, 53–54, 113, 123, 125,179, 204, 221, 238, 245–247*bis*, 248, 249, 251, 253, 304, 506–507
See Industrial Action, Industrial Injury Benefit, Invalidity Benefit, Maternity Rights, Unemployment Benefit
Socialism: 15
Solicitors: 116
Sources of Labour Law: 91–98
Spain: 472
Spare-time Work: 168
Special Register Bodies: 417
Staff Association
See Trade Union
Statement of Terms and Conditions: 115, 118, 132–139, 148, 151, 181, 243, 281, 288
Status: 50–51
Statutory Statement of Terms and Conditions
See Statement of Terms and Conditions
Statutory Maternity Pay (SMP): 249, 251–252
Statutory Sick Pay: 247, 247*bis*, 361*bis*
See Sick Pay
Steel Industry: 26, 399, 471
See British Steel Corporation
Strike: 61, 63, 470–507
miners strike: *See* Miners Strike
'no-strike' clauses in collective agreements: *See* Peace Obligation
picketing: *See* Picketing
'right to strike': 3, 13, 52–54, 63, 473–474
secondary action: *See* Secondary Action
See Industrial Action, Trade Dispute
Students; 144
Summary Dismissal: 147, 160, 167, 171, 216, 264, 294, 303–304, 475
Suspension from Work: 231–239
disciplinary: 288
medical: 254, 290
Supplementary Benefit: 507
Sweated Labour: 206

Tax: 113, 203, 304
Teachers: 65, 107,117, 122, 337, 471
Technology: 23–26, 126
Telecommunications Workers: 504
Temporary workers: 5, 67, 107, 125
Termination of Employment, methods of: 289–299
See Contract of Employment
Time Off Work: 62, 71, 95, 97, 187–195, 448
See Pregnancy, Public Duties, Trade Union
Tort: 34, 52, 80, 81, 95, 176, 179, 242, 248, 420–423, 473–474, 478–483, 501
See Conspiracy, Defamation, Duty of Reasonable Care, Inducing Breach of Contract, Industrial Action, Intimidation, Nuisance, Private International Law
Trade Board: 52, 109
See Wages Council
Trade Disputes: 34, 52, 172, 236, 484–489
ACAS and: 71
definition of: 486–488
'golden formula': 486
private international law: 106
See Industrial Action
Trade Secrets: 169–174, 366
Trade unions: 15, 34, 374–396, 397–438
accounts: 78, 78*bis*, 426
action short of dismissal: *See* Action Short of Dismissal
activities of: 62, 80, 188–189, 376–380, 416
agency: 152
amalgamation of: 78, 405–407
authorisation of industrial action: 421, 495
ballot: 65, 405, 410–414, 416, 420, 426, 433
branch: 458
Bridlington Principles: 403–405
categories of: 399
Certification Officer: 78
check-off: *See* Check-off
closed shop: *See* Closed shop

Index

collective bargaining: *See* Collective Bargaining
compulsory membership: *See* Closed Shop
conspiracy: *See* Conspiracy
constitution: 424
contempt of court: 65
craft union: 399, 401
custom and practice: 424
definition: 408–409
democracy: 493
discipline by: 426, 427
disclosure of information: *See* Disclosure of Information for Collective Bargaining
discrimination by: 426
elections: 78, 426, 431–435
election addresses: 434
election scrutineers: 434
endorsement of industrial action: 421, 495
exclusion from: 87, 393–394, 426
executive committee: 421, 432–434
expulsion from: 87, 393–394, 426
federations: 405
funds: 65, 78*bis*
general trade union: 401
historical background: 15, 52–54, 374 *See* Historical Background
immunity from civil action: 64–67, 420–423
independent: 78, 416, 461
industrial trade union: 400
inter-union disputes: 63, 486
joinder as defendant: 385
Labour Party: relationship with: 15, 409
legal classification: 415–417
legal status: 418–419
listing: 116, 415–416
low pay and: 207, 210
membership: 58, 66, 397, 398
natural justice: 428
number: 398
objects: 408–409
officials: 421, 432 *See* Shop Stewards
political activities: 409, 410
political fund: 78, 220, 410–414, 426
public employees: 118
recognition: *See* Recognition of Trade Unions for Collective Bargaining
redundancy consultation: 80, 325–328
register of members: 434
registration: 415
repudiation of industrial action: 65, 421, 495
right to belong: 376–380
right not to belong: 63, 381–385
rules: 61, 78*bis*, 92, 98, 393, 404, 421, 424–430
safety representatives: 416, 448
sequestration of assets of: 65, 423, 430, 502
shop stewards: *See* Shop Stewards
size: 398
structure: 398–401, 407
time off for trade union activities: 62, 71, 97, 188, 189, 194, 195, 416
tort liability: 420–423
transfer of engagements: 406
transfer of undertakings: 287, 416
trustees: 78*bis*, 419, 423, 426
ultra vires: 419, 430
unfair dismissal: 270, 273, 275, 276, 305, 308, 312, 314, 315, 316, 319, 376, 384, 390–392, 404
union membership agreements: *See* Closed Shop
union-only practices: 396, 492*bis*
white-collar employees: 398, 401
Trades Union Congress (TUC): 15, 70, 402–404, 413, 424, 433, 442
affiliation: 402
Bridlington Principles: 403, 404, 404*bis*
discrimination: 329–332, 336, 348, 352
Disputes Committee: 404
equal pay campaign: 330–332, 336
Independent Review Committee: 395
Labour Party and: 16
policy of non-co-operation with the Industrial Relations Act 1971: 61
'Social Contract': 4
Trainees: 123
See Youth Training Scheme
Training: 77, 77*bis*, 78*bis*, 79, 123
Training Agency: 66, 77, 123, 278
Training and Enterprise Councils (TECS): 77*bis*
Transfer of Undertakings: 4, 18, 19, 275, 283–287, 416, 464

Transport workers: 451
Transport and General Workers Union: 401, 407
Treaty of Rome: 18–19
See European Economic Community
Truck Acts: 66, 104, 120, 121, 217–221
Trust and co-operation, duty of
See Duty of Mutual Co-operation

Unemployment: 26, 27, 63, 66, 67, 77, 212, 278, 320, 337, 471
Unemployment Benefit: 66, 238, 247*bis*, 304, 506
Unfair Dismissal: 60, 69, 95, 115, 167, 185, 262, 269–276, 305–319
appeal to Employment Appeal Tribunal: 311
application to industrial tribunal: 80, 86, 270, 319
apprentices: 123
background to: 269
burden of proof of: 269, 305, 309
closed shop: 269, 276, 308, 314
See Closed Shop
collective bargaining 274: *See* Collective Bargaining
compensation: 273, 310, 314, 315, 317
conciliation: 71
contract of employment: 147, 270, 272
constructive dismissal: *See* Constructive Dismissal
Crown Servants: 118
dismissal: *See* Dismissal
discrimination and: 345, 347
eligibility for: 66, 269, 279–282, 319
exemption from: 69, 274
fixed term contract: 290
impact of: 269–276
industrial action: 307, 324, 477, 499
insolvency: 225
interim relief: 316
part-time workers: 129
pregnancy for: 252, 257, 259, 305, 306, 308
procedural fairness: role of: 270, 272, 276, 310
reasonableness: 270, 272, 305, 309–312
reasons for dismissal: 270, 272, 300–302, 305, 306–308
redundancy and: 270, 305, 308, 312, 315, 317
reinstatement or re-engagement: 270, 273, 284, 313, 314, 315, 380
relationship with other claims: 317
remedies: 269, 273, 314–316
sickness: 256
statistics of claims: 271, 272, 273
territorial scope: 103
trade union membership and activities: 270, 273, 275, 276, 305, 308, 312, 314, 315, 316, 319, 376, 384, 390–392, 404
transfer of undertakings: 283–287, 306
trainees: 123
waiver of rights: 290
week's pay: *See* Week's Pay
Union Membership Agreement:
See Closed Shop
Union of Communications Workers: 400
Union of Democratic Mineworkers: 400
Union of Shop, Distributive and Allied Workers: 336
United Kingdom: 7–9, 10–12
United States of America: 1, 4, 20–26, 37, 54, 61, 205, 503
anti-discrimination legislation: 330, 342, 343, 344, 354
United Nations Internation Covenant on Social and Cultural Rights: 334*bis*
Unofficial Action: *see* Industrial Action – unofficial action

Variation of Contract: *See* Contract of Employment
Vehicle Industry
See Motor Car Industry
Vicarious liability: 34, 179, 248
Victimisation: 121, 341, 346
'Voluntarism': 3, 36, 47, 52–67, 69, 73, 98, 425

Wages: 81
earnings: 53
deductions from: 80, 218, 219
Elizabethan wage fixing system: 50–51
employer's duty to pay: 163; *See* Duty to Pay
guarantee payments: *See* Guarantee Payments
homeworkers: 126
minimum wage legislation: *See* Minimum Wage Legislation

Index

part-time workers: 128
wage restraint: *See* Incomes Policies
wages drift: 57, 61
See Remuneration
Wages Councils: 53, 62, 66, 79, 126, 205–212, 298
Wages Inspectors: 208, 210, 222
Wales: 7–9, 10–12, 17, 99
Water Workers: 451, 504
Webb, Beatrice: 40
Wedderburn, Lord: 152, 486
'Week': 280
Week's Pay: 198, 200, 214, 280, 323
Welfare Law: 3, 39
Welfare Rights: 66
Welfare State: 54
White-collar Employees: 120, 126, 398, 401
Whitley Committee on Relations between Employers and Employees (1916–1919): 450
Whitley Councils: 98, 118
Women Workers: 28, 29, 30, 31 55–56, 67, 335
contractual capacity: 142
discrimination against: *See* Sex Discrimination
equal pay: *See* Equal Pay
ethnic minority: 337
holidays and hours of work: 182
low pay: 209, 335
married women: 29, 142
maternity rights: *See* Maternity Rights
part-time working: 29, 127, 335
pensions: 204, 204*bis*, 346
pregnancy: *See* Pregnancy
protective legislation: 93, 142, 182
sick pay schemes: 243
and trade unions: 336
work absence: 240
Work Experience Schemes: 141
Work Groups: 442
Workers: 107–131, 486
definition: 116
Workers Participation in Enterprise: 59, 439–448
See Industrial Democracy
Working Time:
See Hours of Work, Part-time Work, Time Off Work
Workmans Compensation: 2, 3, 34, 179
Works Councils: 440
Works Rules: 98, 147, 154–156
Written Statement of Terms and Conditions
See Statement of Terms and Conditions
Wrongful Dismissal: 123, 263, 264, 303, 304, 323

Young Workers: 66, 67, 77, 141, 278
age of contractual capacity: 140
protective legislation: 141, 182
unemployment: 27
See Children, Factories
Youth Training Scheme: 66, 123, 277–278